Civic Politics in the Rome of Urban VIII

Civic Politics in the Rome of Urban VIII

Laurie Nussdorfer

PRINCETON UNIVERSITY PRESS

PRINCETON, NEW JERSEY

Library of Congress Cataloging-in-Publication Data

Nussdorfer, Laurie.
Civic politics in the Rome of Urban VIII / Laurie Nussdorfer.
p. cm.
Includes bibliographical references and index.
1. Rome (Italy)—Politics and government. 2. Rome (Italy)—
History—1420–1798. 3. Political participation—Italy—
Rome— History—17th century. 4. Legitimacy of governments—
Italy—Rome— History—17th century. 5. Urban VIII, Pope,
1568–1644. I. Title.
JS5877.A15N87 1992 352.045′632—dc20 91-35635

ISBN 0-691-03182-7 (cl)

In Memory

Emily Cluett Forshew Gips
(1885–1985)

Besides, how was it possible for a Foreigner to pierce thro' their Politicks, that gloomy Labyrinth in which such of the English themselves as are best acquainted with it, confess daily that they are bewilder'd and lost?
—Preface to Voltaire's *Letters Concerning the English Nation*

CONTENTS

ILLUSTRATIONS

MAPS

FIGURES

TABLES

ACKNOWLEDGMENTS

IT HAS BEEN a privilege to be able to write a book about Rome, but it would not have been possible to "pierce through" the politics of seventeenth-century Romans without the help of many individuals and institutions. The research on which this book is based was funded by grants from the American Academy in Rome, the American Council of Learned Societies, the Social Science Research Council, the Newberry Library, and Princeton University, to all of which I am most grateful. My greatest intellectual debts are to two gifted teachers in Princeton University's History Department, Natalie Zemon Davis and Anthony Grafton. Their example, advice, criticism, and encouragement have sustained this project since its inception as a dissertation topic. I have profited from the incisive comments of a number of readers and would especially like to thank Nicholas Adams, Peter Brown, Elizabeth S. Cohen, Sherrill Cohen, Joseph Connors, Dale Kent, Julius Kirshner, Giovanni Levi, John Marino, John Paoletti, and Renato Pasta for their generosity and acuity. I would also like to express special gratitude to Fred Travisano for producing the maps in this book and to Wesleyan University for assisting their production.

In Rome I have been aided to valuable ways by the staffs at several archives and libraries. Dott.ssa Gaetana Scano of the Archivio Storico Capitolino allowed me to work in the archive during the years in which it was closed for repairs and Sig. Basile Donato brought me the documents. Prof. Agostino Paravicini Bagliani and Dott. Luigi Fiorani gave me help at the Biblioteca Apostolica Vaticana as did Sig. Giovanni Saveri at the Archivio Segreto Vaticano. I would also like to thank Frances P. Lederer of the National Gallery Library and Suzanne Boorsch of the Metropolitan Museum of Art. Many friends were pressed into service when I had queries about how to locate illustrations; I am very grateful to Kathleen Weil-Garris Brandt for her assistance and to Nicholas Adams, Joseph Connors, Steven Ostrow, and John Beldon Scott for their efforts. I called repeatedly on the expertise of Tracy Cooper and Francesca Consagra and I am indebted to them for their suggestions. Mirka Beneš, Paul Gehl, Fabrizia Gurreri, James Hankins, and Claudia Jacova also willingly responded when I needed assistance. In Princeton I would also like to acknowledge the aid of Don Breza, Douglas Gowton, and James Townsend. I am grateful to the *Sixteenth Century Journal* for permission to reproduce excerpts from a previously published article. Joanna Hitchcock of Princeton University Press and Ron Twisdale have provided gracious and expert help.

This book about the civic government of Rome owes a number of personal debts. During the time that I worked on it, I had the good fortune to live in two towns that were governed by two exceptional mayors: Luigi Petroselli of Rome and Barbara Sigmund of Princeton. They were leaders of special vision and humanity whose example was, and remains, an inspiring contribution to the possibilities of urban life. I would also like to thank William N. Parker, Karen Brudney, and Thomas and Katherine Cole. I am deeply grateful for the support and friendship of Corinne Rafferty and the support and faith of Fred Travisano and Adrian and Jessica Nussdorfer. This book is dedicated to the memory of my great aunt, Emily Cluett Forshew Gips, in gratitude for what she made possible.

UNITS OF MONEY AND WEIGHT

MONEY

scudo = money of account, equivalent to 100 baiocchi

giulio = 10 baiocchi

grosso = 5 baiocchi

baiocco = 1/100 of a scudo

quattrino = 1/5 of a baiocco

WEIGHT

oncia = 28.2 grams

libbra = 0.339 kilogram

rubbio = 640 libbre; as a measure of capacity also equivalent to 2.3 hectoliters

ABBREVIATIONS

Annales	*Annales Économies Sociétés Civilisations*
arm.	*armarium*
ASC	Archivio Storico Capitolino
ASR	Archivio di Stato di Roma
ASRSP	*Archivio della Societa' Romana di Storia Patria*
ASV	Archivio Segreto Vaticano
ASVR	Archivio Storico del Vicariato
BAV	Biblioteca Apostolica Vaticana
BNC-VE	Biblioteca Nazionale Centrale-Vittorio Emanuele II
bu.	*busta*
cod.	codex
cred.	*credenzone*
MEFRM	*Mélanges de l'École Française de Rome. Moyen âge—temps modernes*
ms.	*manoscritto*
RSRR	*Ricerche per la storia religiosa di Roma*
Studi	*Studi e documenti di storia e diritto*
30 N.C.	30 Notai Capitolini (ASR)
uff.	*ufficio*

Civic Politics in the Rome of Urban VIII

1. The Capitoline hill (Capitolium) as it looked in the first half of the seventeenth century.

INTRODUCTION

THIS BOOK is about the relationship between a city and its ruler in the age of absolutism. The city is Rome and the monarch is Pope Urban VIII, who reigned over one of the most splendid Baroque courts in Europe from 1623 to 1644.[1] "City" in this study refers primarily to the lay municipal administration of Rome, which even today identifies itself by the initials S.P.Q.R., *Senatus populusque romanus*, the Senate and Roman People, supreme political authority of the ancient Roman republic. In the seventeenth century this body was usually referred to more simply as the Roman People, the *Popolo Romano*, and the center of its activities was the Capitol, one of Rome's original seven hills (see Figure 1). The book focuses on the Roman People, institutional embodiment of a lay civic identity, as they interacted with their fellow Romans and their sovereign, the "two-souled" papal prince—holy father and absolute monarch.[2] It treats the political and social dimensions of the adminstration they headed. This is a case study of the relations between the citizens who took part in the local government of a capital city and the early modern state in which they were embedded.

Urban VIII addressed the Roman People as "beloved sons" and civic officials called him "your holiness" and "most blessed father." This pious paternal language signals at once the asymmetrical character of the relationship: the pope was on top, the magistrates were subordinate. The municipal administration of the papacy's capital was supposed to be obedient, reverent, grateful, and loyal, as were all subjects. The etiquette of absolutist discourse characterized the relationship between prince and people as a personal, hierarchical bond.[3] This book explores what the imagery of fidelity successfully masked in Rome: civic institutions had a life and a logic of their own and the social groups that acted through them had something to offer the pontiff and something they expected in return. It is about the politics of an unequal partnership.

[1] Judith Hook, "Urban VIII: The Paradox of a Spiritual Monarchy," in *The Courts of Europe: Politics, Patronage and Royalty 1400–1800*, ed. A. G. Dickens (New York, 1977), 213.

[2] Paolo Prodi, *Il sovrano pontefice: Un corpo e due anime: La monarchia papale nella prima eta' moderna* (Bologna, 1982), now translated into English as *The Papal Prince: One Body and Two Souls: The Papal Monarchy in Early Modern Europe*, trans. Susan Haskins (Cambridge, 1987). See also Hanns Gross, *Rome in the Age of Enlightenment: The Post-Tridentine Syndrome and the Ancien Regime* (Cambridge, 1990), 7, and Peter Burke, "Sacred Rulers, Royal Priests: Rituals of the Early Modern Popes," in *The Historical Anthropology of Early Modern Italy* (Cambridge, 1987), 175.

[3] For a general treatment of the religious sources for this language see Raymond Darricau, "Princes et peuples dans leur réciproque fidélité chez les docteurs catholiques de Bellarmin à Muratori," in *Hommage à Roland Mousnier: Clientèles et fidélités en Europe à l'époque moderne*, ed. Yves Durand (Paris, 1981), 42–55. For a critique of Mousnier's notion of fidelity see Sharon Kettering, *Patrons, Brokers and Clients in Seventeenth-Century France* (Oxford, 1986), 18–19.

I have called Urban VIII an absolute monarch and this book is a contribution to an understanding of an absolutist state and the society that supported it. Yet the term "absolutism" is a debated one and a recent commentator has pointed out that there is little agreement among historians on what it in fact describes.[4] Is it a political philosophy, a rhetorical claim, a type of state? I conceive of absolutism not just as a kind of government but more broadly as a regime embracing both a particular idiom of domination and its diverse social agents throughout a realm.[5] My approach is to concentrate on what absolutism looked like "on the ground," in a specific urban setting, exploring the concrete meanings of the daily operations of municipal officials and their interactions with everyone from the pope and his courtiers to shopkeepers and tradesmen. This way of analyzing early modern government allows a close look at its institutional *and* class character, two key aspects that need to be considered together but are too often treated in isolation.

Civic institutions have not been thought to have fared well under absolutism. The histories of early modern city governments, particularly the capitals of absolute monarchies, usually end on a gloomy note. After achieving power and status in the Middle Ages, free cities lost their independence and fell into servile obsequiousness and submission to the prince. Classic theorists like Max Weber and Lewis Mumford have given us a vivid image of what the suppression of urban autonomy under absolutism cost civic life, and historians have sounded a similar note.[6] The Gothic city hall embodied a creative commercial and republican spirit; its Baroque successor only existed to add luster to royal authority.

Yet several intellectual currents within and outside the discipline of history in recent years converge to make a new examination of civic institutions in the early modern period seem worthwhile. Social history and anthropology have suggested by implication that the history of power and politics is more complicated than the old authoritarian model of Baroque monarchy assumed. Social history has talked about different kinds of power and has pioneered methods for renewing the voices of once silent historical subjects. It has demonstrated the vivid political effects of

---

[4] Richard Bonney, "Absolutism: What's in a Name?" *French History* 1 (1987): 114.

[5] William Beik, *Absolutism and Society in Seventeenth-Century Languedoc* (Cambridge, 1985), offers perhaps the best example of an empirical study based on such a conception. Perry Anderson's *Lineages of the Absolutist State* (London, 1974), while not defining absolutism in exactly these terms, has influenced my formulation in important ways. See also Giorgio Chittolini, "Stati padani, 'Stato del Rinascimento': Problemi di ricerca," in *Persistenze feudali e autonomie comunitative in stati padani fra Cinque e Settecento*, ed. Giovanni Tocci (Bologna, 1988), 12–14. My thanks to Dott. Renato Pasta for this reference.

[6] Max Weber, *The City*, ed. and trans. Don Martindale and Gertrud Neuwirth (Glencoe, Ill., 1958), 74, 185. Lewis Mumford, *The City in History* (New York, 1961), 347, 356. Giulio Carlo Argan, *The Europe of the Capitals 1600–1700*, trans. Anthony Rhodes (Geneva, 1964), 34. Fernand Braudel, "Pre-modern towns," in *The Early Modern Town*, ed. Peter Clark (London, 1976), 76. Roger Chartier and Hugues Neveux, "La ville dominante et soumise," in *La ville classique de la Renaissance aux Révolutions*, ed. Emmanuel Le Roy Ladurie, vol. 3 of *Histoire de la France urbaine*, ed. Georges Duby (Paris, 1981), 157, 180, 191. Guido D'Agostino, "Citta' e monarchie nazionali nell'Europa moderna," in *Modelli di citta': Strutture e funzioni politiche*, ed. Pietro Rossi (Turin, 1987), 395–97.

social networks of kinship and patronage.[7] The anthropological notion of a cultural system offers a way to conceive of politics that embraces diverse forms of expression and participation by a whole community. In his study of kingship in nineteenth-century Bali Clifford Geertz criticizes modern political analysis for its narrow emphasis on "command" as the only important component of rule.[8] Costume, ceremony, and etiquette are not superfluous ornaments but bearers of crucial political messages, not all of which go one way. The impulses arising from social history and cultural anthropology encourage fresh reflection on the relations between absolute monarchs and urban subjects because they raise new questions about society and power.

At the same time historians of the early modern European state have opened methodological paths with important, if undeveloped, implications for understanding capital cities. Analyzing the domestic conflicts of European kingdoms in the first half of the seventeenth century in terms of tensions between state and society, they initially broke ground by bringing political and social forces into the same discussion.[9] Under continued scrutiny the clear dichotomy between state and society that underpinned their analysis began to dissolve and the focus of research shifted toward the interpenetration of political and social structures.[10] Agents of government were obviously members of society and, most relevantly, members of families with concrete social strategies and aspirations. Through purchase of curial or royal offices, later passed on to descendants, private property penetrated to the heart of public administration. A reified notion of the state seems especially inappropriate to an age when powerful individuals owned government posts and rulers auctioned off fundamental activities like tax collection to private entrepreneurs. The emergence of the term "ancien régime state" provides a new way to conceptualize that peculiar mixture of the public and the private in early modern government. Defined as the dominant political formation of the "old regime" society of privileged orders that perished after 1789, the

[7] E. J. Hobsbawm surveys the historiography of social history since the 1950s in his essay, "From Social History to the History of Society," in *Historical Studies Today*, ed. Felix Gilbert and Stephen R. Graubard (New York, 1972), 1–26. See also Ronald Weissman, "Taking Patronage Seriously: Mediterranean Values and Renaissance Society," in *Patronage, Art, and Society in Renaissance Italy*, ed. F. W. Kent and Patricia Simons (New York, 1987), 25–45.

[8] Clifford Geertz, *Negara: The Theatre State in Nineteenth-Century Bali* (Princeton, 1980), 121; for one application of the concept of a cultural system see Clifford Geertz, "Religion as a Cultural System," in *The Interpretation of Cultures* (New York, 1973), 87–125.

[9] For one of the earliest formulations see H. R. Trevor-Roper, "The General Crisis of the Seventeenth Century," *Past and Present* 16 (1959): 38.

[10] See, for example, J. F. Bosher, *French Finances 1770–1795* (Cambridge, 1970); Marino Berengo, "La citta' di antico regime," *Quaderni storici* 27 (1974): 661–92; Jean Claude Waquet, *De la corruption: Morale et pouvoir à Florence aux XVIIᵉ et XVIIIᵉ siècles* (Paris, 1984); Daniel Dessert, *Argent, pouvoir et société au Grand Siècle* (Paris, 1984); Beik; Kettering, *Patrons*; R. Burr Litchfield, *Emergence of a Bureaucracy: The Florentine Patricians 1530–1790* (Princeton, 1986); Donatella Balani, *Il vicario tra citta' e stato: L'Ordine pubblico e l'annona nella Torino del Settecento* (Turin, 1987); David Parker, "Class, Clientage and Personal Rule in Absolutist France," *Seventeenth-Century French Studies* 9 (1987): 192–213.

"state" of the ancien régime could not oppose a "society" external to it because it was so fundamentally embedded within it.

This line of thinking has already begun to reshape the inquiry into the nature of central bureaucracies and the relations between the central administration of the state and the "periphery" over which it reigned.[11] But its insights are equally applicable to the neglected domain of civic administration and the public institutions of the capital city. Capital cities were a new phenomenon, one of the distinctive contributions of the early modern period to urban history, yet we know remarkably little about the internal workings of urban government and society.[12] In those "localities" paradoxically placed at the "center," what exactly was the distribution of responsibilities between civic and state officials? Who was recruited for local government and where did they stand socially? What material and immaterial attractions drew men to municipal administration? What did "power" mean concretely in the complex institutional layering and ambiguous social articulation of dynamic cities? How did the subjects who lived most intimately with absolute rulers express themselves politically?

Baroque Rome, the capital of the Papal States, seat of the head of the Catholic Church, and home to 115,000 people, is a useful case in which to seek answers to questions about the power and politics of the locality in an early modern state. In some ways it resembles those cities—such as Prague, Paris, and Madrid—that were residences of great European monarchs. They shared features that incised urban society in distinctive ways: the presence of a royal court, diplomats and aristocrats of international stature, and the central bureaus and tribunals of a kingdom of far-flung interests. A leader in setting the style for life in the new European capitals, Rome as a civic entity in close proximity to the pope coped with some typical constraints and opportunities.[13]

Focusing on municipal administration, however, reminds us that Rome was a city of a uniquely Italian type too. By the seventeenth century the peninsula was cut up into half a dozen medium-sized territorial states, each with a dominant metropole from which a viceroy, noble senate, grand duke, or pontiff governed. The regimes took different forms, but Naples, Venice, Milan, Florence, and Rome had important elements in common: a strong role for local landed elites in urban administration or traditions of civic independence dating from the Middle Ages, or a combination of both. The peculiar features of these early modern Italian

[11] In addition to some of the studies in the preceding note see the conference papers collected in *La fiscalité et ses implications sociales en Italie et en France au XVIIᵉ et XVIIIᵉ siècles* (Rome, 1980); Elena Fasano Guarini, ed., *Potere e societa' negli stati regionali italiani fra '500 e '600* (Bologna, 1978); Renata Ago, *Carriere e clientele nella Roma barocca* (Bari, 1990).

[12] One exemplary recent study is Robert Descimon, "L'échevinage parisien sous Henri IV (1594–1609): Autonomie urbaine, conflits politiques et exclusives sociales," in *La ville, la bourgeoisie et la genèse de l'état moderne (XIIᵉ-XVIIIᵉ siècles)* (Paris, 1988), 113–50. My thanks to Professor William Beik for this reference.

[13] For Rome's leadership in the new urbanity see Mark Girouard, *Cities and People: A Social and Architectural History* (New Haven, 1985), chap. 6.

regional capitals, which were quite different from Paris, Madrid, Amsterdam, or London, affected their political relations with sovereigns and the structuring of city society.

Destined throughout its history to serve as the symbol for a grand design, Rome is a city whose local past, especially from the sixteenth to the eighteenth centuries, has been startlingly neglected.[14] The historiography of its civic institutions conforms faithfully to the general tradition of urban decay under absolutism, although it puts its own particular "spin" on it. One spin is the view that, unlike other medieval cities, Rome had never enjoyed a period of freedom from the papacy and thus had no glorious communal independence to lose in the early modern period.[15] Another is the ironic contrast between the splendid new town hall on the Capitoline hill that Michelangelo had designed for the civic magistrates in the sixteenth century and the meanness of their actual functions. Their buildings a scenic backdrop for papal gestures, the Senate and Roman People stood uselessly in the wings. The author of the only book devoted to the history of Rome's early modern muncipal officials in fact dismissed them as " 'parade' magistrates" and "high-flown dolls."[16]

Modern scholarship here picks up a topos that was already familiar in the Middle Ages and that grew more vigorous in the Renaissance: Rome's fall from its days of glory as the capital of an ancient world empire. Medieval pilgrim guides played up this point in describing the ruins of once beautiful monuments, temples, and baths.[17] Beginning with Petrarch in the fourteenth century, humanist "pilgrims," paying their respects at the shrine of the cult of antiquity, further embellished the commonplace of decay.[18] Any educated sixteenth- or seventeenth-century commentator on the status of civic institutions would have encountered a constant literary comparison between the greatness of ancient Rome and the debility of the modern city. The contemporary Senate and Roman People would have been judged against the achievements of their illustrious predecessors and been found wanting. Making fun of the lavish costumes worn by civic magistrates who "represented only a certain vain and ridiculous authority," Paolo

---

[14] Gross, ix.

[15] Maria Luisa Lombardo, *La camera urbis: Premesse per uno studio sulla organizzazione amministrativa della citta' di Roma durante il pontificato di Martino V* (Rome, 1970), 32, 40, 46–47.

[16] Emmanuel Rodocanachi, *Les institutions communales de Rome sous la papaute'* (Paris, 1901), 210, 333. See also Massimo Miglio, "Il leone e la lupa: Dal simbolo al pasticcio alla francese," *Studi romani* 30 (1982): 185; Charles Stinger, *The Renaissance in Rome* (Bloomington, Ind., 1985), 257; Christoph L. Frommel, "Papal Policy: The Planning of Rome during the Renaissance," in *Art and History: Images and Their Meaning*, ed. Robert I. Rotberg and Theodore K. Rabb (Cambridge, 1988), 64.

[17] "La piu' antica redazione dei *Mirabilia urbis Romae*," in *Codice topografico della citta' di Roma*, ed. Roberto Valentini and Giuseppe Zucchetti (Rome, 1946), 3:51–53, 65.

[18] See, for example, Francesco Petrarca, "Familiarum rerum liber," in *Codice topografico della citta' di Roma*, ed. Roberto Valentini and Giuseppe Zucchetti (Rome, 1953), 4:10, and Poggio Bracciolini, "De varietate fortunae," ibid., 4:230. See also K. Lloyd-Jones, "Du Bellay's Journey from *Roma Vetus* to *La Rome Neufve*," in *Rome in the Renaissance*, ed. P. A. Ramsey (Binghamton, N.Y., 1982), 307–9.

2. A "modern Roman" and an "ancient Roman" stand
next to each other in a detail from an engraving by
Giacomo Lauro, circa 1618.

Giovio wrote in 1529 that the popes "had left them only the images of ancient
honors."[19] (See Figure 2.) The Venetian ambassador put it similarly in 1560: "Although it is true that the Roman People still have some authority, one sees that
it is more apparent than real and that what it has [la cosa sua] is but a shadow."[20]
Nor was this judgment confined to foreigners, for even Romans who held civic
offices disparaged their shrunken stature when compared to their mythic ances-
tors.[21]

Yet despite the jokes, there was a great deal of vitality to Roman politics. The
capital of the early modern papal monarchy had a celebrated local culture of political irreverence. Pasquino, the remnant of an antique sculptural group unearthed and set up in downtown Rome in 1501, headed a small but audacious
band of "talking statues" who conversed publicly among themselves about the
frailties of the city's great men (see Figure 3). Anonymous satirical comments,
often highly literary, were placed secretly upon Pasquino, Abbot Luigi, Madama

[19] Paolo Giovio quoted by Massimo Miglio, "L'immagine dell'onore antico: Individualita' e tradizione della Roma municipale," *Studi romani* 31 (1983): 264.

[20] "Relazione di Roma di Luigi Mocenigo," in *Le relazioni degli ambasciatori veneti al senato durante il
secolo decimosesto*, ed. Eugenio Albèri (Florence, 1857), ser. 2, 4:30.

[21] Marcello Alberini, *I ricordi di Marcello Alberini*, vol. 1 of *Il sacco di Roma del M.d.xxvii*, ed.
Domenico Orano (Rome, 1901), 483; Giacinto Gigli, *Diario romano (1608–1670)*, ed. Giuseppe
Ricciotti (Rome, 1958), 144.

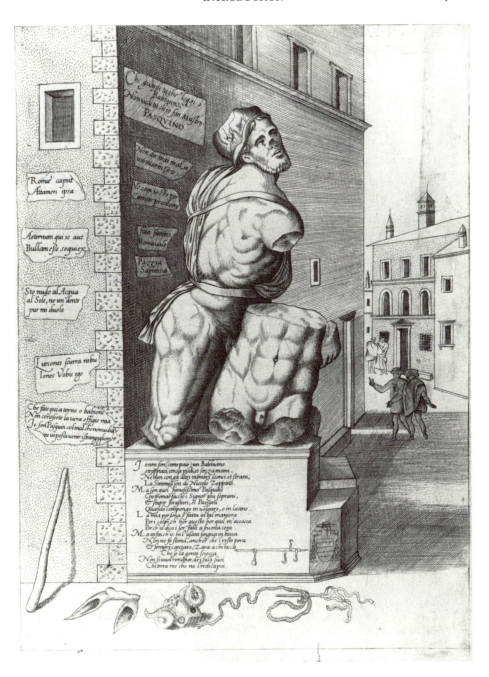

3. The "talking statue" Pasquino with posted pasquinades.

Lucrezia, "il Facchino" (the porter), and Marforio, and read or heard by pas-sersby.[22] Pasquino gave his name to the word for a mocking, clandestine lam-poon, the "pasquil" or "pasquinade," which entered several European languages in the sixteenth century. His was a genre nicely timed for the triumph of absolute monarchy. In Rome the term "pasquinata" soon took on a more general meaning as any written criticism of papal government, even if it was only circulated pri-vately among acquaintances.

Rome's irreverent local culture also included rituals of political indignation. During the weeks between the death of one pope and the election of his successor, Romans had a chance to attack the symbols of the former ruler, to talk back to his once powerful relatives, to make fun of him in songs and verses, and to plot vengeance against his unpopular officials. The Vacant See, as such periods were called, was a traditional vehicle for expressing political grievances that was built into the rhythm of Roman public life.

Civic institutions did have a special role to play in the Vacant See, as we shall see, but it is their role while the pope lived and governed that is the main subject of this study. Rome's underground political culture of satire, gossip, and rumor was notorious in early modern Europe, but its political processes above ground are less familiar.[23] We know very little about what government was like under a sovereign who enjoyed not just royal prerogatives but "the fullness of apostolic power," and who was supreme both in the civil and the ecclesiastical spheres.[24] Who did the work of administration and why? Did the pope and his officials ignore the interests and wishes of local subjects or did they have to cultivate con-sent? Did it depend and, if so, on what? The activities of municipal officials and councils in Rome reveal a few privileged subjects engaged in the practice of gov-ernment within an absolute monarchy. What these subjects did sheds light on how absolutism functioned as a form of rule.

Institutional history has sometimes been criticized as a history that leaves

---

[22] Surviving pasquinades from the sixteenth century have been published by Valerio Marucci, An-tonio Marzo, and Angelo Romano, eds., *Pasquinate romane del Cinquecento*, 2 vols. (Rome, 1983). Peter Burke describes what may be the only surviving manuscript example of a pasquinade actually posted on Pasquino in "Insult and Blasphemy in Early Modern Italy," in *The Historical Anthropology of Early Modern Italy* (Cambridge, 1987), 104 n. 19. For the origins of the practice see Anne Reynolds, "Car-dinal Oliviero Carafa and the Early Cinquecento Tradition of the Feast of Pasquino," *Humanistica Lovaniensia* 34A (1985): 178–208. See also Francis Haskell and Nicholas Penny, *Taste and the Antique: The Lure of Classical Sculpture, 1500–1900* (New Haven, 1981), 291–96. I am grateful to Dr. Chris-topher Moss for this reference.

[23] Giorgio Spini, *Ricerca dei Libertini: La teoria dell'impostura delle religioni nel Seicento italiano*, rev. and enl. ed. (Florence, 1983), 185–99. The underworld of Roman curial life is the subject of many works by the "adventurer of the pen" Gregorio Leti (1630–1701); see the bibliography compiled by Franco Barcia, *Bibliografia delle opere di Gregorio Leti* (Milan, 1981).

[24] Gerhart B. Ladner, "The Concepts of 'Ecclesia' and 'Christianitas' and Their Relation to the Idea of Papal 'Plenitudo Potestatis' from Gregory VII to Boniface VIII," in *Sacerdozio e regno da Gregorio VII a Bonifacio VIII* (Rome, 1954), 59, 66–68. Prodi, 25, provides a number of references to the extensive literature on *plenitudo potestatis*.

"struggle" out.[25] As several imaginative recent studies have shown, however, the "apparatus" of seventeenth-century administration was a living social and political force-field in which political conflict often took the form of institutional competition.[26] In this book institutions are the point of entry into local politics and the full range of relations, harmonious as well as conflictual, between the lay members of the city's patrician classes and the papacy. When we look at civic institutions from many angles, they reveal the meaning and exercise of power in a concrete context.

To clarify that context for Rome's municipal government we need to step back historically to the late medieval papacy and its efforts to turn its fragmented central Italian territories into a strong, independent state. The Senate and Roman People, reappearing in written sources in 1143 after several centuries of obscurity, did not acquire a sharply defined juridical identity until the turn of the fifteenth century.[27] The date is significant because it coincided with the end of the popes' sojourn in Avignon and the crisis of the Great Schism, in which several rival popes contended for the Holy See. Decades of conflict finally concluded in 1417 with the election of the Roman Martin V, who returned the papacy to Rome in 1420. Locally, however, the ground had already been prepared for the pontiffs to enter the city as unchallenged masters by Boniface IX (1383–1404) and the antipope Alexander V (1409–1410). Part of that preparation included making sure that powerful families accepted the sovereignty of the popes and that the lay civic institutions these families controlled reflected their submission. This was achieved through a compromise favorable to the papacy; the pontiffs legally recognized the Senate and Roman People in exchange for its political subordination.[28] The "exchange" allowed the popes to have a key voice, but not an exclusive one, in shaping the institutional physiognomy of the new partnership they were building with

[25] For this critique, made originally in 1960, see Jaime Vicens Vives, "The Administrative Structure of the State in the Sixteenth and Seventeenth Centuries," in *Government in Reformation Europe 1520–1560*, ed. Henry J. Cohn (London, 1971), 60, quoted by Roger Mettam, "Two-Dimensional History: Mousnier and the Ancien Régime," *History* 66 (1981): 221.

[26] In addition to Beik, see also James Allen Vann, *The Making of a State: Württemberg, 1593–1793* (Ithaca, N.Y., 1984), and J. H. Elliott, *Richelieu and Olivares* (Cambridge, 1984).

[27] The first mention of the resuscitated Roman People occurs in Otto of Freising, *Ottonis episcopi Frisingensis Chronica: Sive, Historia de duabus civitatibus*, ed. Adolf Hofmeister (Hanover, 1984), bk. 7, chap. 27, 353. On the fluid nature of the Senate and Roman People in the high Middle Ages see Robert Brentano, *Rome before Avignon: A Social History of Thirteenth-Century Rome* (New York, 1974), chap. 3. For older treatments see Ferdinand Gregorovius, *History of the City of Rome in the Middle Ages*, trans. Annie Hamilton, 4th ed., 8 vols. (London, 1894–1902), and the bibliographical references provided by Eugenio Dupre' Theseider, *Roma dal comune di popolo alla signoria pontificia (1252–1377)*, vol. 11 of *Storia di Roma* (Bologna, 1952).

[28] Lombardo, 46–47; *Codex diplomaticus domini temporalis S. Sedis*, ed. Augustin Theiner (Rome, 1862), 3:172–74; Arnold Esch, *Bonifaz IX und der Kirchenstaat* (Tübingen, 1969); and idem, "La fine del libero comune di Roma nel giudizio dei mercanti fiorentini. Lettere romane degli anni 1395–1398 nell'Archivio Datini," *Bullettino dell'Istituto Storico Italiano per il Medio Evo* 86 (1976–77): 235–77.

Rome's native upper classes. It was a small but important victory in their larger campaign to make themselves effective monarchs in the Papal States.

Creating a state that could compete with what contemporary secular princes were constructing elsewhere in Europe between the thirteenth and the sixteenth centuries took time. Their capital city firmly in hand by the early 1400s, the popes worked until after 1550 to suppress contentious feudal lords and refractory communal governments within their borders. In the process they gave new muscle to "apostolic power," reducing all domestic political rivals to obedience and enlarging their bureaucracy to supervise the expanded temporal domain. Proof of the pontiffs' success was a dramatic increase in the tax revenues yielded by their subjects, who by 1600 provided eighty percent of the income of the Holy See.[29]

Recently historians have disagreed about the degree of "modernity" the Papal States displayed in these political and administrative developments. Some have argued that the papacy was far in advance of other European governments in creating rationalized and effective central state control of its territories.[30] Critics of this view point to the many "backward" features that survived in the Papal States, including weakly organized military forces and extensive feudal and corporate privileges.[31] Both sides will find evidence for their cases in this book, but I am reluctant to debate the existence of "truffles" of modernity in the relationships that I analyze here; proponents and opponents of the thesis of the Papal States' precocious statebuilding both assume a teleological view of history that seems untenable. In the Papal States, political practices we would not deem modern could support changes that we might identify as such, and vice versa. For example, the instinct to defend one's jurisdiction against encroachers had deep roots in medieval custom, but, when experienced by newly created state officers, made them more aggressive in implementing novel modes of control. Appointing powerful, celibate officials whose only loyalty was to the papacy, on the other hand, might seem like a step toward rationalized administration in the Papal States. However, these bureaucrats did not necessarily function as impersonal agents of the state, for many were sons of rich bankers who bought their posts, later resigning them to nephews as they advanced to higher office.[32] By classifying the Papal

---

[29] Jean Delumeau, *Vie économique et sociale de Rome dans la seconde moitié du XVIᵉ siècle* (Paris, 1959), 2:842–43. The literature on the process of state-building in the Papal States is extensive. In addition to many studies of specific localities see Peter Partner, *The Lands of St. Peter: The Papal State in the Middle Ages and the Early Renaissance* (London, 1972), and Mario Caravale and Alberto Caracciolo, *Lo stato pontificio da Martino V a Pio IX* (Turin, 1978). Prodi's *Il sovrano pontefice* is an especially wide-ranging and sensitive reflection on the implications for the pope's ecclesiastical role of the construction of a state.

[30] Jean Delumeau, "Rome: Le progrès de la centralisation dans l'État pontifical au XVIᵉ siècle," *Revue historique* 226 (1961): 399–410.

[31] Caravale and Caracciolo, 352–53; Alberto Caracciolo, "Sovrano pontefice e sovrani assoluti," *Quaderni storici* 52 (1983): 279–86.

[32] Peter Partner, "Appunti sulla riforma della Curia romana," in *Libri, idee e sentimenti religiosi nel Cinquecento italiano*, ed. Rolando Bussi (Modena, 1987), 79. See also idem, *The Pope's Men: The Papal*

States as an ancien régime state and refusing to characterize that entity as either progressive or regressive, I position myself among those analysts whose primary aim is to delineate more sharply a still inadequately understood political and social formation.

Not even the most farsighted leadership could elevate the Papal States above the status of a minor European power. The kingdom's population and resources were meager compared to those of France and Spain in the sixteenth and seventeenth centuries, and it did not have the material base to conduct itself like such states. Yet the early modern popes, like many of their predecessors, continued to seek a grand role in continental politics, both on behalf of the Church they shepherded and to protect their Italian state. Both motives, religious and political, ensured that they would be caught up diplomatically, financially, and even militarily in the great European conflict of the Thirty Years War between 1618 and 1648. Like many contemporary rulers, Pope Urban VIII, whose reign from 1623 to 1644 fell entirely within the period of the war, found himself facing unprecedented demands on his treasury for defense and diplomacy.[33] At the same time he had his own expensive agenda of cultural patronage and family enrichment (see Figure 4). The pontiff charged forward on all fronts without regard for the burdens imposed on taxpayers, who were also suffering the effects of economic depression. He fiercely guarded the integrity of his Italian territory, tried to mediate between warring Catholic princes, promoted the reform vision of the Council of Trent, and made his court the artistic pacesetter of the age. Rome, thanks to the patronage of cardinals and popes, had been the cradle of the artistic style that began to appear around 1600, and Urban VIII surpassed his predecessors in his support for the new movement.[34] This was in part because he was able to dispense commissions for an unusual length of time; few pontificates have lasted over twenty years. The cardinals who elected the pope from their number preferred to choose elderly men so that the Holy See did not remain for too long in the hands of any one family or faction. What was a distinct blessing to artists was less so to officeholders and taxpayers. Urban's longevity stoked frustrations among the ambitious in the central organs of the Church, and his priorities exacerbated pressures on papal subjects from war taxation and agricultural crisis. Although other

---

Civil Service in the Renaissance (Oxford, 1990), 44–46. Prodi, *Pontefice*, 223–24. Prodi argues that the "clericalization" of the administration was necessary to make both lay and clerical subjects submit to the new demands of the modern state, but the Counter Reformation revived opposing demands for clerical privileges, which ultimately foundered the thrust toward modernization in the Papal States.

[33] For the European military and diplomatic context of papal policy during the Thirty Years War see especially Ludwig von Pastor, *The History of the Popes*, trans. Ernest Graf (London, 1938), vols. 28 and 29, and Georg Lutz, "Rom und Europa während der Pontifikats Urbans VIII," in *Rom in der Neuzeit*, ed. R. Elze, H. Schmidinger, and H. S. Nordholt (Vienna, 1976), 72–167.

[34] The literature on Rome's role in the history of Baroque art is vast. For an introduction see Rudolf Wittkower, *Art and Architecture in Italy 1600–1750* (Harmondsworth, England, 1958), and Torgil Magnuson, *Rome in the Age of Bernini*, 2 vols. (Stockholm, 1982–1986), which covers the period from 1585 to 1689.

4. Urban VIII's tomb in St. Peter's designed by the sculptor Gian Lorenzo Bernini.

European peoples suffered more directly from the war, and some reacted more rebelliously as a result, Romans faced real hardships in these years.

Studying the relations between a civic administration and an absolute monarch during a time of stress like that of the Thirty Years War can be useful. We can catch glimpses of the normally elusive politics of local government. Tensions that neither party would wish to show come to light, making it easier to see the process of "negotiation" that the canons of polite address deliberately obscure. The clashing interests of the city's upper-class leaders and more humble inhabitants stand out more clearly. Urban VIII's pontificate is not "typical," but it compensates for that by being more revealing. Its length also "controls" the single most important variable in an absolute monarchy, the person of the ruler, and allows a more sustained investigation of civic activities than would a briefer reign.

While in foreign affairs and cultural developments the decades of the 1620s to 1640s were somewhat unusual, in other respects they display the city in the characteristic form it assumed throughout the early modern period. Demographically Rome was coming to the end of a cycle of rapid growth and settling into a long period of stability. The enduring features of the local economy were also well established by 1620 and would not alter their fundamental outlines in the next two hundred years. At the time of Urban VIII's accession the civic institutional structures that are the focus of this book were already at least two centuries old, as was the political "settlement" between local families and the papacy on which they were based. They too were destined to endure with few substantial modifications until the nineteenth century. Papal or state institutions were more dynamic, and we will have an opportunity to see how this quality manifested itself in the years of Urban VIII's pontificate. Nevertheless, without subscribing to the theory of "immobile history" or to Gramsci and D'Annunzio's image of the "cities of silence," Rome in 1630 was in many ways not terribly different from Rome in 1550 or 1750.[35] While its chronological limits are precise, this study represents an inquiry into a pattern of relations that held firm over several centuries.

It is organized so as to view Rome's civic institutions both in context and up close. The first part sets the scene by describing Rome in the 1620s from a wide variety of perspectives: religious, economic, sociopolitical, and administrative. Chapters 5 and 6 focus on the Senate and Roman People as an institutional structure and as a social phenomenon. In each of the next three parts of the book I take up a different dimension of local governmental activity to show that civic politics can best be understood as three distinct "articulations" of the political: jurisdiction, patronage, and accommodation/protest. Chapters 7 through 9 explore particular Capitoline jurisdictions in detail and Chapter 10 shows civic institutions operating in relation to other institutions—state, corporate, and ecclesiastical—

[35] Emmanuel Le Roy Ladurie, "L'Histoire immobile," *Annales* 29 (1974): 673–92; Antonio Gramsci, *Selections from the Prison Notebooks*, ed. and trans. Quintin Hoare and Geoffrey Nowell Smith (New York, 1971), 91. See also Gross, 8.

in a specific crisis. Chapters 11 and 12 take up the patron-client networks and financial functions of the municipal administration. In the fifth and final part civic institutions are again viewed in context, but this time the context is events in time, the narrative of war and interregnum, which inflect municipal activity in their own unique ways. My double aim is an account of early modern politics in Italy that restores a role to neglected institutions and actors, and an account of early modern Italian government that illuminates the social character of absolutism.

PART I

The Roman Setting

IN THE SECOND QUARTER of the seventeenth century Rome was a city of around 115,000 people that still fit comfortably within the walls built 1,400 years earlier for a population almost ten times larger.[1] A compact urban core, densest where the Tiber River bent to the west, loosened out into a patchwork of villas and vineyards before reaching the city walls. Within the walls the remnants of ancient monuments made room for a promiscuous mix of vegetable stalls, great urban townhouses, taverns, and the newly arrived vehicle of conspicuous consumption, the coach. From this physical tissue rose the belltowers and, increasingly, the domes of more than two hundred churches. From the great basilicas over the tombs of the apostles to the chapels of patrician families and the oratorios of the guilds, the city proclaimed its patronage of the holy. Its topography spoke in brick and stone of its thousand years as a Christian symbol.

The walls of Rome marked a toll barrier and were sometimes a defense against bandits and plague, but they were not really a line between city and country. Through them streamed sheep and vineyard workers as well as couriers, pilgrims, and travelers. Rural life penetrated into the heart of town: in the streets where pigs foraged in defiance of government edicts; in the ancient Forum, now the site of the cattle market; and in the nearby Piazza Montanara where day laborers sought agricultural work.

Religion and agriculture were the material bases of Rome's prosperity in the early modern period. On these twin foundations it could take on a political role in the Europe of the seventeenth century. They powered the splendid court of Urban VIII and his nephews, the majesty of the foreign diplomats and aristocrats whose retinues filled the streets, and the paperwork of lawyers, judges, and officials. The prelates, nobles, and magistrates who carried on the business of government, however, were the social muscle of rule. They made Rome a capital.

In this section we survey the spiritual, economic, social, political, and governmental framework in which Roman civic institutions were set in the 1620s. In Chapter 1 the city's international character as a religious symbol takes center stage and we see the effects upon it of the great movement for Catholic renewal of the sixteenth century. Chapter 2 examines the specific ramifications for Baroque Rome of the seventeenth-century crisis in the Mediterranean and European economies. In Chapter 3 we get a close look at the specific ruler and ruling house that led the Church and city from 1623 to 1644, Maffeo Barberini, Pope Urban VIII. Here the people who concentrated in their persons the greatest social and political

---

[1] Francesco Cerasoli, "Censimento della popolazione di Roma dall'anno 1600 al 1739," *Studi e documenti di storia e diritto* 12 (1891): 175–77 and 170 n. 2, where the city's Jewish population is estimated at an additional 4,500 individuals. Richard Krautheimer, *Rome Profile of a City, 312–1308* (Princeton, 1980), 4.

power are the focus, as well as the members of Roman society who mattered most to them. Finally, in Chapter 4 the structures of urban government—ecclesiastical, papal, and municipal—as a whole come to the fore. This chapter forms the immediate background for the detailed exploration of the Capitoline administration in the sections to follow.

Chapter One

A HOLY CITY

"THIS IS A CITY upon a hill, which is exposed for the whole world to gaze upon." With this pious and timeworn image the bishop of Rome, Pope Urban VIII, announced the beginning of a massive investigation into the religious health of his diocese in 1624.[1] Rome was a symbol of faith. And it was a symbol at the center of religious polemic in the struggle between Catholics and Protestants that marked the sixteenth and seventeenth centuries. "Whore of Babylon" to reformers, the city was an ideological canvas for the Counter-Reformation. Popes and militants made Rome itself the clinching argument in their case for the rightness of Catholic orthodoxy. Publicists of the Counter-Reformation era celebrated "sancta Roma" as a holy city, a community sanctified both by the relics and memories of its buried martyrs and by its ongoing works of devotion and charity. They trumpeted an active faith, not just the dead monuments of the past. "Roman citizens, this is your piety," wrote a pamphleteer preparing pilgrims for what they would find in Rome during the Holy Year of 1625.[2]

Roman piety, however, was never entirely a native construction. The city that had the privilege, and burden, of having the eyes of western Christendom upon it, had so often felt the imprint of outsiders, like the Florentine Pope Urban VIII himself, that to disentangle the local from the universal in its religious culture would be a difficult task. The "holiness" of the holy city was the fruit of intertwining and multilayered impulses—from abroad, from above, and from home— all transformed in their mutual dialogue. The results were not completely under any one person's control, which perhaps accounts for the good bishop's eagerness to investigate in 1624, but also explains the richness, variety, and vitality of spiritual life in Baroque Rome.

The great movement for Catholic renewal of the sixteenth century was international in character but made Rome a special focus. The city drew committed Catholics from all over Europe who saw it as the proper setting for their spiritual vocation. Challenged by Protestants who asserted the primacy of faith over works,

[1] Cf. Matt. 5:14. This passage from the bull inaugurating the visitation is quoted by Luigi Fiorani, "Le visite apostoliche del Cinque-Seicento e la societa' religiosa romana," *RSRR* 4 (1980): 115.

[2] Theodorus Amydenus, *De pietate romana* (Rome, 1625), reprinted in the *Annales ecclesiastici*, ed. Abramo Bzovio (Cologne, 1641), 20:527. For a bibliography of printed guides for pilgrims visiting Rome see Ludwig Schudt, *Le guide di Roma* (Vienna, 1930), 117–23, 321–37. For the first English guide to Counter-Reformation Rome, written in 1581 but not published until recently, see Gregory Martin, *Roma sancta (1581)*, ed. George Bruner Parks (Rome, 1969). See also Gérard Labrot, *Un instrument polémique: L'image de Rome au temps du schisme (1534–1667)* (Paris, 1978).

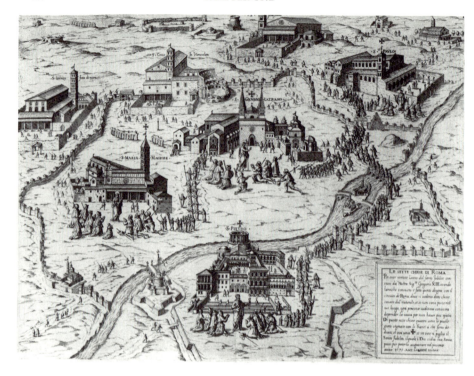

5. Pilgrims during the Holy Year of 1575 make the pilgrimage to Rome's "seven churches."

the Catholic Church reaffirmed its teaching that both were necessary, and that charity to one's neighbor was the sign of faith. A Spaniard and a Florentine were among the most famous of the devout arrivals whose works flourished in Rome; St. Ignatius Loyola and St. Philip Neri were founders of new religious orders that helped to reshape Roman religious life.

The efforts of the Jesuits and of St. Philip's Oratorians took many forms. Jesuits directed the city's most famous schools: the Roman College, with a general curriculum for upper-class Roman youth, and the Roman Seminary, which prepared priests for the cure of souls. They also carried instruction into the piazzas with regular street sermons to rural laborers gathered for hire.[3] St. Philip Neri had inspired one of Rome's most formidable charities, the company of the Trinity of the Pilgrims, which fed, sheltered, nursed, and clothed hundreds of thousands of visiting pilgrims during Holy Years (see Figure 5). His Oratorians were also known for the novel methods they used to bring the word of God to ordinary

[3] For a sympathetic contemporary view of the activities of the Jesuits in Rome see Martin, 71–72, 127–29, 162–79. On the Roman College, founded in 1551, and Roman Seminary, founded in 1565, see Mario Scaduto, *L'Epoca di Giacomo Lainez*, vol. 3 of *Storia della Compagnia di Gesu' in Italia*, ed. P. Tacchi-Venturi (Rome, 1964), 3:271–324, 435–41. See also Gross, 235–36.

people in "familiar sermons" delivered daily at their new church of Santa Maria in Vallicella.[4]

These well-known examples hardly exhaust the list of outsiders who leavened the religious atmosphere in late sixteenth- and early seventeenth-century Rome. St. Camillo de Lellis from the Abruzzi established his healing order, the Ministers of the Infirm, in the city in the 1580s. St. José de Calasanz from Aragon, founder of the Piarist teaching order, made a church in Trastevere the site of his first school for the Roman poor in the 1590s. The English "Jesuitess" Mary Ward also opened one of her popular but ill-fated schools in Rome.[5]

In the 1620s foreigners still found scope for their piety in ministering to the Roman needy. During that decade a Sienese glove merchant made a group of poor girls, whose virtue he thought endangered by their poverty, the object of his charity. Placing them under the protection of St. Philip Neri, who was buried nearby, the glover built a house for the young "filippine," and Urban VIII's brother, the Cardinal Sant'Onofrio, made sure they had enough wool and thread to earn their living together "honestly."[6]

Stimulated by such examples, Counter-Reformation Rome experienced an unprecedented flowering of associational life. New religious orders, innovative charities that specialized in everything from marital peacemaking to converting the Jews, and over 130 new confraternities made their appearance in the sixteenth and seventeenth centuries. Many of these confraternities had novel tasks, such as the company of Christian Doctrine, established in 1560 for the purpose of setting up catechism schools for Roman children, or the confraternity of Pity for the Imprisoned (*pieta' dei carcerati*), founded by a French Jesuit in 1579 to free debtors from city prisons. As elsewhere in Italy, a number of confraternities dedicated to the Eucharist sprang up in sixteenth-century Rome, reflecting the Catholic Church's defense of the mass in the face of Protestant criticism. Even the older confraternities took on commitments that showed the signs of new times; in 1581, for example, Pope Gregory XIII gave the task of ransoming Christians held captive in Muslim lands to the prestigious company of the Gonfalone, whose origins dated back to the medieval flagellants.[7]

---

[4] Martin, 73–74; Delumeau, *Vie*, 1:170–72. Two studies that well situate Neri and his followers within the Roman context are Louis Ponnelle and Louis Bordet, *St. Philip Neri and the Roman Society of His Times*, trans. Ralph Francis Kerr (London, 1932; repr. 1979), and Joseph Connors, *Borromini and the Roman Oratory: Style and Society* (Cambridge, Mass., 1980). On the construction of an image of "holy Rome" in contemporary preaching see also Frederick J. McGinness, "Preaching Ideals and Practice in Counter-Reformation Rome," *Sixteenth Century Journal* 11 (1980): 127.

[5] For a bibliography on the Roman activities of St. Camillo de Lellis, St. Joseph Calasanzio, Mary Ward, and other activist religious see Massimo Petrocchi, *Roma nel Seicento*, vol. 14 of *Storia di Roma* (Bologna, 1970), 193–94. On the Piarists, or "Scolopi" as they were known in Rome, see also Paul Grendler, *Schooling in Renaissance Italy: Literacy and Learning, 1300–1600* (Baltimore, 1989), 381–85. On Urban VIII and Mary Ward's "Jesuitesses" see Pastor, 29:24–34.

[6] On the "filippine" see Pompilio Totti, *Ritratto di Roma moderna* (Rome, 1638), 197; Gigli, *Diario*, 119; Gaetano Moroni, *Dizionario di erudizione storico-ecclesiastica* (Venice, 1844), 24:277–78.

[7] Martin, 109–220; Matizia Maroni Lumbroso and Antonio Martini, *Le confraternite romane nelle loro*

The movement for Catholic renewal in Rome, with its varied aims and impulses, reflected the initiatives of religious and laity from many countries. Similarly international, though more centralized in character, the other arm of the
Counter-Reformation, the Council of Trent, also left its mark on religion in the
city of Rome. The bishops and cardinals who met from 1545 to 1563 in Trent
defined the reforms they wanted in Church institutions. They reaffirmed the importance of the clergy, the traditional ecclesiastical hierarchy, and the units of
parish and diocese for Catholic Christendom. Over the next several generations
the structures of the local Church in Rome began to show the effects of this new
clarity.

An immediate change was the streamlining of Rome's parish topography,
which produced a smaller number of more viable groupings. In 1566 a city of
around 85,000 people had 132 parishes; by the 1620s this number had been
reduced to between 85 and 88, although the population had increased by
30,000.[8] In addition, only eleven churches were now authorized to perform baptisms, which ensured a better measure of control and record-keeping than had
prevailed before.

Behind these steps lay the renewed emphasis on the cure of souls at the parish
level. It was the parish priest's responsibility to make sure his parishioners frequented the sacraments and received basic instruction in religious doctrine. To
carry out these duties, the priest had to know who his parishioners were and to
this end the Council of Trent directed him to keep parish registers of baptisms,
marriages, and burials. In Rome the popes, reinvigorating a traditional but sporadic practice, added yet another instrument, the annual parish census or "state
of souls." From 1614 on, Roman parish priests were to turn in a yearly account
of the number of their parishioners who were qualified to receive communion, the
number of those who actually had, and the number of priests, bishops, members
of religious orders, prostitutes, and unwedded cohabitors.[9] The implementation
of Tridentine policy in Rome brought closer monitoring of papal subjects by ecclesiastical authorities, with the parish priest as the key intermediary. In the years

---

chiese (Rome, 1963), 194–97, 441–44; Gerardo Franza, Il catechismo a Roma e l'arciconfraternita della
dottrina cristiana (Alba, 1958), 70; Vincenzo Paglia, La Pieta' dei carcerati: Confraternite e societa' a Roma
nei secoli XVI-XVIII (Rome, 1980), 93–94. Paglia, 307–21, uses the data in Lumbroso and Martini
to construct graphs of the growth of confraternities in the sixteenth and seventeenth centuries and also
locates them spatially in the city. Two volumes of the journal Ricerche per la storia religiosa di Roma, 5
(1984) and 6 (1985), are devoted to confraternities; vol. 6 contains an invaluable index to all surviving
confraternity archives in Rome.

   [8] Cerasoli, "Censimento," 197; Fiorani, "Visite," 97; Carla Sbrana, Rosa Traina, and Eugenio Sonnino, Gli 'stati delle anime' a Roma dalle origini al secolo XVII: Fonti per lo studio della popolazione di Roma
(Rome, 1977), 132–38.

   [9] Sbrana, Traina, and Sonnino, 50–57, 100–102. Of course not all parish priests obeyed these
directives, as Eugenio Sonnino points out, ibid., 20. Cerasoli, "Censimento," 173–95, gives annual
totals of the Roman stati delle anime for the years 1600 to 1739 and a breakdown by parish for the year
1621.

ahead he would become a tempting figure to endow with other public duties, sometimes only tangentially related to the cure of souls.

The Council of Trent, reaffirming the principle of hierarchy in the Church, had also emphasized the bishop's responsibility for his diocese and his duty to supervise the lower clergy in person. One of the most important vehicles it envisioned was the bishop's "visitation" of the churches and religious institutions in his care, another traditional mechanism that now received new life. The cardinal vicar, deputed by the pope to act as bishop in his stead, had undertaken Rome's first post-Tridentine visitation between 1564 and 1573; after 1592 Roman visitations were entrusted to a congregation, or committee, of cardinals, with the cardinal vicar responsible for executing their decisions. [10]

The visitation that Urban VIII ordered in 1624, however, perhaps thinking of the arrival of thousands of pilgrims for the Holy Year, was the most thorough investigation of the diocese ever attempted. More than two hundred churches and monastic houses in the city as well as prisons, hospitals, and even the taverns near St. Peter's, were to be inspected. The pope was interested in knowing whether divine worship could be carried out properly with the appropriate objects in good repair, whether parishioners were receiving the sacraments, and what measures were being taken for the poor and sick. Urban's detailed instructions to the congregation give a vivid sense of his own vision of a working diocese: a place that had its papers and finances in order. [11] The visitation, which lasted from 1624 to 1632 and resulted in a 2,000-page report, bore the mark of a bishop with an administrative cast of mind.

Despite Rome's reputation as a "city of priests," the clerical component of the population was similar to that of other Italian cities, about two percent. The numbers ranged from 1,500 to 2,300 in the 1620s and 1630s. On the whole, the conditions of Rome's parish clergy satisfied the ecclesiastical inspectors. Rome had benefited from the presence of its Jesuit educators. When they had founded the Roman Seminary in 1565, it was still possible to find illiterate parish priests in Rome who worked at other part-time jobs. By Urban VIII's reign this was no longer the case. The parishioners got a good report as well. In any given year only a few hundred people who were qualified to take communion failed to fulfill their obligation. Moreover, over eighty catechism schools delivered basic doctrinal instruction to boys and girls in the city. The religious orders prompted only a few minor complaints. The pope particularly directed that brothers not ride to races in carriages and that they not go about in public alone. Some communities were

[10] Sergio Pagano, "Le visite apostoliche a Roma nei secoli XVI-XIX: Repertorio delle fonti," *RSRR* 4 (1980): 319; Niccolo' Del Re, *La curia romana: Lineamenti storico-giuridici*, 3d ed. (Rome, 1970), 364–66; Fiorani, "Visite," 64, 92–112.

[11] The pope's instructions are reproduced in Fiorani, "Visite," 124 n. 142; in general on the visitation of 1624 to 1632 see ibid., 112–27. The three-volume record of the visitation can be found in the ASV, Santa Congregazione della Visita Apostolica, vols. 1–3; see Pagano's index of its contents, *RSRR* 4 (1980): 352–55.

deemed too small to live a disciplined life and were asked to take in additional members. The numbers and proportion of religious in the city's population were increasing; in 1630 there were over 5,600 men and women in 103 Roman convents and monasteries.[12]

What Urban VIII's investigation had found was a city that was marked by the dual legacy of the Counter-Reformation, renewal and regulation. The parish was not the only vehicle encouraged by Trent. Catholic revival had impelled "an extraordinary proliferation of structures, institutions, and associations [that] profoundly modified the fabric of Roman religious society."[13] This was a sometimes contradictory inheritance. The effervescence of new devotional and charitable associations and the increase in parochial and diocesan vigilance could be in tension. The ecclesiastical inspectors of 1624 did uncover conflicts between confraternities and parish priests, but, significantly, were directed to resolve them in ways that did not suppress the confraternities.[14] Indeed, the visitors urged priests to start parish confraternities dedicated to the Sacrament in places where they did not already exist.[15] This clerical stratagem acknowledged the power of the bonds formed across territorial boundaries within groups of like-minded men and women, groups often patronized by upper-class families or highly placed prelates.

The Counter-Reformation impressed itself deeply on Roman religious style and practice, providing new models of heroic sanctity and imaginative charity and teaching new habits of bureaucratic attentiveness. But the local Church absorbed its varied thrusts into an already richly textured pattern of piety, something it had in common with many other European communities. Like their contemporaries elsewhere the inhabitants of Baroque Rome located the sacred in hundreds of large and small ways in their daily lives. The civic magistrates presented wax to a saint on a feast day, the butchers' guild paid its chaplain to say extra prayers when plague threatened, patricians joined a confraternity to care for orphans, a religious order sought civic support to promote the sanctity of a member, a confraternity organized a procession to honor a miracle-working picture of the Madonna. Religion was the context for all their activities. Here was another "holy city," rubbing shoulders with the Rome of the pilgrim, sharing the space and time of the Rome of St. Peter's, but translating those universal images into its own native idiom.

---

[12] Fiorani, "Visite," 101 n. 90, 116, 124–26; Franza, 103–4. Cerasoli, "Censimento," 175–77, shows that only 638 out of 91,502 individuals who were qualified to take yearly communion in 1630 failed to do so. See also Guerrino Pelliccia, "Scuole di catechismo e scuole rionali per fanciulle nella Roma del Seicento," *RSRR* 4 (1980): 237–68, and idem, *La scuola primaria a Roma dal secolo XVI al XIX* (Rome, 1985).

[13] Fiorani, "Visite," 140.

[14] Ibid., 90, 124–26.

[15] Ibid., 120.

Chapter Two

THE ECONOMIC CONJUNCTURE

RELATIVE ECONOMIC DECLINE was the fate of the cities of seventeenth-century Italy, but Rome's economy was sturdier than many others and this assured its power to attract newcomers. The peninsula's urban centers lost prosperity and population as southern Europe led the rest of the continent into a period of depression after 1620. Although size was not always a sign of economic health, falling population generally indicated economic malaise, if not disaster. Of a total of seventy Italian towns with a population over 10,000, almost half were smaller in numbers in 1700 than they had been a hundred years earlier. Many others registered no growth. Against that background Rome's modest increase from 105,000 to 138,000 over the century was a mark of comparative good fortune. However, measured against the expansion of the late sixteenth century, when it had doubled its population, and against the coming giants of the age, Paris and London, both of which would number over 400,000 in 1650, Rome's performance was far from brilliant.[1] These statistics highlight the chief characteristics of Rome's urban economy in the Baroque era: its relative strength and its profound weaknesses.

Like all early modern European towns Rome grew because people, especially males in Rome's case, migrated to it. Urban births did not exceed urban deaths and could not have provided a net addition to the city's population. Immigrants were the source of demographic increase. What sort of conditions would they meet in the Rome of the 1620s? They would encounter a highly stratified society with a few fabulously rich people at the top, many gentlemen of moderate wealth, a vast population of artisans and tradesmen ranging from the prosperous to the impoverished, and a noticeable contingent of beggars. They would find in Rome, in short, what they would find in most early modern capital cities. Capital cities grew during the long-term crisis of the seventeenth-century European economy because, as Giovanni Botero remarked in 1588, the presence of a ruler "doth

---

[1] Jan De Vries, *The Economy of Europe in an Age of Crisis 1600–1750* (New Haven, 1976), 4–5; idem, *European Urbanization 1500–1800* (Cambridge, Mass., 1984), 270–77, is my source for population figures. Ruggiero Romano, "L'Italia nella crisi del secolo XVII," *Studi storici* 9 (1968): 725. There is no detailed history of the Roman economy in the seventeenth century to match Jean Delumeau's invaluable study of the late sixteenth century. For a brief overview see Peter J. A. N. Rietbergen, *Pausen, Prelaten, Bureaucraten: Aspecten van de geschiedenis van het Pausschap en de Pauselijke Staat in de 17ᵉ Eeuw* (Nijmegen, 1983), 224–29. A helpful review of recent literature on Italian cities in the "long" Renaissance (mid-fourteenth to mid-seventeenth centuries) is Judith C. Brown, "Prosperity or Hard Times in Renaissance Italy?" *Renaissance Quarterly* 42 (1989): 761–80.

infinitely avail to the magnifying and making cities great and populous."[2] The prince, and the nobles who wanted to be near him, drew wealth to the city and that meant jobs for those who worked for their living, or charity when they could not.

Botero waxed especially eloquent on the pope's role in Rome's prosperity.

> Rome, whose majesty exceeded all the world, would she not be more like a desert than a city if the Pope held not his residence therein? If the Pope, with the greatness of his court and with the concourse of ambassadors, of prelates and of princes did not ennoble it and make it great? . . . If . . . he spent not there a great part of the revenues of the Church?[3]

Being the site of the papal court and the seat of the central administration of the Catholic Church certainly did give Rome an edge over other Italian cities after the Mediterranean economy foundered. Precisely those sectors that had been weakest in Rome were the most vulnerable in the seventeenth-century downturn. Notorious for the feebleness of its commercial and industrial sectors, Rome had never played an important role in international trade and had no export manufactures. It was the northern Italian towns whose medieval greatness had been built on just these foundations, however, that were hardest hit by the crisis.[4] By contrast, an urban economy based on "the trade in stamped parchment," as one seventeenth-century migrant to Rome put it, was more resilient.[5] Bureaucracy, law courts, and state finance continued to provide employment. Patrician families from all over Italy had long been accustomed to send talented offspring to make a career in the Roman Curia and they continued this pattern in the seventeenth century, adding their share of well-born and well-educated immigrants to the pool.

For the plebeian newcomer Rome also offered some distinctive attractions. One was a sizable construction industry, which, despite possible slowing after 1620, still offered plenty of work.[6] Another was relatively cheap and abundant food. Through the papal office of the Annona grain supplies and bread production were

---

[2] Giovanni Botero, *The Greatness of Cities*, trans. Robert Peterson (1606), ed. P. J. Waley and D. P. Waley (New Haven, 1956), 261. For the role of migration in urban growth and the differential growth rates of capital cities see De Vries, *Urbanization*, 141–42, 199–200. For sixteenth-century immigration and the higher proportion of males in Rome see Delumeau, *Vie* 1:188–220, 422; seventeenth-century immigration patterns remain to be studied.

[3] Botero, 273.

[4] Carlo Cipolla, "The Decline of Italy," *Economic History Review*, 2d ser., 5 (1952): 178. Delumeau, *Vie* 1:365–67, 380–82, 501–16.

[5] [Teodoro Ameyden], "Relatione seu Raguaglio compitissimo di tutte le Nobilta' delle Famiglie antiche," ASV, Miscellanea, arm. II, cod. 150, 658v–59r. A. Bastiaanse, *Teodoro Ameyden (1586–1656): Un neerlandese alla corte di Roma* (The Hague, 1967), 408–9, lists twenty-one copies of this manuscript—composed in 1641 and given varying titles—in and outside Rome.

[6] On the importance of the construction industry in Rome see Delumeau, *Vie* 1:380–82. For diverging views on whether or not it was declining in the seventeenth century see Rietbergen, 323, and Paola Scavizzi, "Considerazioni sull'attivita' edilizia a Roma nella prima meta' del Seicento," *Studi storici* 9 (1968): 186.

rigorously monitored in Rome. Brown wheat bread was available at an unvarying price of one *baiocco* a loaf, equivalent to one-fiftieth of a serving girl's monthly wage. Shortages had developed in the late sixteenth century and the popes were now leaving nothing to chance in assuring the food supply of their capital city. Seventeenth-century Romans ate comparatively well. One contemporary source commented that "Rome consumes twice as much meat and wine as Naples, although the latter city is twice as large."[7] Romans' meat consumption was higher than that of other Italians as well and their preferred source of carbohydrates, wheat bread, was a sign of their "privileged diet."[8] Wheat bread, olive oil, local wine, and lamb—in the spring—were staples of the poor; the rich added fish, beef, veal, and pork. Fruits and vegetables from local gardens supplemented bread and meat. In addition to their diet, there were social "cushions" in Rome. When people of the laboring classes fell on hard times, they could count on the habit of giving alms and the large number of charitable services by hospitals, guilds, and confraternities to help ease the fall.

Underpinning this relative prosperity, however, was an economy overwhelmingly dependent on income from land and from a technologically stagnant agriculture. This was a fact that escaped the notice of those who focused on the "trade in stamped parchment" and the glittering presence of the papal court. "Parchment" wealth ultimately rested on land. The taxes paid by agrarian communities to the papal treasury, the tithes owed to the local monastery whose order had a seat in Rome, the rents sent to cardinals from their abbeys and bishoprics around the peninsula, the fees owed to the papal treasury from owners of livestock in transit on Church-owned pastures, the dues collected by feudal lords resident in Rome, and the wine or hay delivered by tenants to their urban landlords were the fruits of rural labors. Rome was a major center of finance in the seventeenth century with a very lively market in private and public debt, but loans, whether to aristocrats or to the state treasury, were secured on grain exports, village taxes, or excises on what urban consumers ate and drank.[9]

---

[7] The unnamed source, quoted by Jacques Revel, is in fact Teodoro Ameyden (see n. 5); Jacques Revel, "A Capital City's Privileges: Food Supplies in Early-Modern Rome," in *Food and Drink in History*, trans. Patricia M. Ranum, ed. Robert Forster and Orest Ranum (Baltimore, 1979), 47. This article originally appeared in *Annales* 30 (1975): 563–74.

[8] Revel, 39–48. Revel makes clear the weaknesses of the available statistical data and eschews efforts to quantify caloric intake or per capita consumption. See also Delumeau, *Vie* 2:598–649; Gross, 114–15. As Revel points out, provisioning Rome was a priority to state officials for which the needs of other towns were sacrificed. See also Yves-Marie Berce', "Troubles frumentaires et pouvoir centralisateur: L'émeute de Fermo dans les Marches (1648)," *École française de Rome, Mélanges d'archéologie et d'histoire* 73 (1961): 471–505, 74 (1962): 759–803, and C. F. Black, "Perugia and Papal Absolutism in the Sixteenth Century," *English Historical Review* 96 (1981): 516, 521, 525. On the *baiocchella*, the small loaf whose price was fixed but whose weight fluctuated, see Maria Grazia Pastura Ruggiero, *La Reverenda Camera Apostolica e i suoi archivi (secoli XV–XVIII)* (Rome, 1984), 83. For wages of serving girl: ASR, 30 N.C., uff. 2 (Bonanni), 1633, pt. 1, 112r–v.

[9] Enrico Stumpo, *Il capitale finanziario a Roma fra Cinque e Seicento* (Milan, 1985). On the world of sixteenth-century finance in Rome see Delumeau, *Vie* 2:751–937.

How healthy was this agrarian base in the seventeenth century? The landscape outside the city gates and beyond the band of vineyards and vegetable gardens (*orti*) had a distinctive physiognomy. Here stretched the five hundred *casali*, or great estates, from which Roman ecclesiastical institutions and patrician families drew their revenues. These revenues had boomed with the European-wide population growth of the sixteenth century.[10] Demand for agricultural products rose, especially around a rapidly growing city, and the *casali* owners profited. Soon after 1600, however, the Mediterranean region felt the first shocks of the agricultural depression that eventually crept across most of the continent. The slowing of population increase in the early decades of the seventeenth century meant that income from land was more precarious. The precise configuration of this conjuncture and its effects on aristocratic and ecclesiastical spending in Rome have yet to be clarified, but most historians agree that there were general signs of an economic downturn after 1620.[11] This is best documented in the production of foodstuffs. Actual quantities of wheat bread and meat available to Romans hit a ceiling in the early 1600s; thereafter any additional mouths had to be content with smaller shares of an inelastic supply. Increasingly in the sixteenth and seventeenth centuries land had passed over from grain to livestock production; by 1700 the area in cereal cultivation had shrunk to one-tenth of what it had been three centuries earlier. Wheat prices climbed rapidly in the 1620s, remaining far above levels of the previous century in the following decades. Although the common person's loaf of bread still cost one *baiocco*, the weight of that loaf fell from twelve to seven ounces.[12]

While the shift to a pastoral economy was a response to market forces and a sign that better profits could be made there than by growing wheat, stockrearing was conducted according to age-old methods that brought no advances in produc-

---

[10] On the landed estates or *casali* see Jean-Claude Maire-Vigueur, "Classe dominante et classes dirigeantes à Rome à la fin du Moyen Âge," *Storia della citta* 1 (1976): 4–5, and Jean Coste, "I casali della Campagna di Roma all'inizio del Seicento," *ASRSP* 92 (1969): 41–115. For the *casali* owned by religious bodies as late as 1873 see Fabrizia Gurreri, "La liquidazione dell'Asse Ecclesiastico nella Campagna romana: Vecchi e nuovi proprietari, cambiamenti e permanenze," *Storia urbana* 12 (1988): 136–43. For a composite price index (without grain) from 1500 to 1630 see Delumeau, *Vie* 2:746; for grain prices from 1460 to 1650, ibid., 2:694–96.

[11] Volker Reinhardt's analysis of the Borghese fortune suggests that real rents were falling in the seventeenth century, *Kardinal Scipione Borghese, 1605–1633: Vermögen, Finanzen und sozialer Aufstieg eines Papstnepoten* (Tübingen, 1984), 195. Ruggiero Romano, "Tra XVI e XVII secolo: Una crisi economica, 1619–1622," *Rivista storica italiana* 74 (1962): 518. De Vries, *Urbanization*, 29; idem, *Crisis*, 4, 54. For grain prices from 1615 to 1691 see Rietbergen, 232. We lack detailed studies of the pattern of prices of other commodities in Rome after 1630 and have little systematic information on the course of rents or landed income in the seventeenth century. Interest rates on public bonds, which were a common form of nonlanded investment, were in steady decline throughout the century; Stumpo, *Capitale*, 296; cf. Delumeau, *Vie* 2:822.

[12] Revel, 41. Emilio Sereni, *Storia del paesaggio agrario italiano*, 3d ed. (Bari, 1976), 245–46. Delumeau, *Vie* 2:527–28, 566. Maire-Vigueur, 6. Gross, 165–66. For the declining size of the *baiocchella* loaf see Gigli, *Diario*, 40, 54, 238, 252.

tivity. Meat supplies, like grain, stagnated, though Romans still consumed more meat than their neighbors.[13] As pasture replaced tillage, fewer workers were needed and swamps spread across what were formerly fields.

On balance the long-term prospects of agriculture around Rome were not good. Commerce and manufacturing had never been strong. Finance remained active, with foreign capital pouring in to purchase papal bonds and offices, but this kind of investment did not promote economic growth. Moreover, in the course of the seventeenth century interest rates dropped steadily as the state's debt reached the maximum supportable by the population.[14] Embedded in an agrarian economy holding little promise for the future, Rome's relatively favorable situation depended too much on the financial health of the papacy; in the eighteenth century the insecurity of this foundation became apparent.[15]

Already by the 1620s the Roman laboring classes, despite their relatively privileged diet, were facing worsening conditions of less food and higher taxes. Their lot had always been precarious in any case. Men and women whose work provided a mere subsistence wage and whose families were thrown into destitution by the calamities of illness, loss of employment, or old age probably made up the majority of the city's population. In one urban parish over seventy percent were listed as too poor to pay a special tax assessment in 1644. It is these people who show up so regularly in the rolls of those imprisoned for debt: a shoemaker who could not pay his rent, a muleteer who borrowed money for a horse, an old man who took out a loan to send his son to school.[16] A large proportion of the unskilled and semiskilled working people of Rome, like their counterparts in most early modern cities, owned little property and had no savings. Chronic debt and the likelihood of complete indigence were the facts of economic life for these urban dwellers. Some of them could certainly expect to find themselves begging in the piazzas during the course of a lifetime.

[13] Revel, 42–43, 47.

[14] Stumpo, *Capitale*, 298–301. For a detailed discussion of increasing fiscal burdens see Chapters 12 and 13.

[15] Gross, 119, 131–49.

[16] Paglia, 62–65. The parish was Santa Dorotea in Trastevere; Sbrana, Traina, and Sonnino, 442 n. 6. While this tax assessment was made by the parish priest, who might have erred on the side of generosity out of sympathy for his parishioners, it does establish an order of magnitude for the proportion of "laboring poor" in at least one Roman neighborhood. A 1627 edict that lists appropriate hospitals for the sick poor assumes that artisans will be included in that category; see ASC, cred. XIII, vol. 30, 260r. According to Paglia, 62–65, debtors made up more than half of Rome's prison population. However, a census of prisoners in the year 1582 records a much higher percentage; indeed Delumeau, *Vie* 1:497–98, estimates that six percent of the city's population in 1582 was imprisoned for debt at one time or another during the year. For some of the natural disasters that befell Romans in the seventeenth century see Luigi Fiorani, "Religione e povertà': Il dibattito sul pauperismo a Roma tra Cinque e Seicento," *RSRR* 3 (1979): 82–84; the entire issue of the journal in which this article appears is devoted to the subject of poverty in Rome from the sixteenth to the twentieth centuries. For a detailed study of the laboring poor in an early modern capital city see Jeffry Kaplow, *The Names of Kings: The Parisian Laboring Poor in the Eighteenth Century* (New York, 1972).

And beggars were everywhere in Rome. While reliable statistical estimates are hard to come by, literary evidence repeatedly underscores how pervasive the presence of beggars was in the churches and squares of the Baroque city. "In Rome you see nothing but beggars," wrote the author of a treatise on charity in 1601, "they are so numerous that it is impossible to walk down the streets without being surrounded by them."[17] For the Holy Year of 1625, when authorities were particularly worried about the impression the city would make on pilgrims, parish priests were asked to make a census of the local poor. The parish priest of St. Peter's reported that beggars accosted people even as they prayed and the Dominican fathers at Santa Maria sopra Minerva hired policemen to keep them out. The very presence of the beggars was perhaps a sign of Rome's comparative prosperity. The crisis elsewhere in the peninsula may have put added pressure on Roman society, as paupers joined the other immigrants thronging through the gates. For some of those who died in the street, or on litters before they reached a hospital, the holy city had been their last hope.[18]

---

[17] Camillo Fanucci, *Trattato di tutte l'opere pie dell'alma citta' di Roma* (Rome, 1601), quoted by Delumeau, *Vie* 1:407. For estimates of the number of poor or of beggars in Rome see Paglia, 51–54; Delumeau, *Vie* 1:403–16; Paolo Simoncelli, "Origini e primi anni di vita dell'ospedale romano dei poveri mendicanti," *Annuario dell'Istituto Storico Italiano per L'Eta' Moderna e Contemporanea*, 25–26 (1973–74): 152. Fiorani records a figure of 10,000 beggars in 1660, "Visite," 128 n. 155; he notes that in 1670 forty-one percent of the population of three urban districts (*rioni*) was described as poor, if not necessarily beggars, "Religione," 99–103.

[18] Fiorani, "Religione," 98–99.

Chapter Three

THE NODES OF POWER

IN THE HOLY CITY earthly status, prestige, and power were unequally distributed. Who was at the top of this hierarchical society? The pope and his close relatives would be the ready answer. Rome was ruled by the supreme pontiff, who made members of his family his closest advisers and assistants. Their temperaments, tastes, and relations with each other absorbed political observers and formed the chief subject of political analysis. Urban VIII had two surviving brothers and three nephews and this troop of Barberini kinsmen dominated the papal capital during his reign. Their power was both informal, in that it was a function of ties of blood, and formal, in that they occupied official posts in the regime. They were the key figures in the city and all eyes were upon them. Any history set in Urban VIII's pontificate begins with Maffeo Barberini and his family.

Our view of the Roman setting, however, should also include their view. In 1623 they were newcomers to the heights, suddenly catapulted to prominence by the accident of papal election. Their gaze took in the permanent features of the city's sociopolitical landscape, lingering longest on those nearest them at the apex of status, prestige, and power. Who did they see there? Not rivals in any overt sense, but figures who conditioned, while not necessarily limiting, the ruler's freedom of action in Rome. These were the Catholic kings and Italian states represented by their ambassadors, the Sacred College of Cardinals, and the high Roman aristocracy. The presence of these nodes of power was a subtle background pressure for a new papal family like the Barberini, shaping in varying degrees their goals, concerns, and methods. These enduring elements helped to give the political topography of Baroque Rome its special contours and this pontificate its particular dynamic.

THE BARBERINI

A story about Pope Urban VIII circulated in Rome in the late 1630s. The son of the Habsburg Holy Roman emperor had been officially designated as heir-apparent to the imperial dignity, a position that bore the title King of the Romans. All friends of the Habsburgs in Rome, and the ambassadors of the empire and Spain, competed to produce the most spectacular celebrations in honor of the event; they fêted the crowds with fireworks, wild animal shows, plays, and showers of coins. When the civic authorities wanted to join in with festivities on the Capitol, however, the pope replied brusquely, "In Rome I am King of the Romans," and the plans were dropped.[1] The story captures some of the pope's qualities as a ruler; he was proud, imperious, and anxious to maintain his prerogatives. Those prerogatives embraced not only his person, office, and kingdom, but, most notably, his family.

Urban VIII was born Maffeo Barberini in 1568, the fifth son of a Florentine wool merchant. In a common pattern for the day Maffeo was chosen to follow in the footsteps of his uncle Francesco, who had opened the family's connections with Rome by becoming a successful prelate in the papal Curia. At his uncle's death in 1600 the thirty-two year old Maffeo inherited his fortune, and he asked his older brother Carlo, with his wife Costanza Magalotti and their children, to move from Florence and join him in Rome. The family's Roman strategy had already touched its third generation. In 1604 Maffeo was consecrated archbishop of Nazareth and sent as papal nuncio to France. Two years later, at the request of King Henry IV of France, he was elevated to the cardinalate. This gave Carlo Barberini and his sons new stature in Roman society and Carlo was soon holding civic office. As Cardinal Maffeo Barberini filled various posts under Pope Paul V (1605–1621) and his successor Pope Gregory XV (1621–1623), he and Carlo supervised the education of the three young boys. The two brothers were accustomed to close collaboration throughout Maffeo's career. It was only natural that their teamwork should continue, with vastly enhanced resources, after 6 August 1623, when Cardinal Barberini was elected pope and took the name Urban VIII.[2]

One of the distinctive features of papal monarchy in the early modern period was that it raised not just a man but a family to the peak of Roman society. It would have disturbed contemporaries if the new pope had not immediately made at least one of his kinsmen a cardinal to act as his second-in-command. It would have surprised them, not unpleasantly perhaps, if the new pope had not bestowed gifts and honors on his relatives. The papal family was expected to play a vital part in any pontificate, and Urban VIII, with two surviving brothers and three nephews, had the necessary personnel at his disposal.

To Carlo Barberini went riches and the highest secular office of state, commander-in-chief of the papal armies, with the title of General of the Church. The most politically vital post, however, could not go to a layman, and it was bestowed instead on Carlo's eldest son Francesco, a youthful twenty-six when his uncle made him cardinal in October 1623. Francesco Barberini assumed an un-

[1] Gigli, *Diario*, 166–68. For references to six printed accounts of *feste* for Ferdinand III in 1637 see Renato Diez, *Il trionfo della parola: Studio sulle relazioni di feste nella Roma barocca 1623–1667* (Rome, 1986), 21–24.

[2] Pio Pecchiai, *I Barberini* (Rome, 1959), 129–51. On Urban VIII's relationships with his family, his early career, and his election as pope see Pastor, 28:1–54. The art patronage of Urban VIII has given rise to an extensive art historical literature. See, among others, Francis Haskell, *Patrons and Painters: A Study in the Relations between Italian Art and Society in the Age of the Baroque*, rev. and enl. ed. (New Haven, 1980), 24–62, 396–98; Marilyn Aronberg Lavin, *Seventeenth-Century Barberini Documents and Inventories of Art* (New York, 1975); Louise Rice, "The Altars and Altarpieces of New St. Peter's (1621–1653)" (Ph.D. diss., Columbia University, 1992).

official position that went by several names, most commonly "cardinal nephew" or "cardinal *padrone*." The word *padrone*, "master" or "boss," suggests what his role was to be as the pope's chief lieutenant. He was the man through whom all business with the pope had to pass.

The informal institution of the cardinal nephew had become increasingly important during the course of the sixteenth century, as the pontiffs sought tighter control of their realm. It was imperative for them to have associates with the range of authority inherent in the office of cardinal, but with greater personal loyalty than most cardinals, their potential successors, could summon up. Ideally the cardinal nephew was a real nephew, although some popes had to adopt a suitable candidate from more distant kin. While much has been written about the abuses of papal nepotism, contemporaries felt that affairs in Rome foundered intolerably if there was no cardinal nephew, or if the man so designated was not the pope's closest adviser. Such a figure was essential to the smooth running of a system in which all authority came from the top.[3]

To Cardinal Francesco Barberini, therefore, the pope ceded "the government of our state, with universal supervision and broadest powers," as he put it in a chirograph of 1632.[4] Intelligent, erudite, and a cultivated art patron, the man known as Cardinal "Barberino" was "closest to the ears of His Holiness" and a person of immense political importance in Urban VIII's Rome.[5] Witnesses described him as someone who veiled his true feelings and submitted completely to his uncle's wishes, but who let nothing get to the pope without his knowledge.

[3] The diarist Giacinto Gigli provides evidence of some of the problems that could occur when a pope did *not* have an effective cardinal nephew, *Diario*, 305, 372–74, 431–32. For a somewhat sensational contemporary view see Gregorio Leti, *Il nipotismo di Roma; o vero, Relatione delle raggioni che muovono i pontifici all'aggrandimento de' nipoti* (Amsterdam, 1667). On the cardinal nephew under Urban VIII see Andreas Kraus, "Amt und Stellung des Kardinal Nepoten zur Zeit Urbans VIII (1623)," *Römische Quartalschrift für Christliche Altertumskunde und Kirchengeschichte* 53 (1958): 239–43; idem, "Der Kardinal-Nepote Francesco Barberini und das Staatssekretariat Urbans VIII," ibid. 64 (1969): 191–208; Madeleine Laurain-Portemer, "Absolutisme et népotisme: La surintendance de l'état ecclésiastique," *Bibliothèque de l'école des chartes* 131 (1973): 518–21. On nepotism under Pope Paul V (1605–1621) see Wolfgang Reinhard, *Papstfinanz und Nepotismus unter Paul V (1605–1621)*, 2 vols. (Stuttgart, 1974), and Reinhardt. Barbara Hallman analyzes the contradictory attitudes of the sixteenth-century Catholic Church on this subject and discusses how the cardinal nephew emerged, *Italian Cardinals, Reform and the Church as Property, 1492–1563* (Berkeley, 1985), 127–28. For a list of cardinal nephews from 1573 to 1689 see Rietbergen, 123. See also Prodi, 190–92.

[4] The chirograph of 17 February 1632 was published by Laurain-Portemer, 561–68. For a critique of Laurain-Portemer's emphasis on the formal powers of the cardinal nephew, however, see Prodi, 193, and Wolfgang Reinhard, *Freunde und Kreaturen: 'Verflechtung' als Konzept zur Erforschung historischer Führungsgruppen Römische Oligarchie um 1600* (Munich, 1979), 61–62.

[5] "Relazione di Giovanni Nani, 1640," in Barozzi and Berchet, 2:25, 34–35. Four other Venetian ambassadors have left assessments of Cardinal Francesco Barberini during his uncle's pontificate, ibid., 1:214–15, 263, 331, 371–72. See also Pastor, vols. 28 and 29, passim; Pecchiai, *Barberini*, 154–59; Laurain-Portemer, 516–18. The cardinal's art patronage is discussed by Haskell, 43–46, 53, 59–61. A source that will undoubtedly prove useful to scholars when it is available for consultation is the Barberini correspondence or *carteggio*, now in the process of being catalogued at the Vatican Library.

Although he lived in the great palace of the Cancelleria, one of the many perquisites of the office of vice-chancellor that he assumed in 1632, Cardinal Francesco Barberini also had an apartment at the papal residence. Compliant and unobtrusive in Urban VIII's presence, he was vastly diligent and well-served in affairs of state by countless informants.

Francesco was the first of the Barberini cardinals; soon there would be two others. In 1624 the pope promoted his brother Antonio, a Capuchin monk, to the purple and, four years later, his youngest nephew, also named Antonio. The elder Antonio, known as the Cardinal Sant'Onofrio for his titular church in Rome, was reluctantly torn from the austere life of his order and played a minor role in his brother's pontificate. His most noteworthy public office, from 1636 to 1642, was substitute cardinal vicar, meaning that he stood in for the cardinal deputed by the pope to supervise the religious life of the diocese of Rome.[6]

The younger Antonio, a mere nineteen years old when elevated to the cardinalate, cut quite a different figure from his severe uncle and hardworking older brother. High-spirited and fun-loving, he sponsored some of the most memorable public festivities of the era.[7] Cardinal Antonio, as he was known, never managed to rival his brother Francesco's intimacy with the pontiff; as one perceptive ambassador noted in 1635, "he does not have a part in government, although he desires it, [because] the Pope knows very well that power [*dominio*] does not want companions."[8] Nonetheless, Urban VIII called frequently on the services of the young Antonio, and in 1638, despite the objections of the Spaniards to this francophile cardinal, appointed him to an important post, cardinal chamberlain of the apostolic chamber. The cardinal chamberlain, who held office for life, had wide-ranging public responsibilities in Rome and played a key role during the periods between pontificates known as the Vacant See. Even without such an appointment, however, Cardinal Antonio could not be ignored, and people seeking favors at the Barberini court did not ignore him.[9] While there may have been tensions at times between the two cardinal nephews, at least during Urban's lifetime they were not permitted to disrupt the larger unity of the family.

To the third nephew and middle brother, Taddeo Barberini, went the task of continuing the lineage. All the power and wealth the pope could bestow upon his kinsmen would come to nothing if someone was not delegated to the task of producing heirs. The choice of Taddeo's wife was made with care; she was a crucial

[6] Pecchiai, *Barberini*, 151–54; Gigli, *Diario*, 161–62. For the Cardinal Sant'Onofrio's activities as "pro-vicario" for Cardinal Marzio Ginetti, who was absent from Rome from 1636 to 1642, see *Regesti*, vols. 4 and 5, passim.

[7] Pecchiai, *Barberini*, 191–213. For his art and festival patronage see Haskell, 54–57, and Ann Sutherland Harris, *Andrea Sacchi* (New York, 1977).

[8] Alvise Contarini in Barozzi and Berchet, 1:372.

[9] See the description of Giovanni Nani, Venetian ambassador in 1640, in Barozzi and Berchet, 2:33–34; Gigli, *Diario*, 200. For civic delegations to express thanks or congratulations to Cardinal Antonio Barberini, see ASC, cred. I, vol. 33, decreti, 0107r (2 June 1631) and 0188v (20 August 1637).

element in the process of social alchemy by which wool merchants were transformed into aristocrats. Taddeo married Anna Colonna in 1627. Daughter of Filippo, the "Contestabile," Colonna, duke of Paliano, Taddeo's bride came from one of the most illustrious families of the Roman feudal nobility. Urban VIII had no intention of leaving his lay relatives without aristocratic titles of their own, however. At his father's death in 1630, Taddeo inherited not only his military duties as General of the Church, but his feudal possessions as well; he now became duke of Monterotondo and prince of Palestrina. One of the richest men of his time, he eventually acquired a total of fifteen fiefs.[10]

It was a heady rise for a family, but one that had ample precedents among papal lineages in the preceding century. The pope offended precedent and shocked the Italian princes and Roman barons, however, when he bestowed the title of "prefect of the city" (*praefectus urbis*) upon Taddeo Barberini in 1631. The honorific title of prefect of Rome had been hereditary in the family of the Della Rovere, rulers of the independent duchy of Urbino in central Italy, until the death of the last Della Rovere on 28 April 1631. The duchy then passed into the possession of the papacy and the ducal title was extinguished. This would certainly have been the fate of the title of prefect as well, whose only distinction was its antique flavor, had Urban VIII not had other plans for it. Having staged a series of solemn public ceremonies in which Taddeo was invested with the "prefecture" of Rome, the pope startled diplomats by announcing that his nephew would have ceremonial precedence over all of them, an honor that no lay papal nephew had ever before claimed or been granted. The ambassadors and high nobility refused to accept Taddeo's new status; some left town to avoid meeting him and others made sure they did not encounter him in public. Taddeo meanwhile did everything he could to defend his novel rights, including bribing the coachman of the Venetian ambassador to pull up his horses as the "prince prefect" passed by.[11]

Urban VIII's creative inflation of a moribund title is a telling glimpse of his ambitions for the house of Barberini. Wealth, fiefs, offices of state, even a marriage alliance with the Colonna were not enough for his family. His sights were set not merely on Rome but on the princely dynasties of Italy: the Medici, the Este, the Savoia, and, above all, the Farnese, descendants of a pope who had reigned less than a century earlier. The Farnese pope Paul III (1535–1549) had actually cut off pieces of the Papal States to create an independent duchy, Parma

[10] Pecchiai, *Barberini*, 159–91. Taddeo Barberini's success in accumulating fifteen fiefs is nonetheless overshadowed by the twenty-eight fiefs acquired by the Borghese, the family of Pope Paul V (1605–1621); Stumpo, *Capitale*, 272–73. On his art patronage see Haskell, 48–52, and John Beldon Scott, *Images of Nepotism: The Painted Ceilings of Palazzo Barberini* (Princeton, 1991). Taddeo Barberini's one public office in Rome was governor of the Borgo, chief civil and criminal magistrate for the Vatican precinct, from 1632 to 1644; his edicts during that period are recorded in *Regesti*, vols. 4 and 5, passim.

[11] Pecchiai, *Barberini*, 166–74. G. Pisano, "L'ultimo prefetto dell'Urbe: Don Taddeo Barberini, e le relazioni tra la corte di Roma e la repubblica veneta sotto il pontificato di Urbano VIII," *Roma* 9 (1931): 103–20, 155–64.

and Piacenza, for his son. His successors made such vandalism illegal; in the seventeenth century papal relatives could no longer hope to have their own sovereign state when their kinsman died. The best they could do henceforth was to marry into the ruling families of Italy. Yet it plainly galled a pope with such an acute sense of his dignity as Urban VIII that his relatives could not command the same honors as rulers who were no mightier, indeed less mighty, than the vicar of Christ.

The pope's concern to advance his lineage, both materially and symbolically, was the dominating political consideration of his reign. If he could have been content with the merely material, his twenty-year pontificate would doubtless have been a great, and tranquil, satisfaction to him. The quest for "symbolic capital," as Pierre Bourdieu has put it, changed all that; it made him perpetually vulnerable, an easy prey to the disdain of real aristocrats.[12] The Barberini nephews, but particularly Taddeo, fully partook of their uncle's obsession, with all its anxious consequences. In an era when the mystique of birth and blood justified the social hierarchy, the smile of fortune that elevated the family of an elected monarch was not purely beneficent. They had their work cut out for them.

No discussion of the Barberini family would be complete without mention of their "friends," for they were the hub of a wider patronage network. If a career was to have any hope of success a system of patron-client relations had to be built up in its course. Any ambitious prelate would have been part of someone's clientele, and Maffeo Barberini was no exception. While he owed his start to his uncle, his first major advance came in the 1590s thanks to services rendered to Cardinal Pietro Aldobrandini, the nephew of Clement VIII (1592–1605). A second powerful patron was the king of France, to whom his attainment of the cardinal's cap was due; the Bourbon connection would continue to be important for the Barberini even after Urban's death. In the same manner the rising cardinal Maffeo befriended others lower down on the ladder, such as Carlo's brother-in-law Lorenzo Magalotti of Florence, who served him loyally in various posts.

After Urban VIII's election and the elevation of the Barberini nephews, the Barberini client network, now with several strands, grew broader and more complex. In general, however, the pontiff's warmest ties after kinsmen were to other Florentines. The banking family of the Sacchetti profited handsomely from their old friend's new position. Marcello Sacchetti became the papal banker and treasurer, and his brother Giulio was made a cardinal. Florentine financiers and tax-farmers like Piero and Orazio Falconieri and Orazio Magalotti found lucrative opportunities in Urban VIII's Rome. The "honorary Tuscan" Cassiano dal Pozzo, an important figure in the city's cultural life, assisted Cardinal Francesco Barberini in several capacities and Tuscan artists and poets like Pietro da Cortona and Francesco Bracciolini also enjoyed Barberini patronage.[13]

---

[12] Pierre Bourdieu, *Outline of a Theory of Practice*, trans. Richard Nice (Cambridge, 1977), 178.

[13] For a general discussion of papal client networks in Rome see Reinhard, *Freunde*, 47, 64–71, and

THE FOREIGN POWERS

The Barberini and their Florentine friends and relatives were the most highly charged power node in Rome during the years 1623 to 1644. That charmed circle drew the attentions of bad poets, hopeful scholars, ambitious curialists, promising soldiers of fortune, impoverished refugees, and even duplicitous bandits. The Barberini court so dazzles scholars that we need to remind ourselves to look out at the world they themselves surveyed. It was a political landscape that necessarily embraced the whole of western Christendom, with particular regard for the three greatest Catholic monarchs of the age: the "most Christian" king of France, the "most Catholic" king of Spain, and, to a lesser extent, the Holy Roman emperor. Louis XIII of France and the Habsburg cousins Philip IV of Spain and Emperor Ferdinand II—until 1637, then Ferdinand III—were at war during the entire length of Urban VIII's pontificate. While their military conflicts never touched Rome directly, they disturbed life in the papal capital in many indirect ways, as we shall see in later chapters.

The "powers" were a palpable presence in Rome through their ambassadors. These envoys, whether on routine assignment or special missions, made dramatic ceremonial entries into the city, gave lavish public fêtes, and carried on distant wars by other means in the Vatican halls and Roman streets. Rome still figured in the calculations of international diplomacy, perhaps for the last time, and during the long decades of the Thirty Years War Catholic rulers lobbied tenaciously for political and financial favors from the papacy.

Such efforts often took the form of competitive display. When the French ambassador made his formal cavalcade through the city in 1633, it was a fact of some diplomatic importance that his horses were shod in silver and his footmen wore livery embroidered with real gold.[14] While the intended audience for such a spectacle was undoubtedly the pope and other foreign agents in Rome, ambassadors were not above courting the Roman populace. The Spanish envoy celebrated the birth of a son to Philip IV with the usual fireworks and showers of gold coins, but he also sent eighteen mules loaded with foodstuffs to the prisons, *after* they had circulated "with great pomp" through the city streets.[15]

If diplomacy at a Baroque court was one part display, it was another part intrigue, and the latter shaped the political atmosphere of Rome as surely as the former. Spanish agents, who were distressed at what they perceived to be Urban VIII's pro-French policies in the late 1620s, hoped to terrify him mortally by

---

on the Barberini in particular the graphic rendering on p. 71. See also Haskell, 38–39, 51, 98–100. Cassiano dal Pozzo, born in Turin, spent much of his youth in Pisa; for his participation in plague prevention efforts under Cardinal Francesco Barberini see Chapter 10.

[14] Gigli, *Diario*, 134–35. The most complete account in English of great power rivalry at Urban VIII's court may be found in Pastor, vols. 28 and 29.

[15] Gigli, *Diario*, 108. It is important to note that the prison population was largely composed of people who could not pay their debts and who would thus have appreciated gifts of food.

paying astrologers to forecast his imminent demise. The pontiff was frightened, but not fatally. He issued stern edicts making it treasonous to predict the deaths of popes and their kinfolk, and closeted himself with the gifted astrologer Tommaso Campanella for some timely countermeasures.[16] Foreign monarchs tried to influence papal policy in less occult ways too. They routinely offered gifts and pensions to the powerful Barberini nephews, and they expected to count a few cardinals of their choosing in the Sacred College.

Rome was disordered in more overt ways by the presence of foreign diplomats and the shadow of their international rivalries. When the Spanish ambassador tried to assassinate the rebel Portuguese ambassador on his way home from lunch, a foreign quarrel turned into a dangerous shootout in the city streets.[17] Then there was the whole matter of diplomatic immunity. An ambassador's palace was legally exempt from any Roman criminal jurisdiction, and thus was a refuge for anyone fleeing the papal police. It also offered tempting sanctuary for illicit enterprises. Spanish agents used their envoy's residence, which gave its name to the whole neighborhood of the Piazza di Spagna, to hide young Romans they had kidnapped for the armies of the "most Catholic" king. The exact boundaries of a palace were somewhat fluid; they often extended to neighboring streets and piazzas, which were thus "off limits" to even the meager law enforcement efforts that Roman constables (*sbirri*) could muster.[18]

Although the pope's view took in all of Christendom, by the seventeenth century it fell with greatest attentiveness on the Italian peninsula. Here lay a mosaic of states: the republics of Venice, Genoa, and tiny Lucca, Piedmont under the dukes of Savoy, the duchy of Parma and Piacenza under the Farnese, the duchy of Modena under the Este, the grand duchy of Tuscany under the Medici, the state of Milan under its Spanish governor, and the "regno" or kingdom of Naples and the island of Sicily, both under Spanish viceroys. The Italian states, in all their variety, may not have counted for much in Europe, but they loomed very large in the eyes of the successor to St. Peter and in the politics of the Roman court.

The Italian powers made their weight felt in Rome not only through their ambassadors but also through the College of Cardinals, of whose seventy members over eighty percent were Italian by 1650.[19] There was always a cardinal from each of the princely families—Medici, Este, Farnese, and Savoy—and the Venetian republic also had its cardinals.[20] The cardinals from Italy's ruling families and

[16] D. P. Walker, *Spiritual and Demonic Magic: From Ficino to Campanella* (London, 1958; Notre Dame, Ind., 1975), 205–7. For Urban VIII's bull of 4 January 1631 against astrologers see *Regesti* 4:120.

[17] Gigli, *Diario*, 209–11.

[18] Ibid., 367–69. Leopold von Ranke, *History of the Popes*, trans. E. Fowler, rev. ed. (New York, 1901), 3:374–75. Niccolo' Del Re, *Monsignor Governatore di Roma* (Rome, 1972), 44. Gross, 215. Leonard Kociemski, "Un fattaccio di cronaca del Seicento," *Strenna dei romanisti* 23 (1962): 184–87.

[19] Rietbergen, 88–90.

[20] On this phenomenon in the sixteenth century see Prodi, 175. Pietro Contarini, Venetian ambas-

leading states had not only dynastic interests to protect but also the multiple strands of ecclesiastical business that touched their clients and countrymen, both at home and in the Curia. The Cardinals Este, Medici, Farnese, and Savoia were the chief power brokers at Rome for those of their subjects who sought pensions, benefices, curial offices, or papal dispensations. With their superior aristocratic credentials and independence they were also potentially serious adversaries should they oppose Barberini ambitions.

THE CARDINALS

Venetian political observers in the late sixteenth and seventeenth centuries were fond of repeating that the Sacred College of Cardinals had lost any independent voice in the government of the Church and simply went along with whatever the pope wanted.[21] Both the older forum of the consistory and the more recent cardinalatial congregations were, they asserted, completely subservient to the papal will. Except during the Vacant See, when the college chose the next pope, "the only role given to the cardinals is in matters that are already decided, and at times even already carried out."[22] Such charges were substantially true, for the Sacred College as an institution had become a clearly subordinate body within an absolutist papal monarchy. Even the Venetians would have admitted, however, that as individuals the cardinals could not be so easily dismissed, and the careful descriptions of each cardinal in their diplomatic reports attest to that. As social figures and as foci of political intrigue, the cardinals were a far from negligible force in the life of the Roman court and in the city of Rome.

Of the seventy possible cardinals who might exist at any one time, around two-thirds could be found resident in Rome. In the seventeenth century, as in the sixteenth, they tended to be drawn from the urban upper classes of Italy and to have had legal training rather than a purely literary or theological education.[23] Elevation to the purple for such men represented the summit of a successful administrative career in the Papal States, and, of course, a chance at the chair of St. Peter. If few would attain that prize, most could be certain of achieving at least the improvement of their family's status and fortune.

Like good courtiers at a secular court, most cardinals at the papal court, whatever their official functions, were absorbed in furthering career and family. What tended to happen, however, was a process of centrifugal fragmentation, a curious accompaniment to the increasing centralization of authority under absolutism. As

sador to Rome in 1627, described the Venetian cardinals there as "true and worthy sons of this homeland," in Barozzi and Berchet, 1:213.

[21] Prodi, 170, 179; Barozzi and Berchet, 1:142, 2:25.

[22] Alvise Contarini, Venetian ambassador to Rome, in his report of 1635 in Barozzi and Berchet, 1:355. See also Prodi, 169–80.

[23] Hallman, 5, 8, 15; Rietbergen, 96–98, 102; for the education of prelates, who often became cardinals later on, see Ago, *Carriere*, 16–18.

the council halls of the papacy grew silent and the cardinals limited their public voice to "mute approbation" of papal decisions, a constellation of miniature "courts" grew up around the cardinals.[24] To the extent that individual incomes would allow, the cardinals in Rome conducted themselves like ecclesiastical lords. The greatest collected paintings, books, and manuscripts, planned villas, built churches and chapels, and employed a retinue of dozens if not hundreds of servants.[25]

The role of such courts was not purely decorative, however, for each cardinal functioned as the center of his own patron-client network. Just as he was the "creature" of the pope who had promoted him, he had his informal "creatures" who owed him gratitude and loyalty for advancing them at the papal palace or in the Curia. As the sixteenth-century biographer of one cardinal put it, in Rome, "although all the power belongs to one [prince] alone, each [cardinal] has his little court and his personal authority, and his popularity, even among the people, can be considerable."[26]

In reality the cardinals constituted dozens of minor nodes of influence and prestige in the city. Even as their collective institutional role withered, their informal patronage powers received quasi-official recognition in the developing status of "cardinal protector." Each foreign power had its pensioned cardinal protector to serve as its agent in the Sacred College and the Curia. More to our purpose, however, most Roman churches, welfare institutions, confraternities, and colleges also had cardinal protectors, whose "protection" took a rich variety of forms. Cardinal protectors lobbied for and supervised the institutions under their aegis, and in some cases exercised both civil and criminal jurisdiction over them. From the side of the "protected" a stream of requests for favors and money flowed upward to the cardinal, sometimes for the group's buildings or pious works, but often for the personal needs of members.[27]

---

[24] Barozzi and Berchet, 1:355. On the constellation of courts see n. 26.

[25] Kathleen Weil-Garris and John F. D'Amico, "The Renaissance Cardinal's Ideal Palace: A Chapter from Cortesi's *De Cardinalatu*," in *Studies in Italian Art and Architecture, 15th through 18th Centuries*, ed. Henry A. Millon (Rome, 1980), 49–50. Hallman, 158–61, and passim, since her whole book is devoted to the cardinals' ecclesiastical income in the first half of the sixteenth century. Delumeau, *Vie* 1:274–79, 433–35, 447–57 (a list of the revenues of the cardinals in 1571 follows p. 452). See also Markus Voelkel, "Haushalt und Gesellschaft. Römische Kardinalsfamilien des 17. Jhs. Unter besonderer Berücksichtigung der Borghese, Barberini und Chigi" (Habilitation thesis, University of Augsburg, 1991).

[26] Antoine Maria Gratiani (1537–1611), *La vie du cardinal Jean Commendon* (Paris, 1671), 25, cited by Pierre Hurtubise, "Familiarité et fidélité à Rome au XVIe siècle: Les 'familles' des cardinaux Giovanni, Bernardo et Antonio Maria Salviati," in Durand, *Hommage*, 336.

[27] Prodi, 186; Giovanni Battista De Luca, *Il Dottor Volgare overo il compendio di tutta la legge civile, canonica, feudale, e municipale, nelle cose piu' ricevute in pratica* (Rome, 1673), bk. 15, pt. 3, chap. 38, p. 344. The selection of a cardinal protector was made with care; see, for example, Franza, 236–37. The private papers of cardinals would be interesting to explore for such requests. A cardinal nephew such as Cardinal Francesco Barberini was much in demand as a protector during his uncle's pontificate; see the alms volume of his correspondence (*carteggio*) in BAV, Barb. lat. 10636 (provisional). I am grateful

Despite the satisfactions of power broking and patronage that the cardinalate offered the ambitious churchman, it could not compete with the rewards of election to the Holy See itself; this naturally was the dream of most members of the Sacred College. It was also the dream of their clients and relatives, who sometimes simply could not wait. Giacinto Centini, nephew of the Cardinal d'Ascoli, was executed in 1635 for trying to clear his uncle's path to the papacy by making a pact with the devil to kill Urban VIII.[28] Papal elections were much more subtly engineered than Centini, in his innocence, realized. Each cardinal nephew of a previous pope controlled the votes of his uncle's "creatures" and bargained with the other cardinal nephews on the choice of a candidate. Political observers devoted minute attention to the leanings of each faction of the Sacred College and to the character and allegiances of each *papabile*, as especially promising aspirants were called, but there was no formula for victory. After the election was over, whatever its outcome, each cardinal scrambled to pledge undying loyalty to the new pope and his nephew; it was the minimum required to keep a "court" in business.

THE "TITLED LORDS"

As the pope and his nephews completed their survey of the topography of power in Rome, they would have paused over a final group of a dozen or so Roman families. These were a composite aristocracy of feudal stock enriched by more recent papal blood.[29] To distinguish them from the larger body of "gentlemen" who play the key role in civic institutions in Rome, and whom I discuss in detail in Chapter 6, I will follow the practice of seventeenth-century commentators and call these families the "titled lords" (*signori titolati*).[30] These were aristocrats bearing only the highest titles: princes and dukes, not the less exalted marchesi, counts, and cavalieri. The feudal component consisted of eight medieval baronial houses, of whom the most prestigious were the Orsini and Colonna, followed by the Conti and Savelli.

The newer element, dating from the second half of the sixteenth century on, was the "papal nobility," descendants of the six popes preceding Urban VIII. Here the outstanding names were Aldobrandini, Borghese, and Ludovisi. Members of these families had set an example for the Barberini by arranging marriage alliances with the feudal nobility, amassing great fortunes, and building monumental sub-

---

to Professor Agostino Paravicini Bagliani and Dr. Luigi Fiorani for allowing me to consult these papers.

[28] Gigli, *Diario*, 145, 152–54; Ranke, 3:398.

[29] For this analysis of Rome's social hierarchy I depend on the Flemish lawyer Teodoro Ameyden (1586–1656), ASV, "Relatione," 662r–75r.

[30] For contemporary examples of this use of the term *signori titolati* see Gigli, *Diario*, 139; Francesco Cerasoli, "Diario di cose romane degli anni 1614, 1615, 1616," *Studi* 15 (1894): 293–94; and see Figure 8 where one group in the procession of 1623 is so designated.

urban villas and urban palaces. Although it may well have dismayed an age that believed so fervently in "birth," the elevation of someone to the papacy effectively added a new family to the roster of the Roman aristocracy.

Of course, as the Barberini marriage to the Colonna indicates, the papal nobility were in an excellent position to acquire the blood of high birth, at least for their children. Their social ascent was made smoother by the fact that many of the Roman baronial lineages found themselves overwhelmed by debt in the late sixteenth century. Faced with acute financial difficulties, some were willing to barter breeding for the wealth that a papal family commanded. But in the minutely calibrated status consciousness of this group the Barberini were not entirely accepted. When the young Cardinal Antonio sponsored a lavish chivalric tournament in one of the city's grandest piazzas in 1634, the titled lords were conspicuous by their absence.[31]

The pope and the Barberini family and friends were the political epicenter in Baroque Rome. On their periphery, however, were other sources of status, prestige, and power that had the capacity to ripple if not embroil the waters through which they steered. The envoys of foreign rulers, cardinals from the major Italian princely houses, and feudal barons and the new papal aristocracy were factors to be reckoned with in the social geography of influence and authority in the papal capital. Urban VIII and his nephews kept them in view. Their presence inflected the aim and the reach of absolute monarchy, forcing the attention of the ruling family, inscribing their fears and hopes, and impinging on the space in which they maneuvered.

[31] Delumeau, *Vie* 1:457–62, 469–85. The lone baronial family participating in the Barberini tournament was the Colonna; Martine Boiteux, "Carnaval annexé. Essai de lecture d'une fête romaine," *Annales* 32 (1977): 370.

Chapter Four

A WEB OF JURISDICTIONS

NO SINGLE OFFICIAL or office "governed" the city of Rome. Even dividing governmental tasks for analytical purposes between papal and civic authorities does not do justice to the complex configuration of government in the papal capital. In describing it, seventeenth-century commentators made two sets of distinctions: they divided temporal affairs from spiritual affairs, and, within the broad category of temporal affairs, they distinguished between that which concerned the Roman Curia and that which, for the most part, did not.[1] Here we will survey the whole array of institutions falling under the heading of the temporal. In later chapters I will take up those that were specifically civic in greater detail. We begin with the Roman Curia and those members of its staff who had any duties at all touching the city of Rome. Then we turn to what lay outside the Curia: those officials, tribunals, and bodies, chosen either by the pope or the municipality, which saw to the "domestic" needs of the town. As contemporaries understood the distinction, these were needs that any city in the Papal States might have, regardless of whether the Curia of the Holy Roman Church made its home there.

It is important to keep in mind that Roman urban administration was a creation that had been built up over time, not according to a rational overall schema but in response to historical contingencies. As William Beik has found in studying the provincial government of seventeenth-century France, each institution "held a slightly different kind of power," granted because of the particular needs of the monarch and not with an eye to the powers held by other institutions.[2] Officials had overlapping spheres of responsibility in Rome because early modern government was a cumulative not a Cartesian construction. No one thought about what it meant to already existing authorities that another set was added. Change of an organic and incremental sort left unresolved the precise relationships between all the elements in the mix, as well as the exact nature of the autonomy each possessed. Working this out was a process of political negotiation on a slippery and mobile chessboard.

---

[1] In his legal handbook the jurist and cardinal Giovanni Battista De Luca (1614–1683) calls the former "pontifical tribunals" (*tribunali pontificij*) and the latter "particular tribunals" (*tribunali particolari*), *Il Dottor Volgare*, bk. 15, pt. 3, chap. 40, pp. 357–58.

[2] Beik, 177. See also Rietbergen, 207–8. As early as 1948 Mario Romani noted the ill-defined competencies of units of administration in Rome and pointed out the scholarly neglect of this administrative history in *Pellegrini e viaggiatori nell'economia di Roma dal XIV al XVI secolo* (Milan, 1948), 166–67.

CURIA AND CITY

A modern historian of the Roman Curia defines it as the totality of organs that assist the head of the Catholic Church in carrying out his work.[3] In the seventeenth century, as today, the Curia was made up of tribunals, offices, cardinalatial committees called congregations, and secretariats, with all their attendant personnel. Each supervised some aspect of papal business, and the mandates of some of these organs included matters related to the city of Rome. No curial office or official was completely responsible for the city, however, not even the so-called governor of Rome, about whom we will hear more later. The curial office that had the most to do with Rome was the apostolic chamber (*camera apostolica*), the agency in charge of the Church's temporal, and especially its economic and financial, affairs. The head of the apostolic chamber was the cardinal chamberlain, who purchased his office and held it for life. A source from the 1630s quotes a price of 50–70,000 *scudi* for this post. A few months before Urban VIII's election in August 1623, Ippolito Aldobrandini, nephew of Clement VIII's cardinal nephew, became cardinal chamberlain. After his death in 1638 Cardinal Antonio Barberini the younger succeeded him. While not the highest priced curial office, the cardinal chamberlain's was expensive enough to require at least a papal fortune to finance it.[4]

Associated with the cardinal chamberlain in managing the apostolic chamber were twelve clerks of the chamber (*chierici di camera*), a vice-chamberlain who bore the title governor of Rome, a treasurer general, a depositary general, and a magistrate called the auditor of the chamber (see Table 1). Together they made up the "full chamber" (*piena camera*). With the exception of the governor of Rome and the depositary general, who was the pope's personal banker as well as cashier for the apostolic chamber, all these were venal offices. The treasurer general and the auditor of the chamber paid the most for their offices, 60–70,000 scudi; often in the seventeenth century they were members of Genoese banking families. In 1628 the post of clerk of the chamber cost 36,000 scudi.[5]

---

[3] Del Re, *Curia Romana*, 3.

[4] The price of the chamberlain's office, according to a manuscript of 1631, is given by Fausto Piola Caselli, "Aspetti del debito pubblico nello Stato Pontificio: gli uffici vacabili," 55–56 n. 4. The copy of Piola Caselli's article that I have used is catalogued under the author's name in the Vatican Library. Peter Partner cites the article as follows: *Annali della Facolta' di Scienze Politiche dell'Universita' degli Studi di Perugia*, n.s., i (1973): 99–170, in Peter Partner, "Papal Financial Policy in the Renaissance and Counter Reformation," *Past and Present* 88 (1980): 18. On the cardinal chamberlain see also Girolamo Lunadoro, *Relatione della corte di Roma* (Venice, 1661), 32–33; Del Re, *Curia Romana*, 297–98; Ruggiero, 63–75.

[5] On the apostolic chamber see Del Re, *Curia Romana*, 295–309, and Ruggiero's now indispensable study. Rietbergen, 234–35, lists the treasurers general from 1565 to 1715. For the prices of venal offices see Lunadoro, 47–50, 64–66, and Piola Caselli, 55–56 n. 4. The manuscript newsletters known as *avvisi* quote prices for offices that are slightly lower than those given by these two sources. According to an *avviso* of 1627 the post of treasurer was bought for 60,000 scudi, BAV, Urb. lat.

TABLE 1
The Apostolic Chamber

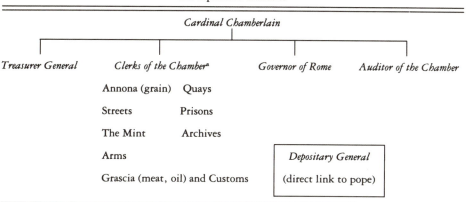

Cardinal Chamberlain

Treasurer General	Clerks of the Chamber[a]		Governor of Rome	Auditor of the Chamber
	Annona (grain)	Quays		
	Streets	Prisons		
	The Mint	Archives		
	Arms		*Depositary General*	
	Grascia (meat, oil) and Customs		(direct link to pope)	

[a] I have listed only those offices in existence by 1650.

Legislation of 1621, intended to clarify the cardinal chamberlain's competence with respect to the other officials of the chamber, gives an idea of the range of concerns that the temporal domain embraced. The chamberlain was responsible for supervising the collection of taxes, tolls, duties, and feudal dues, as well as rents owed by tenants of properties owned by the chamber. He was also the competent judge for any cases involving these fiscal and financial matters in the Papal States, as well as for disputes concerning roads, water supplies, quays, construction, archives and notaries, mints and coinage, and those foodstuffs subject to state control. He could raise armies and name their officers and authorize communities to borrow money, sell town lands, or hold a fair. In Rome he could hear appeals against sentences handed down by guild and civic tribunals and he administered the vegetable market in Piazza Navona and the cattle market in the Forum.[6]

In practice many of the specific tasks entrusted to the apostolic chamber, over which the cardinal chamberlain was nominally in charge, were really the responsibility of his semiautonomous associates. Each of the clerks of the chamber, for example, might serve in rotation as president, prefect, or commissioner of the chamber's various departments: Annona (grain supplies), Grascia (meat, cheese, and oil provisions), streets, quays, prisons, archives, the mint, and arms.[7] The

1097, 466v; sixteen years later Gigli says it sold for 80,000 scudi, *Diario*, 226. For the price of the office of clerk of the chamber in 1628 see the *avviso* in BAV, Urb. lat. 1098, pt. 1, 90v. It is worth noting that all these posts, except that of depositary general, were held by clerics rather than laymen; see Prodi, 222–23, on the "clericalization" of the bureaucracy of the Papal States.

[6] Ruggiero, 67–68. The edicts of the cardinal chamberlain registered in *Regesti*, vols. 4 and 5, provide another view of his responsibilities.

[7] These departments are discussed in detail in Ruggiero, 75–166. According to Ruggiero, 68–69,

governor of Rome had civil and criminal jurisdiction over anyone charged with a crime in Rome and its district. The treasurer general authorized expenditures, administered state loans (*luoghi di monti*) and the government pawnshop (*monte di pieta'*), and awarded tax-farming contracts. The depositary general, usually a layman and banker with personal ties to the pope and thus only formally linked to the chamber, was the papacy's central cashier. The auditor of the chamber seems to have begun life as the judge of cases brought before the full chamber, but by the seventeenth century he had become the head of his own tribunal with civil and criminal jurisdiction in cases arising anywhere in the Papal States.[8]

In general, with the exception of the governor of Rome, the mandates of the officials of the apostolic chamber extended throughout the state, although certain departments focused more on Rome and its nearby provinces than others. The prefect of the Annona, for example, collected data on the amount of cereals sown and harvested everywhere in the papal territories, but he could compel the sale of grain only in the regions surrounding Rome. If dearth threatened, his first task was to feed the capital, even if it meant depriving the provinces or spending large sums from the state treasury. The Annona, like the departments of the Grascia and the streets, had originated to meet the needs of the city of Rome, gradually extending its authority geographically in order to do its job more effectively. Other departments headed by clerks of the chamber, however, might have few or no responsibilities in Rome. The prefecture of the archives, for example, supervised all the archives in the Papal States *except* those in Rome and Bologna.[9]

One of the most dramatic bureaucratic developments of papal administration in the sixteenth century was the increasing articulation of the departments within the apostolic chamber and specifically of the competencies of the clerks of the chamber. Nevertheless, it would be a mistake to see this phenomenon as an unambiguous sign of modernity, for we are still well within the world of the ancien régime state. With a few exceptions these offices were privately owned by their holders, were often resigned to relatives, and could be counted on to produce handsome personal profits.[10] Moreover, when a clerk of the chamber took on an area of public life that the apostolic chamber had not previously regulated, such as Roman streets in the sixteenth century or urban water supplies in the seventeenth century, he joined a set of already existing civic officials with the same responsibilities. The preexisting authorities were never abolished and the clerk of the chamber had to figure out how best to coordinate with the relevant municipal officials over time. For example, the prefect of the Annona, who set grain and

---

the evolving relationship between the cardinal chamberlain and the clerks of the chamber exemplifies the notion of "cumulative [juridical] competence." On the clerks of the chamber see also Ago, *Carriere*, 20, 43. Many future cardinals rose from their ranks; Rietbergen, 106.

[8] Ruggiero, 211–17.

[9] Ibid., 76, 85, 135, 145–46.

[10] Lunadoro, 32, 48. Ruggiero, 31 n. 26. For these patterns in the fifteenth century see Partner, *The Pope's Men*.

bread prices, eventually excluded civic officials entirely from his decisions, while the president of the streets met regularly with civic officials to set tax rates for street improvements.[11] The various prefectures, presidencies, and commissions of the apostolic chamber were not yet rationalized vehicles of modern government. They each had a different historical, and indeed juridical, physiognomy and distinct relations of power with their non-curial counterparts.

In addition to the apostolic chamber the Roman Curia also included a number of committees or congregations composed predominantly of cardinals. The cardinalatial congregations had appeared sporadically over the course of the sixteenth century until the great administrative reorganization by Sixtus V in 1588. At that time the pope systematized the duties of fifteen of these committees and gave them a new legal stature.[12]

Over the decades new congregations were created and old ones withered away; they varied strikingly in the extent of their energy and authority. At the apex of power and prestige were the congregations of the Holy Office, responsible for detecting and punishing heresy, and the Index, which determined what books Catholics could publish or possess. At the bottom of the hierarchy were ephemeral congregations like the Abbondanza, briefly concerned with grain provisions, and the short-lived congregation for roads, whose mandates were already being more efficiently executed by the clerks of the chamber and their departments. The vitality of a congregation had a great deal to do with who headed it and their preoccupations. The congregation of health (*Sanita'*) under Cardinal Francesco Barberini was extremely active when plague threatened the Papal States from 1629 to 1632. The congregation of the Annona and Grascia met infrequently when Cardinal Antonio Barberini the younger chaired it because he was busy with the war of Castro.[13]

Like most of the departments of the apostolic chamber, the cardinalatial congregations generally embraced the whole of the Papal States. Roman matters jostled with those of the provinces on their agendas. As we have seen, one exception was the congregation of the apostolic visitation (*Visita apostolica*), which conducted the investigation of religious institutions in the diocese of Rome ordered by Urban VIII in 1624. In general the congregations did not devote themselves so single-mindedly to the papal capital, and some, like the congregation of Buon Governo or the Consulta, were explicitly excluded from responsibility for Rome.[14]

The College of Cardinals, taken as a collegiate body, would not usually be considered a part of the Curia, and under normal circumstances it did not have authority over the city of Rome. For the sake of completeness, however, we should

---

[11] Ruggiero, 76. ASR, Presidenza delle Strade, verbali, vol. 8 (1616–1628).

[12] Del Re, *Curia Romana*, 321–442. Del Re, 505–21, reproduces Sixtus V's legislation of 1588. Ruggiero, 47–51.

[13] Del Re, *Curia Romana*, 337. Ruggiero, 51, 79–80, 88, 103. The congregation of health is discussed in more detail in Chapter 10 and the congregation of the Annona and Grascia in Chapter 7.

[14] Del Re, *Curia Romana*, 347, 352, 364–66.

note that, on occasion, the cardinals did claim such authority. During the periods between the death of a pope and the election of his successor the Sacred College governed the Church, and thought it should control the city as well. [15] As we shall see in more detail in a later chapter, civic officials refused to accept this latter claim, so the question of who governed Rome during the Vacant See remained contentious.

THE "PRIVATE CITY"

In the seventeenth century the city of Rome happened to be the home of the papal court and thus of the Roman Curia. This had not always been the case in history and, when the pope went elsewhere, so did the Curia. Jurists, therefore, separated those institutions active in Rome because of the presence of the papal court from those officials and tribunals given responsibility for the city whether or not the pope was physically present. As Cardinal Giovanni Battista De Luca put it in the 1673 edition of his legal handbook, *Il Dottor Volgare*, these latter organs had authority in Rome, "considered . . . as a private city [*citta' privata*] and not as the Curia of the pope." [16] De Luca distinguished the "particular tribunals" of the "private city" from the curial authorities discussed in the preceding section. Some of these "particular tribunals" were staffed by ecclesiastics and some by men in the secular state (see Table 2). For him the important distinction was not that a cleric or layman was the judge, but that these magistracies concerned themselves with local matters in Rome rather than the universal matters absorbing the Curia. De Luca, intent on producing a guide for lawyers with curial business, describes urban institutions from the perspective of the central administration of the state. Not all of the city's "particular tribunals" found a place in his manual.

One that did was the ecclesiastical court of the cardinal vicar, the Vicariato, which had jurisdiction over spiritual matters in the holy city. As we have seen, since the bishop of Rome had to carry out more far-reaching tasks as head of the Catholic Church, he delegated a cardinal as his vicar and acting bishop in the diocese of Rome. Most of the day-to-day business of the diocese, however, fell to the vicar's increasingly autonomous assistant, the vicegerent. It was the vicegerent who heard marriage and morals cases, attended monthly discussions of cases of conscience by the Roman parish priests, issued licenses for schoolmasters, midwives, exorcists, and confessors, and made decisions about which books could be published in Rome. [17]

---

[15] Ibid., 457–502. Prodi, 188–89.

[16] De Luca, *Il Dottor Volgare*, bk. 15, pt. 3, chap. 34, pp. 308–9; see also chap. 40, p. 351, and chap. 43, pp. 415–16.

[17] Niccolo' Del Re, *Il Vicegerente del Vicariato di Roma* (Rome, 1976), 9, 17–22. Virgilio Caselli, *Il Vicariato di Roma* (Rome, 1957), devotes only a few pages to the functioning of the office between 1400 and 1700. Basilicas and some hospitals might also have their own judges; De Luca, *Il Dottor Volgare*, bk. 15, pt. 3, chap. 40, p. 358.

TABLE 2
Rome's Local Tribunals

Headed by Laymen	Headed by Ecclesiastics
Senator of Rome	Vicariato
Conservators	Governor of Rome
Master Justicieries	
Street Masters (*maestri di strada*)	
Agriculture	
Governor of the Borgo	
Marshall of the Roman Curia (*Corte Savella*)	
Individual guilds	
Giudice dei mercenari	

Note: Romans might also appear before the tribunals of the various officials of the apostolic chamber.

In the temporal realm the governor of Rome was an important official. The governor, who has already appeared in his aspect as a "vice-chamberlain" of the apostolic chamber, actually operated in virtual independence of the chamber and chamberlain, reporting directly to the pope twice a week. For this reason De Luca thought that he was more appropriately located among the authorities of the "private city" than among those of the Curia. From a structural point of view the governor's position in Rome was similar to that of the governors dispatched to lesser towns in the Papal States. He was a prelate appointed by the pope who administered justice in the locality on behalf of the central government. Such governors rarely had exclusive jurisdiction, even in criminal cases, because they were usually superimposed on already existing local magistrates who were not abolished. The governor of Rome, an official who had first appeared in the fifteenth century, was no exception to this rule; he shared civil and criminal cases in Rome and its district with the Capitoline tribunal headed by the senator of Rome. At the same time, from within the apostolic chamber itself had arisen a new contender for the same business, the court of the auditor of the chamber.[18]

[18] For an attempt to sort out the competencies of these and other Roman tribunals see Paul V's bull of 1 March 1612 in *Bullarium diplomatum et privilegiorum sanctorum Romanorum pontificum* (Turin, 1867), 12:58–111. On the governor of Rome see the following: Del Re, *Governatore*, 11 and passim; De Luca, *Il Dottor Volgare*, bk. 15, pt. 3, chap. 33, pp. 295–301; Prodi, 224–25; Irene Polverini Fosi, *La societa' violenta: Il banditismo dello Stato Pontificio nella seconda meta' del Cinquecento* (Rome, 1985), 39–44, and his edicts in *Regesti*, vols. 4 and 5. In 1624 the apostolic chamber rented a palace for the governor on the street then known as the Via di Parione or Via Papalis; this served as the location of the governor's

Nonetheless, the popes had steadily built up the prestige and resources of the governor. The post was an important step on the career ladder that led to the cardinalate, and the governor was given ceremonial precedence over all officials and ambassadors, coming right after the cardinals. The governor of Rome had the edge on the senator in that he could hear cases involving clerics and religious entities as well as lay people. De Luca thought he also had one other notable advantage over his competitors, more spies—"both public and secret"—so he was the first to know about crimes and was in a position to capture more criminal business than other Roman judges.[19]

All the other "particular tribunals" of Rome were headed by laymen, a significant juridical distinction because their jurisdiction was limited thereby to those of lay status. The senator of Rome headed the Capitoline tribunal, about which we will hear more in the next chapter, and had the right to make judgments in civil and criminal matters concerning lay Romans. The senator, a layman appointed by the pope, had to come from at least forty miles outside Rome so that he could be an impartial arbiter in urban disputes. The tribunal of the street masters and the tribunal of agriculture by contrast were staffed by Romans, approved by the pope, who came from the city's landed upper classes.[20]

Other "particular tribunals" added to the mesh of local institutions. The civic magistrates known as conservators had their own court, and there was another for the master justicieries that handled conflicts associated with vineyards. The governor of the Borgo, a layman while the pope was alive who was replaced by an ecclesiastic during the Vacant See, had civil and criminal authority over the Borgo, the quarter around the Vatican palace. Taddeo Barberini held this office under Urban VIII. Lay employees of the papal court had their own specific judge, a lay nobleman called the marshal of the Roman Curia. For almost three centuries this office belonged to a member of the Savelli family, and the "Corte Savella," complete with prisons, was located in the Savelli palace on Via Monserrato. In addition many artisans and tradesmen had their own guild tribunals and there was a special civil court for debt-ridden agricultural laborers presided over by the *giudice dei mercenari*.[21]

---

tribunal; Del Re, *Governatore*, 40. On governors elsewhere in the Papal States see, among others, Prodi, 226–230, and Black, 518. De Luca lists some of the governorships to which clerks of the chamber were appointed; others were held by lesser curial officials, *Il Dottor Volgare*, bk. 15, pt. 3, chap. 30, p. 271.

[19] De Luca, *Il Dottor Volgare*, bk. 15, pt. 3, chap. 33, pp. 295–302. The governor also had the largest force of *sbirri* or police; Steven C. Hughes, "Fear and Loathing in Bologna and Rome: The Papal Police in Perspective," *Journal of Social History* 21 (1987): 97–98. At least three of the five governors of Rome during Urban VIII's pontificate were made cardinals. For a description of the ceremony in which a new governor of Rome, Giovanni Battista Pallotto, was invested with his office see BAV, Urb. lat. 1098, pt. 1, 84r (*avviso* of 16 February 1628).

[20] De Luca, *Il Dottor Volgare*, bk. 15, pt. 3, chap. 40, p. 351. On the senator and street masters see the detailed discussion in Chapter 5. On the tribunal of agriculture see Armando Lodolini, "Il tribunale dell'Agricoltura," *Agricoltura* 2 (1953): 79–80. See also Delumeau, *Vie* 2:584–85.

[21] On the duties of the conservators see Chapters 5, 7–10. On the master justicieries see Chapter 5.

Curial prelates, cardinalatial committees, and the lay and clerical judges of the city's "particular tribunals" together made up a tissue of multiple, overlapping jurisdictions. A crime committed in a convent, for example, might be investigated by either the cardinal protector, the congregation of the apostolic visitation, the vicegerent, the governor of Rome, or some combination thereof. The cardinal chamberlain, the president of the streets, the congregation on waters and roads, and the street masters might each give orders, or, what was even more disruptive, exemptions to orders, to clean up the city streets. Moreover, in the background lurked the shadow of seigneurial jurisdictions. The cardinal chamberlain tried to keep feudal lords in the district of Rome from throwing their tenants into jail during the threshing season. The auditor of the chamber competed with the conservators' court to hear a case from a fief belonging to the civic magistrates.[22]

What did it mean to "govern" in this setting? In practice government was a dispersed activity carried on simultaneously in numerous locations. It was always incomplete. Decisions were contested by appeal to a different tribunal; orders were frequently contradicted or undermined by special exemptions; judgments were eluded by petition to a higher official. It was inherently political, a discourse about power, even if what was at stake was not power in material terms but in the symbolic terms of institutional prestige. Since the relationships among all the various fragments of public authority set up over time were ambiguous, the exercise of jurisdiction was far from a routinized, bureaucratic procedure. The cloudier the boundary between one office and another, the more jealously each guarded what it hoped others would accept as its judicial prerogatives. This fluid administrative landscape shaped the language of politics in Baroque Rome in its own image, making jurisdiction a source of honor and a subject of rivalry and compromise.[23]

In the next section we will be exploring the place of the Capitol in this broader configuration of papal, curial, ecclesiastical, and corporate institutions. After meeting the city as a religious, economic, sociopolitical, and governmental whole, it is now time to look more closely at a part, that part represented by the Senate and Roman People. I have briefly mentioned tribunals on the Capitoline hill and civic officials; now we can flesh out what they were and what they meant in more detail. What exactly was "civic" in a web of such complexity?

On the governor of the Borgo see Del Re, *Governatore*, 46 n. 109. On the guild tribunals see Chapter 8. See also Niccolo' Del Re, "La curia Savella," *Studi Romani* 5 (1957): 390–400; idem, *Il maresciallo di santa romana chiesa, custode del conclave* (Rome, 1962); on the *giudice dei mercenari* see idem, "L'Abate Ottavio Sacco ed una singolare magistratura romana," *Studi romani* 3 (1955): 12–26.

[22] For the cardinal chamberlain and the barons see *Regesti* 4:41. For the auditor's competition with the conservators see Chapter 9.

[23] For a similar view of seventeenth-century French institutions see Beik, 179–80, 185–86.

PART II

The Roman People

THE SEARCH FOR THE CIVIC in Baroque Rome begins with a title, the *Senatus populusque romanus*, the Senate and Roman People, and a place, the Capitoline hill. The Capitol, a tranquil and somewhat isolated slope above the ancient Roman Forum about a half-hour walk across town from the Vatican palace, was the spatial locus of the Roman People, as the Senate was called in daily seventeenth-century parlance (see Map 1). The Roman People were both an institutional and a social identity.[1] In Chapter 5 I discuss the nature and activities of the Roman People as a municipal administration: the buildings, laws, electoral mechanisms, officials, councils, committees, and funds that constituted its setting and existence. But the Roman People were also individuals, or better, families, and in Chapter 6 we meet them as social flesh and blood. There we will explore what sort of men made their way to the Capitol and ask what civic participation meant in the society of Baroque Rome.

The assortment of tribunals, officials, duties, and privileges associated with the Capitoline hill added up to the densest node of purely local concerns that existed in the complex network of Roman government. It was not a sovereign administration in any sense and fully acknowledged the authority of the pope, which gave legal force to its judgments and decisions. What distinguished civic from other bureaucratic structures in the city was a strong secular or lay component. Men in holy orders, with some exceptions, could not participate in Capitoline affairs and Capitoline judges had no jurisdiction over ecclesiastics, unless, as with the street masters, a papal official was attached to them. This did not mean, of course, that civic magistrates eschewed pious responsibilities; they felt it an honor to keep the keys to the reliquary at St. John Lateran that held the heads of the city's patron saints, Peter and Paul, and they regularly made offerings at dozens of Roman churches.[2]

In keeping with this lay orientation, however, we might understand the civic as embracing associations and festivities of a nonecclesiastical character, such as the artisan corporations, the fourteen urban districts known as *rioni*, and the pre-Lenten races at Carnival. Specific objects in the urban landscape were pre-eminently, if not exclusively, a municipal concern: ancient ruins, walls, gates, fountains, markets, salt, and weights and measures.[3] Water distribution and

---

[1] For a similar point made about the communal institutions of a town in the Romagna in the fifteenth century see Ian Robertson, "Neighborhood Government in Malatesta Cesena," in *Patronage, Art, and Society in Renaissance Italy*, ed. F. W. Kent and Patricia Simons (New York, 1987), 100.

[2] Rodocanachi, *Institutions*, 198. See also Chapter 5 and Chapter 11.

[3] Michele Franceschini, "La magistratura capitolina e la tutela delle antichita' di Roma nel XVI secolo," *ASRSP* 109 (1986): 141–50; Amydenus, *Pietate*, in Bzovio, 20:561.

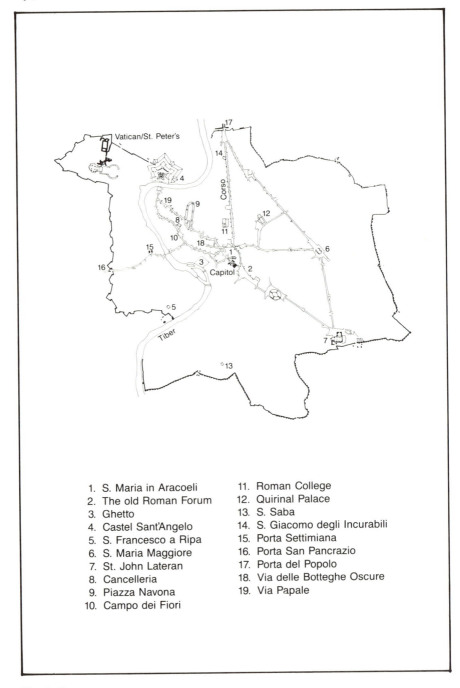

Map 1. Rome

1. S. Maria in Aracoeli
2. The old Roman Forum
3. Ghetto
4. Castel Sant'Angelo
5. S. Francesco a Ripa
6. S. Maria Maggiore
7. St. John Lateran
8. Cancelleria
9. Piazza Navona
10. Campo dei Fiori
11. Roman College
12. Quirinal Palace
13. S. Saba
14. S. Giacomo degli Incurabili
15. Porta Settimiana
16. Porta San Pancrazio
17. Porta del Popolo
18. Via delle Botteghe Oscure
19. Via Papale

the local militia also came under its aegis. What unified a motley accumulation of institutions was a setting (the Capitol), a text (the city statutes), a sense of dignity supported by structures of limited self-government and overtones of antique and seigneurial majesty, and the concerns of the local landed classes.

Chapter Five

A CIVIC SPACE

THE CAPITOL

The Capitoline hill was Rome's civic space. Here in 1143 a group of Romans proclaimed the restoration of the ancient Senate and Roman People, a body that had not been heard from for several centuries. They installed themselves in the ruins of a feudal fortress on the hill, overlooking the Forum, which had been sacred to Jupiter in antiquity, when it was called the "head of the world" (*caput orbis*). Medieval memory had rearranged ancient topography and twelfth-century guidebooks to Rome identified the Capitol as the seat of secular government, not as the site of the imperial city's most important temple. Whatever the truth, the hill plainly had powerful and charismatic associations with antiquity and the renewed Senate wanted them.[1]

There were few buildings on the Capitol in 1143: only the stronghold built into the ruins of the ancient Tabularium, which rose directly above the Forum, and a small Benedictine church dedicated to St. Mary on the rise to the north. The Senate and Roman People, a rather amorphous entity in their early years, were themselves rather slow to establish an architectural presence on the hill.[2] They possessed a ready-made assembly ground in the declivity between the Capitol's two crests and they evidently made use of the existing fortress and the church. It was not until the late thirteenth century that they at last had a new palace on the site of the fortress-Tabularium. When the Senate was transformed into a single senator, a foreign—and hopefully impartial—judge, this became the seat of the senator and his tribunal.

During the fourteenth century, as the senator became the city's chief judicial official, a new set of urban magistrates emerged who had responsibility for town finances and administration. These were the three conservators, local men who were chosen by lot for terms of two, later three, months. The conservators acquired increasing authority in the century between 1350 and 1450, and under

---

[1] Valentini and Zucchetti, 3:51; Otto of Freising, 353. A. Frugoni, "Sulla 'renovatio senatus' del 1143 e l' 'ordo equestris,' " *Bullettino dell'Istituto Storico Italiano per il Medioevo* 62 (1950): 161–62. Pierre Toubert, *Les structures du Latium médiéval*, 2 vols. (Rome, 1973), 2:965–66. See also Luigi Pompili Olivieri, *Il senato romano nelle sette epoche di svariato governo*, 3 vols. (1886; repr., Bologna, 1972–73); Alfonso Salimei, *Senatori e statuti di Roma nel medioevo* (Rome, 1935); Arrigo Solmi, *Il senato romano nell'alto medio evo* (Rome, 1944); Laura Moscati, *Alle origini del comune romano. Economia, societa', istituzioni* ([Rome], 1980).

[2] Krautheimer, 197, 206–7; Brentano, 93–97.

Pope Nicholas V (1447–1455) they also finally obtained a building of their own; it was to the south of the senator's palace on the site of the temple of Jupiter Capitolinus.[3]

In addition to the church, now in Franciscan hands and renamed Santa Maria in Aracoeli, the Capitol now had two secular structures clearly distinguished in function. The senator's palace with its castle-like towers and live lion, symbol of Roman justice, was preeminently a judicial building closed off from the space before it. Here prisoners awaited trial, sentences were read, and executions were performed. To the right the palace of the conservators, with its open portico, corner loggias on the second floor, and interior courtyard, was more accessible to the throng of petitioners, guild members, and notaries who sought out its officials on varied business.[4] The uneven ground in front of the two buildings served as a public gathering place and market, and on the hill's western slope a lumpy trail led down to the more densely populated quarter in the Tiber bend (see Figure 6).

The fifteenth-century Capitol had thus completely turned its back on the Forum, now the Campo Vaccino, and oriented itself toward the new city that had grown up near the river in the Middle Ages. Though retaining its ancient name, it had taken on a secular significance as the lay center of civic life quite unlike that of its classical past. The Senate and Roman People, now known more simply as the Roman People, had reappeared but also in a translation. The magistracies of the senator and the conservators took final shape in the critical years of struggle for the papacy, during the Great Schism and the definitive return to Rome. Their emergence meant the end of several centuries of fluid experimentation with forms of civic government, and coincided with the new stability of papal rule in Rome. From 1410 the juridical and political relationship between the Capitol and the popes was clear: civic officials were subject to the lordship (*signoria*) of the pontiffs, who imposed limits on their independence and the range of their activities.[5] The

[3] Carroll Westfall, *In This Most Perfect Paradise: Alberti, Nicholas V, and the Invention of Conscious Urban Planning in Rome, 1447–1455* (University Park, Penn., 1974), 92–100. See also Charles Burroughs, *From Signs to Design: Environmental Process and Reform in Early Renaissance Rome* (Cambridge, Mass., 1990), 126-27. According to Pio Pecchiai, the first documentary reference to the conservators dates from 1311, *Roma nel Cinquecento*, vol. 13 of *Storia di Roma* (Bologna, 1948), 241. Esch, *Bonifaz IX*, 612–19, includes a list of conservators from 1389 to 1404. Lombardo publishes a documentary appendix that refers to their activities during the reign of Pope Martin V (1417–1431), see nos. 6, 18, 25. For the later fifteenth century see Rodocanachi, *Institutions*, 174, 197–99. The loss of the civic archives in the sack of Rome of 1527 means that reconstructing the history of the conservators in the fourteenth and fifteenth centuries requires an indirect approach, mostly through papal and private documents.

[4] Carlo Pietrangeli and Guglielmo De Angelis D'Ossat, *Il Campidoglio di Michelangelo* (Milan, 1965), 104. For the symbolism of the lion see Miglio, "Leone," 178, and Shelley Perlove, "Bernini's Androclus and the Lion: A Papal Emblem of Alexandrine Rome," *Zeitschrift für Kunstgeschichte* 45 (1982): 293.

[5] Theiner, 3: 172–74; Lombardo, 46–47; Esch, "Fine," 235–77. On the fourteenth-century political order see Maire-Vigueur, "Classe dominante;" *Statuti della citta' di Roma*, ed. Camillo Re (Rome,

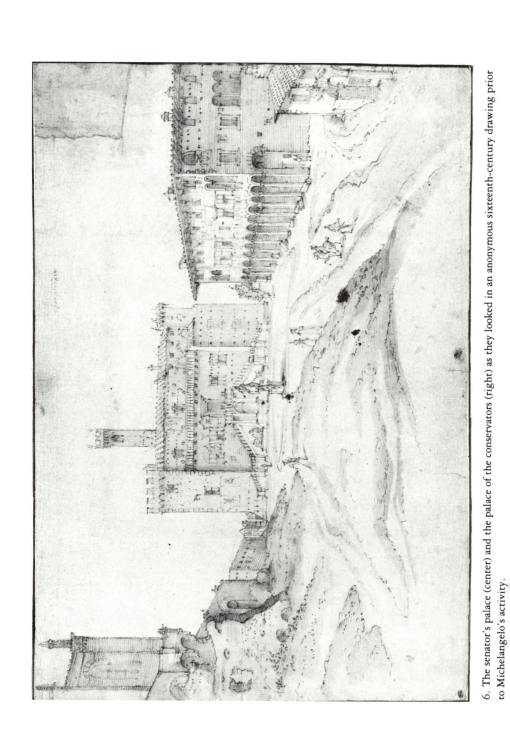

6. The senator's palace (center) and the palace of the conservators (right) as they looked in an anonymous sixteenth-century drawing prior to Michelangelo's activity.

Roman People had thus come to resemble not the Senate that ruled republican Rome but the patrician magistrates who served under the emperors.[6] Subordinate to rulers absorbed with a world dominion, the Roman People continued in the tradition of their late antique forebears to represent the aims and interests of the city of Rome.

By the early sixteenth century, Renaissance notions of grandeur and propriety had pervaded Rome and the ragged, if serviceable, appearance that the Capitol had assumed under Nicholas V no longer satisfied either the civic magistrates or the popes. In 1536 the impending visit of the Habsburg emperor Charles V prompted Pope Paul III to commission from Michelangelo a new design for the whole complex of secular buildings on the hill. The first step in the Capitol's transformation, though too late for the emperor's eyes, took place in 1538 when the pope moved a bronze equestrian statue of Marcus Aurelius from the Lateran to the newly leveled piazza in front of the palace of the conservators.[7]

In the decades that followed the artistry of Michelangelo turned the Capitoline's rough slopes and motley medieval structures into a masterpiece of unified urbanism. The execution of his project required several generations, and several architects, as well as papal funds and the active supervision of civic officials. By 1600 the senator's palace with its bell tower had been rebuilt and the palace of the conservators had been wrapped in a new facade. A magnificent ramp whose balustrades were adorned with ancient marble sculptures had replaced the uneven path down toward the center of town, and several fountains tossed water from a new aqueduct that had reached the Capitol in 1587. On the north side of the piazza, below the Aracoeli church, Michelangelo had planned a third building to "balance" the palace of the conservators (see Figure 7). When this had not yet been started in 1595, a large antique statue of a river god whom the Romans called Marforio was moved to the site and became another fountain. With a majesty unequalled since the days of imperial Rome the Capitol thus greeted the seventeenth century.[8]

1880); A. Natale, "La felice societa' dei Balestrieri e dei Pavesati e il governo dei Banderesi dal 1358 al 1408," *ASRSP* 62 (1939): 1–176.

[6] On the imperial senate up to 238 CE see Richard J. A. Talbert, *The Senate of Imperial Rome* (Princeton, 1984).

[7] In addition to Pietrangeli and De Angelis D'Ossat, the basic reference on Michelangelo's design for the Capitol is James Ackerman, *The Architecture of Michelangelo*, 2 vols. (London, 1961). See also James Ackerman, "Marcus Aurelius on the Capitoline Hill," *Renaissance News* 10 (1957): 73; Herbert Siebenhüner, *Das Kapitol in Rom* (Munich, 1954), 17–36; Fritz Saxl, "The Capitol during the Renaissance—A Symbol of the Imperial Idea," in *Lectures*, 2 vols. (London, 1957), 1:200–14; Stinger, 254–64. On the emperor's entry in 1536 see Bonner Mitchell, "The S.P.Q.R. in Two Roman Festivals of the Early and Mid-Cinquecento," *Sixteenth Century Journal* 9 (1978): 99–100. See also the sarcastic comment of Paolo Giovio quoted by Jacob Hess, *Kunstgeschichtliche Studien zu Renaissance und Barock*, 2 vols. (Rome, 1967), 1:349 n. 5. I am grateful to Professor Joseph Connors for bringing this passage to my attention.

[8] For the interior decoration of the palaces see Roger Aikin, "The Capitoline Hill during the Reign of Sixtus V" (Ph.D. diss., University of California, Berkeley, 1977). See also Emmanuel Rodocanachi,

CAPITOLII·ROMANI·VERA· IMAGO·VT·NVNC·EST·

7. Michelangelo's redesigned Capitoline hill showing the planned third palace (left), which was not executed until after 1644.

THE STATUTES OF 1580

The reconstruction of the Capitol was a coming of age for the civic administration whose framework had been established at the turn of the fifteenth century and the city statutes reflected this moment of maturity. In 1580, the very year that the palace of the conservators was completed, a final revision of Rome's municipal laws appeared that would direct the operation of Capitoline institutions for the next two hundred and fifty years.

The impulse behind the creation of statutes had always sprung from the city rather than the papacy and this new edition also arose at civic initiative. But city laws had no legal force without the approval of the pontiffs. Like the Capitol's renovation itself, though over a longer period, the text defining the domain of civic government was the product of cooperation between citizens and popes. In both form and content it represented a compromise with the papacy and an acknowledgment of its sovereignty.

Le Capitole romain antique et moderne (Paris, 1904); Pio Pecchiai, *Il Campidoglio nel Cinquecento* (Rome, 1950); Klaus Güthlein, "Der 'Palazzo Nuovo' des Kapitols," *Römisches Jahrbuch für Kunstgeschichte* 22 (1985): 83–190. On Marforio see Haskell and Penny, 258–59.

By comparison to other Italian city dwellers Romans had been slow to write down their local legal customs. It was not until the 1360s, during the absence of the popes in Avignon, that Rome acquired its first statutes. In three books they defined municipal civil and criminal procedure and the powers of the urban magistrates. By the time the popes recognized this legislation, however, the civic self-government assumed in the texts of the 1360s had collapsed. Pope Alexander V was the first to accept the Roman statutes, but in his 1410 bull he asserted his right to appoint civic officials and collect city revenues into the papal treasury.[9] Characteristically in late medieval Italy, this fundamental constitutional change did not produce new statutes. Papal edicts simply ignored laws they found inappropriate and the others remained in force.

In the course of the fifteenth century many papal regulations adjusted, extended, or restricted the functions of the civic administration and the competence of the Capitoline tribunal. Pope Paul II issued a new compilation of existing laws in 1469, which was printed shortly thereafter. The shower of pontifical acts continued in the following decades, however, and in 1518, when the conservators resolved to reprint the 1469 statutes, they had to add three volumes of papal legislation to the original three books.[10]

By the mid-sixteenth century civic authorities sought a more unified solution to their legal status. In the 1560s, as palace reconstruction began, they undertook a study of their current administration that recommended a complete revision of the city statutes. New officials and institutions had come into being since 1410 that were not adequately covered by extant regulations. The powers of the conservators had increased, two urban councils had been formalized, and electoral procedures giving local families control over civic offices had crystallized. The untidy accumulation of laws over two centuries offended a sense of administrative decorum.[11]

At the same time the urban magistrates were on the defensive. Since 1500 the popes had increasingly delegated officials of the Roman Curia, particularly the clerks of the chamber, to posts supervising aspects of city life previously overseen by the Capitol. The creation of these rival officials threatened civic administrative and judicial competence, and the desire for new statutes reflected an instinct for institutional self-preservation in the face of papal encroachment. Moreover, some sixteenth-century popes had played fast and loose with civic elections; local families wanted to ensure that their voice would be heard on the Capitol.[12]

---

[9] Lombardo, 46–47; Theiner, 3:172–74; for the fourteenth-century statutes see *Statuti*, ed. C. Re.

[10] Rodocanachi, *Institutions*, 165, 185–86, 216–19, and passim for a detailed study of the successive statutes of the fifteenth and sixteenth centuries.

[11] Ibid., 283; Laurie Nussdorfer, "City Politics in Baroque Rome, 1623–1644" (Ph.D. diss., Princeton University, 1985), 44–45, 61.

[12] Clara Gennaro, "La 'Pax Romana' del 1511," *ASRSP* 90 (1967): 17–60; Alberini, 483; Giacinto Gigli, "Cronologia dei Consoli, Priori, e Magistrati di Roma, e Statuti propri," BNC-VE, Sess. 334, 258r–v, 279v–80r; Nussdorfer, "City Politics," 41–42. A similar reaction among the local ruling

In 1580 the revised statutes received papal approval. They condensed earlier editions and codified existing procedures, incorporating the self-study of the 1560s but largely avoiding other innovations. They retained even the fourteenth-century article offering a bounty on wolves killed within the city walls. Three centuries of relevant papal bulls were attached in a separate section.[13]

As a description of Rome's city government, the statutes of 1580 are of course one-sided. They do not mention curial officials, covered by papal ordinances, and ignore many aspects of the daily operations of the civic administration. What the statutes provided was the authoritative statement of municipal law until the nine-teenth century in cases of dowry or rent dispute, homicide, bribery, and vendetta. They also described the expanded responsibilities of the conservators and the two councils and reminded anyone who needed it what the procedures for choosing civic officials were supposed to be. This text did what it could to delineate, and so to protect, what were called the "jurisdictions of the Roman People."[14] Since the new statutes could not, by their nature, make the jurisdictional relationships between the Roman People and other bodies clearer, the institutional terrain of the Roman People retained a permeable boundary. In practice it admitted varied arrangements of shared authority with papal officials, while preserving a distinct identity.

THE ROMAN PEOPLE

But just who were the Roman People? In the bull of 1580 with which Pope Gregory XIII made the statutes lawful he addressed his "beloved sons the Roman People." Yet nowhere does the document state explicitly whom it meant by that title. It was an elastic term in sixteenth- and seventeenth-century usage, ranging in meaning from the strictly historical magistracy of antiquity to "all Rome," everyone currently living in the city.[15]

Helpful for our purposes however is the distinction made in a public edict of 1642, which refers to the militia "of the People and inhabitants of Rome."[16] Here

---

classes of Milan after the Visconti established their *signoria* is noted by Cesare Mozzarelli, "Strutture sociali e formazioni statuali a Milano e Napoli tra '500 e '700," *Societa' e storia* 3 (1978): 434.

[13] *Statuta almae urbis Romae* (Rome, 1580). The papal bull of confirmation is published in *Bullarium* 8:330–32. One "innovation" the new statutes did include restricted the jurisdiction of the guilds and they appealed successfully to the pope to restore it; Rodocanachi, *Institutions*, 309–10, and in general on the 1580 edition of the statutes, ibid., 283–308, especially 298 n. 1. Nussdorfer, "City Politics," 23–24.

[14] This was the phrase used when defending civic privileges. See, for example, ASC, cred. I, vol. 33, decreti, 0029r (31 October 1625) and 0052r (26 August 1627).

[15] *Bullarium* 8:330–32. For examples of varied uses of the phrase "Popolo Romano" see Cardinal Roberto Bellarmine, quoted by Luigi Fiorani, "Visite," 86 n. 55, and Pietro Romano [Pietro Fornari], *Quod non fecerunt barbari . . . (Il pontificato di Urbano VIII)* (Rome, 1937), 93.

[16] "Militia . . . del Popolo & habitanti di Roma," ASR, Biblioteca, Bandi, Campidoglio, vol. 436, 8 October 1642.

the "People" of Rome were not the equivalent of "all Rome" but something more exclusive. It was this restricted *Popolo* or *Populus* who had initiated the drafting of new statutes, "desiring that their law be rendered in a fixed form."[17] The "People" of edict and statute were a notion ultimately derived from classical thinkers. Cicero, who provided the elites of early modern Europe with most of their political concepts and vocabulary, formulated it nicely. "The people [*populus*] are not every assemblage of men associated in any way whatsoever, but an assemblage of many men associated by common acceptance of the law and the sharing of a useful service."[18] By this definition the Roman People were a vague but privileged body with the right to represent the city of Rome and act through their councils and officers.[19] Juridically they were much like the civic corporations that governed towns throughout late medieval and early modern Europe. Their relation to the popes was similar to that of these other intermediate bodies to their rulers; they accepted whomever had sovereign power in the state without contest but expected to be consulted on policies disposing of their lives and property.[20]

Despite the broad inclusiveness of the term Roman People, only a few Romans actually took part in the offices, councils, and committees that directed civic affairs. How few? Perhaps five or six hundred in a population of 115,000 participated in a given two-year period during Urban VIII's reign.[21] More significant, if it were known, would be the number of people *permitted* to take part. Lists of Romans eligible for the public council, the largest of the two civic assemblies, were made in 1569, 1581, and 1584.[22] The public council did not have a fixed

---

[17] "Populus cupientes . . . ut ius proprium in certam formam redigeretur." *Bullarium* 8:330–32. See also Krautheimer, 106. For a similarly restricted sense of "people" in early modern English usage see Christopher Hill, "The Poor and the People in Seventeenth-Century England," in *History from Below*, ed. Frederick Krantz (Oxford, 1988), 30–31.

[18] Cicero, *De republica* 1.25.39, quoted by George Boas, *Vox Populi: Essays in the History of an Idea* (Baltimore, 1969), 46. According to Moses Finley, however, in both Greek (*demos*) and Latin (*populus*) the word seems to have had a socially double meaning, referring both to the people as a whole and to the poor, *Politics in the Ancient World* (New York, 1983), 1–2.

[19] For examples of this sense see Gigli, *Diario*, 237, 255, and ASC, cred. I, vol. 34, decreti, 0021v–22r (16 March 1641). For a similar understanding of the Parisian town government see Descimon, 131.

[20] Vicens Vives, 63. De Luca, *Il Dottor Volgare*, bk. 15, pt. 3, chap. 34, pp. 319–20. Roland Mousnier, *The Institutions of France under the Absolute Monarchy, 1598–1789*, 2 vols. (Chicago, 1979), 1:563–65.

[21] For these statistics and the samples on which they were based see Nussdorfer, "City Politics," 129–30, 132. I would like to thank Dr. J. Jefferson Looney for his help.

[22] ASC, cred. I, vol. 4 (1569, 1584), vol. 5 (1581). On the councils see discussion later in this chapter. I have also found lists from three urban districts (*rioni*) of men eligible for the public council in the late 1550s: the *rioni* of Parione in 1557 and of Ponte and Trevi in 1558; see ASC, cred. VI, vol. 63, interessi diversi della camera capitolina, 121r–28v. One clue as to why such lists may not be readily available for later years is provided by Giovanni Battista Fenzonio in his commentary on the Roman city statutes in 1636; he writes that the notary who served each *caporione* was to keep the list of those eligible to attend the public council. Systematic research in the notarial archives might therefore bring these lists to light. Giovanni Battista Fenzonio, *Annotationes in statuta, sive ius municipale*

number of seats but was open to any Roman citizen over twenty years old who was deemed eligible by a group of five gentlemen from the *rione* in which he lived. This flexibility stands in interesting contrast to membership in the Parisian town council of the seventeenth century, which demanded prior purchase of civic office. The 1580 statutes required that the names of those qualified to sit in the public council be drawn up every year, but since so few lists survive this stipulation may well have been ignored. It was not unheard of for people who were ineligible, such as barons and artisans, to attend a meeting of the public council, but they would not have been considered members.[23]

In 1581 and 1584 respectively a total of 1,799 and 1,836 citizens were eligible for the largest Capitoline council. These figures were higher than the number qualified in 1569—only 1,256—suggesting that the process of clarifying procedures, which resulted in the new statutes, might have made the district committees more assiduous about their lists, at least for a few years.[24] Although we lack censuses that give the total population of Rome in the 1580s, a commonly cited count for 1592 is 98,625 Christian inhabitants. If a rough estimate of the adult lay male proportion of this figure is 14,000 to 19,000, about ten to twelve percent of adult laymen were eligible to participate in Capitoline affairs in the late sixteenth century. Civic councils in Baroque Rome were thus less open than in a republican regime like that of Renaissance Florence, where twenty percent of adult males were eligible, but more accessible than in the aristocratic republic of Venice, where only the five percent of adult males of noble birth had political rights.[25] As we shall see in Chapter 6, peculiar social features of the papal capital help to account for this relatively high proportion.

The Roman statutes grew more restrictive when they moved from the qualifications for the public council to those for elected office. However, in an era when, for example, Parisian civic offices were for sale and were becoming family prop-

---

romanae urbis (Rome, 1636), 613. It should be noted that Roman citizenship was different from membership in the public council and easier to acquire; see *Statuta almae urbis*, bk. 3, chap. 57.

[23] For barons see ASC, cred. I, vol. 15, decreti, 116r–v (17 November 1523). For guild officers see cred. I, vol. 28, decreti, 0021r–24v (1 February 1580). For Paris see Descimon, 149.

[24] Other explanations are also possible. The number eligible may have expanded either because of population growth or a widening of access to the council. However, it seems unlikely that demographic rates, which in the second half of the sixteenth century caused the total number of inhabitants to double in fifty years, could have had such impact in only twelve years. Nor has evidence of a dramatic opening up of civic institutions to previously excluded families between 1569 and 1581 yet come to light.

[25] Petrocchi, 175. Litchfield, 16, estimates that in fifteenth-century Florence males between the ages of twenty-five and seventy, "the customary age for officeholding," made up fifteen to twenty percent of the total population. Petrocchi does not break down the population figure for 1592 by age and gender, but the Roman census totals from 1600 to 1739 published by Cerasoli do include gender and also indicate the number of clerics. In 1605, for example, sixty-two percent of the total non-Jewish population of Rome was male; six percent of the males were clerics; Cerasoli, "Censimento," 174. The number of Venetian nobles is given in Richard T. Rapp, *Industry and Economic Decline in Seventeenth-Century Venice* (Cambridge, Mass., 1976), 24.

erty, the fact that electoral rather than venal methods of recruitment prevailed in Rome is worth noting. To be eligible for elected offices a Roman citizen had to be of legitimate birth and living with his household (*familia*) in his own house or rented quarters. He could not be a servant or craftsman. If a foreigner had acquired Roman citizenship by grant of a privilege, at least five years had to elapse before his nomination as conservator or *caporione*. While gentlemen living on their rents were undoubtedly preferred, merchants and men in the liberal professions were not excluded by this text and notaries and lawyers did occasionally serve in the seventeenth century.[26]

The Roman People were thus a legally privileged body whose social contours extended towards the upper end of city society. There is nothing especially surprising about the fact that the direction of civic affairs in early modern Rome went to men of the substantial propertied classes and that the vast majority of the urban population had no formal voice in them. By 1600, oligarchies controlled most town governments in Europe and artisans, hired workers, and, of course, women were kept out of council chambers almost everywhere. What is striking about these regulations in the Italian context is their silence on native roots. Nowhere did the statutes require that one be born in Rome in order to play a role on the Capitol. While local families going back several generations did predominate, as we shall see in the next chapter, they did not monopolize civic office as did their counterparts elsewhere in Italy. Indeed, stipulations for annual eligibility lists and a five-year waiting period before foreigners could fill an office suggest that newcomers were expected, and they did not disappoint such expectations. The Roman People were not a closed corporation.[27]

THE SENATOR

The most visible emblem of the civic government was the senator, although he was actually the official most remote from local society. Here was an office steeped in antique associations that had undergone a quite remarkable metamorphosis, becoming a single judgeship, held by a foreigner, with civil and criminal jurisdiction over lay Roman men and women. The senator's physiognomy is immediately recognizable as the Roman equivalent of the *podesta'*, a ubiquitous judicial

---

[26] *Statuta almae urbis*, bk. 3, chap. 28, 57; Rodocanachi, *Institutions*, 292. For the procedure to become a citizen see Nussdorfer, "City Politics," 26. The 1580 statutes stipulated no length of residency for citizenship, though those of the fourteenth century had required three years' residency. In sixteenth-century Florence citizenship qualifications included a thirty-year residency requirement; Litchfield, 46. On Paris see Descimon, 121–22, 144–45.

[27] See Chapter 6 for a more detailed discussion of this point. Craftsmen were excluded from civic offices in Rome by 1440; Rodocanachi, *Institutions*, 154–55. For exceptions to the exclusion of artisans from European urban governments see James S. Amelang, *Honored Citizens of Barcelona: Patrician Culture and Class Relations, 1490–1714* (Princeton, 1986), 219–21.

magistrate in late medieval Italian towns. In Rome's fourteenth-century city stat-utes he was elected by local "knights."[28]

When the popes returned to Rome in the fifteenth century, they took over the selection of the senator. This change followed logically from the notion, which they shared with other rising monarchs, that justice was the prince's domain. The senator's tribunal was called the Capitoline Curia and consisted of four judges (including the senator), reduced from six by the 1580 statutes. Although the statutes provided for nomination of two of the judges by the civic councils, with the choice left up to the pontiff, in the 1620s and 1630s candidates skipped the councils and simply petitioned Cardinal Francesco Barberini directly. The senator and his three associates held sessions twice a week in the great central chamber of the senator's palace, a few steps from the prison and "examination" room.[29]

By the seventeenth century learned jurists had reclassicized the senator, tracing his genealogy to the urban prefect (*praetor urbanus*), an imperial official who ad-ministered justice in ancient Rome. The senator's dress and insignia evoked those of the ancient prefect, and his link to the sovereign was underscored by the fact that he was not a Roman. The senator, despite a ceremonial role that posed him as a representative of the city, was actually the embodiment of papal justice on the Capitol.[30]

Not all the Capitoline judges whom the pontiffs appointed were as closely as-sociated with the sovereign, however, as the four judges of the senator's tribunal. Two other sets of magistrates had courtrooms in the senator's palace: the street masters (*maestri di strada*) and the master justicieries (*maestri giustizieri*). Unlike the senator, an outsider and a doctor of laws, these judges were Romans who were not necessarily trained in law. Like the senator they were laymen named by the pope, but their offices were technically elected, as we shall see, and during Urban VIII's reign candidates continued to be nominated by electors from the local Ro-man upper class. The street masters, who shared duties with the clerk of the chamber called the president of the streets, gave out building permits and assessed

[28] *Statuti*, ed. C. Re, bk. 3, chap. 8.; *Statuta almae urbis*, bk. 1, chap. 3. The statutes stipulate that the senator be from a town at least forty miles away from Rome. During Urban VIII's reign the three senators were all from towns in the Papal States: Baldo Massei from Camerino, Giulio Cartari from Orvieto, and Orazio Albani from Urbino; Nussdorfer, "City Politics," 32.

[29] *Statuta almae urbis*, bk. 1, chaps. 4–6, 41; nomination of two judges by the councils did take place in 1580, ASC, cred. I, vol. 28, decreti, 0054r (28 November 1580); petitions to Cardinal Francesco Barberini in BAV, Barb. lat. 10634 (provisional), sheets were without numeration. See also Niccolo' del Re, *La curia capitolina* (Rome, 1954); Ameyden, ASV, "Relatione," 683r–v; De Luca, *Il Dottor Volgare*, bk. 15, pt. 3, chap. 34, pp. 318–19; Nussdorfer, "City Politics," 31–35. On the senator's palace see Pecchiai, *Campidoglio*, 94, 99–100. See also Güthlein, 104–6, 109–13; I am grateful to Professor Mirka Beneš for sharing this information with me.

[30] Fenzonio, 25–28. Fenzonio held the post of senator from 1616 until 1623. For a different view see Westfall, 97–98. To show his connection to civic interests, however, the senator took an oath of office from the conservators after receiving his appointment by papal *breve*; see, for example, ASC, cred. I, vol. 33, decreti, 0070r–71r (28 February 1629). The archives of the senator's tribunal are in the ASR.

taxes for road repairs; in their tribunal they heard cases arising from these activities. The master justicieries pronounced sentence in disputes relating to the vineyards. The senator's palace was thus a palace of justice, imbued with papal authority, whose tribunals differed from those of the Roman Curia in their procedures—governed by the city statutes—and in their exclusively lay jurisdiction.[31] There was a great deal more judicial business on the Capitoline hill, however, than took place in the palace of the senator. For that we look to the adjacent palace dominated by the three magistrates known as the conservators.

THE PALACE OF THE CONSERVATORS

If municipal tradition in all its permutations resounded through the senator's halls, local society found its mouthpiece in the palace of the conservators. This building was the heart of that process of limited self-government through which the Roman People deliberated and acted in their two councils and many committees and elected offices. It was the residence of the three most important elected officials, who served together for three-month terms, and the hub of their judicial, ceremonial, and administrative activities. The palace was also the preeminent architectural representation of the Roman People, their space of display par excellence. Rooms for assemblies and banquets, for rendering justice, and for storing records bespoke these varied needs.

But the palace was not used only by the civic administration. It was also a meeting place for the largest corporation of city notaries, known as the Thirty Capitoline Notaries; it sheltered the many small courtrooms where artisan guilds judged their members' and clients' disputes; and it was the site of the tribunal of agriculture, where the patrician owners of the great landed estates gave judgment in cases involving livestock and cultivated fields. In its functions, spaces, and objects the palace condensed the range of meanings attached to the civic in Baroque Rome.[32]

The conservators' palace also conveyed the flavor of this particular municipality. It housed a renowned collection of Roman antiquities, originating in a gift from Pope Sixtus IV in 1471. A special pride was the famous *fasti consulares*, tablets with the names of the ancient consuls that had been unearthed nearby in 1546; the conservators liked to think of their magistracy as descending from the consuls of the Roman republic. The palace courtyard featured a colossal head of

[31] Totti, 404. For discussion of a sixteenth-century drawing in which the senator's palace is labeled "palazzo della ragione" see Güthlein, 87. The records of the tribunal of the master justicieries are in the ASR; a great deal of material on the activities of the street masters in the seventeenth century can be found in ASR, *fondo* Presidenza delle Strade.

[32] Rodocanachi, *Institutions*, 302; idem, *Capitole*, 165–67. For guild tribunals see chapter 8 and Carlo Pietrangeli, "Iscrizioni inedite o poco note dei Palazzi Capitolini," *ASRSP* 71 (1948): 129–30, 132–33. On the jurisdiction of the tribunal of agriculture see *Statuta nobilis artis agriculturae urbis* (Rome, 1627), chaps. 22, 23.

the emperor Constantine and a gigantic marble foot mounted on a pedestal. Reflecting the city's Christian heritage, a painting of the Madonna, later credited with saving Rome from an earthquake, hung on the internal staircase. Between 1645 and 1648 the palace chapel would acquire portraits of four local holy people: Saints Alessio, Cecilia, and Eustachio, plus a not yet officially beatified Ludovica Albertoni.[33]

A household staff or *familia*, many of them vassals from Capitoline fiefs outside Rome, maintained the building, fed the conservators, played music at their meals, accompanied them on ceremonial occasions, and informed them of what went on at meetings of artisan guilds. A chaplain, archivist, and team of scribes and secretaries worked in more specialized capacities. The civic administration had its official architects and lawyers (two prelates called the advocates of the Roman People), plus its official carpenter, mason, and fishmonger. Out in the city streets and neighborhoods the conservators relied on several other groups of employees: the market police called *straordinari*, who looked for infractions of market regulations; the mandataries of the fourteen *rioni*, who carried messages and notified people of meetings; and the drummers of the Roman People, whose drums added a civic presence to public functions.[34]

Attached to the Roman People, but physically distributed around the city's fourteen urban districts, was an artisan militia called "the company of *contestabili* and *capotori*." The company numbered 320 and was composed of bands of twenty or thirty working men from each of the *rioni* (see Map 2). The militia helped to represent the Roman People in major city processions, but played its most important role as a neighborhood patrol during periods of the Vacant See. Although each district's contingent was headed by a *caporione*, an elected civic official who rotated in and out of office every three months, it was his subordinate, the *capotoro*, who was the backbone of the militia. The *capotori* were independent master craftsmen, supposedly chosen yearly by the higher-status caporioni from nominations submitted by the company. In fact they had gradually taken control of the selection process themselves and exercised their office for life, forming a small corporation of their own complete with written statutes. The capotori were a route by which civic patronage extended into the artisan class; one of their major annual

[33] Totti, 402–7; Stinger, 255; Carlo Pietrangeli, "La 'Madonna delle Scale' nel Palazzo dei Conservatori," *Strenna dei romanisti* 17 (1956): 244; the four paintings are attributed to Giovanni Francesco Romanelli, idem, " 'Cappella vecchia' e 'capella nuova' nel Palazzo dei Conservatori," *Capitolium* 35, no. 2 (1960): 15. For a recent room-by-room description of the palace of the conservators see idem, ed., *Rione X—Campitelli*, 2d ed., 4 pts., Guide rionali di Roma (Rome, 1979), pt. 2: 86–112. See also Haskell and Penny, 15.

[34] Nussdorfer, "City Politics," 59–60, 69–70; *Statuta almae urbis*, bk. 3, chap. 28, lists officials of the palace; Emmanuel Rodocanachi, *Les corporations ouvrières à Rome depuis la chute de l'empire romain*, 2 vols. (Paris, 1894), 2:417; Alberto Cametti, "I musici di Campidoglio," *ASRSP* 48 (1925): 119. ASC, cred. XI, vols. 19 and 20, registers of letters patent (1615–1645), are a good source for civic appointments of mandataries, *straordinari*, masons, carpenters, etc.

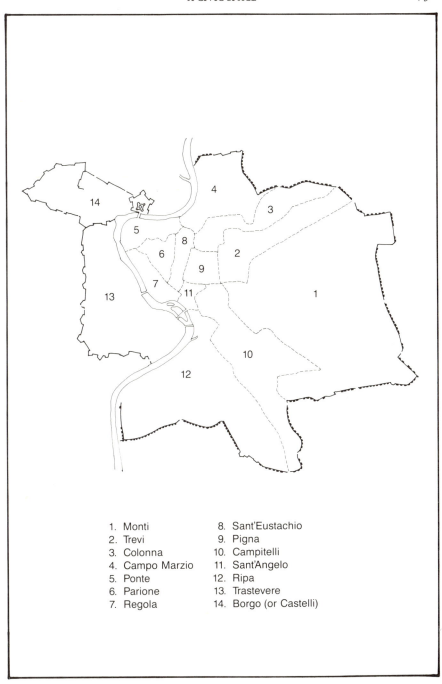

1. Monti	8. Sant'Eustachio
2. Trevi	9. Pigna
3. Colonna	10. Campitelli
4. Campo Marzio	11. Sant'Angelo
5. Ponte	12. Ripa
6. Parione	13. Trastevere
7. Regola	14. Borgo (or Castelli)

Map 2. Rome's Fourteen *Rioni*

preoccupations was bestowing dowries from public funds on fourteen marriage-able girls.[35]

The palace of the conservators was the link between the extended jurisdiction of the Roman People—into markets and neighborhoods and as far as rural fiefs—and that vague but privileged group of citizens who had the right to take part in civic affairs. Inside its halls upper-class laymen conducted the closest approxima-tion to representative local government that existed in the papal capital, even if those they represented were the propertied few. We now look more closely at the opportunities Capitoline institutions gave them to participate in public life.

OFFICEHOLDING

In impact, prestige, and numbers officeholding was the most important way for a well-born layman to take part in civic affairs in the seventeenth century. Of around 550 men who appeared in some formal role on the Capitol in two samples taken in the 1620s and 1640s, over sixty percent did so as candidates for office or as elected officials.[36] Exercising a particular function rather than attending coun-cils or serving on committees was what engaged the greatest number of upper-class Romans. Not all civic offices were equal of course. The candidate pool for top offices held different names than that for minor ones. In social status and judicial competence the three conservators, two street masters, and two master justicieries were the highest magistrates. The conservators served for three months; the street masters and master justicieries, in theory, for a year. Overlap-ping with them to some degree, but on the whole a less prominent group of substantial citizens, were the fourteen district caporioni, who also held office for three months. They were led by an official called the prior of the caporioni, who shared ceremonial rank with the conservators (see Figure 8).

A group of less important elected posts consisted of the four reformers of the university, the marshals (often children and the sons of the sort of people likely to be conservators), the peacemakers (*pacieri*), and the syndics with their notaries. The functions of the reformers of the university and the peacemakers dated back

<hr />

[35] Nussdorfer, "City Politics," 71–73. A painting of the procession honoring Taddeo Barberini at his investiture as prefect of Rome in 1632 shows the rione banners in the foreground. It is attributed to the workshop of Agostino Tassi and owned by the Cassa di Risparmio di Roma, Gruppo Banca di Santo Spirito; the painting is reproduced on the cover of Cassa di Risparmio di Roma, ed., *Via del Corso* (Rome, 1961). The capotoro of rione Regola attended a meeting of the gentlemen of the rione to choose an elector (*imbussolatore*) in 1631; he is listed as a witness to the notary's record of the meeting; ASR, 30 N.C., uff. 2 (Bonanni) 1631, pt. 3, 882v. See also ASC, cred. IV, vol. 128, cedole di sussidi dotali, and the newly inventoried capotori dowry subsidy documents in ASC, cred. XXII. For a discussion of how marriageable girls used similar dowry subsidies see Marina D'Amelia, "La conquista di una dote: Regole del gioco e scambi femminili alla Confraternita dell'Annunziata (secc. XVII-XVIII)," in *Ragnatele di rapporti: Patronage e reti di relazione nella storia delle donne*, ed. Lucia Ferrante et al. (Turin, 1988), 305–43.

[36] Nussdorfer, "City Politics," 130–34.

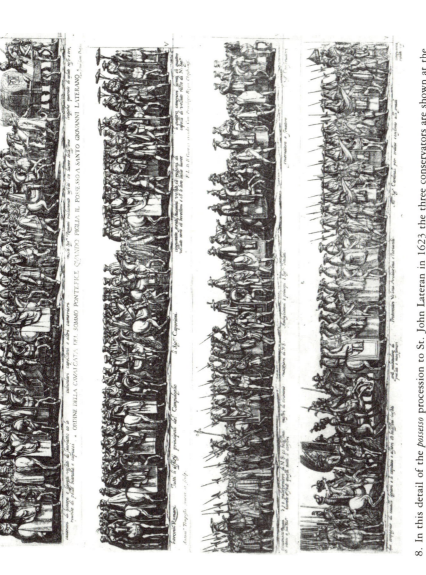

8. In this detail of the *possesso* procession to St. John Lateran in 1623 the three conservators are shown at the extreme right of the third strip, just before the governor and senator of Rome. The caporioni ride further back (second strip) between fifty "gentlemen" and the Capitoline employees.

to the fifteenth century, but had failed to sustain themselves, in part because of the rise of cardinalatial congregations or curial officials with similar mandates. The election of syndics to audit the accounts of the elected magistrates was an old-fashioned method of financial control that had been superseded by a standing civic committee. The post of marshal, whatever it had once been, was now a gesture of honor and tiny source of patronage, eleven scudi, to the most prominent civic families. While all these officials received money and perquisites in the form of pepper and sweetmeats on holidays, their actual duties in the seventeenth century were few. In an economizing move Pope Innocent X suppressed these lesser offices in late 1644 and diverted their income to construction of the third palace on the Capitol.[37]

How were the elected officials elected? The system was a combination of nomination and sortition. One elector or *imbussolatore* was chosen by an informal group from each of the city's fourteen rioni to draw up a list of nominees for each of eleven offices.[38] The fourteen electors and the conservators then voted on the electors' combined nominees and made up a master list from which officials would be chosen by lot. This master list was called the *bussola* and it was drafted every two years during Urban VIII's reign. Drawing officials by lot from a group of approved candidates was a common mode of election in late medieval and early modern Italy; the purpose of the sortition method, usually coupled with very short terms of office, was to ensure that civic offices circulated widely and rapidly among those eligible. While it helped prevent the overweening influence of a few families, this procedure could be manipulated politically, as Nicolai Rubinstein has shown in a classic study of Medicean Florence.[39] Nevertheless it gave significantly more men the chance to hold office than a system based on heredity or venality would have done.

How much control did the pope and his relatives exercise over civic elections? In the early sixteenth century the pontiffs had sometimes completely ignored the bussola, treating Capitoline offices as an extension of their own patronage re-

---

[37] Ibid., 145–47, 51–52, 56–59; Gigli, *Diario*, 265. For perquisites see ASC, cred. IV, vol. 106, tabella (1641), 115r–26r. For salaries see the discussion on finances later in this chapter.

[38] The eleven elected offices yielded 109 positions in a given year. Five offices were for three-month terms (three posts as conservator, fourteen as caporioni, two as syndic of the officials, one as the syndics' notary, and four as marshal) for a subtotal of 96 positions to which were added the thirteen men who served in the six annual offices (two street masters, two master justiciaries, two peacemakers, four reformers of the university, two syndics of the Roman People, and their notary) for a total of 109. See Nussdorfer, "City Politics," 36–37.

[39] *Statuta almae urbis*, bk. 3, chaps. 27, 28; Nussdorfer, "City Politics," 37–39; ASR, 30 N.C., uff. 2 (Bonanni) 1633, pt. 3, 649r. A biennial *bussola* held from 310 to 360 names for a total of 218 offices. All but one (for 1630–1631) of the *bussole* from the years 1623 to 1644 can be found in BAV, Barb. lat., 2211, 2213–16, 2218, 2221–23. No new *bussola* was created for 1644 and the one that preceded it was used for a third year to draw officials for 1644. On political manipulation of a sortition system see Nicolai Rubinstein, *The Government of Florence under the Medici (1434–1494)* (Oxford, 1966), 4–8 and passim.

sources. During the push by the Roman People in the 1560s to get their procedures in order, they painted an embarrassing picture of "our citizens . . . seen every day . . . with great lack of dignity wearying the doorkeepers of His Holiness, the cardinals and all the other princes who turn up in town, in order to be made officials by favor outside the *bussola*."[40] To remedy this the civic councils solicited papal support for the very precise instructions enshrined in the 1580 statutes.

It was true that in the seventeenth century neither the nomination vote nor the sortition, or "extraction" as it was commonly called, took place on the Capitol. Papal officials were present and a papal setting can be assumed for both stages in the election process, though this in itself was not a violation of the statutes.[41] There were at least three vulnerable points in the Roman system that offered opportunities for more or less covert tampering: the choice of electors, the vote to determine who the candidates would be, and the actual extraction of successful nominees. The Roman diarist Giacinto Gigli charged one of Cardinal Francesco Barberini's assistants with mistreating him in the drafting of one bussola and he accused another official of taking bribes from would-be candidates. His contemporary Teodoro Ameyden baldly asserted that "although the elector places the names of the best citizens in the urn only those requested by the [papal] Palace come out."[42]

Yet these complaints exaggerate the degree of interference. Gigli's own account, as well as notarial sources, attests that electors were still chosen by informal groups from the rioni; presumably they furnished most of the over three hundred names that went into the urn, even if other officials fiddled with the list later on.[43] Then too, pure chance favored anyone who was a nominee, since over sixty percent of the men in a given bussola were needed just to fill the 109 offices a year. The civic councils in 1625 reminded Urban VIII that the bussola should be drawn up according to the statutes, but it only did this once during his reign.[44] The lamentable incidents that had occurred in the preceding century did not recur and very few officials in the Barberini decades were actually appointed outside the bussola.[45] Occasionally a friend of the Barberini received a civic office—Gigli

[40] Gigli, BNC-VE, Sess. 334, 279v–80r, 258r–v; Alberini, 481, 483, 491; Nussdorfer, "City Politics," 41–42.

[41] ASC, cred. I, vol. 13, matricole di consegli [sic] (1613–1639), 106r; Ameyden, ASV, "Relatione," 684r; *Statuta almae urbis*, bk. 3, chap. 28; Nussdorfer, "City Politics," 39–40.

[42] Gigli, BNC-VE, Sess. 334, 210v; idem, *Diario*, 259; Ameyden, ASV, "Relatione," 684r–v.

[43] Gigli, BNC-VE, Sess. 334, 219v; ASR, 30 N.C., uff. 2 (Bonanni) 1633, pt. 3, 648r–49v (meetings in rione Regola and rione Sant'Angelo).

[44] ASC, cred. I, vol. 33, decreti, 0029r (31 October 1625).

[45] Nussdorfer, "City Politics," 41. While the total number of offices to be filled each year (see n. 38) was fixed, the actual number of officials who served varied because sometimes an entire group of incumbents was confirmed for another term in office. In the two-year period from 1 July 1623 to 31 July 1625 a total of 153 men served in elected offices; only four of these men (three caporioni and one master justiciery) were not in the bussola of candidates drawn up by the process outlined above. In the

himself was so rewarded—but for the most part the electors' list, with possible editing, served as the basis of the sortition. If Ameyden was right and successful candidates needed papal favor, there was a rather large group of Romans in this category. The Roman People seemed to have had a substantial, if not exclusive, voice in choosing their officials, though they undoubtedly produced nominees acceptable to the pope.[46]

The electoral system successfully functioned to keep civic offices moving around among the lay urban elite. The statutes required that at least two years pass before an officeholder could be placed in a new bussola, and sampling found close adherence to this rule in the Barberini era.[47] Thirty-seven men out of a total of 167 conservators held the office more than once between 1623 and 1644, and only eight repeated a third time, always at widely spaced intervals. No small group monopolized civic office, and every other year the bussola contained dozens of new names. Interestingly, the choice of electors, which was made at an informal district meeting and was not strictly regulated by statute, followed a similar pattern, although one exceptional elector served eight times.[48]

Two elected offices were an exception to the general pattern. Nominees for the annual posts of street master and master justiciery appeared faithfully in each new bussola. Because of the judicial character of these offices, however, they received appointment from the pope, who probably did not select them by lot and who did permit them to hold office for several years at a time. For these posts the pontiffs chose local men of social distinction, "always . . . gentlemen and the highest nobility, of a mature age and good reputation," who were likely to serve as conservators when they were not street masters and master justicieries.[49] But

---

two-year period from 1 July 1642 to 31 July 1644 a total of 128 men served in elected offices; although we lack the names of thirty-one of those men, of the ninety-seven names we can identify thirteen were appointed outside the bussola (five caporioni, three syndics, two reformers, one marshal, one conservator, and one street master). The period 1642–1644 was somewhat anomalous because of the war of Castro and the pope's death and these events may have caused some deviations from normal electoral procedures.

[46] Gigli, BNC-VE, Sess. 334, 213r; Gigli had previously been drawn in the normal manner. One papal "friend" who profited in this way was the official known as the fiscal procurator of the Capitol, who is discussed in more detail later in this chapter. The relationship between the king and municipal elections in Paris was remarkably similar; Descimon, 130–31.

[47] *Statuta almae urbis*, bk. 3, chap. 28; Nussdorfer, "City Politics," 141, 145.

[48] Nussdorfer, "City Politics," 38. At two such meetings in rione Sant'Angelo in 1633 and 1635, between one and two dozen men are represented, but only two of them attend both meetings; ASR, 30 N.C., uff. 2 (Bonanni) 1633, pt. 3, 649r–v, and uff. 2, (Bonanni) 1635, pt. 3, 806r–v. In Sant'Angelo in 1637 thirteen men actually attend the meeting, but two come with *procure* or power of attorney for a total of twenty-six additional men; ibid., uff. 2, (Bonanni) 1637, pt. 3, 741r–v, 758r.

[49] Ameyden, ASV, "Relatione," 687v–88r. The street masters are listed each January in the decrees of the Capitoline councils, ASC, cred. I, vols. 32–34 (1612–1660). For the master justicieries, whose lengthy tenures appear to have been a peculiarity of Urban VIII's reign, see also Carla Nardi, "La campagna nella citta': L'opera dei maestri giustizieri (secc. XV–XVIII)," *Storia della citta'* 29 (1984): 55, 59.

maintaining the fiction that these were elected offices was an important symbolic gesture on the part of the Roman elite. Both were sensitive magistracies, able to damage the interests of local property owners. The master justicieries headed a tribunal intended to protect the proprietors of the vast web of vineyards that surrounded the city both inside and outside the walls; they prosecuted thefts, settled boundary disputes, and regulated the grape harvest. The street masters had an extremely broad mandate not only to maintain roads and bridges but also to grant land from the public domain to those wishing to build on it and to assess taxes to pay for repairs and demolitions that "improved" the value of surrounding property. This latter power inspired several pages of regulations in the 1580 statutes, designed to make owners feel included in the tax assessment process.[50] Such officials had to have the confidence of the urban upper classes or they could not do their jobs, and the pope recognized this by appointing men of "good reputation." The Roman gentlemen who compiled nominees for an election by lot that never took place were indicating appropriate choices.

Normal electoral procedures operated for the conservators and caporioni, who rotated promptly in and out of office every three months. The conservators led the Capitoline government; one of the three lived in the palace of the conservators for one month of each term. It was their responsibility to see to the upkeep of the palace, making a yearly inventory of its furnishings and silver. The conservators' names were on the edicts emanating from the Roman People and they had regular audiences with the pope. They also formally represented the city at mass in the papal chapel or at great religious ceremonies such as the beginning of a Holy Year, and of course they made offerings to local churches on special saints' days. The conservators presided over their own tribunal, located in the room now known as the Sala dei Capitani, which heard cases concerning market infractions, evasion of civic taxes, conflicts between gatekeepers and travelers or between guilds and city employees, as well as appeals from decisions of guild tribunals.[51] They governed the four fiefs of the Roman People and expedited letters patent for all city offices that were not elected. The conservators chaired meetings of the smaller of the two

[50] On the office of street master see *Statuta almae urbis*, bk. 3, chap. 39; *Regesti* 4:7, 14, 25, 40; Nussdorfer, "City Politics," 52–55. On the office of master justiciery see Nardi; *Statuta almae urbis*, bk. 3, chap. 40 and p. 206; *Regesti* 4:121, 160; Nussdorfer, "City Politics," 55–56.

[51] Nussdorfer, "City Politics," 44–47. I have seen the few surviving records of the conservators' tribunal from 1623 to 1644, which are located at the ASR, Tribunale dei Conservatori; I have not seen the newly inventoried materials pertaining to this tribunal in the ASC, Cred. XXII. In the 1630s the Flemish lawyer, Teodoro Ameyden, was the conservators' *assessore* or legal consultant; Bastiaanse, 45. *Statuta almae urbis*, bk. 1, chap. 15, and bk. 3, chaps. 4, 29; Totti, 406; ASC, cred. I, vol. 32, decreti, 0287v (7 November 1624); Rodocanachi, *Institutions*, 304; Carlo Pietrangeli, "La sala dei capitani," *Capitolium* 37 (1962): 640–48. The colored marble revetment with the inscription "Diligite iustitiam" ("Love justice") is still in place; it bears the names of the three conservators who served from October to December 1628. An engraving by Ambrogio Brambilla, printed by Lafréry in 1582, of the pope celebrating mass in the Sistine Chapel at the Vatican palace shows the conservators among other laymen seated on a dais at the foot of the papal throne.

civic councils and set its agenda. They were often charged with executing its decisions as well, which might include selecting citizens to accompany them when they made a special delegation to the pope or his nephews. But there were many things they did without the participation of the councils, such as their notorious grant of the bronze from the beams of the Pantheon to Urban VIII for making cannon in 1625.[52] The conservators, the only elected officials who received no salary, had considerable latitude to use their brief periods in office to advance their family's stature in nonpecuniary ways, as we shall see in later chapters.

Twelve men served as conservator each year; fifty-six held the office of caporione, head of one of fourteen rioni. The caporioni did not necessarily live in the districts over which they presided. Their duties were more intermittent than those of the conservators; they were often younger men or somewhat lower in social status. A notary might fill the post of caporione, or a not very prominent gentleman poet and antiquarian like the diarist Giacinto Gigli. Nevertheless the conservators were prepared to argue that holding the office of caporione was a mark of prestige.[53]

What did the caporioni actually do in the seventeenth century? Because they were scattered around the city few records of their activities survive in the municipal archives. Like all civic officials they took an oath of office, which could be administered either by the pope, the cardinal chamberlain, or the senator.[54] They were required to attend the civic councils, although they did not always do it, and they convened the meetings at which the rione elector was chosen.[55] The statutes indicate that they judged minor civil cases arising in the district, and in fact Gigli did appoint a lawyer or *assessore* and a notary to assist him when he held the office, but I have not found direct evidence of such trials.[56] Less frequently than the conservators they participated in important public ceremonies, such as

---

[52] Pietro Romano, 44–56; Gigli, *Diario*, 93–94; Nussdorfer, "City Politics," 219–21. One newly available source for the activity of the conservators that I have not seen is the acts of the notary of the conservators; thirteen *protocolli* survive for the years 1626 to 1746 in the ASC, Archivio del Protonotaro del Senatore, Sezione I, Atti del notaro dei conservatori.

[53] A letter from the conservators dating from 1617 attests to the nobility of a certain G. Gomes on the basis of the fact that he had held the office of caporione the year before; ASC, cred. IV, vol. 96, istrumenti (1610–1640), 32v. By the early eighteenth century, however, the conservators no longer supported claims to noble status based on election to this office; see Luigi Guasco, *L'archivio storico capitolino* (Rome, 1946), 36. Lorenzo Bonincontro, a member of the college of Thirty Capitoline Notaries, held the office of caporione in 1626.

[54] Nussdorfer, "City Politics," 43–44. ASC, cred. I, vol. 13, matricole, 89r, 116r, 120v, record some of these oaths in the 1620s and 1630s. In 1626, and again in 1638, the cardinal chamberlain issued edicts chastising civic officials for failing to take their oaths; ASV, arm. IV, vol. 32.

[55] *Statuta almae urbis*, bk. 3, chaps. 2, 3. In 1633 the gentlemen of rione Sant'Angelo convened in the house of their caporione to choose a new elector (*imbussolatore*); ASR, 30 N.C., uff. 2 (Bonanni) 1633, pt. 3, 649r; in 1637 they met in the cloister of Santa Maria in Aracoeli; ibid., uff. 2 (Bonanni) 1637, pt. 3, 741r.

[56] *Statuta almae urbis*, bk. 1, chap. 18; Gigli, BNC-VE, Sess. 334, 214v; see also Alberini, 485.

the *possesso* procession in which the pope took formal possession of his diocese. During the Vacant See the role of the caporioni is better documented; then they definitely heard legal cases arising in the rione and commanded the artisan militia contingent that patrolled its borders at night.[57]

COUNCILS AND COMMITTEES

The two civic councils that had taken firm institutional shape in the fifteenth century, the broad public council (*consilium publicum*) and a smaller private council (*consilium secretum*), generated little interest in the seventeenth century. Although almost 1,800 men had qualified for the public council in 1581, and an average of seventy members had shown up for its sessions, attendance in the Barberini era was down to around twenty. Despite the statutory requirement of a monthly meeting, the public council usually met no more than three or four times a year. The private council appealed slightly more to Romans than its sister body; while it did not meet as often as the statutes stipulated, its attendance had held steady since the 1580s and exceeded that of the public council. Still, of almost 250 people eligible for the private council no more than half turned up at its sessions in a two-year period in the 1620s and 1640s.[58]

The councils were dying by 1620, and the statutes suggest why. Subject to minute regulation that dictated how members should comport themselves and prohibited from raising any issue not on the agenda prepared by the conservators, the councils did not offer much opportunity for unauthorized expression of opinion. Under normal circumstances their duties were fairly routine, for example, approving new grants of Roman citizenship; they acquired greater significance however when it was a question of approving "extraordinary" expenditures by the civic government. In addition, at the beginning of the Vacant See the public council took on a transformed role as source of the authority of the Roman People.[59]

[57] Gigli, *Diario*, 159; idem, BNC-VE, Sess. 334, 219v. For the role of the caporioni during the Vacant See see Chapter 14.

[58] The records of the decrees of the two councils for 1623 to 1644 are located in ASC, cred. I, vols. 32–34. The same statistical study also showed that between twenty and forty percent of those who *did* attend the private council were not technically eligible; Nussdorfer, "City Politics," 61–66, 134–38. *Statuti*, ed. C. Re, 44; Rodocanachi, *Institutions*, 188, 307. The private council met in the same room as the conservators' tribunal, the so-called Sala di Udienza now known as the Sala dei Capitani; Pietrangeli, *Campidoglio*, 120. On the decoration of this room see Roger Aikin, "Christian Soldiers in the Sala dei Capitani," *Sixteenth Century Journal* 16 (1985): 206–27, and Maria Elisa Tittoni, "Gli affreschi di Tommaso Laureti in Campidoglio," in *Roma e l'antico nell'arte e nella cultura del Cinquecento*, ed. Marcello Fagiolo (Rome, 1985), 211–34. The public council met in the so-called Sala Grande, now the Sala degli Orazi e Curiazi; Pietrangelo, *Campidoglio*, 119. See also Aikin, "Capitoline Hill," 125, and the exhibition catalogue, *Gli affreschi del Cavalier D'Arpino in Campidoglio: Analisi di un'opera attraverso il restauro* (Rome, 1980), 9–10.

[59] *Statuta almae urbis*, bk. 3, chaps. 2, 3; Nussdorfer, "City Politics," 62–63 and 49 n. 79. More than eighty citizens attended the public council at the beginning of the Vacant See of 1623 and more

The Romans themselves were at least partly responsible for circumscribing and neutralizing the potential impact of these assemblies. Since no council decrees from before 1515 survive, it is difficult to know what the councils were like in their early days. Yet one suspects that the process of defining their membership and fixing their procedures in writing, which culminated in the statutes of 1580, had a dampening effect.[60] Giving the conservators complete control over the councils may have increased decorum but did not stimulate excitement; gradually people voted with their feet and stayed away. Not even all the caporioni attended meetings in the seventeenth century, despite their legal obligation to do so.

Yet the councils were important, notwithstanding faltering interest, because they provided the one formal mechanism for collective discussion available to eligible Romans. Civic emergencies usually provoked the convening of the councils and decisions about extraordinary expenditures could ignite lively debate. In a sense, they were the only vehicle of public, or at least semipublic, political negotiation that existed in Baroque Rome, the means by which to establish the consent or rally the resistance of the upper classes to controversial requests. This function remained essential even when the councils as such disappeared after 1669, when, I suspect, informal adhoc assemblies were required to take their place.[61]

The men who were most actively involved with Capitoline business were members of standing or adhoc committees. Neither those elected to brief terms in office nor people who attended the councils were as likely as committee members to take part in an additional form of civic activity. The standing committees in particular, known as "annual deputations," were flexible instruments of administration, lightly regulated and offering a useful degree of continuity in a system of rotating offices. The statutes said little about the committees, and their number and competencies changed over time in response to current needs. In the first half of the seventeenth century fifteen annual deputations functioned, ranging in size

than sixty that of 1644; ASC, cred. I, vol. 32, decreti, 0267r–v (9 July 1623) and vol. 34, 0069v (29 July 1644). For more details on the public council during the Vacant See see Chapter 14. See also Antonio Spaziani, *Cenni sul potere del senato di Roma considerato in rapporto allo statuto del S. P. Gregorio XIII e alle vigenti leggi comunali* (Rome, 1864), 12.

[60] See, for example, efforts "to avoid tumults that could arise from calling frequent councils" during the Vacant Sees of 1590 and 1591; ASC, cred. I, vol. 29, decreti, 0253v (28 August 1590) and 0304v (16 October 1591). On the councils in the thirteenth and fourteenth centuries see Brentano, 112–15, and *Statuti*, ed. C. Re, 216 and passim. For theories about the councils in the sixteenth century see Güthlein, 85–115.

[61] See, for example, the reference to a meeting in 1736 in ASC, cred. VI, vol. 108, trattato, 16r–v. De Luca, writing in 1673, also makes it sound as if the councils still met, though rarely; De Luca, *Il Dottor Volgare*, bk. 15, pt. 3, chap. 34, p. 319. From 1669 the decrees of the councils are no longer recorded, although new officials and new grants of citizenship continue to be listed. The public councils also continued to meet after the deaths of popes at the beginning of the Vacant See; ASC, cred. I, vol. 35. In 1694 a series of decrees of the Capitoline "congregation" begins; ASC, cred. I, vol. 40. For the councils' role in relation to extraordinary expenditures and civic emergencies during Urban VIII's reign see Chapters 11–13.

from two to sixteen members. Ninety-two slots were filled each year by civic officials and ten gentlemen whom they named. In the 1580s citizens who were chosen by lot, not by the conservators, had nominated the annual committees.[62]

Two committees totaling twenty-two members had responsibilities connected to the operation of two of Rome's three recently completed aqueducts, the Acqua Vergine and the Acqua Felice. These committees had expanded rapidly in the preceding half century due to the dramatic increase in the city's water supply; two men had sufficed on a single fountains' committee back in 1580.[63] The largest deputation of the Barberini era was also new since 1580; it was the sixteen men who supervised the yearly Carnival races. Smaller groups screened applicants for Roman citizenship, oversaw municipal finances, and ensured the proper maintenance of the conservators' palace. Two deputies went over the accounts of the street masters and two others served as administrators on the board of the public beggar's hospice, the *ospedale dei mendicanti*.[64] Often a citizen participated on several committees in the same year, and it was common for a member to keep his place for several years. The four-man committee that reviewed applications for citizenship stayed the same for a decade. In addition to the annual deputations a standing committee of eight members, responsible for distributing the customary gifts (*regaglie*) to officials each year at Christmas, held their posts for life. It cost the tidy sum of over 3,100 scudi to provide the gloves, wax, pepper, and sweetmeats given out annually. Only gentlemen from prestigious families, like the Massimi, Albertoni, and Costaguti, were chosen for this committee.[65]

This structure of formal committees did not preclude creation of adhoc groups to meet temporary or unexpected needs. Staging a solemn funeral ceremony for Urban VIII's brother in 1630 required the efforts of eight citizens, and every

[62] The main source on the committees is the decrees of the civic councils, ASC, cred. I, vols. 32–34. Nussdorfer, "City Politics," 66–68, 139–40; table 7 (p. 140) shows that about seventy percent of committee members also attended council sessions or were candidates or officials. One of the annual deputations was the "forty additional councillors," a group who were individually named each year as eligible to attend the private council; with this group the total number of places on annual deputations during Urban VIII's reign was 132. For an example of the three-step procedure by which the committee spots were filled see ASC, cred. I, vol. 32, decreti, 0275v–78r (23 March 1624). To compare the procedure in the 1580s see ASC, cred. I, vol. 28, decreti, 0028v, 0060r.

[63] See, for example, ASC, cred. I, vol. 32, decreti, 0277r–v (23 March 1624). The civic treasury seems to have received income from water distribution; C. Paola Scavizzi, "La rete idrica urbana in eta' moderna," *Storia della citta'* 29 (1984): 80. Although the third aqueduct, the Acqua Paola, did not have a committee, deputies of the Roman People did have certain responsibilities during its construction; see edict of 11 August 1609 in ASC, cred. XIII, vol. 30, 169r.

[64] See, for example, the meeting to set up the committees for 1634, ASC, cred. I, vol. 33, decreti, 0142v–44v (29 April 1634). For the papal bull of 1587 that authorized this civic role in managing the *ospedale dei mendicanti* see Simoncelli, "Origini," 132–34; see also edict of 6 October 1634, ASR, Biblioteca, Bandi, Campidoglio, vol. 436. See also *Regesti* 2:50.

[65] Nussdorfer, "City Politics," 68 n. 132. For the *regaglie* committee members and their annual meeting in 1624 see ASC, cred. I, vol. 32, decreti, 0275v, 0276v, 0289r (27 November 1624). For the amount spent on these gifts see ASC, cred. IV, vol. 106, tabella, 113v.

delegation that went to the pope on the Roman People's behalf included from four to fourteen gentlemen as well as the conservators and prior. Like the members of the *regaglie* committee, men chosen for these special tasks tended to be from the more distinguished families of local society. Conversely, since the choice of their personnel was entirely up to the Romans, these adhoc committees help to identify the citizens who stood at the center of civic affairs and whose influence counted the most, a group that was by no means an oligarchy, but which shaped the social and political profile of the Capitol in the seventeenth century.[66]

GO-BETWEENS

Lay Romans could take part in Capitoline institutions in diverse ways and had many-sided responsibilities in public life. Much of the time this cluster of duties, offices, and bodies hummed along like any administrative structure, not overly affected by larger political contexts or events. When the magistrates or the councils felt very worried about something or had a special request, however, they turned toward the Vatican. Action or favors came from the prince. The Roman People used several methods to take their messages to Urban VIII. If it was a minor issue, the conservators might bring it up at their audience with the pope. On more delicate matters they preferred to surround themselves with several other well-born Romans in a special delegation, as we have seen, and perhaps also visit Cardinals Francesco and Antonio Barberini the younger. To beef up a delegation or serve as intermediaries on their behalf they also relied on their two attorneys, the "advocates of the Roman People," Giulio Cenci and Domenico Cecchini. Prelates and members of the college of consistorial advocates, the city's most prestigious group of barristers, Cenci and Cecchini came from Roman families with traditional civic ties.[67]

For their part the popes liked to keep an eye on what went on at the Capitol. This government of lay amateurs might not offer any political threat, though one

[66] Nussdorfer, "City Politics," 140–41. Fifty-seven men were chosen for "special deputations," as the ad hoc committees were called, between 1623 and 1644. Seven served in this capacity four or more times: Lorenzo Altieri, Giovanni Francesco Palazzola, Giacomo Velli, the brothers Agostino and Bernardino Maffei, and two cousins from the Massimi family, both named Massimo.

[67] ASC, cred. I, vol. 33, decreti, 0051r (23 August 1627); 0121r (19 April 1632); 0162v (22 September 1635); 0242v–43r (24 September 1640); Ranke, 3:410; Pietro Romano, 115; Rodocanachi, *Institutions*, 347. Both Cenci and Cecchini, who was a Capizucchi on his mother's side, came from Roman families going back more than 300 years; Ameyden, ASV, "Relatione," 676v–77r. Their forebears were conservators as early as the fourteenth and fifteenth centuries; Giacomo Pietramellara, *Il libro d'oro del Campidoglio*, 2 vols. (Rome, 1893–97), 2:185, 190, 192. Giulio Cenci's father Girolamo served as street master from 1631 to 1633 and his brother Virgilio held the same post from 1634 to 1640. Both Girolamo and Virgilio Cenci were chosen for special civic delegations several times during Urban VIII's pontificate. On Cecchini, who became a cardinal in 1645, see also Lorenzo Cardella, *Memorie storiche intorno ai cardinali di santa romana chiesa*, 10 vols. (Rome, 1792–97), 7:53–54, and Luigi Fumi, "Il Cardinale Cecchini romano secondo la sua autobiografia," *ASRSP* 10 (1887): 287–322.

could never be too careful, but it did need to be kept to proper judicial and financial procedures. Then too, sometimes a pontiff wanted something from the Roman People and on those occasions it was handy to have someone who could act as go-between. So the pope had a man of his own in the heart of the civic administration and this official was called the fiscal procurator. The fiscal procurator of the Capitol was a lawyer who was appointed by the pontiff and vested by the city statutes with wide-ranging legal powers to protect the financial interests of the Roman People. This broad mandate to defend the civic treasury by judicial means meant that he was sometimes cast in an adversarial role to the magistrates themselves. For instance, he had to see to it that the fines levied by the conservators on artisans or tradesmen for marketplace infractions were fully collected and not lowered or quashed by a sympathetic magistrate. His zeal was presumably encouraged by the fact that his salary was partly drawn from such fines. He also made sure the conservators drew up the yearly inventory of the valuable collection of furnishings, antiquities, and silver in their palace, and did not walk off with any of it. But the fiscal procurator's presence on the Capitol was much more pervasive than these examples suggest. While the conservators rotated in and out of office every three months, he might serve for many years. He lived in the senator's palace, attended most council sessions, and grew very well informed about all aspects of the Roman People's affairs. At the same time he was also in close contact with the pope, often acting as the agent by which papal wishes were conveyed to the Capitol.[68]

A new fiscal procurator of the Capitol was usually named soon after the election of a new pontiff. By December 1623 Urban VIII had appointed Pietro Fontana in place of Polidoro Nerucci, the choice of his predecessor Gregory XV. Fontana was followed in late 1627 by the man who became a fixture of civic politics for the next ten years, Monsignor Pietro Colangelo, a native of Cascia in present-day Umbria. Colangelo, "having acquired the ears of the pope and Cardinal Barberino," according to the disaffected diarist Gigli, left the Capitoline post when Cardinal Antonio Barberini assumed the office of cardinal chamberlain in 1638 and made him his auditor. Gigli happily reported that Colangelo was found suffocated in his own blood in April 1639, which he thought was divine retribution for Colangelo's misdeeds as fiscal procurator.[69] Angelo Giardino of Macerata in the Marche succeeded Colangelo from 1639 to 1644, but was no more popular,

[68] The fiscal procurator of the Capitol, *fiscale del Campidoglio*, should not be confused with the fiscal procurator of the apostolic chamber, who was known as the *fiscale generale* or *fiscale di Roma; Bullarium* 12:71, 82–84. On the Capitoline official see *Statuta almae urbis*, bk. 1, chap. 19; bk. 3, chaps. 10, 92; Rodocanachi, *Institutions*, 246, 283, 292, 297, 325; ASC, cred. IV, vol. 106, tabella, 106v; ASC, cred. IX, vol. 21, pene (1683–1684), 11v; ASC, cred. I, vol. 28, decreti, 0039r (20 June 1580); Gigli, *Diario*, 168, 178; ASC, cred. I, vol. 6, decreti in *sede vacante*, 0298r (28 September 1644); Biblioteca Corsini, ms. 1654, "Relatione," 177.

[69] My source for names of fiscal procurators and their terms in office is the decrees of the civic councils; ASC, cred. I, vols. 32–34. Gigli, *Diario*, 184–85.

and was replaced as a favor to the Roman People by the new pope Innocent X in September 1644. He too seems to have been a Barberini client, reminding Cardinal Francesco in an undated letter that he had been promised the post of auditor of the first clerk of the chamber that became available.[70] The job of fiscal procurator of the Capitol was a step on the career ladder of ambitious papal bureaucrats, a fact not lost on the Romans who dealt with them and who, as we shall see, both needed and feared their services as go-betweens.

THE CAPITOLINE TREASURY

Both papal debt and taxation of papal subjects leaped sharply under Urban VIII; the years from 1623 to 1644 marked a new era in the state's fiscal pressure upon society.[71] In Chapter 12 I explore the interaction between the pope and the Capitol on money matters in these critical decades. Here we look at the structure of the Capitoline treasury from an analytical perspective, isolating its stable features from their dynamic context. Civic finances were intimately bound up with the finances of the papacy, but at the same time distinct from them. Scholars have downplayed this distinction, claiming that the Roman People had no revenue of their own, or that they had some but were hopelessly in debt to the papal treasury, or that financial relations between the city and the pontiffs were so complicated that it was impossible to distinguish municipal sources of income from those of the state.[72] But in fact the Capitol had its own budget, its councils often considered how to raise money, and the popes repeatedly sought funds from the Roman People.

In Rome, as in many medieval and early modern cities, no one treasury controlled all public revenues and expenditures. A civic treasury, the *camera urbis*, had emerged alongside the papal treasury or apostolic chamber by the thirteenth century. Although its precise institutional physiognomy varied in different epochs, one enduring trait was that it was closely monitored by other authorities: by Charles of Anjou for a few years in the thirteenth century, and by the papacy

---

[70] BAV, Barb. lat. 10634 (provisional). Gigli, *Diario*, 259–60. Gigli felt that he had suffered personally at Giardino's hands for, among other reasons, blocking his plans to publish a chronology of the Capitoline magistrates; idem, BNC-VE, Sess. 334, 210v. It is interesting to note that the fiscal procurators were able to obtain extra income for themselves and members of their families by "election" to civic offices. Colangelo was one of four "reformers of the university" every year from 1628 to 1638, for which he collected twenty-six scudi annually. His nephew Carlo was marshal three times (earning eleven scudi each term) between 1629 and 1635 and caporione for rione Pigna in 1636 (earning fourteen scudi). Both Angelo Giardino and his son Emilio held the office of "reformer of the university," for six and five years respectively; ASC, cred. I, vols. 32–34. Emilio served as caporione for the rione of Campo Marzio in 1639, although he was not in the bussola of candidates that year; Gigli, BNC-VE, Sess. 334, 208v.

[71] Lutz, 119, 123–24; Partner, "Financial Policy," 27; Stumpo, *Capitale*, 124, 131–33.

[72] Rodocanachi, *Institutions*, 327; Pecchiai, *Roma*, 263–64, 273; Peter Partner, *The Papal State under Martin V* (London, 1958), 166; Delumeau, *Vie* 2:751–53; Lombardo, 61; Hook, 214; Gross, 116.

the rest of the time. The thirteenth-century popes claimed that the revenues Rome collected from towns it had conquered since the mid-twelfth century belonged to them, but at the same time they recognized the existence of a distinct financial organ on the Capitol by agreeing to pay its officials.[73] This mixture of acquisitiveness and obligation continued to mark papal behavior toward the *camera urbis*, later known as the Capitoline chamber, in succeeding centuries.

The civic treasury gained independence during the fourteenth century, when the popes were in Avignon, and had to accommodate itself to renewed intimacy when Martin V returned in 1420.[74] Nevertheless, the process of building up the Papal States in the fifteenth and sixteenth centuries, while assuring the subordination of the Capitoline fisc, did not extinguish it. Even historians who argue for the dominance of the central government over municipal revenues would have to admit with Jean Delumeau that "certain taxes were collected in the name and by the efforts of the city of Rome."[75] Just as civic tribunals functioned separately from papal ones, a civic treasury operated distinctly from the apostolic chamber.[76]

In the mid-seventeenth century the Capitoline chamber was a financial entity, neither wholly dependent on papal support nor completely free of it, administering an annual budget of over 150,000 scudi, about one-tenth the size of the papal budget.[77] It had its own revenues, obligations, financial officers, and budget, but

[73] Alain de Boüard, *Le régime politique et les institutions de Rome au moyen-âge, 1252–1327* (Paris, 1920), 48–49, 170–73; Mario Caravale, *La finanza pontificia nel Cinquecento: Le province del Lazio* (n.p., 1974), 26–27.

[74] Sigismondo Malatesta, *Statuti delle gabelle di Roma* (Rome, 1885). An instance in the 1420s in which the apostolic treasurer drew funds directly from the *camera urbis* for the pope's private expenses is noted by Partner, *Papal State*, 167. I have found no evidence of such a practice in the seventeenth century and it does not seem to have become the norm.

[75] Delumeau, *Vie* 2:750; Partner, *Papal State*, 166. Lombardo, 61, describes civic income as "fittiziamente municipali ma sostanzialmente statali." One of the themes of the various contributions collected in *La fiscalité et ses implications sociales en Italie et en France au XVIIᵉ et XVIIIᵉ siècles* is the greater survival of the municipal presence in fiscal matters in early modern Italy than in France. In the Venetian *terraferma* this resulted in "considerable bargaining power" for local town governments in tax dealings with the Venetian state; Michael Knapton, "City Wealth and State Wealth in Northeast Italy, 14th-17th Centuries," in *La ville, la bourgeoisie et la genèse de l'état moderne* (Paris, 1988), 201–2.

[76] On the apostolic chamber see Partner, "Financial Policy;" Reinhard, *Papstfinanz*; idem, "Finanza pontificia e Stato della Chiesa nel XVI e XVII secolo," in *Finanze e ragion di stato in Italia e in Germania nella prima eta' moderna*, ed. Aldo De Maddalena and Hermann Kellenbenz (Bologna, 1984), 353–87; Rietbergen, 159–240. Although there is no study of Capitoline finances in the early modern period, Maria Luisa Lombardo has investigated specific aspects of the *camera urbis* in the fifteenth century using documents in the ASR. This is an important effort because the Capitoline government's records before 1500 in the ASC have not survived. Pecchiai bases his estimate of Capitoline revenue in the sixteenth century on inadequate documentation, *Roma*, 263–64. Delumeau made use of a series (*fondo*) in the Archivio di Stato called *Camera Urbis*, which listed the prices of the Christmas gifts (*regaglie*) presented to officials between 1505 and 1613, *Vie* 2:710–19. The figures for municipal receipts and expenditures from this series are much too low to constitute the entire municipal budget, however, and probably represent the accounts of just one of the civic financial officers; ibid., 2:753.

[77] This annual budget will be discussed in greater detail below. For a table of papal revenues see Partner, "Financial Policy," 49. For the 1607 Parisian municipal budget, which was about a tenth

it also had numerous links to the finances of the larger state in which it was embedded. One such tie was the regular payments that the apostolic chamber made to the civic treasury of around 12,000 scudi a year. Another was the gifts the Capitoline chamber provided to papal officials each Christmas. There were many less predictable contacts too, for, as we shall see in Chapter 12, both city and papacy looked upon each other as a source of funds when the unexpected occurred and urgent new needs developed.

The Capitoline chamber had four principal officials, each presiding over his own income, expenditures, and accounts. These four were the chamberlain of the Roman People, the depositary of the Roman People, the depositary of the wine tax (*gabella dello Studio*), and the depositary of the meat tax (*gabella della carne*). Exercising a more limited role were the two chamberlains of the Testaccio games, pre-Lenten contests on Monte Testaccio that had been converted in 1567 into races on the Corso. The Roman Jewish community paid a games tax of 531 scudi to these chamberlains each year to spend on the festivities; they also paid 1,456 scudi to the depositary of the meat tax. A seventh official had become, despite his title, more a judicial than a financial figure: the *gabelliere maggiore* acted as chief enforcement officer for wine tax collection, with his own investigators and tribunal.[78]

In 1641, the one year during Urban VIII's reign for which we have a municipal budget (*tabella*), the civic treasury's receipts were 143,168 scudi.[79] (See Table 3.) This document was a projection, not an actual account, of income and expenditures for each of the four main financial officers mentioned above. The *tabella* omits payments of 7,174 scudi made by the apostolic chamber directly to Capitoline officials;[80] it also leaves out the Jews' payment of 531 scudi.[81] The com-

---

that of the French state, see Henri de Carsalade du Pont, *La municipalite' parisienne à l'époque d'Henri IV* (Paris, 1971), 181.

[78] ASC, cred. VI, vol. 30, registro di mandati, 461–62, records payment of 531 scudi by four officials of the Jewish community to the two chamberlains of the Testaccio games in January 1625, as well as disbursements from these funds. On the games tax see also Kenneth R. Stow, *Taxation, Community and State: The Jews and the Fiscal Foundations of the Early Modern Papal State* (Stuttgart, 1982), 170. The chamberlains of the Testaccio games were one officer or consul of the elite guild of agriculturalists (*arte dell'agricultura*) and one consul of the merchants' guild. For the Jews' payment to the depositary of the *gabella della carne* see ASC, cred. IV, vol. 106, tabella, 134v. On the *gabelliere maggiore* see *Statuta almae urbis*, bk. 3, chap. 11, and ASC, cred. IV, vol. 97, istrumenti, 257v.

[79] ASC, cred. IV, vol. 106, tabella, 112v–38r. I have dated it to 1641 on the basis of the signatures of the conservators (112v), who served from January to March 1641. On the nature of early modern "budgets" see Partner, "Financial Policy," 35, and Rietbergen, 175. Fragments of the actual accounts of the depositary of the Roman People and the chamberlain of the Roman People survive for the years 1621–1625 and 1627–1629; ASC, cred. VI, vol. 48, ristretti di dare et avere, 85v–112r.

[80] These payments for 1623 may be found in ASR, Camerale II, Conti di entrata e uscita, bu. 1, no. 8, 107v–8v. A similar account for the year 1619 was published by Reinhard, *Papstfinanz* 2:327–28. The total here of 10,103 scudi remained virtually unchanged from year to year. The *tabella* of 1641 includes payments from the apostolic chamber to the chamberlain of the Roman People (112v) and to the depositary of the Roman People (136v) totaling 5,207 scudi.

[81] In addition to the games tax the Jews paid the Roman People 1,456 scudi a year, which was credited to the meat tax; ASC, cred. IV, vol. 106, tabella, 134v.

TABLE 3
Civic Revenues in 1641 *Tabella* (scudi)

Chamberlain of the Roman People	5,351.23[a]
Depositary of the Roman People	5,294.36[b]
Depositary of the meat tax	101,465.10[c]
Depositary of the wine tax (*Studio*)	31,057.95[d]
Total	143,168.64
Additional Civic Revenues Not Listed in the *Tabella*	
Apostolic chamber (direct provisions)[e]	7,174.22
Jews' games tax	531.00[f]

Note: The 1641 *tabella* is found in ASC, cred. IV, vol. 106, 112v–38r.

[a] Includes payment from apostolic chamber of 2,928.86.

[b] Includes payment from apostolic chamber of 2,279.10.

[c] Of this sum the contract for the meat tax (which was combined with a tax of 4 *giuli* per barrel on foreign wine imports) provided 87,666.67 scudi annually.

[d] In 1641 the wine tax-farmer was running at a deficit; his contract stipulated that he would pay 33,972.23 scudi a year.

[e] "Direct provisions" were payments to specific officials rather than to the depositaries. For sources see n. 80.

[f] See n. 78.

bined total of civic revenues is thus slightly over 150,000 scudi. Eighty percent of this sum came from the taxes on meat and wine; the 121,638 scudi they provided had almost doubled since the end of the sixteenth century.[82] The popes, through the apostolic chamber, paid 12,382 scudi or eight percent of the total. Smaller amounts came from: leases of the offices of notary of the conservators and notary of the Ripa (the riverine port); rent for three public scales; fines imposed by the conservators, the master justicieries, and the *gabelliere maggiore*; a yearly payment of 400 scudi from the Thirty Capitoline Notaries for their rights to those offices; and feudal dues.

The two main forms of taxation collected by the Capitoline chamber, the meat and wine taxes, did not by any means account for all the public charges paid by Romans. Individual householders were assessed improvement taxes, called *gettiti*, for street repairs and demolitions in their neighborhood.[83] In addition, many im-

[82] A joint total of 65,000 scudi in 1594 is given by Delumeau, *Vie* 2:751–52. For the history of the *gabella dello Studio*, which dated from the early 1430s, see D. S. Chambers, "Studium Urbis and *gabella studii*: The University of Rome in the Fifteenth Century," in *Cultural Aspects of the Italian Renaissance: Essays in Honour of Paul Oskar Kristeller*, ed. Cecil H. Clough (New York, 1976), 70–71. This was a tax on imported wine (i.e., not wine from Roman vineyards or from the hilltowns [*castelli*] nearby) sold in Roman taverns. On the *gabella della carne* see Stumpo, *Capitale*, 117–18; Delumeau, *Vie* 2:795, 831; Lutz, 124; Caravale, 91–92. While all these studies date the beginning of this tax to the early or mid-1550s, there is a reference to a *gabella della carne* in *protocollo* no. 3913 in the ASC under the date 14 June 1522; at the ASR, inventory no. 112/30 lists a *liber gabellarum carnium* dating from 1459.

[83] The volumes of *gettiti* for the years 1612–1677 can be found in ASR, Presidenza delle Strade, vols. 445 bis to 450; Partner, *Rome*, 166; *Statuta almae urbis*, bk. 3, chap. 39; Emilio Re, "Maestri di

posts went directly to the apostolic chamber and never concerned the civic treasurers. The customs duties on goods entering the city brought 209,000 scudi
yearly to the papacy in the 1620s, a sum greater than the annual civic budget.
Providing much smaller amounts were a tax paid by shopkeepers, several further
payments by the Jewish community, required purchases of salt, and charges on
public bonds, firewood, ice, and fishselling. There were also papal excises on
wine, in addition to the civic wine tax. Even the Roman clergy contributed to the
apostolic chamber. Although there were a few direct taxes, there was no general
tax on heads or real property; urbanites made their greatest contribution to the
papal budget through indirect taxes on consumption items.[84]

Like those of the apostolic chamber, the civic treasury's indirect taxes were
collected by tax-farmers who bid competitively for contracts. The Capitoline wine
tax was leased for nine years in 1628 by Cesare Arigone and the Genoese banker
Giovanni Domenico Pagliari. In 1637 the papal notary Felice de Totis won the
contract for another nine years, but renounced it after a short stay in prison in
1642; later that year Arrigo Arigone picked it up.[85] The larger meat tax was
farmed by partners Giulio Magalotti of Florence and Giovanni Rotoli of Bergamo
from 1620 to 1629, by Gasparo Rivaldi from 1629 to 1639, and by the son of a
Genoese financier, Francesco Ravenna, from 1639 to 1654.[86] De Totis was not
the only one to encounter problems in the course of his contract; in 1659 the
Capitol sued Ravenna for 27,000 scudi in back claims.[87]

The depositary of the meat tax and the depositary of the wine tax were the

---

strada," *ASRSP* 43 (1920): 49, 56, 78. In addition, Roman shopkeepers paid a tax of four *giulii* per
shop (*bottega*) for street cleaning, which was disbursed by the street masters; Rodocanachi, *Institutions*,
275.

[84] Rome and Bologna were often treated distinctly from the provinces in papal taxation; Stumpo,
Capitale, 97, 101–2. A budget for the apostolic chamber in 1619 is published by Reinhard, *Papstfinanz*
2:310–22. The papal budget of 1624 is analyzed in detail by Rietbergen, 192–95. He cites (p. 193)
a document that lists separately income drawn from the city of Rome by the apostolic chamber and
the Roman People; ASR, Archivio Santacroce, D 141, 182r–87v. Although it bears no date, I would
place it between 1630 and 1637. For a schematic rendering of revenues collected from Rome by the
apostolic chamber at selected dates between 1587 and 1657 see Stumpo, *Capitale*, 141–45. For the
Jews' contribution to the papal fisc see Stow.

[85] An edict of 28 January 1628 announcing rules for the wine tax names the tax-farmers (*appalta-
tori*). On Pagliari see Ameyden, ASV, "Relatione," 681r. De Totis was one of the prestigious notaries
of the apostolic chamber from 1614 to 1633. For traces of his activities as tax-farmer see *Regesti* 4:229,
and ASC, cred. IV, vol. 97, instrumenti, 213r. He petitioned Cardinal Antonio Barberini for release
from prison on 16 March 1642. On Arrigo Arigone see ASC, cred. VI, vol. 63, interessi diversi, 47r.

[86] ASC, cred. IV, vol. 96, istrumenti, 40r–61v, contains copies of these three contracts (*appalti*).
On Magalotti see ASR, 30 N.C., uff. 25 (Scala) 1645, pt. 1, 382r. A copy of Giovanni Rotoli's will
dated 9 December 1627 is located in ASC, cred. III, vol. 22, testamenti, 58r–67v. It provides rich
detail on the management of a seventeenth-century Roman bank. On Rivaldi see Ameyden, ASV,
"Relatione," 682r. Ravenna's father Filippo was granted Roman citizenship in October 1578; ASC,
cred. I, vol. 1, p. 149. See also 30 N.C., uff. 18 (Bonincontro) 1630, pt. 1, 272r–73v, 298r.

[87] The conflict with Ravenna is documented in ASC, cred. VI, vol. 58, giustificazioni diverse,
275r–98v.

Capitoline officials responsible for receiving payments from their respective tax-farmers. Specific items in the municipal budget were to be paid from each tax and the depositaries made and recorded these disbursements. The chamberlain and depositary of the Roman People fulfilled similar functions for the many smaller sources of revenue that belonged to the Capitoline chamber. It was the chamberlain's responsibility, for example, to provide money for the Christmas gratuities (*regaglie*) of pepper, wax, gloves, and sweetmeats that went to over four hundred civic and papal officials each year. He paid partial costs of the Carnival races from funds provided by the apostolic chamber, while the chamberlains of the Testaccio games made additional payments from the Jews' games tax. The depository of the Roman People had charge of most payments for the staff and maintenance of the Capitoline palaces, as well as for the conservators' entertainment expenses.[88]

Even more than the notoriously indebted papal treasury, Rome's municipal treasury sometimes seemed like an agency that existed to transmit money from taxpayers to creditors. Over seventy percent of its receipts went to pay interest on sums the Capitoline government had borrowed on the public bond or *monti* market; the equivalent figure for the apostolic chamber was about a third. Despite the prohibition in canon law on charging interest for loans, the market in the public debt—both papal and civic—had been very lively in Rome for almost a century. Although the total amount of municipal debt under Urban VIII is not known, in 1604, when annual interest payments equaled 62,500 scudi, it was 850,000 scudi.[89] In the 1641 budget the Roman People were paying off eleven separate bond issues. The upward increase in the meat tax from 20,000 scudi a year in 1555 to 89,000 in 1620 surely reflects increased borrowing since most of its revenue was earmarked for interest payments to bondholders.[90]

The 108,000 scudi the Capitol spent to pay *monti* owners in the 1641 *tabella* does not even fully indicate the extent of the burden of debt service on the municipal budget; another six to eight thousand scudi annually provided annuities to owners of fictitious offices known as *uffici vacabili*. These were called *vacabili* because they were theoretically "vacated" at the death of the owner, though in practice they were often extended to heirs. Before developing the *monti* system, the Roman Curia had discovered a way of borrowing money by instituting venal posts in the temporal sphere and selling them; purchasers received fixed annual

[88] For Christmas *regaglie* in 1641 see ASC, cred. IV, vol. 106, tabella, 113v; for personnel see ASC, cred. I, vols. 32–34.

[89] Stumpo, *Capitale*, 247–64; Rietbergen, 230; Partner, "Financial Policy," 28. The first civic *monti* date from the 1550s; Stumpo, *Capitale*, 117, and Delumeau, *Vie* 2:794–97. On the *monti* system, with its peculiar terminology for evading the prohibition on usury, see Delumeau, *Vie* 2:783–823. It should be noted that total papal debt service on both *monti* and offices amounted to around fifty percent of income in these decades; Partner, "Financial Policy," 27. In 1619 alone the apostolic chamber paid out over 800,000 scudi to creditors; Reinhard, *Papstfinanz* 2:342.

[90] ASC, cred. IV, vol. 106, tabella, 132v, 135r; Delumeau, *Vie* 2:831; ASC, cred. IV, vol. 96, istrumenti, 40r (contract for *gabella della carne* collection dated 9 October 1620). For the implications of increasing municipal debt in the towns of the Papal States see Rietbergen, 222.

payments.[91] The Capitoline administration eventually followed suit, creating many such offices.

It is difficult to know precisely how many *vacabili* the Roman People had sold, since it is often impossible on the basis of their titles to distinguish venal offices that were mer~ investments from those with administrative duties. To complicate matters furthc., real posts could be purchased, with a substitute performing the actual job. In 1626, for example, the "architect of the Roman People" was really an architect, but the Capitoline bellringer and the four trumpeters were gentlemen whose social standing was obviously too exalted for such tasks. Substitutes rang the bell and did the trumpeting; the gentlemen collected an annual sum and Christmas gifts.[92] Perhaps three-quarters of the over four hundred offices that received Christmas gratuities from the municipal treasury were purely financial in nature. The street master Virgilio Cenci, for example, owned seven civic *vacabili* with a total annual yield of over 500 scudi. Many of these offices had been in the families of men who served in high elected positions on the Capitol for several generations, although sculptors like Gian Lorenzo Bernini and his father had also acquired them.[93] A Roman savant humorously described his post as one of four "commissioners" of a stream called the Marrana or Mariana just outside the Lateran gate: "Of what my office consists I have never known nor what this Marrana is, where it comes from, where it goes [or] what use the Roman People make of it." But the man complained bitterly when his annual payment of 98 scudi, and the allotment of salt, wax, pepper, sweetmeats, and wine that went with it, were suppressed in the late 1640s.[94]

After paying all its creditors the Capitoline chamber had around 33,000 scudi left of its 150,000 annual income. In 1641 the civic administration took about half of this sum; salaries to elected officials and palace employees, and the costly Christmas gratuities accounted for most of it. From the receipts of the wine tax the Roman People also provided almost 8,000 scudi a year for professors' and staff salaries and expenses at Rome's university. They put on the Carnival races, made

[91] On papal *vacabili*, which date from the fifteenth century, see the following: Piola Caselli; Partner, "Financial Policy," 21–25, and idem, *The Pope's Men*, 12, 16, 38; Stumpo, *Capitale*, 228–47. For Capitoline offices see Rodocanachi, *Institutions*, 213–16; ASC, cred. IV, vol. 106, tabella, 112v–38r. In addition to those listed in the *tabella* the apostolic chamber paid about 2,000 scudi a year to owners of two dozen venal Capitoline offices; these sums were included in the annual payment made to the Capitoline chamber, which is published in Reinhard, *Papstfinanz* 2:327–28. See also Francesco Cerasoli, "Lista di uffici di Campidoglio (a. 1629)," *ASRSP* 12 (1889): 373–76.

[92] ASC, cred. IV, vol. 16, cartoni delle regaglie del sale.

[93] The 3,100 scudi spent on Christmas gifts to civic officeholders should perhaps also be considered part of the cost of debt service; ASC, cred. IV, vol. 106, tabella, 113v. For Cenci's offices see ASC, cred. VI, vol. 114, uffici capitolini, 225r. For the Bernini offices and others see the 1626 salt list, ASC, cred. IV, vol. 16. For comparison see the published civic budget of 1593 in ASV, arm. IV, vol. 32, 255r.

[94] Luigi De Gregori, "Cariche da burla del comune di Roma," *Strenna dei romanisti* 3 (1942): 268; De Luca, *Il Dottor Volgare*, bk. 3, pt. 2, chap. 34, p. 327. See also Piero Becchetti, "L'Acqua Mariana," in *Il Tevere*, ed. Bruno Brizzi (Rome, 1989).

annual gifts of silver chalices and candles to thirty-seven Roman churches, and paid the organist at nearby Santa Maria in Aracoeli. The 18,000 scudi a year it cost to run the municipal government could have purchased three statues by the celebrated Bernini or one aristocratic town residence.[95]

There was obviously not a lot left over for "extras," yet the Capitoline authorities had to repair city walls, drain ditches, build plague hostels, put on special celebrations for the pope or local saints, and outfit themselves occasionally in new robes. None of these items had a place among the ordinary expenses anticipated in the budget, but rather fell under the rubric of extraordinary expenditures. To meet these as they arose, the civic councils or magistrates resorted to a variety of financial devices, most of which entailed some manipulation of their debt. In this they were very like the papacy itself, which needed to borrow whenever a big project, be it artistic or military, loomed.[96] We will look more closely at this aspect of finance and at how the Roman People and Pope Urban VIII confronted their extraordinary needs in later chapters.

In concluding this chapter on civic institutions we might look back for a moment on the political implications of the way in which civic officials were recruited. The broad circulation of office among upper-class Romans that was ensured by the electoral system, fragmented local influence and kept the Capitol out of the hands of any one family. While it granted a share of temporary public authority to more people, it also ensured that the popes would have no competitors in Rome and prevented the kind of political agitation they disliked.[97] The papacy approved a quite different type of civic regime in Bologna, the Papal State's second largest city. There it turned local government over to a hereditary senate of seventy families and a papal legate. In Rome, which had not been as rebellious as Bologna in recent centuries, the popes favored the divide-and-rule strategy. Both cities stand in sharp contrast to Paris, where venality was transforming an older system founded on elections into one based on purchase and

---

[95] For the price of Bernini's statues see Gigli, *Diario*, 195; for the price of an urban *palazzo* see Cerasoli, "Diario," 283. All elected officials except the conservators received a salary. These ranged from 7.5 scudi a year for the notary of the *pacieri* to 47 scudi for the street masters; the 320 artisans who made up the company of *capotori* and *contestabili* earned 60 *baiocchi* a year (0.6 scudo), the equivalent of about one loaf of bread a week; Nussdorfer, "City Politics," 78. A caporione received 14.66 scudi per trimester from the apostolic chamber and an additional 4.85 scudi from the proceeds of the *gabella dello Studio*; Gigli, BNC-VE, Sess. 334, 220r–v.

[96] Stumpo, *Capitale*, 121.

[97] Pope Gregory XIII made this last point explicitly in 1580. He complained to the magistrates that he had heard that many Romans were gathering on the Capitol to vote for members of the annual civic committees (discussed earlier in this chapter). In high umbrage the pope commanded that these posts be distributed by lot, "as they had previously, since this method removes electioneering deals [*pratiche*]," and, presumably, the "great confusion and assemblies of people" that he found so distasteful. Gregory was so annoyed that "he would have done it himself," the conservators reported to their fellow citizens, "but we wanted to be the ones to tell you to choose the said committees in the manner ordered by His Blessedness." ASC, cred. I, vol. 28, decreti, 0028r (3 March 1580).

inheritance.[98] The tendency to make offices into property was strong inside the papal administration, but it had not yet extended its reach into civic spheres. Despite their differences, urban elites in Rome and Bologna retained more influence over their own processes of self-definition and relied more heavily on traditional sources of prestige than their Parisian counterparts.

Now it is time to find out more about the actual men who constituted the abstraction we call the Roman People. Meeting in the council chamber decorated with frescoes of the early history of Rome, sitting in judgment at the conservators' tribunal, parading in costume behind the red and gold banner of the Senate and Roman People, publishing meat prices and awarding prizes to the winners of the Carnival races: it was they who made the Capitol a civic space and not simply an architectural setting. In their persons they brought the social tissue of the city onto the ancient hill and marked its structures, physical and institutional, with the concerns of their class and families.

[98] On Bologna see Mario Fanti, "Il governo e classi sociali di Bologna," *Strenna storica bolognese* 11 (1961): 133–79, and Paolo Colliva, "Bologna dal XIV al XVIII secolo: 'Governo misto' o signoria senatoria?" in *Storia della Emilia Romagna*, ed. Aldo Berselli, 3 vols. (Bologna, 1977), 2:13–34. On Paris see Descimon, 144–45.

Chapter Six

A CIVIC NOBILITY

HERE WE EXPLORE the social contours and connotations of civic participation. Who were the Capitoline officials as members of Roman society? What role did the Capitol play in the articulation of status in the unusually dynamic social landscape of seventeenth-century Rome? What did it mean to be associated with the Roman People? The men who participated in civic affairs reflected the distinctive features of Rome's material life: dependence on agriculture and the Church, and Italian traditions of civic nobility. Both influenced concretely the social physiognomy of the Roman People.

Although the offices of the Capitoline administration circulated rapidly and widely among a small segment of Rome's wealthier inhabitants, some citizens still attempted to bribe their way into the bussola.[1] Why was election to municipal office so desirable? What was at stake for aspiring candidates was family honor. By the seventeenth century two hundred years of political, cultural, and demographic changes had reshaped the upper levels of the urban class structure in Rome, with important consequences for the Roman People. The emergence of a fluid but status-conscious elite gave the Capitol a social as well as institutional role in the Baroque city. Noble status in Italian cities did not depend on possession of an aristocratic title. The late medieval city-state had conferred nobility by a process of public recognition of a family's rank as expressed in access to governmental office. In the early modern era this flexible mechanism had tightened, but the criterion for a certain kind of nobility, "civic nobility" (*nobilta' cittadina*), remained the right to take part in city government.[2]

---

[1] Gigli, *Diario*, 259.

[2] Carlo Mistruzzi, "La nobilta' dello Stato Pontificio," *Rassegna degli Archivi di Stato* 23 (1963): 239–40; Danilo Marrara, "Nobilta' civica e patriziato. Una distinzione terminologica nel pensiero di alcuni autori italiani dell'eta' moderna," *Annali della Scuola Normale Superiore di Pisa*, 3d ser., 10 (1980): 219–20; De Luca, *Il Dottor Volgare*, bk. 3, pt. 2, chap. 9, p. 155. For the treatise literature on the general topic of nobility see Claudio Donati, *L'Idea del nobilta' in Italia, secoli XIV-XVIII* (Bari, 1988). More attention has been focused on the social status of the men who staffed the central organs of state administration in early modern Italy than those of civic adminstration. Among others see Marino Berengo and Furio Diaz, "Noblesse et administration dans l'Italie de la Renaissance. La formation de la bureaucratie moderne," in *XIII International Congress of Historical Sciences* (Moscow, 1970), 1:151–63; Mozzarelli, "Strutture;" Giovanni Muto, "Gestione del potere e classi sociali nel Mezzogiorno spagnolo," in *I ceti dirigenti in Italia in eta' moderna e contemporanea* (Udine, 1984), 287–301; Enrico Stumpo, "I ceti dirigenti in Italia nell'eta' moderna. Due modelli diversi: Nobilta' piemontese e patriziato toscano," in ibid., 151–98; Litchfield; Ago, *Carriere*; Partner, *The Pope's Men*.

An Open Elite

The economy of early modern Rome, as we have seen, was based on two main sources of income, agriculture and the business of the Catholic Church. From the time the popes returned in the fifteenth century it was the latter, Church employment and finance, which was the most dynamic of the two. New careers in the ecclesiastical bureaucracy opened up in the 1400s and 1500s as the papacy consolidated its temporal domain and Tridentine reforms intensified supervision of the spiritual life of the faithful. Men of ambition from all over Italy increasingly sought to make their fortunes in Rome. They flocked to posts in the Curia and to service in the households of a growing body of cardinals.[3]

At the beginning foreigners seemed to make their way into Church employment more successfully than native Romans. Prominent local families in the fourteenth century had occupied themselves with agriculture rather than the acquisition of the skills needed by learned clerics.[4] Although a disgruntled sense of competition lingered among some members of the native elite well into the sixteenth century, they had more reason for optimism than they realized.[5] Some local families quickly adapted. By the mid-fifteenth century the Santacroce, for example, who were landowners and merchants holding important civic offices, also included lawyers with curial appointments.[6] The reinvigoration of Rome's university in 1431 promised eventually to produce more native youths trained for bureaucratic service. More significantly, the decision by Sixtus IV in 1474 to allow clerics in the Curia to bequeath real property to their relatives gave foreigners an incentive to put down roots in the city.[7] The lay kinsmen of curialists who had found employment in Rome followed the clerics, and intermarried with Roman families.

The Maffei of Verona, who arrived in Rome in the second half of the fifteenth century, illustrate this gradual integration. Two brothers in the first generation

[3] Indeed it is Partner's thesis that Italian elites made a sustained and successful effort to gain control of the offices of the papal court in precisely this period, *The Pope's Men*, 13–18. See also John F. D'Amico, *Renaissance Humanism in Papal Rome: Humanists and Churchmen on the Eve of the Reformation* (Baltimore, 1983), 65–67. For the continuing attraction of the Curia as late as 1700 see Ago, *Carriere*, 16.

[4] Maire-Vigueur, 5–8.

[5] The disgruntled view of local Romans is best represented by the social commentary of Marc'Antonio Altieri (1450–1532), *Li Nuptiali*, ed. E. Narducci (Rome, 1873). Altieri's text is discussed by Christiane Klapisch-Zuber, "An Ethnology of Marriage in the Age of Humanism," in *Women, Family, and Ritual in Renaissance Italy*, trans. Lydia Cochrane (Chicago, 1985), 247–60, and Stephen Kolsky, "Culture and Politics in Renaissance Rome: Marco Antonio Altieri's Roman Weddings," *Renaissance Quarterly* 40 (1987): 49–90. See also Miglio, "Leone," 182, and the comment of Paolo Giovio in idem, "L'immagine," 264; Rodocanachi, *Institutions*, 204; Gennaro, 37.

[6] Anna Esposito, "Famiglia, mercanzia e libri nel testamento di Andrea Santacroce (1471)," in *Aspetti della vita economica e culturale a Roma nel Quattrocento* (Rome, 1981), 199–211.

[7] D'Amico, 70; Chambers, 84. It is interesting to note that by 1700 the university was playing a significant role in training non-Romans for curial careers; see Ago, *Carriere*, 16.

held curial posts, although only one of them was a priest. The lay brother Benedetto married into the Roman Conti family and his grandson became a street master and father of two cardinals.[8] Two descendants in the seventeenth century, Agostino and Bernardino, were repeatedly chosen for special civic delegations; both served as conservator and Bernardino was an active committee member as well as street master from 1631 to 1640.

But it was not just Church office that drew newcomers to Rome in the early modern period. The papacy's financial business was also a powerful lure as it developed a succession of sophisticated mechanisms for borrowing money and increased the tax bite on its subjects by 200 percent in the course of the sixteenth century.[9] The creation of venal offices, the launching of a market in the state debt, and, above all, the profits of tax-farming proved irresistibly attractive to foreign investors. Bankers from Florence, Tuscany, and later Genoa emigrated to Rome to take advantage of lucrative opportunities in a city that was still in the seventeenth century the premier money market in Europe.[10] They too found their way to the Capitol.

The expansion of the Roman Curia and the Sacred College in the fifteenth and sixteenth centuries, and the Church's continual need for money and manpower, produced a class structure in Rome that was somewhat unusual by the standards of Italian cities. Elsewhere in Italy, over a period of several hundred years, urban ruling groups had attempted to close themselves off to immigrants from other nations and ranks. This *serrata* or "locking up," as it was called in Venice when instituted in 1297, named a fixed number of families who alone had the right to consider themselves noble and participate in public councils and offices. In this moment of exclusion the civic aristocracy defined itself for all time, freezing the governing class to those who qualified at a given date. In the sixteenth century Genoa also cut non-nobles out of high offices and Milan and Bologna passed laws restricting access to key civic posts to a limited number of families.[11]

In contrast to many other major centers in the seventeenth century, Rome had no fixed list—either official or unofficial—of noble families who had the right to take part in city government. As we recall, the roster of Roman citizens who were

---

[8] D'Amico, 265 n. 36. The connections between family and Church office in fifteenth- and sixteenth-century Rome are extensively documented in D'Amico, chap. 3, and Hallman, chap. 5.

[9] Delumeau, *Vie* 2:843.

[10] This was of course partially due to the increase in government borrowing under Urban VIII, which is discussed in Chapter 12. Ameyden, ASV, "Relatione," 680v–82r, 711r–v. Delumeau, *Vie* 2:772–820, 878–93; Rietbergen, 232–33.

[11] For Milan see Giulio Vismara, "Le istituzioni del patriziato," in *Il declino spagnolo (1630–1706)*, vol. 11 (1958) of *Storia di Milano*, ed. Giovanni Treccani degli Alfieri, 16 vols. (Milan, 1953–62), 226, 244–46. For Bologna see Alfeo Giacomelli, "La dinamica della nobilta' Bolognese nel XVIII secolo," in *Famiglie senatorie e istituzioni cittadine a Bologna nel Settecento* (Bologna, 1980), 59, 62. For Genoa see Maria Nicora, "La nobilta' genovese dal 1528 al 1700," *Miscellanea di storia ligure* 2 (1962): 233–35. See also Frederic C. Lane, *Venice: A Maritime Republic* (Baltimore, 1973), 111–14; Amelang, 25–26, 31, 217–18; Mozzarelli, "Strutture," 438–40; Muto, 290–91.

eligible for the public council was supposed to be re-made every year, and there were no formal criteria for inclusion, eligibility being determined annually by a rione committee. There was no Roman equivalent to Venice's "golden book" in which the births and marriages of the nobility were carefully recorded to preserve the purity of the caste.[12]

In Rome there was an underlying expectation that social and political status were subject to change and that new families needed regularly to be taken into account. This openness and flexibility reflected the dynamism of Roman society after the papacy's return in the fifteenth century, and was intensified by rapid population growth in the late sixteenth century. It was a commonplace then to call Rome a city of foreigners. Even if this was only true in a relative sense, newcomers certainly had opportunities to move in and move up that were much rarer elsewhere in Italy.[13] Now we will look at where the men who represented the Roman People fit in this mobile yet hierarchical society.

GENTLEMEN OLD AND GENTLEMEN NEW

Even without a "golden book" we can get some sense of how status distinctions were conceived in Rome from seventeenth-century chronicles and diaries. In the contemporary language of rank, well-born laymen were divided into two main groups, "titled lords" (*signori titolati*) and "gentlemen" (*gentiluomini*). The diarist Giacinto Gigli's description of the Polish ambassador's entry into Rome in 1633 illustrates this usage. Since social status determined one's place in a public procession, Gigli narrated the order of the march with great precision. Early on came the "Roman and Italian gentlemen," while much later, just before the climax constituted by the envoy himself, rode the "titled lords." Similarly an anonymous chronicler, describing a less successful procession in 1615, comments on the disappointingly plain outfits of the "Roman gentlemen" and notes how few "titled" took any part at all. The distinction between gentlemen and titled lords corresponds to that between "private nobility" and "public nobility" in Cardinal De Luca's legal handbook of 1673. Private nobility, according to De Luca, was the possession of those who were deemed noble in their own city "and in Italy are called gentlemen." He contrasted it to public nobility, the status of the baronage or titled aristocrats honored throughout a kingdom.[14]

---

[12] Delumeau refers to a "golden book of the Roman patriciate," but his source cites no contemporary evidence for its existence, *Vie* 2:776–77.

[13] For Marcello Alberini's (1511–1580) oft-quoted remark that Romans were a minority in Rome see Alberini, 279. See also Delumeau, *Vie* 1:189, 217–18. This issue has been discussed critically by Egmont Lee, "Foreigners in Quattrocento Rome," *Renaissance and Reformation*, n.s., 7 (1983): 135–46. See also Hallman, 161. On the singular openness of nobility in Rome see De Luca, *Il Dottor Volgare*, bk. 3, pt. 2, chap. 9, pp. 144–45.

[14] Gigli, *Diario*, 139; Cerasoli, "Diario," 293–94; Pecchiai, *Roma*, 220; Hallman, 9; De Luca, *Il Dottor Volgare*, bk. 3, pt. 2, chap. 9, pp. 163, 154. Of course in social actuality what constituted

Teodoro Ameyden (1586–1656), a Flemish lawyer who worked for a while as legal consultant to the conservators, lived most of his life in Rome and compiled a list of the city's most "conspicuous" families in 1640.[15] It is a highly personal catalogue, appropriate for a city where no objective standard of status existed, that was part of a lengthy report prepared for his Spanish patron, the Marquis of Leganés. The ambiguity of the notion of nobility in Rome pervades Ameyden's own criteria for including a family on his list. The 215 names he records were, in his words, "noble or, if not [noble], at least well-bred and of honorable position."[16]

This is a heterogeneous upper class composed of varied ethnic and occupational elements; Ameyden must devise fourteen subdivisions for his roster. The greatest diversity of course is found among the eighty-two newcomers to Rome since the mid-sixteenth century. Frenchmen, Flemings, and Portuguese jostled with Genoese and Florentines in a group called to the papal capital for trade, finance, or business with the datary and chancellery. The largest category in Ameyden's report were the 116 families who had been in Rome for over a century but were not members of the feudal nobility. Ameyden disparages their origins, "the majority . . . [though] esteemed noble in Rome come from low beginnings, such as notary, grocer and the smelly art of leather-tanner."[17] At the apex of Ameyden's ranking, and of Roman society, was a group of seventeen families descended from medieval Roman barons and sixteenth- and seventeenth-century popes.[18]

None of these last seventeen lineages, the "titled lords" whom we have already met, would have had a formal civic role, but members of the other two major categories did. Of 167 conservators elected between 1623 and 1644, ninety-eight (58 percent) appear on Ameyden's list of families. Eighty conservators came from families living in Rome for over a century, while eighteen fell among the newcomers. There were of course other recent immigrants who became conservators in these years who did not make it on to Ameyden's list.

Were we to apply contemporary status terminology to Ameyden's 215 families,

---

nobility was less rigid than De Luca's categories imply; see the critique in Donati, 293–94. Stumpo cautions against overly simple definitions of what were in fact composite elites, "Ceti," 151–55.

[15] Ameyden, ASV, "Relatione," 646r–716r. The date of 1640 comes from internal evidence (681v); this particular copy was transcribed after 1644 (674v). Ameyden (1586–1656) arrived in Rome in 1600; Bastiaanse, 9–10. Ameyden's connections to the Capitol: granted Roman citizenship in 1625, ASC, cred. I, vol. 33, decreti, 0026r (19 July 1625); legal *assessore* to the tribunal of the conservators from 1633, ASV, "Relatione," 685r; his son Urbano, aged nine, in the bussola for the office of marshal in 1634, BAV, Barb. lat. 2216, 15r.

[16] "Queste sono le famiglie di Roma cospicue, o' che sono, o' si picicano [?] se non di Nobilta' almeno di civilta', et honorevolezza;" Ameyden, ASV, "Relatione," 682r.

[17] Ibid., 675v.

[18] Ibid., 676v–82r. A recent dissertation chronicles the rise of one of these papal families, that of Innocent X Pamphili (1644–1655), from gentlemanly status to the top rank of the nobility; see Mirka Beneš, "Villa Pamphilj (1630–1670): Family, Gardens and Land in Papal Rome" (Ph.D. diss., Yale University, 1989).

we would find the top group of feudal and papal families among the "titled," with the native-born families going back for more than a century designated as "Roman gentlemen," and visitors and recent newcomers among the "Italian gentlemen." In reality, minor aristocratic titles were beginning to spread among the "gentle-men" in the early decades of the seventeenth century, but they did not yet elevate them much above their peers.[19]

The families who predominated on the Capitol were those with Roman roots for a hundred years or more who were not descended from great feudal houses. They provided almost half the conservators during Urban VIII's reign and, when they were not in office, they were usually the men chosen by the councils or magistrates to speak for the Roman People as part of special delegations.[20] In its geographical origins this group is not entirely homogeneous for it includes lin-eages like the Maffei of Verona or the Pamphili of Gubbio who arrived in the fifteenth and early sixteenth centuries to work in the Curia. Yet half this group, and almost a quarter of the conservators from 1623 to 1644, came from Roman stock dating back three centuries or more. These families were rarely involved in finance or law, but they had strong ties to local agriculture. Over a quarter of the conservators from 1623 to 1644 held the office of consul of the guild of agricul-turists; in this post they judged disputes arising over livestock grazing and culti-vated land in the agricultural tribunal that had its sessions at the palace of the conservators.[21] Families like the Altieri, Albertoni, Boccapaduli, Massimi, and Cenci owned and leased the great estates called *casali*, and sold the hay, meat, butter, and cheese they produced on the Roman market.[22] Such families, who often led prestigious local confraternities, did not neglect Church employment

---

[19] By "minor" aristocratic titles I mean count, marchese, and cavaliere as opposed to duke or prince; Mistruzzi, 227. Rodocanachi, *Institutions*, 336. I am grateful to Richard Ferraro, who is at work on a doctoral dissertation on the Roman nobility, for information on the conferral of titles on Roman gentlemen in the early seventeenth century. R. Burr Litchfield's recent study of the early modern Florentine elite gives a detailed picture of the transition from a community of honor collectively generated to one based on the gift of the sovereign. Without a formal register it is difficult to quantify the number of Roman "gentlemen." Two pieces of evidence shed some light on the quantitative dimensions of this group. At some point during Urban VIII's reign "gentlemen" (*gentilhuomini*) in Rome capable of bearing arms were counted and the total came to 548; BAV, Barb. lat. 4835, 5r, published by Paglia, 285. In 1661 another list of "gentlemen," drawn up for an unspecified purpose, included 359 names; BAV, Chigi, H II 55 (iv).

[20] Nussdorfer, "City Politics," 139–41.

[21] *Gli statuti dell'Agricoltura* (Rome, 1718), 221–28.

[22] On the Cenci see Maire-Vigueur, 10; Mario Bevilacqua, *Il Monte dei Cenci: Una famiglia romana e il suo insediamento urbano tra medioevo ed eta' barocca* (Rome, 1988), 18–22; Cesare Fraschetti, *I Cenci* (Rome, 1935), 148; ASR, 30 N.C., uff. 2 (Bonanni) 1632, pt. 3, 10r–v. Systematic research in the notarial archives would yield much more information on agricultural exploitation not only by the Cenci but by families of similar status. On Boccapaduli see David Coffin, *The Villa in the Life of Renaissance Rome* (Princeton, 1979), 21; as master justiciery from 1633 to 1639 Teodoro Boccapaduli punished vineyard transgressions. On Massimi see ASR, 30 N.C., uff. 20 (Camillus), 1630, pt. 1, 316r, and Thomas Ashby, *La Campagna romana al tempo di Paolo III* (Rome, 1914), 82–90. On Alber-toni and Altieri see ibid., 85–91.

either; increasingly their names also turn up in the Curia, some finding their way to the College of Cardinals and even to the papal throne itself.[23] Their hold on civic offices stretched back many generations and the lay members of these houses continued in the seventeenth century to constitute the core of Capitoline leadership.

By comparison to the "old" Roman families Ameyden's newcomers were not, of course, as able to make their weight felt in civic office. Yet their presence was significant. Eighteen families, twenty percent of the "conspicuous" arrivals since the mid-sixteenth century, produced conservators during Urban VIII's reign. And Ameyden's criteria, which favor prominent immigrants over the less conspicuous, probably obscure the extent to which newcomers reached the Capitol.

Unlike their native Roman counterparts these men tended to have backgrounds in finance, though they also invested in agriculture. Wealth, numerous male offspring, and connections to a reigning papal family, or at least a cardinal, were the most effective assets for newcomers who wanted access to civic office. The Costaguti were a dramatic example because they combined all three; they put together the profits of tax contracts, sheep raising, and papal service to parley Genoese banking wealth into Roman civic prominence. While Vincenzo Costaguti was made a Roman citizen in 1571, it was the next generation that really put down roots. Giovanni Battista Costaguti, a cleric, owned large flocks of sheep and served in the household of Pope Paul V (1605–1621); his two brothers, Ascanio and Prospero, worked as the pope's bankers and tax-farmers. As early as 1618 Ascanio Costaguti appeared as a conservator and he soon became a member of the important *regaglie* committee. In 1626 and 1640 his brother Prospero was also a conservator. The first Costaguti cardinal was appointed in 1643.[24]

Francesco Ravenna was another son of a Genoese financier whose wealth propelled him into key local institutions in the seventeenth century. His father Filippo had acquired Roman citizenship in 1578 and was one of the main purchasers of a papal loan in the early 1590s. Francesco was actively involved in agriculture, renting estates from Rome's largest landowners, the Borghese family, and selling the grain and butter they provided. He was consul of the guild of agriculturalists five times between 1629 and 1645 and held civic offices in the same years: caporione in 1633 and conservator in 1631, 1639, and 1649. Ravenna was the only Capitoline official between 1623 and 1644 who also leased civic tax-farms, though the father of another conservator did as well. A few months after his term as

---

[23] For the officials of the prominent confraternity of the SS. Salvatore see Giovanni Marangoni, *Istoria dell'antichissimo oratorio o cappella di S. Lorenzo nel Patriarchio lateranense* (Rome, 1747); Partner, "Financial policy," 61; Pecchiai, *Roma*, 330–32; Filippo Renazzi, *Storia dell'universita' di Roma*, 4 vols. (Rome, 1803–1806), 3:81; Pietro Visconti, *Citta' e famiglie nobili e celebri dello stato pontificio*, 3 vols. (Rome, 1847), 3:510–24; Haskell, 114–18; BAV, Urb. lat. 1095, avvisi (22 November 1625), 700v.

[24] ASC, cred. I, vol. 1, cittadini, 115; ASC, cred. XIII, vol. 30, edicts, 144r; Rietbergen, 181, 208; Reinhard, *Papstfinanz* 2:263, 330; Ameyden, ASV, "Relazione," 681r; Gigli, *Diario*, 233; ASR, Cam. I, mandati camerali, no. 1008 (1634).

conservator ended in 1639 he contracted to collect the meat tax for fifteen years and in late 1643 a milling tax newly imposed to fund the war of Castro. He was heavily involved in papal finance too in the early 1640s, as papal debt soared to record levels to pay for military expenses.[25]

Giovanni Francesco Palazzola was a newcomer who rose not through finance but through ties to a pope. He was from a Milanese family originally drawn to Rome by their links with Pope Pius IV (1560–1565). His father was made a Roman citizen in 1590. Palazzola, who married into the local Cenci family, held the office of conservator three times and was chosen for civic delegations five times between 1623 and 1644. At his death in 1645 his property included a hayloft, a vineyard, a canebrake (*canneto*), farm animals and implements, jewels, several houses, dozens of paintings, many shares of venal offices, and 215 bonds (*luoghi di monti*). The fact that Palazzola, like Ravenna, served as consul of the guild of agriculturalists shows that some immigrants quickly adapted to the economic patterns of Roman gentlemen. Notarial documents confirm their success, identifying both these men as "noble Romans."[26]

These were three "conspicuous" immigrant houses who found a place among the Roman People in the seventeenth century. What about the sixty-nine conservators whose families Ameyden did not see fit to mention? For the most part we do not know their social and geographical origins, although detailed study of the notarial protocols would undoubtedly illuminate them. Four of these men were lawyers, five others were "cavalieri," and several had come from other parts of Italy.[27] Papal connections helped. Both Pietro Mazzarini of Sicily and Prospero Giori of Camerino rode the coattails of sons or brothers who served the Barberini to brief stints in civic office during Urban VIII's reign.[28] Their arrival on the Capitol was a sign of the sensitivity of those who made up the bussole to families on the rise. Curial connections were also influential; newcomers whose clerical relatives scored a career advance attracted the attention of Roman gentlemen. Urban VIII's own story illustrates this process. Three years after Maffeo Barberini was made cardinal in 1606, his brother Carlo became a conservator, after residing in Rome for less than ten years.

---

[25] ASC, cred. I, vol. 1, 149; Delumeau, *Vie* 2:890; *Gli statuti dell'Agricoltura* (Rome, 1718), 221–28; ASR, 30 N.C., uff. 18 (Bonincontro) 1630, pt. 2, 608r, and pt. 5, 101r; ASC, cred. IV, vol. 106, tabella, 134v; Gigli, *Diario*, 238; BAV, Chigi, H III 68, 32v, 33v, 48v, 56v, 66r; Ameyden, ASV, "Relatione," 681r.

[26] On Palazzola: Ameyden, ASV, "Relatione," 680v; ASC, cred. I, vol. 29, decreti, 222; Nussdorfer, "City Politics," 141–42; ASR, 30 N.C., uff. 18 (Bonincontro) 1630, pt. 3, 118r; ASR, 30 N.C., uff. 18 (Pacichelli) 1645, pt. 1, 527r–29v, 536r–v. On Ravenna: ASR, 30 N.C., uff. 18 (Bonincontro) 1630, pt. 1, 272r.

[27] De Luca, *Il Dottor Volgare*, bk. 3, pt. 2, chap. 9, pp. 144–45; Pecchiai, *Roma*, 242.

[28] Ameyden, ASV, "Relatione," 680r–v, 681r, 682r; Georges Dethan, *Mazarin et ses amis: Étude sur la jeunesse du Cardinal* (Paris, 1968), 13; Haskell, 180; Gigli, *Diario*, 233.

CIVIC STRATEGIES

The absence in Baroque Rome of a legally designated aristocratic estate did not mean that people in Rome were any less concerned about noble status. They may well have had an even more intense interest in the issue because in their city it was so indeterminate. With so many immigrants and so much mobility built into Roman society both old families and new felt pressed to make constant public demonstration of their rank. In this context, and given the traditional Italian association of civic office and nobility, election to a Capitoline post was a significant claim to honor. While landed families with long roots in Rome had the most conspicuous share of civic offices, newcomers from diverse nations and occupations also found room. In a city that drew many enterprising and patrician immigrants, place of birth was not permitted to bar access to government. During Urban VIII's reign two foreigners, from Florence and Barletta, actually took their oath as conservator before they had become citizens.[29]

The unusual porousness of Rome's civic administration made the Roman People function as an instrument of social integration. To appreciate this role, we should bear in mind the importance of family even to the career of a celibate churchman. Need or ambition propelled many seventeenth-century men to seek their fortunes near the pope, but success, especially material success, at court or in the Curia, would have proved fleeting indeed if it could not have been anchored in a family. The celibate governance of the Church had a social shadow in dozens of Roman households headed by the brothers and nephews of clerics. Establishing a family in Rome was almost a necessary concomitant to a successful ecclesiastical career.[30] The life of the Florentine Urban VIII illustrates this two-pronged strategy. The priest Maffeo Barberini had moved his brother Carlo's family to Rome even before he became a cardinal in 1606. While Maffeo served the papacy in various distant posts, Carlo educated his three sons, held civic office, and kept Maffeo informed of what was happening in Rome. Once elected to the Holy See, Maffeo Barberini turned to his brother and nephews to fill key government offices and to forge matrimonial ties with the great feudal lords. The Barberini's rise in Roman society, though its climax in 1623 was more dramatic than most, followed a common pattern. In this strategy the churchman's prosperity was initially consolidated by the layman's progeny and civic honors, later by marriage alliances and aristocratic titles. Success at the papal court was a family matter.

As the Barberini case suggests, establishing a family in Rome involved more than just finding a place to live. It also meant making a statement about family status. The Capitol was a resource for the aspiring, for the Roman People con-

---

[29] ASC, cred. I, vol. 32, 0285r (28 September 1624), and vol. 33, 0181v (9 February 1637); Litchfield, 364.

[30] D'Amico, 69; Hallman, 129–30, 161; Ago, *Carriere*, 90.

trolled not only nomination to public office but also grants of Roman citizenship. Both were indicators of social prestige that were meaningful to the lay branch of a churchman's family or to laymen settled in Rome for papal business.

During the period 1623 to 1644 the Capitoline authorities created an average of forty-one new citizens a year. The basic requirement for a role in civic institutions was Roman citizenship, but few of these new Romans actually participated at the Capitol; indeed, some of them were ecclesiastics.[31] For them citizenship was a sign of civic honor rather than a passport to local political responsibility; it marked the family's arrival and provided a touchstone for future generations. For newcomers, citizenship and office were two significant forms of prestige in the secular realm. By acquiring them immigrants could hope to be acknowledged eventually as "noble Romans."

Sometimes, however, this acknowledgment needed to be made explicit in a hurry. Then the conservators were the resource, writing letters attesting to the nobility of a particular family. Their phrases emphasize public recognition of status and the priority of officeholding. The Buti are "noble men," they write, with full access to the Capitol, "as is notorious and manifest not only to us but also to all the other nobles of our city of Rome." The Salamoni "are noble and among the principal [families] of our city and have always enjoyed and enjoy presently all the ranks, offices, honors and dignities that our first citizens and gentlemen enjoy and in particular the dignity of the conservatorship."[32]

Recognition could be won in other ways, of course. Wealth made it possible to purchase an aristocratic title, found a local charity, join a prominent confraternity, or build a chapel, palace, or villa. Not everyone sought out the Capitol; some families skipped that step altogether. Unlike the Costaguti under Paul V,

[31] The source for grants of Roman citizenship between 1623 and 1644 is the decrees of the Capitoline councils, ASC, cred. I, vols. 32–34. To test the degree of civic participation by newly created citizens I followed the thirty-five men made citizens at the public council of 15 December 1623 (ASC, cred. I, vol. 32, 0272r–v) through the records of the Capitoline councils until 1644. In most cases they did not appear at the Capitol. One exception was Pirrhus de Guadagnus of Arezzo, who was elected *paciere* in 1624. Different authorities had bestowed citizenship in fifteenth-century Rome, but the 1580 statutes formalized procedures; *Statuta almae urbis*, bk. 3, chaps. 56–58. The pope, of course, retained the right to make grants of Roman citizenship; for an interesting use of this power in 1641 see Ameyden, "Diario," Biblioteca Casanatense, cod. 1831, 93r. Acquired citizenship did not confer fiscal advantages; *Regesti* 2:6, 27. Citizenship was occasionally granted to clerics; see, for example, ASC, cred. I, vol. 32, 0281r (18 June 1624). De Luca suggests that an additional motive for acquiring citizenship was to inherit property in a place in which one had not been born, but, as we have seen, this had been permitted in Rome since at least 1474. *Il Dottor Volgare*, bk. 3, pt. 2, chap. 12, p. 196.

[32] ASC, cred. IV, vol. 96, istrumenti, 61r, 49v. There are also occasional "fides nobilitatis" among the volumes of letters patent. See, for example, ASC, cred. XI, vol. 20, letters patent, 91r. The 1601 list of fees charged by the secretary of the conservators indicates that a "fides nobilitatis" cost ten *giuli* or one scudo; ASV, arm. IV, vol. 45, 116r. An undated and uncited source from the ASC quoted by Ferdinand Gregorovius refers also to "litterae civilitatis," which establish noble status and cost up to thirty-five scudi, but I suspect these documents date from a later era; Ferdinand Gregorovius, "Alcuni cenni storici sulla cittadinanza romana," *Atti della R. Accademia dei Lincei*, 3d ser., 1 (1876–77): 346.

the lay members of the Florentine Sacchetti family, for example, Urban VIII's personal bankers, seemed to have no interest in civic offices. They manifested their status in local society through inspired patronage of the arts and remained entirely within the circle of the Barberini.[33] For the majority without such privileged ties or riches, however, the Roman People had a role to play in transmuting talent, celebrity, or administrative success into family honor.[34]

DEFINITION AND COMPETITION

Rome, like many early modern cities, was an unstable medium in which to shape a social identity, which had consequences for the Roman People. Fluid conceptions of nobility and competition for family honor gave Capitoline institutions social significance, but also produced tensions within them. The integrating and legitimating role that holding civic posts played in the larger society was not always smoothly experienced on the Capitol; conflicts surfaced in the form of efforts to restrict access to offices and limit opportunities for family publicity.

The permeable Roman elite generated internal attempts to clarify its boundaries. Since the fifteenth century the Roman People had continually tried to become more exclusive; they had barred artisans from offices in 1440 and protested the inclusion of "plebeians" in the bussola in the early sixteenth century. In 1562 they decreed that the electors had to be gentlemen. The most dramatic step occurred in 1614 when the councils resolved that only nobles might be nominated to civic office. They ordered that if the electors named anyone who was not a *vir nobilis* to the bussola, the magistrates could substitute someone else who was.[35]

Yet, as we have seen, much Capitoline policy and practice worked against exclusivity. The statutes of 1580 with their flexible criteria for admission to the public council had left the door open to newcomers. During Urban VIII's reign rich and well-connected foreigners were able to gain entry to civic offices. In 1640, when Ameyden commented that candidates were nominated for different posts on the basis of their "quality," he implied that there was still a range of

[33] Haskell, 38–39.

[34] Carlo Antonio Dal Pozzo, brother of Cassiano, the learned Piedmontese scientist and artistic adviser to the Barberini, came to Rome in 1620, but did not become a conservator until 1656; Giacomo Lumbroso, "Notizie sulla vita di Cassiano dal Pozzo," *Miscellanea di storia italiana*, 1st ser., 15 (1876): 146–47. I am grateful to Professor Joseph Connors for this reference. See also Donatella L. Sparti, "Carlo Antonio dal Pozzo (1606–1689) An Unknown Collector," *Journal of the History of Collections* 2 (1990): 7–19. Haskell, 44, 98–114. Gian Lorenzo Bernini, since the 1620s the most celebrated sculptor of his era, was an old and long-knighted man when he was nominated for the post of conservator in 1667; his name was not drawn from the bussola of nominees; BAV, Chigi, H III 56 (7), 3r.

[35] "Ex S.C. Decretum est quod imbussolatores non possint imposterum imbussolare in illis officijs, quo[rum] nominatio ad ipsos absque Bussula spectat nisi viros nobiles, alias nominatio sit, nulla"; ASC, cred. I, vol. 32, 0081v–82r (14 November 1614). Rodocanachi, *Institutions*, 282–83; Pecchiai, *Roma*, 241.

social rank in any given bussola, an impression confirmed by detailed analysis.[36] When speaking of the office of conservator in that year, the Fleming emphasized its social ambiguity.

> Formerly this magistracy was the ambition of the first families, who today disdain it, because of the admission of low men and new, and this by artifice of the [papal] government, which finds itself more secure with the low. It remains [true] however that they only ask gentlemen, also of the old nobility [nobilta' antica], not however the titled.[37]

The problem with the resolution of 1614 of course was that any restriction of civic office to "noble men" was unenforceable as long as there was no objective determination of noble rank in Rome. The bussola, which included as many as 350 names and changed every two years, was voracious. Given the large number of offices to fill and the uncertainty of status in Rome, someone whose "nobility" was disputable would more than likely find his way to Capitoline office. Ameyden detected a political motive to this heterogeneous recruitment. To the political fears of the popes, however, we must add the social ambitions of patrician families seeking banking profits or an ecclesiastical career amidst the diminishing economic opportunities of seventeenth-century Italy. These all helped to keep civic officeholders in Rome diverse, despite increasing consciousness of rank. The council's attempt in 1614 was a sign that the social and geographical mobility of early modern Rome did not meet with uniform approval on the Capitol, but it could not succeed in its aim without a tighter definition of nobility. This was not forthcoming for another century.

The families that collectively made up the Roman People were internally divided over another issue in the sixteenth and seventeenth centuries. Accepting an electoral system that gave them brief and widely spaced opportunities to hold civic offices, they imaginatively sought ways to perpetuate the memory of a fleeting honor that had long-term social implications. For many decades it had been the custom for officials to paint their family crests in diverse locations around the palace of the conservators. This practice was prohibited in 1588 and the ban against it was carved in marble and posted in the great hall of the palace.[38] Behind

---

[36] Ameyden, ASV, "Relatione," 684r; Nussdorfer, "City Politics," 146–47.

[37] "Anticamente questo Magistrato era ambito dalle prime famiglie, che hoggi lo sdegnano, venendo ammessi huomini bassi e nuovi, e cio' p artificio del Governo, che si trova con li bassi piu' sicuro, Non resta pero' che non lo chieda Gentilhuomini anche della Nobilta' antica, non pero' Titolati"; Ameyden, ASV, "Relatione," 685r. Cf. Pecchiai, however, who makes it clear that conservators were socially heterogeneous in the fourteenth century too; Pecchiai, Roma, 241.

[38] ASC, cred. I, vol. 29, decreti, 0175v (1 December 1588); Rodocanachi, Institutions, 320; Alessandro Ademollo, Giacinto Gigli ed i suoi diarii del secolo XVII (Florence, 1877), 42. The public placement of family crests was also a volatile issue in other Italian cities; Richard Trexler, Public Life in Renaissance Florence (New York, 1980), 94.

this action lay the conflict between the formal equality of the individual families that composed the Roman People and the pressure for social distinction felt by those same families.

The pressure proved too great. In 1626 the councils repealed the resolution against posting names and coats of arms on the Capitol and competition for space proceeded unhindered.[39] As any visitor to the palace of the conservators today can attest, the magistrates rapidly began to carve their way back into posterity. Almost every antique sculptural fragment in the piazza or palace courtyard received a pedestal inscribed with the names of the three conservators and the prior of the caporioni for the given trimester, sometimes adorned with four diminutive stone coats of arms as well (see Figure 9). Gifts to the Capitoline palace could also serve as a chance to leave behind a record of one's family. The marble revetment behind the seats where the conservators dispensed justice, and the four paintings of Roman saints in the palace chapel each permitted the public inscription of their donors' names.[40] The one compromise of course was that gifts and commemorative memorials bore collective inscriptions. The three conservators and the prior of the caporioni who held office together for three months all shared the space on the wall or monument.

A new resolution to the conflicting demands of equality and honor emerged in 1640. In that year the civic authorities revived the classical Roman practice of recording the names of their magistrates annually in stone. Since their rediscovery in the sixteenth century, the tablets of the ancient *fasti consulares* had decorated the courtyard of the palace of the conservators. The decision of 1640 ensured that henceforth the names of all conservators and priors of the caporioni would also be engraved on the walls of the Capitol; now the highest civic officials had a guarantee that their names would go down in history. The new policy decreased competitive tensions and confirmed the Capitol's important role in buttressing family status. Significantly, when nobility was at last restricted to a particular group of families in eighteenth-century Rome, being inscribed in the new *fasti* was the proof demanded for inclusion in the "golden book."[41]

[39] ASC, cred. I, vol. 33, 0040v (3 December 1626).

[40] Many of the inscriptions on the Capitol can be found in Vincenzo Forcella, *Iscrizioni delle chiese e d'altri edifici di Roma dal secolo XI fino ai giorni nostri*, 14 vols. (Rome, 1869–84), vol. 1 (1869). For the inscription on the marble revetment in the old tribunal of the conservators see ibid., 1:52, no. 120. For the inscriptions accompanying the four paintings of Roman saints or cult figures in the old chapel of the palace see ibid., 1:57, no. 141 (where Rutilio Specchi's name appears again, this time honoring Sant' Alessio "confessor of Roman patricians"); 1:58, no. 143 (Ludovica Albertoni, unofficially bearing the title "Blessed"); 1:59, no. 147 (Sant' Eustachio) and no. 148 (Saint Cecilia).

[41] Mistruzzi, 238; see also Susanna Pasquali, "Il patriziato romano secondo il 'libro d'oro' di Benedetto XIV," in *L'Angelo e la citta'*, 2 vols. (Rome, 1987), 2:41–43. The "modern" *fasti consulares*, which are still in situ, drew Gigli's scorn. He regarded them as an attempt to fool posterity into thinking that the conservators were the equivalent of the ancient consuls; Gigli, *Diario*, 196. In fact,

9. The pedestal supporting a fragment of the foot of a colossal antique statue in the courtyard of the palace of the conservators bears the names and crests of the conservators and
prior who held office in March 1635.

Giacinto Gigli

An analysis in broad strokes of the social connotations of civic participation in early modern Rome leaves many questions still unanswered. In a given two-year period from 1623 to 1644 five to six hundred men had some role in Capitoline affairs—not just holding an elected office but attending a council meeting, serving on a committee, being listed as a candidate, or being named to a special delegation. Who were these mostly obscure lay gentlemen? What did they think of the institutions in which they had a hand? What did the Roman People mean to them?

One Roman who played a bit part on the Capitol during Urban VIII's reign has left us a record of his life, which, while not offering exhaustive answers, gives us at least a point of entry into these questions. Giacinto Gigli (1594–1671), whose diary I have frequently cited, was a gentleman of middling rank who lived on the Via delle Botteghe Oscure, a five-minute walk from the Capitoline hill. Gigli was a poet, doctor of laws, and avid chronicler of Roman doings. Were it not for his writings—an autobiography, a diary, historical notes, and manuscripts, all unpublished during his lifetime—he would be as unknown to us as most other Romans of the seventeenth century. Gigli's experiences provide a window on the Roman People not because he was a prominent or even typical member of the society of his time, but because his life is more accessible to us than the lives of most of his contemporaries.

Born in the central rione of Pigna in 1594, Gigli was the only surviving child of Giovanni Battista Gigli and Plautilla Bongiovanni. Both families were Roman from the late fifteenth century, which was as far back as Gigli could find record; it is an indication of Gigli's atypical scrupulousness as a genealogist that he was unwilling to make further claims without evidence. An inscription dating from 1490 on the family tomb in the Dominican church of Santa Maria sopra Minerva remembered Marianus Lilius, "Mercator Ro[manus]." No longer merchants, the Gigli family was well-off, if not rich. At the time of his marriage Gigli enjoyed an income of about 1,000 scudi a year. His father had left him an estate worth 12–13,000 scudi; this included a vineyard outside the Lateran gate and a number of houses in the city. Educated at the Jesuit college in Rome, Gigli went on to earn his doctorate in laws in 1616.[42]

Kinship connections were as important an attribute of social standing in seventeenth-century Rome as riches, and Gigli carefully noted the families to whom he was related either by blood or marriage. His wealthy grandfather Orazio Gigli had married Flaminia del Bene, "of a noble and very honorable family," but Orazio had consumed his inheritance in protecting himself from his enemies. Gi-

---

the inscriptions did have a role to play in rewriting the past, but it was the social history of the individual families that was rewritten, not the historic powers of the conservators.

[42] Ademollo, *Gigli*, 12, 39, 43–44, 50–52, 61; Giuseppe Ricciotti, Introduction to Gigli, *Diario*, 2. I have not yet found evidence that Gigli ever practiced law; his interests were mainly literary.

gli's father Giovanni Battista had to struggle to pay his father's creditors and to marry off his sisters decently. Giovanni Battista's virtue was rewarded by the favorable notice of Orazio Fosco, the man who took the official minutes of the civic council meetings, whom Gigli described as "old, wise and of great authority with the Roman People and well acquainted with the nobility of Giovanbattista." In 1591 Fosco did Gigli's father the honor of bestowing on him the hand of his ward and niece by marriage, Plautilla Bongiovanni. Through the Bongiovanni Gigli was a great-nephew of Monsignor Alessandro Mileti, who occupied the high curial post of referendary of the Segnatura, an office once held by Maffeo Barberini himself.[43]

Shortly after his father's death, when Giacinto was twenty-five, he married Virginia Lucci, who brought him a dowry of 3,500 scudi. This was far from a princely sum—in his diary Gigli mentions a prosperous local bookseller who had planned to give his daughter 8,000 scudi—but it was a respectable figure. A mason's wife might have a dowry of 650 scudi, and a lacemaker's bride one of 230 scudi.[44]

The first notice we have of Gigli's civic career was his election as caporione of Campitelli, the rione in which the Capitol was located, in January 1631. Earlier public offices exercised by the Gigli family are uncertain. Gigli mentions at some length a kinsman, Antonio Gaulo of the house of Racotolli de Guidoni, "very noble, very rich and of great reputation," who died serving as a Roman magistrate. He states proudly that Antonio's coat of arms could be seen in several locations at the Capitol prior to the time of Sixtus V (1585–1590). Gigli says nothing about the Giovanni Battista Gigli who was conservator in 1597; one suspects he might have had this been his father. Three Giglis, including a Giovanni Battista, were among the Romans who had the right to attend the public council in 1581.[45]

Giacinto was thirty-six years old in 1631 when he became caporione, and for the next fifteen years his name reappears several dozen times in the Capitoline registers. He went to several meetings of the private and public councils and served on the Carnival races committee in 1638 and 1639. In 1636 Gigli held the office of syndic of the Roman People, though he was in the bussola for a different position, that of *paciere*. He served as prior of the caporioni in 1638 and 1641.[46]

Gigli's public career suggests that an ambitious citizen could use the papacy to

[43] Ademollo, *Gigli*, 40, 42.

[44] Ibid., 42, 51, 64–71; Gigli, *Diario*, 140. Artisan dowries: ASR, 30 N.C., uff. 2 (Bonanni) 1633, pt. 2, 260r (lacemaker's bride), and pt. 3, 46v (mason's bride).

[45] ASC, cred. I, vol. 33, decreti, 0100v. Details of Gigli's civic activities are drawn from the decrees of the Capitoline councils for the period 1623–1644, ASC, cred. I, vols. 32–34. Ademollo, *Gigli*, 41–42. The closest approximation to Gigli's ancestor that I have been able to find is an Antonio Saba Facottoli de Guidoni, who was conservator in 1515; see Pietramellara, 2:194, 204. ASC, cred. I, vol. 5. The minimum age of the Roman citizens who had the right to attend the public council was twenty; Giacinto's father Giovanni Battista would only have been nineteen years old in 1581 when this list was compiled.

[46] ASC, cred. I, vols. 33–34. BAV, Barb. lat. 2218 (bussola of 1636).

get ahead at the Capitol. The first council meeting that Gigli attended as a private citizen, in March 1634, three years after his first term as a civic official, had two items on the agenda. One was an effort to avoid a new tax by the owners of stalls in the fish market. The second, which probably drew Gigli, was the question of whether to post memorials to the pope and to Cardinal Francesco Barberini in Santa Maria in Aracoeli. Gigli, with twenty-three others, registered his support for both motions and followed this up three months later by voting to rescind a prohibition against putting testimonials to "living princes" on the Capitol.[47]

In these same years Gigli composed and presented a seventeen-page verse eulogy to Urban VIII called "La Gloria barberina, song in praise of the holiness of Urban VIII."[48] Poetry could be an effective form of self-promotion at the court of a pontiff who was a poet himself and Gigli did not miss his opportunity. In 1634 he illustrated a poem he had written for a Barberini cardinal, probably Cardinal Francesco, with elaborate floral allusions to his own name, which meant hyacinth and lilies, and to the bees that were the Barberini family emblem (see Figure 10). Beneath the garden scene in which plump bees minister to a long-stemmed lily, Gigli writes, "I can securely hope for my comfort in the drops of choice honey."[49]

Gigli's efforts seem to have paid off. Once he was made caporione even though he was not in the bussola. More importantly, as we have seen, Cardinal Francesco Barberini named him prior of the caporioni in 1638 and again in 1641. "I am the first to have this honor twice in two successive bussole," he proudly recorded in his diary.[50] A man of Gigli's modest, though gentlemanly, status might never have expected to become conservator, but thanks to papal patronage he briefly enjoyed equivalent rank as prior.

In light of this connection with the Barberini, it is worth noting that Gigli held no civic offices after 1644. Apparently he did not intend to withdraw from public activity immediately for he kept his caporione outfit for another decade. Perhaps ill health prompted his retirement for we know he was suffering from failing sight a few years later.[51]

On the other hand he may have been too closely identified with Urban VIII's family to prosper in the next pontificate. Gigli never made explicit reference to his own public role in commenting about Pope Innocent X Pamphili (1644–1655), a Roman whose brother and nephew had served as conservators. Yet he remarked that Innocent X did not appreciate poets and that it was useless to

[47] ASC, cred. I, vol. 33, decreti, 0141v–42r (27 March 1634); ibid., 0145r–47v (23 and 26 June 1634).

[48] Ademollo, Gigli, 101–3.

[49] BAV, Barb. lat. 9910, 20r. I am grateful to Professor Joseph Connors for bringing this drawing to my attention.

[50] Gigli, Diario, 198–99.

[51] Gigli, BNC-VE, Sess. 334, 220v, records Gigli's sale of his caporione uniform to Rutilio Specchi, caporione of Trastevere, on 7 May 1655, for which he received 30 silver scudi. See also idem, Diario, 473.

Gigli, Giacinti, e Rose,
In angusto Giardin chiuse, e serrate,
Solo il mirar, solo all'odor son grate.
Ma se fian trasportate
In un prato, due sian l'Api Ingegnose:
Potrà l'Agricoltore
Sperar; oltr'alla Vista, oltr'all'Odore;
Di raccorre anco il Miel dolce, e perfetto.
Tal Io; che dal mio retto
Questi Fioretti porto
Nel Prato BARBERINO Almo, e Ridente,
Doue albergan le PECCHIE al Ciel dilette;
Potrò sicuramente
Sperar, per mio Conforto,
Di dolcissimo Miel le Stille elette.

10. Giacinto Gigli's illustrated poem for a Barberini cardinal.

compose verses in his honor. He was also outspokenly hostile to the pope's sister-in-law, the imposing Donna Olimpia Maidalchini Pamphili, who was thought to be the power behind the tiara.[52]

Whatever the reasons for the termination of Gigli's civic career, his pride in and fascination with the Roman People emerge very clearly in his writings. He did extensive research in the Capitoline archives and authored at least two manuscript histories of the civic magistrates. In the late 1630s he had high hopes to publish one of these, the "Cronologia Romana," and had gone so far as to design an ornate frontispiece for the work before his hopes were dashed, a failure he blamed on the machinations of the fiscal procurator.[53]

Gigli's respect for the civic authorities is apparent even when he criticizes them. He thought the Roman People made a poor impression when they sponsored a procession giving thanks for Rome's deliverance from the plague, but did not pay for the candles the artisans carried. Similarly he censured the conservators for missing an opportunity to show "magnificence and largeness of spirit" when they failed to invite the pope to dine with them after he had said a special morning mass at Santa Maria in Aracoeli.[54]

Gigli took delight in his caporione uniform and described with pride the jeweled band his wife had sewed on his cap and the gilded sword he carried in procession.[55] He treated his participation in Capitoline activities seriously. Above all he wanted the Capitoline magistrates to represent themselves publicly in the most dignified way possible. The issue of civic power or impotence was not nearly as pressing to Gigli as that of civic decorum.

Gigli was scandalized when the prior of the caporioni, Valerio dei Massimi, was arrested for debt. Capitoline officials should have been immune from prosecution while in office and the affront to civic dignity was blatant. The constables had stopped a carriage in which two conservators were riding along with Massimi.

Such a thing was highly unusual, [for] the magistrates have always been respected and secure from insult, particularly in a civil case. But the majesty of the Roman People has been reduced to this state and will demean itself still further, through the meanness [*vilta'*] and ineptitude of those who are admitted to this magistracy.[56]

---

[52] Gigli, *Diario*, 264, 305. Perhaps Gigli's luck with the Pamphili would have prospered if his brother-in-law, Giovanni Battista Lucci, a priest who was secretary to the pope's adopted cardinal nephew Camillo Astalli, had not died in 1651, after only one year in his advantageous post; ibid., 389.

[53] Ademollo, *Gigli*, 16. The design of the frontispiece included the figure of Saint Peter, beside whom was a small angel bearing a coat of arms with the letters "S.P.Q.R." Here the familiar initials stood for the words "Sanctus Petrus Quirites Regit": "Saint Peter rules the citizens of Rome." Gigli's two manuscripts bear the titles "Cronologia dei Consoli, Priori, e Magistrati di Roma, e statuti propri," (BNC-VE, Sess. 334), and "Cronologia Romana di Giacinto Gigli," (BNC-VE, Sess. 375).

[54] Gigli, *Diario*, 129–30.

[55] Gigli, BNC-VE, Sess. 334, 219v.

[56] Gigli, *Diario*, 144. The unfortunate official arrested for debt in 1634, Valerio dei Massimi (1587–1658), who hailed from a distinguished Roman family, seems actually to have been imprisoned

Proud of his association with the Roman People, Gigli did his part to promote civic majesty in Baroque Rome.

Giacinto Gigli's life allows us to see one of the participants in civic institutions in greater detail than is possible for most citizens, and to suggest the means and motivations that could lie behind a civic career. Although he never held the Capitol's most prestigious posts and his degree of public activity was not dramatic, Gigli reminds us that the Roman People stood for something important to men like himself. However he might grumble about contemporary realities, Gigli felt linked by the Capitol to the majestic Senate and Roman People of antiquity. In other European cities the governing elites might have to invent myths to ennoble their rule, but in Rome the greatest secular myth of all was conveniently at hand.

---

in the Capitoline jails but to have escaped; Ademollo, *Gigli*, 79. Although he held a number of civic posts and served on six different committees prior to this incident, he never again took part in Capitoline activities.

PART III

The Politics of Jurisdiction

WHAT DID CIVIC OFFICIALS actually do? We know that they occupied a famous site and set of buildings, that they had printed statutes delineating their procedures, and that their offices gave them a claim to social prestige. They shared government in complex ways with members of the Curia. But in the daily routine of administration, or in a public crisis, what did the "jurisdictions of the Roman People" really mean? This section explores that question by looking at the Capitol in action in four different contexts.

One is the urban marketplace, where civic magistrates supervised commerce like their counterparts in many other early modern towns. The second is the corporations of artisans and tradesmen, which had a special position of subordination to the Roman People. The third context takes us to the lands beyond the walls where four towns or *terre* were feudal subjects of the municipality. The fourth is the plague threat of 1629 to 1632—a chronological context—which provides a case study of civic interaction with the whole range of other institutions and officials in Rome.

In each of these four contexts, though its claims were not absolutely exclusive, the Capitol had the special weight of tradition behind its exercise of jurisdiction. The Roman People existed as one source of public authority among many in the Baroque city. They always had rivals. But their rivalries were precise. The dynamics of the relationship between civic officers and other bodies were closely calibrated to the kind of jurisdiction they possessed. Since "jurisdiction" was not merely a technical legal phenomenon, but the term in common parlance denoting a sphere of power, to see how magistracies sorted out their respective duties is an investigation into an elusive yet characteristic form of political activity. In these four chapters we can trace the domains of responsiblity that were particular—in diverse ways—to the Roman People. Talking about what civic officials actually did illuminates their class interests, their languages of power, the mechanics and symbols of their administrative authority, and their meaning in the lived reality of daily life.

Chapter Seven

MARKETPLACE

To such wretchedness has the empire of the world been
reduced that we think much of ourselves for fining the thefts,
frauds and tricks of greedy tradespeople, doing battle every
hour with bakers, grocers, innkeepers or butchers.
—Marcello Alberini

THUS WROTE the sometime civic officeholder Marcello Alberini in 1548, invoking the topos of decline beloved of commentators on Rome's municipal institutions in the early modern period.[1] His irony nicely conveys the condescension Roman gentlemen felt towards "tradespeople," and he correctly highlighted a domain of activity that loomed very large indeed for Capitoline officials. In Rome landed gentlemen kept watch on the encounter of buyer and seller in the city marketplaces.

What was the Capitoline role in the marketplace? To begin with butchers, bakers, and grocers is appropriate, for the conservators' obligation to set standards for these tradesmen and root out their crimes against consumers was written into specific articles of the city statutes. However, their mandate, though not given statutory expression, extended beyond the three important provisioning trades to embrace everyone from candlemakers to fodder merchants. Their primary job was to enforce existing rules on commerce, whether these governed prices, purity, weight, location, or timing.[2]

Thus streams of edicts (*bandi*) regularly poured forth from the Capitol alerting the public to the prices of meat, chestnuts, coal, hay, soap, candles, stabling, milling, and wine. To ensure that buyers were not defrauded the magistrates directed that all scales used in Rome must conform to the authorized "scales [*stadera*] of the Roman People." Foodstuffs brought into the city had to be weighed on these official scales as well. They also dictated product quality, forbidding the

[1] Alberini, 483. See also the allegorical depiction of the conservators, called *poliarchi*, in this role in Ianus Nicius Erythraeus [Giovanni Vittorio Rossi], *Eudemiae libri VIII* (n. p., 1637), 153–55.

[2] *Statuta almae urbis*, bk. 3, chaps. 5–7; Rodocanachi, *Institutions*, 291–95, 306. This kind of regulation was a ubiquitous feature of town government in medieval and early modern Europe. For the operations of state and local authorities in the marketplaces of Paris see de Carsalade du Pont, 119–47, and Steven L. Kaplan, *Provisioning Paris: Merchants and Millers in the Grain and Flour Trade during the Eighteenth Century* (Ithaca, N.Y., 1984), 33–39. For regulation of butchers, bakers, and food purveyors see also James R. Farr, *Hands of Honor: Artisans and Their World in Dijon, 1550–1650* (Ithaca, N.Y., 1988), 37. For the conservators' commercial edicts see *Regesti*.

use of pig feet in pork sausages, for example, or decreeing the legal ingredients of butter. Sometimes their notices warned against practices that threatened future food supplies, such as telling fishermen not to throw weeds and lime into the mouth of the Tiber during the spawning season. Sometimes they resolved disputes, such as the conflict in 1629 between myrtle sellers and tanners over the price of myrtle, a vital ingredient in tanning.[3]

Making these announcements was seen as part of the process of enforcement. It was understood, by the 1620s if not before, that the Capitol did not set prices. In a meeting of the congregation of the Annona and Grascia in 1628, at which the conservators were present, this point was clarified in the case of fruit and vegetable prices. While "in the past" civic officers had fixed these rates, "presently" this was done by two clerks of the apostolic chamber, the president of the Grascia and the prefect of the Annona. The conservators were charged with writing up the price lists and emitting them as public edicts.[4] As we shall see, they were also responsible for seeing that these orders were obeyed.

Enforcement fell to Capitoline officials as part of a broader understanding of the division of labor between them and papal officers. The cardinal chamberlain, the president of the Grascia, the prefect of the Annona, the congregation of the Annona and Grascia, even Cardinal Francesco Barberini himself, could all make decisions affecting local market practices. But the civic administration was to execute any decree they put forth. Cardinal Francesco simply told the conservators when he wished to change a given policy; they in turn told the public. While the cardinal chamberlain could and did send out posters on some of the same matters, his regulations usually stated that the conservators were to implement them. What that meant besides publishing the bulk of edicts on trade matters was policing the markets and punishing transgressors.[5]

---

[3] *Regesti* 2:233; 4:39, 94, 229; 5:12, 38, 55, 73, 74. Curial officials, especially the cardinal chamberlain of the apostolic chamber, occasionally published edicts on these matters too. Bread prices were not publicized since they did not vary; the weight, not the price, of a loaf rose and fell with grain prices and the weight was set by the papal Annona office. Antonio Martini, *Arti, mestieri e fede nella Roma dei Papi* (Bologna, 1965), 65.

[4] ASC, cred. VI, vol. 63, interessi diversi, 18r. See also ASC, cred. I, vol. 33, decreti, 0125r (15 February 1633). De Luca, *Il Dottor Volgare*, bk. 15, pt. 3, chap. 34, pp. 324–25. Del Re, *Curia Romana*, 337. The congregation, established by Sixtus V in 1588, seems to have experienced episodic activity. Although Del Re says it did not long outlast the reign of Paul V (1605–1621), the "liber decretorum congregationis super concernentibus annonam et grasciam urbis" located in ASC, cred. VI, vol. 63, 16r–52r, covers the period 1628 to 1646. Apparently reinvigorated in 1628, with the resolution to meet twice a month, it soon fell to assembling twice a year, with gaps of several years due to the illness or other preoccupations of the cardinal chamberlain who led it. Cardinal Ippolito Aldobrandini was the head of the congregation from 1628 to his death in 1638; Cardinal Antonio Barberini the younger succeeded him in 1638. See also Ruggiero, 79–80.

[5] ASC, cred. VI, vol. 63, interessi diversi, 16r–52r. Biblioteca Corsini, ms. 1654, "Relatione," 178. In an edict concerning hay and straw emitted by the cardinal chamberlain in 1637, he makes it clear that if violators were reported to the conservators they had the authority to execute penalties for transgressions of his edict. "All'essecutione delle sopradette pene si procedera' in ciascuno delli detti

The role of "executors" embraced more varied functions too. The resolutions of the congregation of the Annona and Grascia, a committee headed by a cardinal and composed mainly of clerics but on which the conservators also sat, nicely illuminate some of these. For instance, the congregation might direct the conservators to follow up on a dispute, such as the one over myrtle, and mediate between the guilds involved. It might leave to them the job of setting a penalty, if, as was feared in one case, the wine wholesalers tried to overcharge the retailers. Or it might have them communicate a change in policy: when the grocers' permits to sell fresh buffalo cheese were revoked, the congregation charged civic officials with informing them. Sometimes an investigative role was thrust upon the conservators. During a hay shortage in 1636, the Annona and Grascia congregation wanted the conservators to inquire "personally" at all the haylofts in the city to find out the true state of supplies and to make sure that new prices were being observed. Hay wholesalers were to give written testimony to the notary of the conservators as to whether they were providing fodder to the public or to the horses of the postmaster, since they were not permitted to do both.[6]

The anonymous author of a diatribe against the high cost of foodstuffs in Rome pointed out the perils for the consumer of making the Capitoline authorities responsible for enforcement. "The clerks of the chamber set the prices for meat, but their execution is reserved to the conservators, and, since ordinarily the meat is theirs and [so is] the hay . . . they do not have the orders observed."[7] There were perhaps other reasons why policing mechanisms might fail, as we shall see. But the charge that patrician Romans traded in meat and hay was undoubtedly true, though it seems likely that the clerks of the chamber did too. The language of marketplace edicts, however, masks this reality and presents a quite different image of the civic magistrates.

These conventional phrases portray officers who are deeply suspicious of retailers and the ways of the market, and anxious to defend urban consumers from being cheated. Verbally Capitoline officials project themselves as moral authorities. "It is our duty," went one of the formulaic letters patent issued by the conservators to their agents in the markets, "to ensure that . . . every person has his complement of justice."[8] A venerable tradition in European thought, still alive in seventeenth-century Rome, subordinated the free play of commerce to a higher moral code. As a recent historian of the Parisian provisioning trades put it, "the social

---

casi, non solo da Noi, ma anco . . . da Signori Conservatori, quando si faranno inventioni o denuntie avanti di loro." ASC, cred. XIII, vol. 30, edicts, 224 (27 May 1637). For the full range of authorities making market rules in Rome see *Regesti*, vols. 4 and 5, passim. For the notion in seventeenth-century France that executing royal authority "completes" it, see Beik, 177.

  [6] ASC, cred. VI, vol. 63, interessi diversi, 20r, 26r, 40r, 45r.

  [7] "Modo per tor via che i prezzi delle cose magnative non stiano alti in Roma"; BAV, Chigi, N III 84, 126r. Although this document bears no date, the hand appears to be that of the late sixteenth or seventeenth centuries.

  [8] ASC, cred. XI, vol. 20, letters patent, 7v.

organization was not submerged in the market principle, as it is in most modern 'market' societies today. Rather, the distribution of certain goods . . . was determined by the social organization."[9] The Roman People stood here for the community as a unit of social needs rather than economic interests.

Civic authorities constrained exchange in the name of equity. This principle underlay those rules that tried to preserve the buyer's access to goods at the public stalls, setting fixed times and places of sale and banning such practices as forestalling and engrossing that gave the few an unfair advantage over the many. It also helps to explain the special concern the edicts show for the behavior of hotelkeepers and innkeepers. These large-scale purchasers of victuals and hay could keep supplies from reaching other consumers and might resell products, such as bread, pickled fish, or cheese, at the expense of the legitimate members of the guilds specializing in those items. Pronouncements against urban middlemen who sold rotten food at high prices to rural laborers expressed the same ideal of justice.[10]

What were the resources the Capitoline magistrates could bring to their job of enforcing marketplace morality? The mechanisms of enforcement were the public edict, a staff of commercial policemen called *straordinari maggiori* and *straordinari minori*, and the conservators' tribunal, which operated together as a total system. The edict established lawful prices and practices. The market police then busied themselves searching for violations of the posted rules. Working a given zone each day they functioned as teams of two or three, first checking the weight of bread sold by the bakers, then looking for goods smuggled in without payment of entry duties, testing the scales shopkeepers used, and demanding to see licenses to buy and sell. The term for an infraction was *invenzione* or "finding," for the straordinari had literally made a finding when they detected a crime. Those cited for transgressions usually had to pay a fine, although corporal punishment via the strappado was an option. The straordinari received the bulk of the penalty with about a third going to the civic treasury. Tradesmen could appeal to the conservators against the straordinari, and, if they did not like their judgment, they could appeal to the auditor of the cardinal chamberlain. Rare appeals went further and were heard by the congregation of the Annona and Grascia itself.[11]

The market police were clearly the key to the effectiveness of the enforcement effort. Yet their job was a hard one. An edict of 1643 shows what the straordinari had to go through in order to earn their share of the fines. In looking for cheating grocers, for example, they were permitted to enter shops and also to question

---

[9] Kaplan, 29; Romani, 167. The notion of the "just price" is of course associated with Saint Thomas Aquinas.

[10] *Regesti* 2:90; 4:78, 116, 210, 220, 242; 5:68, 181. Romani, 167.

[11] Pecchiai, *Roma*, 257–58. Rodocanachi, *Institutions*, 295–96. *Statuta almae urbis*, bk. 3, chaps. 19, 33. ASC, cred. IX, vol. 21, pene (1683–1684), 1r. ASC, cred. VI, vol. 63, interessi diversi, 18r, 33r. Biblioteca Corsini, ms. 1654, "Relatione," 173. See, for example, the edict of 19 July 1639, ASV, arm. V, vol. 233.

customers outside about what they had bought and how much they had paid. Then, assuming a willing customer, they could check the weight of the merchandise themselves and, if necessary, take the defrauded buyer back to the seller prior to citing him or her for a violation. That a willing customer could not always be assumed was attested by the existence of edicts ordering customers to answer the straordinari's inquiries. To add to their frustrations, when a shopkeeper arrived at the Capitol to pay the fine, the conservators, ignoring their own regulations, sometimes lowered it, cutting down the take both of the agent and the fisc. Given the rewards, it was not surprising that the market police occasionally invented illegal methods of securing their living, either by harassing tradesmen or by colluding with them. After one of them was dismissed for his abuses, the mercers and several other guilds brought suit against him. Edicts prohibiting the straordinari from accepting bribes were frequent, and on one occasion in 1628 the temptation seemed so inevitable that they were actually forbidden to enter the bakers' shops.[12]

Fragmentary records of the cases heard by the conservators' tribunal in the 1630s and early 1640s show the straordinari at work. Often these cases involve countryfolk; the market agents apparently knew that rustics were frequent victims of sharp practices by townsmen. What the judicial acts also reveal is the close attention straordinari paid to tavernkeepers. Sometimes this was for routine cheating of customers, as when a certain Leone at the sign of the Carrozze overcharged a clown's apprentice for the wine he had just bought. But there was also a fiscal motive for keeping tabs on taverners. The tax on wine sold at retail in the city's inns was a major revenue source for the Capitoline treasury. Although its collection was leased to a private tax-farmer, the conservators guaranteed the latter's rights so their police were supposed to hunt for innkeepers who evaded paying. Knowing that at times they were up against big operators, the straordinari were themselves capable of the grand gesture. In one investigation in 1641 the straordinario maggiore put together a team consisting not only of his own two subordinate straordinari minori and two others belonging to another agent, but also a notary. They headed for the caverns cut into the Janiculum hill at the Porta Settimiana where innkeepers stored their wine, and went through the caves looking for casks that did not sport the proper ticket from the tax-farmer. Having the

---

[12] ASR, Bandi, vol. 18, 28 March 1643. *Regesti* 4:169; 5:57. Regulations prohibiting the conservators from lowering fines date from at least 1571; ASC, cred. I, vol. 38, decreti, 312r. In 1618 they were ordered not to impose fines in their own houses, but only in their official audiences at the Capitol in the presence of the appropriate officials. However, they were offered some latitude to reduce the fines of offending artisans. They were limited to reducing a ten scudi fine by no more than three scudi; fines from three to ten scudi might be lowered by no more than two scudi. How reductions affected the amount going to the *straordinari* is not mentioned in this 1618 resolution; ASC, cred. IV, vol. 106, tabella of 1618, 106v. ASC, cred. VI, vol. 63, interessi diversi, 31r, 28r. ASV, arm. IV, vol. 80, edict of 8 August 1628.

notary with them meant they could immediately begin the process of documentation necessary to bring the smugglers to trial.[13]

While I have been unable to locate records of the "findings" or *invenzioni*—the term both for an infraction and the fine it entailed—for the first half of the seventeenth century, some do survive for intermittent years between 1683 and 1735. These are a useful register of what the market police were actually doing while the flow of edicts in rarely changed language eddied around them. The forty-four infractions listed in January 1695 included a butcher for rotten meat and prohibited "additives," a baker for thirty underweight loaves, a tavernkeeper for using a false wine measure, a chickenseller for not showing his scales, and a seller of candles for not having the official candle prices posted. The fines levied on *invenzioni* in 1683 and 1684 are reported in more detail than in the later volume. Few exceeded one scudo and most ranged from 30 to 50 baiocchi. Bread infractions carried higher penalties, however, of two or three scudi. A tavernkeeper was caught overcharging clients by fiscal agents who collected eight scudi and a further sum to pay a notary. Romano Trabucco, coal merchant, paid the largest fine, 12.5 scudi, for contravening the edicts and "impertinence" to the market police; his case, like that of the tavernkeeper, was destined for the courts. On a penalty of 50 baiocchi the civic treasury received 23 and the straordinari 27, to divide among a team of three men. When a fine totaled 30 baiocchi, the fisc garnered 13.[14]

The sums generated by market infractions seem small, yet they occupied a large place in the outlook of civic officials. A report they prepared for a meeting of the congregation of the Annona and Grascia in April 1644 reveals their anxiety about the loss of *invenzioni* to papal officials "usurping" their jurisdiction. While the political implications of the problem were important, financial ones also clearly bothered them. At issue was the conservators' right to collect fines on the violations of all market edicts, whether or not they had published them. The report argued that *invenzioni* by the agents of the president of the Grascia and the prefect of the Annona in particular belonged to the civic treasury. The money involved was significant. In 1614, it claimed, infractions of an edict emitted by the president of the Annona against the sale of a certain type of bread by innkeepers had netted more than 600 scudi for the Capitoline fisc. Similarly a single fine levied by the president of the Grascia and turned over to the conservators had produced the 200 scudi needed to construct rooms for the fiscal procurator at the Capitol.[15]

Why civic officials might be concerned about the funds generated by tradesmen's penalties is suggested by an emergency meeting of the committee on *rega-*

[13] ASR, Tribunale dei conservatori, vol. 49, atti frammenti, includes several leaves, dating from 1634 and after, which refer to activities of the *straordinari maggiori*. See also ASR, Tribunale dei conservatori, vol. 59, processi, 1641, pt. 2, 6 August 1641. Romani, 169.

[14] ASC, cred. VI, vol. 88, invenzioni (1695–1735), 1r–2v; ASC, cred. IX, vol. 21, pene (1683–1684), 1r, 3r, 8v.

[15] Biblioteca Corsini, ms. 1654, "Relatione," 170–71.

glie in 1618. Confronting a shortfall in the money available to purchase *regaglie*, these thousands of scudi worth of nougat, pepper, gloves, and wax given to a vast array of real and venal civic and papal officeholders each Christmas, they stressed the fact that fines were their principal revenue source. The committee, which included the papal treasurer general but was otherwise a Capitoline body, recommended strong measures to ensure that *invenzioni* did not disappear into the conservators' pockets or slip into other expenditure items. They knew the magistrates had to raise at least 2,000 scudi a year from penalties to balance the *regaglie* portion of the budget.[16]

Of course fines were a political matter too. The pro-Capitoline authors of the complaint made to the congregation of the Annona and Grascia in 1644 cried out against invasions of their rights. They accused four different papal officials of recent violations of established civic prerogatives. The governor of Rome, the prefect of the Annona, and the president of the Grascia had all been guilty of receiving the fines paid by artisans for infractions of market edicts. They charged a fourth official, the auditor of the cardinal chamberlain, with usurping their role as the court of first instance in such cases. To these encroaching officers they held up an exemplary one. When the agents of the cardinal chamberlain made *invenzioni* for violations of edicts posted by "cardinals and chamberlains [sic]," the report claimed, they took them to the conservators to be fined. It urged the prefect of the Annona and the president of the Grascia to instruct their men to do the same.[17]

The congregation of the Annona and Grascia was not eager to undermine the authority of the conservators. At the meeting held on 7 April 1644 it responded favorably, if dryly, to the civic arguments, reminding all concerned to observe the guidelines set forth in 1618. It also repeated an instruction made in 1635 to the auditor of the chamberlain that, when hearing appeals from the conservators' market judgments, he could confirm a fine they had set, or revoke it, but he could not lower it.[18]

The resolutions the congregation made in 1644 were consistent with a general pattern of support for the authority of the Capitoline officials over the two decades covered in the record. In 1628 the congregation decreed that judges of the Roman Curia could not issue exemptions from the marketplace regulations contained in the conservators' edicts. Twice in one year they upheld the jurisdiction of the civic magistrate responsible for enforcing the municipal wine tax against the cardinal chamberlain and the auditor of the apostolic chamber. In 1630 they decided favorably in the appeal of a *straordinario* imprisoned by the auditor of the apostolic chamber and released by the conservators. No one could follow the congregation's

[16] ASC, cred. IV, vol. 106, tabella of 1618, 105r–8r.
[17] Biblioteca Corsini, ms. 1654, "Relatione," 169–74.
[18] ASC, cred. VI, vol. 63, interessi diversi, 33r, 47r.

deliberations over these years and claim that the papal government was riding roughshod over local officials.[19]

Yet there were real tensions at the point at which the conservators' jurisdiction met that of the two clerks of the apostolic chamber responsible for food supplies. The first of these papal officers to appear in the sixteenth century was the prefect of the Annona; awkwardly at times, the Capitol gradually made its accommodation with him, slowly turning over grain pricing and supply supervision. The second, the president of the Grascia, who dealt with meat, oil, and cheese, separated himself from the prefect of the Annona sometime after 1575. Relations between him and the conservators were more intimate and more ambiguous than with the keeper of the grain. One thing that kept them intimate was that the prices of meat, cheese, and oil were allowed to respond in some measure to the law of supply and demand; since they changed frequently papal and civic officers had to act in a coordinated way on a regular basis. Then too the conservators had lost their authority to decide these fluctuating prices within the past few decades and the memory of the loss may still have rankled.[20]

A deeper source of tension lay in the whole principle of having one group of authorities set rules and prices and another group enforce them. How such a system broke down the jurisdiction of the conservators was starkly revealed in the complaint prepared for the congregation of the Annona and Grascia in 1644. When, according to its author or authors, the market police cite bakers for making "bad" bread, the bakers sometimes argue that they had been given spoiled grain by the office of the Annona and have the prefect send word to the conservators to lift the penalties. Trying to pin down the truth in such situations, the conservators "tire themselves out going in circles every day." Worse follows, for "the prefects draw [the cases] to themselves, and do not send word and begin themselves to exercise and extort the jurisdiction."[21]

The operation of marketplace controls on less controlled products like oil had the same results for different reasons. Take another example in the 1644 report. Since oil prices might change daily depending on the arrival of supplies at the river port, the civic market agents took to checking directly with the president of the Grascia on the current legal limits. From there it was a simple step—much simpler than making the trip to the Capitol—to have him fine the transgressors

[19] Ibid., 17r, 23r, 24r, 27r. For a different view see Ruggiero, 76.

[20] Ruggiero, 78–79, 91. Ruggiero's discussion highlights the relative obscurity of the president of the Grascia by comparison to the prefect of the Annona. She quotes an eighteenth-century treatise that reveals the continued close relations of the president of the Grascia and the conservators (p. 90). See also Revel, 37–38; Gross, 178–81, 189–90; Marina D'Amelia, "La crisi dell'egemonia urbana: Approvigionamenti e consumo della carne a Roma nel XVIII secolo," *MEFRM* 87 (1975), pt. 2: 495–534. In the present state of research it is not yet possible to date precisely the conservators' loss of the power to set prices, but it was definitive by the 1620s; ASC, cred. VI, vol. 63, interessi diversi, 18r. Cf. Rodocanachi, *Institutions*, 320, 337.

[21] Biblioteca Corsini, ms. 1654, "Relatione," 172.

they had detected. "And so the *straordinari* begin to bring *invenzioni* to the presidents and thus this jurisdiction is usurped."[22]

Given the complexities of the Roman system of regulation and the fact that it was undergoing change, Capitoline jurisdiction was hard to define and easy to violate. The conservators' frequent charges that the auditor of the cardinal chamberlain was overstepping his bounds, by hearing cases of market infractions before they had or by lowering the fines they had imposed, were another sign of its vulnerability. On the other hand, cases going to the "wrong" tribunal were a threat to prestige that agitated papal officials just as often as civic ones, so Capitoline complaints on that score were scarcely unique. Yet the conservators had cause to be nervous about the encroachments of the clerks of the chamber, whom many early modern commentators saw as their rivals. Despite the support of the congregation of the Annona and Grascia, they found themselves losing business to the prefect of the Annona and the president of the Grascia for humdrum and utterly practical reasons.[23]

It is useful to return for a moment to the critic of Capitoline market regulation who pointed out that the conservators' own estates supplied the products whose prices they were supposed to control. He was unhappy with the situation of course and wanted the Romans out of this arena of government, recommending that a higher authority in the form of a cardinalatial congregation be placed over them.[24] But as we have seen, there was already a cardinalatial congregation supervising provisioning, the congregation of the Annona and Grascia, which was at least intermittently active. It not only included the civic magistrates in its deliberations but upheld their role in the marketplace. Did the idea that the conservators might have a conflict of interest in enforcing market regulation ever occur to papal officials? If it did, it did not bother them enough to alter existing arrangements. Judging from their general practice, the theory of administration to which curial and civic officials alike adhered was that "interested" parties knew best how to monitor themselves. Landowning patricians were the experts in matters relating to agriculture, and by extension in the urban venues at which its produce was marketed. Although I have focused here on the role of the conservators, the same men might be found judging cases of damage to vineyards when they held the office of master justiciery or assessing penalties for thefts of livestock when they served as consuls of the guild of agriculturalists. These Roman gentlemen would perhaps have answered their critic by saying that the privileges of jurisdiction were a form of self-policing.

In the next chapter patricians meet "greedy tradespeople" again, but this time

[22] Ibid., 172–73. See also Revel, 47.

[23] Biblioteca Corsini, ms. 1654, "Relatione," 170, 173–74; ASC, cred. VI, vol. 63, interessi diversi, 33r, 47r; Rodocanachi, *Institutions*, 337 n. 4.

[24] BAV, Chigi, N III 84, 126v.

inside their guilds rather than outside in the marketplace. The Capitol's jurisdiction over the organizations of Roman artisans and tradesmen had a slightly different character than that traced here, but the theme of privilege and police emerges forcefully. So too does the image of social superiors directing their plebeian neighbors.

Chapter Eight

GUILDS

WHILE THE CAPITOLINE role in the marketplace clearly expressed the principle that it was the executor and enforcer of laws emanating from other authorities, its jurisdiction over the guilds of tradesmen and craftsmen was more extensive, open-ended, and intrusive. The conservators had a great deal of freedom in their relations with the corporations; they were the immediate *signori superiori* who gave them orders and monitored the minute details of their internal life.[1] Only with their feudatories did the Roman People exercise power with so untrammeled a hand as with the artisans. While papal officials also dealt with the guilds, the division of labor between curial and civic officials gave the Capitol more consistent responsibility for them. Here their authority was less circumscribed both in theory and in practice than that which they wielded in the marketplace.

Guilds were increasingly numerous in the Rome of the late sixteenth and seventeenth centuries. Associations of tradesmen dated back to medieval times in many cases, but they multiplied, often by dividing into more specialized groups, in the decades around and after the Council of Trent. Legally the guild or *universitas* was distinct from the confraternity or *societas*, but the links between them were manifold and complex. Often a corporate or guild organization developed out of a prior association of men in the same trade who gathered regularly for pious purposes. At the moment a collective structure was first imposed on a given group of workers it might be difficult indeed to distinguish the religious from the professional motivations; trade guilds may even have prompted the founding of new confraternities at times. Because of the fluidity of relations between religious sodalities and occupational corporations, the great boost that Catholic renewal gave to associational life in sixteenth-century Rome must have contributed to the proliferation of guilds. Population growth may well have too. By the 1620s some 24,000 masters and workers composed at least seventy-one corporations, and perhaps two-thirds of these had been created since 1500.[2]

---

[1] Referring to an edict of the conservators three days before, the officers of the masons' guild tell members that the "lord superiors" (*signori superiori*) have ordered them to take charge of one of the city gates in a plague prevention measure. They then go on to say that this task must be carefully organized, "so as to be able promptly to serve the *signori superiori*." ASR, 30 N.C., uff. 25 (Raymundus) 1630, pt. 1, 155v (9 January 1630). See also the statutes of the fishmongers' guild (1636), ASR, Biblioteca, Statuti, 449/7, chap. 6. For municipal policing of guilds in other European cities see Gerald L. Soliday, *Community in Conflict: Frankfurt Society in the Seventeenth and Early Eighteenth Centuries* (Hanover, N.H., 1974), 139; Richard Mackenney, *Tradesmen and Traders: The World of the Guilds in Venice and Europe c.1250–1650* (London, 1987), 25; Farr, 35.

[2] These figures for masters, workers, and guilds are provided by an undated six-page manuscript in

The Capitoline administration supported the formation of guilds of artisans and traders, backed up their privileged authority over those exercising a particular craft, helped to mediate their disputes, and policed them. Civic and curial policy harmonized perfectly in favoring corporate forms of organization and in giving the conservators special control over them. While a guild intent on revising or formalizing its procedures would seek papal confirmation of its statutes as well as that of the senator and conservators, and would freely appeal for papal assistance in a serious conflict, papal officials generally had limited and uneven contacts with corporations. What determined the degree of curial intervention in an artisan association were fiscal issues or concern about food prices and supplies. Surveillance and discipline of the internal life of the guilds as such were duties that fell to the Roman People, undisturbed by the predatory clerks of the chamber.[3]

Policing craft corporations began with reviewing any new or revised guild statutes before they could take effect. Once approved, these rules could not be changed in any detail without endorsement by the conservators. Increasing annual dues, raising fines on members, altering election procedures, and, occasionally, lowering apprentices' wages entailed getting the civic magistrates' permission. The conservators wanted to know who held guild offices and, when they were not kept informed, issued a public edict ordering all corporations to forward the names of their consuls and chamberlain to the Capitol.[4]

BAV, Barb. lat. 4835, 1r–5v, published by Paglia, 282–85. I have tentatively dated the manuscript to the 1620s, but the period of the war of Castro in 1641–1644 cannot be entirely ruled out. This short document, which includes a count of the number of horses and carts available in the city, the number of men in the militias of Rome's four vassal towns, and the number of Roman gentlemen capable of bearing arms, seems to have been drafted with an eye to some sort of threatened civil emergency, perhaps invasion or plague. The document mentions Gregory XV (1621–1623), which establishes the *terminus a quo* as 1621. Two crises in the Valtellina, in 1621 and 1625, as well as the war of the Mantuan succession in 1628–1630 and the accompanying plague in 1630, could have been the occasions for making this count. Cf. Rodocanachi, *Corporations* 1:xxiii–xxiv; Delumeau, *Vie* 1:377–79.

The first to note that the peak period of growth in the number of guilds was the sixteenth and seventeenth centuries was Amintore Fanfani, *Storia del lavoro in Italia*, 2d ed., enl. and illust. (Milan, 1959), 175. Estimates of the number of guilds and craft-based confraternities in Rome vary. Martini reproduced figures showing that forty-seven new guilds were founded in the sixteenth and seventeenth centuries in Rome, for a total in 1700 of seventy-nine, *Arti*, 40. Rodocanachi listed ninety-six guilds in *Corporations* 2:58. See also Delumeau, *Vie* 1:369–70. Paglia provides chronological graphs of the foundations of new craft confraternities, 320–21; these are based on the data of Maroni Lumbroso and Martini, 441–45.

[3] For relations between guilds and the pope or papal officials see *Regesti* 4:185, 224; 5:13, 51. I am presently at work on a more detailed study of the relations between the Roman guilds and the civic administration, the clerks of the chamber, and the pope.

[4] Many manuscript copies of guild statutes preserve written confirmations by the conservators, as well as by the senator and sometimes by papal brief (*breve*). Martini provides the most complete list of the locations of these statutes, *Arti*, 267–302. The secretary of the conservators charged guilds five *giuli*, or half a scudo, for the document of confirmation, according to a fee list of 1601 in ASV, arm. IV, vol. 45, 116r. ASC, cred. I, vol. 28, decreti, 0067v (29 May 1581); ASC, cred. XI, vol. 15, lettere, 161 (1661); *Regesti* 4:165. The conservators seem to have proposed new election procedures to

Monitoring guild meetings was a priority for the civic magistrates for which they had two main instruments. A trade corporation had to get a written permit signed by one of the conservators before an assembly of its members. Often these permits stipulated the topics that could be discussed at the meeting and they always required that one of the conservators' staff of retainers, the *fedeli*, be in attendance. Thus Capitoline officials not only controlled the agenda but kept themselves informed at first hand about what transpired in the gatherings of Roman artisans and tradesmen.[5]

These procedures for guild surveillance were in full vigor in the first half of the seventeenth century. Many permits for assemblies survive, and guild minutes often record that the conservators' license with the list of topics approved for discussion at a meeting was read aloud as the first item of business. In 1630 the butchers objected to the fact that the conservator, Giacomo Filonardi, had restricted their agenda to discussion of how many lambs they were purchasing for the spring slaughter and refused to hold their meeting as an indication of their displeasure. Meeting minutes also attest to the regular attendance of the conservators' agents. The *fedele* was usually tolerated and sometimes even played a role in the business of the gathering, by extracting names in sortition elections or acting as witness to the notary's record. Sometimes, however, he was a source of tension; the blacksmiths objected so vociferously to the *fedele*'s presence at a meeting of guild officers in 1630 that the case eventually wound up before the tribunal of the conservators.[6]

There were loopholes in the system. If a guild called itself an "academy," as did the artists of the Academy of St. Luke, or a "college," as did the notaries or the wool merchants, rather than a corporation (*universitas*), it did not need to obtain a permit or endure the watchful eyes of a civic agent. Such terms connoted an association of men of greater social status, and perhaps education, than did a trade guild. Nor were such checks necessary if workers met as a confraternity rather than a guild, though sometimes a priest or sacristan is recorded in attendance at business meetings of tradesmen's confraternities. Sometimes too the con-

---

the fishmongers: ASR, 30 N.C., uff. 2 (Bonanni) 1631, pt. 2, 540v (24 July 1631). For the lowering of wages by the master doughnut makers (*ciambellari*) in 1643 see ASC, cred. XI, vol. 14, lettere, 93r–v.

[5] Delumeau, *Vie* 1:390. Rodocanachi states that the senator or cardinal protector could also authorize meetings, but I have not yet found any permits in the notarial archives that bear their signatures, *Corporations* 1: lxxxvii–lxxxiii.

[6] I have departed somewhat from the standard view summarized by Delumeau, *Vie* 1:390–91. The sources I have found most useful for detailing the interaction between civic authorities and artisan corporations are the minutes of guild meetings taken down by notaries and found among the notarial records of the 30 Notai Capitolini in the ASR; see Nussdorfer, "Writing and the Power of Speech: Notaries and Artisans in Baroque Rome," in *Culture and Identity in Early Modern Europe, 1500–1800*, ed. Barbara Diefendorf and Carla Hesse (forthcoming). For the butchers: ASR, 30 N.C., uff. 25 (Raymundus) 1630, pt. 3, 27r–29r. For the *fedele*'s role in a sortition at the soapmakers' meeting: ASR, 30 N.C., uff. 25 (Raymundus) 1630, pt. 3, 706v. For the blacksmiths' protest: Tribunale dei conservatori, vol. 57, processi, 1630. The case bears the date 20 June 1630.

servators seem to have accepted the custom of having just the officials of very large guilds, such as the tailors or carpenters, gather for "private" meetings without the usual restrictions. This practice may explain the anger of the blacksmiths' officers when the *fedele* insisted he should attend their gathering.[7]

Despite these avenues of escape, however, the Capitoline magistrates kept in touch with the internal operations of many associations of working people in Baroque Rome. When the conservators heard in 1627 that the fishmongers had chosen a chamberlain who did not know how to write for the second year in a row, they intervened to make them elect someone who did. And they warned that if their *fedele* reported that there was any "noise" at the meeting, two men speaking at the same time, for instance, they would swiftly impose punishment. When the vegetable sellers (*ortolani*) could not find any willing replacements for their outgoing officers in 1634, they recorded that they would give a full account of the situation to the conservators, who in fact seem not to have done anything in particular about it.[8] What is significant here is not that civic officials always interfered when a guild had internal difficulties, but that the leadership of the vegetable sellers considered informing the "lord superiors" of problems that arose, or at least could invoke such a possibility as a threat. Such habits suggest that the formal Capitoline mechanisms for controlling guild life encouraged self-policing by guild officials, and could even be a resource for them when facing recalcitrant members.

Surveillance and discipline of the corporations were a major concern of the civic magistrates, but their involvement with the guilds extended beyond this in two broad directions. The first followed logically from their role as enforcers of the rules of the marketplace and led to their giving orders, or making adjustments in orders already given, to particular trade organizations about the commerce in their products. The second took relations between the Roman People and Roman workers out of the immediate economic sphere to a more lofty plane of communal needs, on which, however, the guilds were expected to contribute their members' decidedly down-to-earth muscle.

The Capitoline authorities found artisan and tradesmen's corporations a useful adjunct to the other instruments with which they regulated the marketplace. Guild officers functioned as channels of communication between the conservators and their members, and meetings fulfilled a similar purpose on a larger scale. Sometimes this meant more effective policing. Instead of waiting to catch vegetable sellers who threw their refuse underneath their stalls—a practice that contemporaries feared bred disease miasmas—the fiscal procurator of the Capitol sent

---

[7] Meetings with no permit or *fedele* are recorded in the following citations: ASR, 30 N.C., uff. 20 (Camillus) 1630, pt. 1, 411r–v, 436r; ASR, 30 N.C., uff. 2 (Bonanni) 1633, pt. 3, 392r; ASR, 30 N.C., uff. 25 (Raymundus) 1630, pt. 4, 493r.

[8] For the fishmongers: ASR, 30 N.C., uff. 2 (Bonanni) 1626, pt. 2, 331r; ASR, 30 N.C., uff. 2 (Bonanni) 1627, pt. 2, 785r–v, 786r. For the vegetable sellers: ASR, 30 N.C., uff. 2 (Bonanni) 1634, pt. 1, 43r–44v, 71r.

them a stern warning at their monthly meeting in May 1633.[9] The fact that the orders came from the civic prosecutor gave them extra bite, and the fact that they appeared on the consuls' agenda implicated the guild's own representatives in their enforcement.

Two-way communication between civic officials and trade corporations also helped to soften a market policing system based on public edicts and prosecution and make it somewhat more flexible. Thus, when the gardeners wanted to shift the location at which they unloaded their vegetable-laden mules, they chose a new site and sought approval from the civic magistrates. Whatever practices the conservators' *bandi* addressed were a potential object of negotiation between the Capitol and the guild in question. This expectation was explicit in the language of an edict aimed at the millers in 1639, for it demanded that millers who wanted to sell flour as well as simply grind grain, must obtain written permission from the conservators. On behalf of its members the millers' corporation then petitioned the magistrates for such permission, which was granted for a provisional period of six months. The butchers launched an effort to "moderate" several key articles of an edict from the conservators in 1630 in a more strident tone. They complained that they labored from dawn to dusk "so that everyone would be well served," and if they had to bear the further restrictions imposed by the recent *bando* they would all go out of business. Protests from the butchers' guild were chronic. One of the city's most tightly regulated trades, they were almost always lobbying public officials to ease their rules. Like other corporations, they saw two-way communication with the Capitol as a vehicle for changing policies as well as submitting to them.[10]

The second broad category of civic engagement with the guilds was of a different nature. The Capitoline administration, and papal officials as well, regarded the tradesmen's associations as mobilizers of labor for a startling variety of public "needs," from military to ceremonial. Though the notion was never articulated, it seems to have been understood by all parties involved in government in Rome that the conservators were the proper officials to organize such efforts. Sometimes they acted on their own initiative and sometimes they conveyed instructions from other authorities, but in both cases they relied on guild officers to see that their wishes were carried out.

Their wishes covered a wide array of benefits to the community. In the sixteenth century they included requests for funds to pay for a new printing of the city statutes, for example, or to maintain several hundred sick beggars in the new beggar hospital. These informal methods of raising money for civic necessities were shouldered out as the seventeenth century advanced, however, and the papal

---

[9] ASR, 30 N.C., uff. 2 (Bonanni) 1633, pt. 2, 30v.

[10] For the vegetable sellers: ASR, 30 N.C., uff. 2 (Bonanni) 1630, pt. 3, 534v. For the millers: ASC, cred. XI, vol. 14, lettere, 79r; ASV, arm. IV, vol. 63, p. 201, edict of 8 October 1639. For the butchers: ASR, 30 N.C., uff. 25 (Raymundus) 1630, pt. 5, 446v, 449r–v; ASV, arm. IV, vol. 52, p. 34, edict of 8 October 1630.

treasury began imposing regular fiscal levies on the guilds. What the Capitoline magistrates most frequently called for from the guilds was unpaid services. Sometimes this was festive service. When the Roman People wanted to mount a large civic procession, they ordered the guilds to round up their members and turn out. In 1536 the corporations figured in one of the last great Carnival parades of the Renaissance papacy. Artisans, grouped by guild, made up the bulk of the celebratory procession the Roman People promoted in 1632 to give thanks that plague had spared the city. A petition of 1570 nicely illuminates the assumptions people in Rome made about the relations between the Capitol and the craft corporations and about the artisans' ceremonial obligations. In that request the Franciscans at Santa Maria in Aracoeli asked the conservators to command all guild consuls to attend the solemn mass at the beginning of the year in their church, "since it is the most important one performed there."[11] In many eyes a distinctive component of the municipality's arsenal of spectacular resources was public display of urban workers.

More frequent than festive labor was military and, especially, public health service. Written into the statutes of some corporations was the expectation that the Roman People might require them to send members to do gate duty or respond to other civic "needs."[12] A list of nine trades "not enrolled as soldiers" in the 1620s leaves the impression that the several dozen others preceding these *were* so enrolled and contributed to urban defense.[13] Artisans did make up a hastily assembled militia when the city faced a hostile army in 1642, but the guild role in organizing this effort, if any, is obscure. The guild role is strikingly clear, however, during the early 1630s when the plague outbreak in northern Italy threatened Rome. Then, standing guard at the city gates became an active responsibility of the corporations with each of twelve gates assigned to a particular trade, as we shall see in Chapter 10. "Other needs" in that effort, such as mattresses for the pesthouses, drew on guild requisitions too.

On a more mundane level civic needs translated into many small, sometimes irritating, demands. Guilds were supposed to hire the official "drummers of the Roman People" whenever they held a procession, usually on the feast of their patron saint. In 1618 the blacksmiths got so angry at the conservators for insisting that they pay for the drummers' cloaks as well that they took their protests to

---

[11] Rodocanachi, *Institutions*, 220, 274–75; Delumeau, *Vie* 2:415; Reinhard, *Papstfinanz* 2:311; Rietbergen, 193; Filippo Clementi, *Il carnevale romano nelle cronache contemporanee* (Rome, 1899), 301; Fortunato Crostarosa, *Le milizie urbane della citta' di Roma* (Rome, 1897), 69; Gigli, *Diario*, 128; ASC, Protocolli, 2999; cf. Delumeau, *Vie* 1:390. Exceptionally, the guilds were called on to contribute funds to the papal treasury during the war of the Mantuan succession in 1630; see fishmongers' meeting, ASR, 30 N.C., uff. 2 (Bonanni) 1630, pt. 1, 652r–v, 685r. For guild service to the Venetian state in the sixteenth and seventeenth centuries see Mackenney, 219–20.

[12] See, for example, those of the mattress makers (1515), ASR, Biblioteca, Statuti, 571, 17.

[13] Paglia, 283, 285. Of course artisans organized by rione rather than guild made up the 300-member civic militia known as the company of capotori and contestabili; for more on this militia see Chapters 5 and 14.

the cardinal chamberlain. Corporations had to handle some of the logistics of the annual Carnival races. An item in the Capitoline budget allotted ten scudi to the blacksmiths to supply horses for these contests each year. According to a complaint from the hotelkeepers, taverners, and hay sellers in 1643, however, the smiths were keeping the money and taking *their* horses without any remuneration. Not being subject to the blacksmiths' guild, the petitioners argued, they did not see why they should be harassed in this fashion, a view that found support among the conservators.[14]

The special subordination of the artisans and tradesmen to the Roman People was emphasized architecturally in the layout of the palace of the conservators itself. On the ground floor beneath the dignified public spaces of the *piano nobile*, where the councils met and the magistrates sat in judgment, were the tribunals or *consolati* of the guilds with their doors opening onto the portico and the plaza beyond. These small courtrooms were the site at which commercial disputes involving sums below fifty scudi found an airing before the officials of the relevant trade.[15] Although some corporate judicial activity may have gone on elsewhere, the civic authorities wanted to have guild sentences pronounced on the Capitol. Since a percentage of guild fines usually went to the Capitoline treasury, emitting judgments in the *consolati* helped to ensure that a revenue source did not slip away unnoticed. While most associations met in the chapels or churches of their patron saints, some corporations also used the tribunals for their general meetings or rented quarters in the "new palace" across the plaza after its completion in the 1650s. Rather than avoiding proximity to the civic magistrates, they seemed to view the Capitol as a location lending them added prestige.[16]

Accepting their formal subjection, Roman artisans knew that their statutes allowed them to define a sphere of "private law" for their trade and that it was the Roman People that protected that sphere. In exchange they tendered deference and obedience to the *signori superiori*. The anonymous critic we have already met in the preceding chapter reminds us not to let the asymmetry of this relationship

[14] Rodocanachi, *Corporations* 2:417. For the blacksmiths: ASR, Camerale II, Arti e mestieri, vol. 15, bu. 35. For the hotelkeepers: ASC, cred. XI, vol. 14, lettere, 80v. Since the fourteenth century, city statutes had required guilds to pay a tax for the traditional Carnival games at Monte Testaccio; *Statuta almae urbis*, bk. 3, chap. 87.

[15] Pietrangeli, "Iscrizioni," 129–33; Rodocanachi, *Corporations* 1:lxvi–lxvii. For guild tribunals see also *Statuta almae urbis*, bk. 1, chap. 90; bk. 3, chap. 42. Book 3, chapter 42 of the city statutes was expanded to cover disputes between guilds and clients who were not members of the trade in the papal bull confirming the city statutes in 1580; this expanded jurisdiction was reaffirmed the following year in a papal brief; *Bullarium* 8:332–35. Rodocanachi, *Institutions*, 309. For the few surviving judicial records of the guild tribunals see the series in ASR, Universita' di arti e mestieri.

[16] *Statuta almae urbis*, bk. 3, chap. 45; *Regesti* 6:170; ASC, cred. IV, vol. 106, tabella, 106v; ASC, cred. I, vol. 32, decreti, 0082r (14 November 1614); Gonippo Morelli, *Le corporazioni romane di arti e mestieri dal XIV al XIX secolo* (Rome, 1937), 12; Rodocanachi, *Capitole*, 166. Examples of guild statutes with provisions that a percentage of fines go to the civic treasury include the masons (1639, chap. 5) and the fishmongers (1636, p. 30); see Martini for locations of unpublished guild statutes.

blind us to what its parties had in common. Attacking the guilds in the same terms as the conservators, he saw both Roman gentlemen and Roman tradesmen prospering at the expense of the consumer. "These guild officers [*consolati*] are the ruin of everything and they do nothing but buy forty or fifty straw mattresses for soldiers when needed, which, with all the extortions [they inflict] they make us pay for at a very high price."[17]

In sum, the Capitoline jurisdiction over the corporations overlapped with that over the marketplace in many details, but was also subtly distinct from it. Civic officials certainly could play the same role with the guilds that they played in the markets, enforcing or executing the orders of others, but their relationship with the corporations was not confined to that. They were free to examine very closely what the artisans were doing as collective bodies, and to allow them to do it or not. They could call on the unpaid services of guild members, and the help of guild officers in coordinating it, for whatever they decided were civic needs. They approved their rules and they heard appeals from their judgments; they fined them and collected those fines into the Capitoline treasury. Other people assumed that the conservators were the brokers, the appropriate intermediaries, to whom they could turn if they wanted something from the craft corporations.

How would we characterize the hierarchical relationship embodied in this behavior, acknowledging its similarity to that between municipal governments and guilds in many other European cities? It was faintly seigneurial in flavor, although it was not a feudal tie in any precise juridical sense. As we shall see, the Roman People had real vassals and they were not guilds. Yet the subordination of associations of artisans and tradesmen to an administration of landed gentlemen dated back at least to the fourteenth century in Rome and, while not a formal seigneurial bond, it had many of the same features. The papal administration did not disturb these traditional relations, but instead took advantage of them, as we find during the plague threat discussed in Chapter 10. The powerful forces keeping social hierarchy in place in seventeenth-century Rome ensured that laboring people would not challenge the "lord superiors," especially since they protected guild privileges.

For a different evocation of hierarchy, that between city and country, we turn now to consider the power that the Capitol wielded outside the walls of Rome. The Roman People possessed four fiefs in the surrounding territory, making them lords in legal as well as social terms. There, like any titled individual, they exercised a full-fledged feudal jurisdiction, dispensing seigneurial justice to their rural vassals.

[17] BAV, Chigi, N III 84, 126v–27r. For two examples of civic guarantees for guild privileges see Romani, 171, and the statutes of the soapmakers (1605, 6r).

Chapter Nine

VASSALS

THE ROMAN PEOPLE as a corporate body held in fief four towns scattered in the city's environs to the north and south: Magliano in Sabina, Vitorchiano, Barbarano Romano, and Cori. In these territories the Roman civic magistrates acted as lords in the same manner as contemporary aristocratic feudatories. In each subject community statutes provided for some local control via elected councils and officials called priors, but the Capitol sent a Roman as chief criminal magistrate or *podesta'* and supervised finance, justice, politics, and administration. Like other lords in the early modern Papal States, however, the Capitol acknowledged the ultimate sovereignty of the pope. This showed up in small but important details. A council decision to make an official visitation of the fiefs in 1625, for instance, added the formulaic "if it pleases His Holiness." The podesta' whom the conservators sent to their vassal towns held their offices both by letters patent from the Roman People and by papal brief.[1] This sort of lordship owed something to medieval communal traditions of dominating nearby towns, but it borrowed chiefly from the vocabulary of feudalism with its language of fiefs, vassals, and seigneurs. It carried rights of jurisdiction and sometimes service obligations. But it was lordship articulated within a different political context than that of the Middle Ages. Early modern popes operated as sources of sovereign power, not as heads of a vassal hierarchy of shared authority. Although they allowed fief holders to exercise traditional rights, they kept a sharp eye out for any infringement of princely prerogative.

Late sixteenth-century pontiffs had in fact attacked private jurisdictions in the Papal States, seeking to eliminate these intermediate authorities between them and their subjects. Ironically this policy bore its scantiest fruit in the region closest to Rome, which we know today as Lazio.[2] Here feudal relations continued to predominate under a variety of feudatories, from old baronial families like the Orsini and Colonna to corporate bodies like the great Roman hospital of Santo Spirito and, in the seventeenth century, new papal dynasties like the Borghese and Barberini.

---

[1] ASC, cred. I, vol. 33, decreti, 0027v (29 October 1625); cred. XI, vol. 15, lettere (1648–1704), 3–4. On the fiefs of the Roman People see Pecchiai, *Roma*, 265–66 and Cesare D'Onofrio, *I vassalli del Campidoglio* (Rome, 1965).

[2] Roberto Volpi, *Le regioni introvabili: Centralizzazione e regionalizzazione dello Stato Pontificio* (Bologna, 1983), 66–68. For enduring feudal jurisdictions further afield, in the former duchy of Urbino, see Bandino Giacomo Zenobi, *Tarda feudalita' e reclutamento delle élites nello Stato Pontificio (secoli XV–XVIII)* (Urbino, 1983).

While more limited than medieval lordship, therefore, early modern lordship was pervasive and much sought after. The power wielded over vassal communities and the fees from seigneurial justice might bring concrete benefits; the aura of aristocratic prestige undoubtedly did. The fiefs of the Roman People kept the Capitoline magistrates busy with countless details of administration and public order, from appointing Lenten preachers to repairing communal walls. Subjects they could not touch in Rome, like homicide and grain provisioning, were part of their daily fare as seigneurs.[3] Feudal jurisdiction unquestionably brought them closer to the full exercise of what contemporaries understood as *governo* in their fiefs than their status as the heirs of the Roman Senate did in the city of Rome.

The Roman People had never taken their seigneurial prerogatives lightly. When in 1143 the *Senatus populusque romanus* reappeared in history after their Dark Age silence, the occasion that brought them back into written records was their effort to hammer the vassal town of Tivoli into line. They had entered the sixteenth century with control over at least six towns—including Tivoli and Velletri. Given their historically contentious relationship, it must have been a bitter blow when the Capitol lost Tivoli in 1522 and Velletri in 1537. Velletri at least continued to make a gesture of homage in the form of a yearly payment of forty-five scudi to the Capitoline treasury.[4]

Four towns thus remained in civic hands in the seventeenth century: Magliano in Sabina, overlooking the Tiber northeast of Rome, Barbarano and Vitorchiano off the Via Cassia to the north near Viterbo, and Cori, high on the steep western slopes of the Lepini mountains south of the city (see Map 3). Magliano and Cori had the juridical status of city (*citta'*), while Vitorchiano and Barbarano were less exalted *castelli*. Not much is known about the size and wealth of the subject towns in this period, though Magliano and Cori were presumably the two largest. Magliano had a population of 20,000 in the late sixteenth century, but experienced a drastic decline when the Tiber changed its course after 1605. Barbarano, the one fief for which a population figure exists, had 168 male heads of household in 1645.[5]

The Roman civic treasury drew little from its feudal possessions. Barbarano, the most lucrative of the four, was expected to yield only 105 scudi, the third part of its fines (*pene*), in the 1641 budget. The budget may not fully represent Bar-

---

[3] The richest source for daily relations with the subject towns are the summaries of letters of the conservators in the ASC. Five volumes of these summaries ("registri di lettere e memoriali con res-critti") survive for the period 1595 to 1735, with lacunae from 1604 to 1631. The ones I consulted in particular were ASC, cred. XI, vol. 13 (1595–1603) and vol. 14 (1632–1647).

[4] Otto of Freising, 353. Pecchiai, *Roma*, 265; Volpi, 65; Caravale, *Finanza*, 31; ASC, cred. IV, vol. 106, tabella (1641), 112v.

[5] For the late sixteenth-century population of Magliano see Giulio Silvestrelli, *Citta', castelli e terre della regione romana*, 2d ed., 2 vols. (Rome, 1940; repr., 1970), 2:473–74; for Barbarano see ASC, cred. XI, vol. 40, statuti della terra di Barbarano, 257r. The raw materials for a more detailed social, economic, and demographic portrait of these four communities await the researcher in the holdings of the ASC.

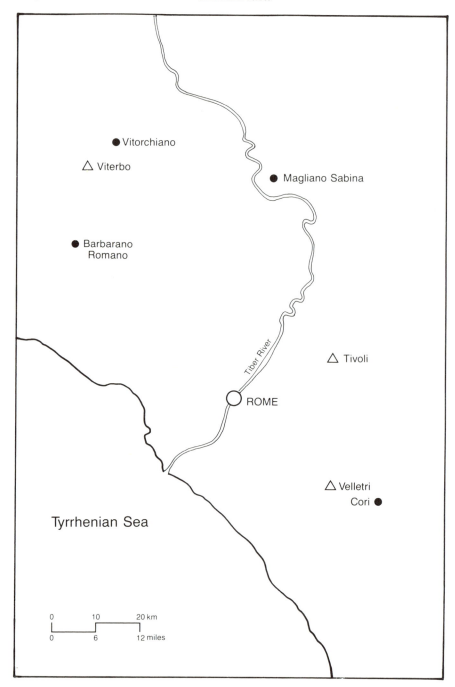

Map 3. Rome's Vassal Towns

barano's obligations, however, for an agreement of 1523 gave the Roman People the right to one-third of the town's income, which may have led to the assignment of certain properties to the Capitoline chamber.[6] The civic magistrates regularly auctioned off their Barbarano revenues to the highest bidder, the only fief for which they did this, and perhaps these included the rents from their landholdings in the town. Vitorchiano made annual payments to the Roman People for the salaries and costs of the conservators' palace majordomo and the twelve *fedeli* who served them, all of whom were natives of Vitorchiano. Neither Magliano nor Cori owed regular yearly sums to the Roman civic treasury, though they did have to pay the podesta' and the staff he employed to carry out his duties in the locality. Together the four fiefs provided a military force of over six hundred infantry and fifty cavalry, with the largest contingent coming from Cori. This was captained by Romans and included in papal calculations of Rome's defensive units.[7]

In each of the subject towns local statutes described the sources of public revenue—transit tolls, indirect taxes on goods bought or sold in the market, and monopolies such as the communal ovens—and prescribed their collection or lease by tax-farmers. The money raised provided for town needs or taxes owed to the apostolic chamber, while fines were expected to cover the costs of justice. As feudal lords, the Roman People were constrained both by the jealousy of the papal treasury and their vassals' statutes from exploiting their fiefs as sources of income. The conservators' chief financial concern was to make sure the towns did not overspend their income and go into debt, so they drew up their budgets and reviewed their accounts each year.[8]

It was not the money these towns provided the city treasury that made them important, but the seigneurial role in which they cast the civic authorities. The most important feature of lordship was jurisdiction, the strictly judicial activity of hearing cases and giving judgment and the broader mandate of keeping order in the vassal territory.[9] As we have seen, jurisdiction was a commodity highly

[6] ASC, cred. IV, vol. 106, tabella (1641), 136v. See also Pecchiai, *Roma*, 264 n. 1. The 1523 document was published in Cametti, 109. The Capitoline administration did own property in Barbarano in 1695, which was leased to local tenants. Cadastral surveys from Barbarano, but not, as far as I can tell, from the other fiefs, are in the ASC. The drafting of a new cadastral survey for Barbarano in 1695 is mentioned in cred. IV, vol. 2, decreti della congregazione, 2v, and the survey itself is found in cred. IV, vol. 92.

[7] In 1628 a man from Vitorchiano purchased one of the twelve posts as *fedele* from the widow of its previous owner for twenty scudi, according to the contract of sale in ASR, 30 N.C., uff. 2 (Bonanni) 1628, pt. 1, 289r–v. ASV, arm. IV, vol. 32, edict dated 3 December 1627 announces the Roman People's auction of Barbarano's revenues. ASC, cred. IV, vol. 106, tabella (1641), 136v; cred. VI, vol. 48, ristretti di dare et avere (1623–1625), 93r–94v; cred. XI, vol. 64, statuti di Vitorchiano, bk. 4, chap. 1.

[8] Statutes for Vitorchiano: ASC, cred. XI, vol. 64 (1614); for Magliano, cred. IV, vol. 90 (1575), and cred. XI, vol. 49 (1594); for Barbarano, cred. XI, vol. 103 (1484) and vol. 40 (1613 with additional provisions from 1645); for Cori, cred. IV, vol. 91 (1732). Copies of the statutes of 1549 and 1732 for Cori are also found in ASR, Biblioteca, Statuti.

[9] ASR, Biblioteca, Statuti, 795/1, *Statuta civitatis corae* (Rome, 1732), 252, 257. ASC, cred. XI,

prized in Rome and the value placed upon it sometimes charged relations between the Roman People, their subject towns, and papal officials.

The key agent in the exercise of the Capitol's feudal jurisdiction was the podesta' whom the conservators dispatched to each fief for terms of six or twelve months. The podesta' was recruited from the same Roman families that provided conservators and caporioni; he headed a staff that included a judge, a notary, a captain, and several constables (*birri* or *sbirri*). [10] He was a typical ancien régime magistrate in his combination of policing and criminal investigation with the job of pronouncing sentence. In practice his freedom of action was limited from below by the statutes of the vassal towns, which claimed varying degrees of authority for local officials, including the right to hear cases in disputes involving sums below a specified amount. His powers were further constrained from above by the fact that vassals continually appealed his sentences to the conservators in Rome. In 1606 the press of these appeals brought a ruling in the Capitoline council that feudal subjects could present their petitions to civic officials only on Fridays. [11]

The conservators, when they were not mitigating the penalties the podesta' imposed, depended on him to hunt out criminals, keep an eye on town councils and officials, and help settle local conflicts. In 1595, for example, when trouble arose with some priests in Barbarano, they directed the podesta' to follow the instructions sent him by the ecclesiastical authorities and to choose some townsmen to negotiate a settlement. In 1632 when a certain Antonio of Pescia asked them to lift a fine imposed on him "for passing through a meadow," the Roman officials were suspicious and requested that the podesta' investigate. Since the lord was unquestionably a potent resource in village disputes, they received countless petitions to take action on one side or another in local quarrels. Portia Riozzi of Cori, for example, appealed to the conservators to stop Antonio Luzzi from building next to her house. [12] In the sometimes delicate balancing act they had to perform the podesta' was the conservators' eyes and ears in the subject town.

Faced with the snarls of small town politics and anxious to protect their seigneurial position, civic officials looked closely at any proposals to change local statutes in their fiefs. When Vitorchiano in 1644 wished to raise the fines for damaging the flax fields, it first had to get the conservators' approval. Barbarano's

---

vol. 14, lettere, 4r. Serving as judges was also the most prestigious attribute of Parisian civic officials; Descimon, 119.

[10] The names of podesta' can be traced in the registers of letters patent issued by the conservators, ASC, cred. XI, vol. 19 (1615–1630) and vol. 20 (1632–1645). However, one must keep in mind that after 20 June 1624 it was permissible for the conservators to appoint "supernumerary podesta' " who did not perform official functions; the relevant civic decree is found in ASC, cred. I, vol. 32, 0282v. A council decree of 1614 describes the podesta' as having obtained their offices in one of two ways, "by bussola or by letters patent and papal brief;" ASC, cred. I, vol. 32, 0075r. I have found no other mention of the first method, which certainly did exist in the sixteenth century, in the seventeenth-century documents.

[11] ASC, protocollo no. 2202, 5 December 1606; ASC, cred. XI, vols. 13 and 14, lettere.

[12] ASC, cred. XI, vol. 13, lettere, 16v; cred. XI, vol. 14, lettere, 1r, 3r, 4r–v, 29v.

attempt to alter its constitution by electing forty councillors in perpetuity was quickly suppressed by the Capitoline councils in 1640.[13]

Innovation was suspect but not impossible, especially if lords and vassals both participated in the process. In the late sixteenth century Magliano successfully lobbied for new statutes by stressing that the initiative arose from "substantial men" in the community and that existing documents were so old and torn that the town was living "almost . . . without law." They prudently brought their proposed revisions to the Roman People for review, while expressing the pious hope that with new statutes "the city can live in a more orderly fashion [*piu' politicamente*]."[14] In the mid-1640s Barbarano confronted problems of tax collecting and property damage that were unforeseen at the time it received new town laws in 1610. The conservators ultimately added twenty-four "decrees" to Barbarano's statutes, carefully noting that the pope had told them verbally to resolve the difficulties.[15] They then convoked a general assembly of all male householders in the village, at which the podesta' and four local priors were present, to make sure that the community also approved the changes.

Politically the podesta', as the lord's agent in the locality, was the figure around whom tensions that rippled their way to the Capitol often erupted. The chancellor of the town of Vitorchiano in 1632, for example, a man named Giovanni Sacchi, did not want the podesta' to act as judge in several cases in which he was involved. At the same time he wished to be reconfirmed as chancellor and evidently suspected that the podesta' would not support him. Sacchi turned to the conservators, requesting both that his cases be removed to another tribunal and that he be retained as chancellor. The officials in Rome were faced with a choice: uphold their representative at the risk of alienating an influential figure in Vitorchiano or undercut the podesta' merely because of one individual's hostility. They took the middle course, backing the podesta's right to hear the case and granting Sacchi's petition that the statutes be observed in electing a new chancellor.[16] It was prudent, in the Roman context, for lords not to behave in too high-handed a manner because vassals might seek redress in another tribunal or from a higher authority. In response to complaints about the Roman deputies in 1581 Pope Gregory XIII had warned the Capitoline councils that they had better select as podesta' "men of substance [*da bene*] who knew how to govern" or he would pick them himself.[17]

At times the podesta' had to be sacrificed. In 1630 Cori's priors brought their case against the podesta' Filippo Ugolino to the conservators' tribunal in Rome.[18]

---

[13] ASC, cred. XI, vol. 14, 132r; cred. I, vol. 33, decreti, 0230r (8 February 1640).

[14] ASC, cred. I, vol. 28, decreti, 0043r–48r (7 September 1580).

[15] ASC, cred. XI, vol. 40, statuti della terra di Barbarano, 251r–57r. The additional decrees date from 1645. The wording of the passage strongly suggests that the context was a papal audience at which the conservators themselves brought up the matter.

[16] ASC, cred. XI, vol. 14, lettere, 1v–2v.

[17] ASC, cred. I, vol. 28, decreti, 0093v (9 December 1581).

[18] ASR, Tribunale dei conservatori, vol. 57, processi, 1630. The case begins under the date 28 July 1630.

The priors accused Ugolino of twice administering corporal punishment to townsmen, one an old man, without trial. He had forcibly entered houses with his constables and afterwards hens were found to be missing; he and his men were blamed. Furthermore the podesta' had let suspected criminals off without examining them, failed to take action against a notorious thief, and extorted money in legal proceedings. To clinch their case the officials from Cori played shrewdly on the conservators' jealousy of their seigneurial authority. Ugolino, they charged, not only disobeyed the conservators' instructions but also reported cases for appeal to other tribunals rather than theirs, "in prejudice to their jurisdiction." Something in the argument worked. The podesta' tried to defend himself, but despite serving twice as caporione in the 1620s, Ugolino never again held a Capitoline office after this episode.[19]

Whatever the truth of the charge, Cori's claim that the podesta' had deserted the civic court showed its skill at the game of jurisdictional blackmail. More restive than the other fiefs, it frequently appealed over the heads not only of its podesta' but also of the conservators, sometimes to the Capitoline councils and sometimes to the pope himself. At least twice in the early 1640s the community initiated suits in a papal tribunal rather than in the conservators' court. The network of overlapping authorities operating in the Roman district provided wily vassals with opportunities to subvert their feudal lord. The auditor of the apostolic chamber who competed with the conservators did not resist the temptation, but Urban VIII intervened in the 1640s and sent Cori's cases back to the Capitoline tribunal, to the delight of the civic councils who sent him a delegation of thanks.[20]

Why did the pope maintain the privileges of a feudatory over the claims of his own court? The image some historians have given us of early modern monarchs "building" states at the expense of their feudal subjects does not easily accommodate this gesture. But the real attitudes of absolute rulers, and certainly of seventeenth-century popes, toward seigneurial rights were more complex than the conventional view allows. Papal families like the Borghese and Barberini eagerly bought fiefs as part of their strategy of social ascent, and Urban VIII not only helped his brother acquire principalities but made the acquisition of feudal titles easier for all subjects. In general, feudal privileges, like other forms of privilege, were supported, not undermined, by the early modern papacy.[21] The fact that the feudatory in this case was the Roman People certainly inflected the incident but

---

[19] Cf. Renata Ago, "Conflitti e politica nel feudo: Le campagne romane del Settecento," *Quaderni storici* 63 (1986): 865.

[20] ASR, Biblioteca, Statuti, 795/1, *Statuta civitatis corae* (Rome, 1732), 258. ASC, cred. I, vol. 28, decreti, 0093v (1581); cred. I, vol. 33, decreti, 0234v (1640), and cred. XI, vol. 20, letters patent, 165r (1644); cred. IV, vol. 2, decreti della congregazione, 1v (1695).

[21] Mistruzzi, 210–12, 221, 227. See Urban VIII's brief of 17 May 1639 regarding the transfer of feudal titles, cited in *Regesti* 4:264. For the argument that feudalism and absolutism were compatible rather than antagonistic see Beik, 27–33.

not to their disadvantage. Recognizing their rights in relation to Cori gave the pope a chance to strengthen those feelings of gratitude in his "beloved sons" that were the tissue of fidelity. It was a gracious benefaction that put the civic magistrates in his debt and with which he agreed in principle anyway. And, as we have seen, neither he nor the cardinals nor even the clerks of the chamber, for all their competitiveness, pursued an intentional policy of diminishing Capitoline authority, whether in Rome or outside it.

Lordship offered Capitoline officials more scope for rule and a freer hand in the four fiefs than did their statutes and the web of jurisdictions within the city itself. The contrast between the conservators' powers to bring criminals to justice in the subject towns and within Rome is striking. The magistrates' status as seigneurs also enhanced civic prestige and endowed the Capitol with an aura of institutional nobility. Perhaps this neutralized any discomfort arising from proximity to the "ignoble" domain of "greedy" urban tradesmen.[22] The language of feudalism suited city gentlemen in an era in which the court set the tone for elite self-expression and aristocratic values permeated the Italian upper classes. For this reason, while drawing small monetary reward from their vassals, civic officials did not like them to neglect the payment of symbolic dues. The fiefs owed presents of wild game and hens to the conservators at Carnival and the magistrates issued sharp reminders if their gifts lagged.[23] Magliano's offering of four chickens and twenty-five tiny table birds dramatized a relationship that had strong appeal in Baroque society.

Having explored the duties of the Capitol in the marketplace, the guilds, and the fiefs we have seen the civic administration exercising three different kinds of jurisdiction, each with its own nuance. Jurisdiction in the markets highlighted the civic role as an executor, enforcing the will of curial and cardinalatial authorities. To execute policies was perhaps a more robust notion in this period, when it usually involved a physical relationship between enforcers and their targets, than it has since become. In this arena the Roman People acted to fill out and thus complete the authority of concerned papal officials. The civic jurisdiction over the corporations of artisans and tradesmen, on the other hand, was a complicated mixture of discipline, support, and demands. Although it had its judicial aspect, it was infused with the spirit of a more informal, if still hierarchical, relationship. The magistrates were like a well-born master with the social inferiors he commands, inspects, punishes, and protects. In a third articulation of jurisdiction, that over the fiefs, the Capitol was a full-fledged lord with the ample juridical breadth of that status. The exercise of jurisdiction was here seen in its classic incarnation: overseeing justice, which in fact meant managing all aspects of what we might think of as local government. It was paradoxical, but fitting in the early

---

[22] This civic taste for gestures of feudal homage may also have extended to the Roman Jewish community; see Martine Boiteux, "Les Juifs dans le Carnaval de la Rome moderne," *MEFRM* 88 (1976): 754. Cf. Trexler, 258.

[23] ASC, cred. II, vol. 101, bilanci della camera capitolina, 2r; cred. XI, vol. 14, lettere, 4r.

modern context, that civic magistrates operated with the freest hand outside the city walls.

Isolating the Roman People in these three contexts has illuminated the varied meanings of jurisdiction in practice. But where did the Capitol, in operation, stand in the total nexus of institutions that had public responsibilities in the city of Rome? To answer this question we will take a specific crisis and examine civic responses to it in relationship to those of papal, curial, and ecclesiastical authorities. The plague threat of 1629 to 1632 will serve as our case study.

Chapter Ten

PLAGUE

PLAGUE DID NOT break out in Rome during Urban VIII's reign, but from 1629 to 1632 the city lived in fear that it would. In those years an especially severe epidemic devastated northern and central Italy as far south as Tuscany. In Rome civic, ecclesiastical, and papal officials threw all the physical and spiritual means they could think of into the attempt to keep plague out, organizing through institutions and rituals to protect their community. This time they were fortunate and it was spared. Their response and the measures they took help us to see what a network of jurisdictions looked like in action, illustrating how public tasks were divided up between the papacy, the Capitol, and the local Church. This crisis reveals something else, however. A large segment of the population that had no governmental authority helped to guard against the epidemic, whether as members of confraternities, guilds, religious orders, or simply alert neighbors. Their contribution shows us how thin ordinary administrative resources really were and how dependent a state of this kind was on society's participation in public causes. The Roman People stand out as the agents of a significant proportion of that mobilization.

In early November 1629 the news sped south that Habsburg troops sent to Italy to fight for one of the claimants to the duchy of Mantua in the second war of the Mantuan succession had carried the plague infection into Lombardy. Three centuries after the Black Death such tidings disturbed Italian cities in profound but predictable ways. Though ignorant of its real causes and without effective therapy against it, urban governments had developed an elaborate, and occasionally successful, system to prevent the spread of plague. Their principal tactic was to avoid contact with whatever might carry infection, so on 14 November 1629 edicts appeared ordering Romans to suspend commerce with towns where outbreaks of illness had been reported.[1]

Shortly afterward, Urban VIII revived the ad hoc commission that usually supervised epidemic prevention measures in the Papal States whenever they were needed. It was called the congregation of health (*Sanita'*) and he put the energetic

---

[1] For plague deaths in northern Italy in 1630 see Lutz, 111–12. For literature on the plague in seventeenth-century Italy see Pastor, 29:370 n. 3. In addition to Carlo M. Cipolla, *Fighting the Plague in Seventeenth-Century Italy* (Madison, 1981), see also Paolo Preto, *Epidemia, paura e politica nell'Italia moderna* (Bari, 1987), and Giulia Calvi, *Histories of a Plague Year: The Social and the Imaginary in Baroque Florence* (Berkeley, 1989). For a recent edition of an eyewitness account of the plague in Milan in 1630, the setting for the great nineteenth-century novel *I promessi sposi*, by Alessandro Manzoni, see Cardinal Federico Borromeo, *La peste di Milano* (Milan, 1987).

Cardinal Francesco Barberini at its head. The commission met twice weekly and had complete authority to issue the orders and enforce the laws required to protect Rome and the Papal States from disease. Its membership consisted of Barberini nephews and friends, and about equal proportions of curial and non-curial officials. The cardinal vicar took part, as did several clerks of the apostolic chamber, the governor of Rome, the governor of the nearby port of Civitavecchia, and the president of the customs office. In addition to some of the Barberini entourage, lay members included three physicians, the master of the posts, the three conservators and the prior of the caporioni, the fiscal procurator of the Capitol, and five Roman gentlemen. Monsignor Giovanni Battista Spada, a future governor of Rome, served as secretary. Like the congregation of the Annona and Grascia this was a joint body of clerics and laymen, but with a much stronger representation from the Barberini family and circle. Their presence promised fast and decisive action at the top.[2]

While the Sanita' commission held ultimate power in matters relating to plague prevention, it did not execute the policies it made, except on the borders and major highways of the Papal States. The congregation of health usually limited its role to publishing edicts and the names of new cities struck by the pestilence, and to checking up on guards posted at the gates. Occasionally, however, it promoted innovative schemes, such as investigating the urban poor, which it expected existing institutions to carry out. The Sanita' took the broad view of the problem, issuing traditional directives or generating new ones, leaving the countless details of enforcing them to local authorities in villages and towns.[3]

In Rome this job fell mainly to the Capitol. As in the marketplace, the conservators were responsible for executing the orders of a higher body of which they

[2] BAV, Barb. lat. 5626, 3r–4r. The *Sanita'* was established by papal brief, 27 November 1629. In 1635 Monsignor Spada collected the official documents and reports of the congregation from 1629 to 1634 into three volumes and added the plague edicts in a fourth. These provide a detailed summary of the anti-plague measures taken by the papal government during these years; they are found in BAV, Barb. lat. 5626–29. The members of the Barberini circle on the congregation included Giovanni Francesco Sacchetti, Cassiano dal Pozzo, and Orazio Magalotti, who was also the papal postmaster.

[3] An edict at a time of an earlier plague threat has the conservators renew health *bandi* issued by the congregation of the Sanita' "in execution of the aforementioned regulations and in accordance with the duty of their office." ASV, arm. IV, vol. 61, edict of 2 February 1625. For a similar division found in other European states of this period see Brian Pullan, "The Roles of the State and the Town in the General Crisis of the 1590s," in *The European Crisis of the 1590s*, ed. Peter Clark (London, 1985), 287.

Two recent accounts of the plague of 1656–1657, which claimed over 9,000 lives in Rome, credit the measures of the Sanita' with keeping mortality in Rome significantly lower than that of other cities; Eugenio Sonnino and Rosa Traina, "La peste del 1656–57 a Roma: Organizzazione sanitaria e mortalita'," in *La demografia storica delle citta' italiane* (Bologna, 1982), 440, and Alessandro Pastore, "Tra giustizia e politica: Il governo della peste a Genova e Roma nel 1656/7," *Rivista storica italiana* 100 (1988): 126–27. See also Pietro Savio, "Ricerche sulla peste di Roma degli anni 1656–1657," *ASRSP* 95 (1972): 113–14. Without denying the key policy role of the congregation of the Sanita', I suspect that research in Capitoline documents would reveal a larger civic role in the plague of 1656 than one would guess from an exclusive reliance on papal records.

formed a part, though the scale of the effort here was far vaster. Capitoline officials had the tasks of preventing infected goods or persons from entering the city gates, issuing travel certificates to residents who needed to leave, constructing quarantine areas outside the gates and paying for their upkeep, and feeding Roman beggars rounded up and confined for the duration of the threat. To do this they coordinated the unpaid labor of thousands of residents of different classes and, when things looked especially grim, tried to enlist the aid of celestial forces as well.

According to seventeenth-century medical understanding, the plague originated in poisonous atoms that infected the air, creating disease "miasmas." The miasmas could stick to fur, letters, or skin and were spread by physical contact or inhalation.[4] Given this theory, public health depended on keeping out contagion from abroad and suppressing its possible sources at home. Attention naturally turned first to the city's walls and their twelve openings. The plan called for careful scrutiny of anyone and anything that arrived at the gates; if travel certificates or package addresses showed that a person or object had come from or passed through an infected town, they must wait for inspection or fumigation in special enclosures or pesthouses (*lazzeretti*) beyond the urban entrances. Doctors checked travelers for signs of exposure or required them to stay in the enclosures for their period of quarantine. Unlike people, animals, goods, and letters could be made safe by sulfurous smoke and vinegar baths, procedures also performed outside the walls.

The importance of the city gates to plague prevention meant they could not be left in the hands of the toll-collectors and gatekeepers who usually manned them. Instead the Capitol organized the gentlemen and artisans of Rome to attend each entrance that remained open in a daily rotation. The conservators moved to set up this system, which was routine when epidemic menaced, on 6 January 1630, with an edict ordering one gentleman and two artisans to each of the twelve gates. The job of the gentlemen was to check that everyone entering Rome had a certificate attesting to her or his good health. Anyone without a document or anyone from an area where plague had been reported had to wait for the doctor in the nearby enclosure. To avoid contact with miasmas, the gentlemen had instructions to question travelers from a distance; they inspected certificates personally only if new arrivals were not from a suspect area. A few Corsican mercenaries employed by the pope backed up their authority. Once each day a member of the Sanita' commission was to ride by each gate to see that all was well; on Thursdays this duty fell to the conservators.[5]

---

[4] Cipolla, 8.

[5] On Tuesdays and Fridays the fiscal procurator of the Capitol had the job; BAV, Barb. lat. 5626, 7r. ASV, arm. IV, vol. 61, edicts of 7 September 1607 and 26 July 1624. ASR, Bandi, vol. 436, Campidoglio, edict of 6 January 1630. The printed form left blanks for the name of the gentleman, the gate, and the date; see Nussdorfer, "City politics," 191, which translates ASV, arm. IV, vol. 61, 45r (a form from 1599). See also Gigli, *Diario*, 111.

Each night a public messenger employed by the Roman People carried the gate key to the gentleman designated for duty at dawn the next day. The Capitoline edict of January 6th made it clear that it wanted only men of rank in charge; it stipulated that gentlemen were not to use substitutes without written permission from the conservators and that such a substitute must be of equal status. To have teeth, the regulations had to be enforced by men of a certain degree of social authority, especially when aristocrats were transgressors. An incident in May 1630 drives this point home. A count and his party returned from the countryside on a spring day without health certificates and were quite annoyed when the gentleman in charge refused to admit them. A lively exchange of insults ensued, ending up as a court case before the conservators' tribunal. In such circumstances it was important that whoever was responsible for the gate not be easily intimidated or bought off. Giacinto Gigli was one of this group of patrician gatekeepers, who remained on call for the next two years.[6]

Travelers who wanted to avoid trouble procured health certificates from the municipal authorities of their town of origin, which they then had stamped by commissioners at the gates of each village or city through which they passed. Capitoline officials were responsible for issuing these documents for Romans who needed to travel. The two scribes of the Senate directed this bureaucratic labor, managing a team of fifteen copyists. The certificates were written in Italian for those journeying within the Papal States, and Latin for those going beyond its borders. In July 1630 the Roman People paid Andrea Brugiotti over 200 scudi for printing health certificates in the two languages; he was one of their own financial officers, but also happened to hold the lease of the apostolic chamber's printing press at the time. Should anyone with a suspicious-looking document try to reenter Rome, the gentleman who was in charge that day was to send it with one of his two artisan assistants to the Capitol for inspection, while the party in question waited outside the walls.[7]

As we have seen, the Roman People had a special responsibility for the city's artisan and trade guilds: now they gave the guilds the task of mustering their members for gate duty. One gate was assigned to each of twelve guilds, but more than these twelve may actually have been involved in 1630–1632.[8] The guild consuls drew up a roll designating two artisans for service each day and handed it over to the fiscal procurator of the Capitol each week. The fact that the fiscal procurator kept the list signified to the recalcitrant that they would be prosecuted if they did not show up. When members had each taken their turn, the gate passed to another guild.

As gatekeepers, artisans had the unusual privilege of wearing a sword, but their

[6] ASR, Tribunale dei conservatori, vol. 57, processi, 1630. Gigli, *Diario*, 120; ASR, Bandi, vol. 436, Campidoglio, edict of 6 January 1630.

[7] ASR, Bandi, vol. 436, Campidoglio, edict of 6 January 1630; ASC, cred. IV, vol. 112, mandati per sanita' e sede vacante, 2r, 10v.

[8] BAV, Barb. lat. 4835, 5v, published by Paglia, 285. For the conservators' directions to the guild consuls see ASR, Bandi, vol. 436, Campidoglio, edict of 6 January 1630.

main job was the unglamorous one of obeying the gentleman in charge and running back and forth to the Capitol with dubious health certificates. The sculptors did not complain about what they had to do, but they did object to being classified with the tradesmen and asked the conservators to be called as gentlemen, "in the usual manner."[9] The masons however, at almost four hundred strong one of the largest craft associations, moved swiftly to respond. On 9 January 1630, only three days after the conservators' first plague ordinance, their consuls met to organize gate patrols. They authorized one guild official from each of the city's fourteen rioni to make a list of all the masons in his district. The order of service was arranged by drawing the names of the rioni randomly from a hat. Thus the masons of rione Campitelli reported first and, when no more were left, then the masons of Trevi began their turn.[10] While the civic magistrates' primary need was for men to assist at the gates, they did not hesitate to make other requests of the guilds. In June, for instance, they called on the mattress dealers to supply sixteen beds "for present needs," probably in quarantine areas.[11] The volunteer effort against plague was not limited to labor.

The gentlemen and artisans served without pay, but the Roman People had to provide supplies and wages for many other activities essential to keeping disease away. With funds from their meat tax and also from the apostolic chamber, the Capitol paid the carpenters and blacksmiths who constructed the three pesthouses and four enclosures at the seven gates that remained open after April 1630. They also provided food, fuel, and vinegar to the Theatine fathers who ran the large quarantine area near Porta San Pancrazio and to the Camilliani order, which supervised purgation and cared for visitors at two centers outside busy Porta del Popolo. The physicians at the other gates received a salary of ten scudi a month, health certificate copyists got three, and a certain Jacomo, whose job it was to fetch the night gatekeeper when couriers arrived at Porta del Popolo after dark, got two. Civic money paid Brugiotti for printing edicts and the orders that informed gentlemen of their gate assignments as well as health certificates.[12]

The special responsibility of the governor of Rome in the plague prevention effort was the river that cut through the city. He authorized the gentlemen posted at three gates closest to the Tiber to check the health certificates of boatmen. At night ropes stretched from one bank to the other kept out water borne traffic (see

[9] ASR, 30 N.C., uff. 15 (Salvatori) 1630, pt. 2, 343v.

[10] ASR, 30 N.C., uff. 25 (Raymundus) 1630, pt. 1, 155r–56v. The workshop "census" of the 1620s counts 388 master masons; BAV, Barb. lat. 4835, 4r, published by Paglia, 284.

[11] ASR, 30 N.C., uff. 26 (Scoloccius) 1630, pt. 1, 660v–61r (18 June 1630).

[12] ASC, cred. IV, vol. 112, mandati per sanita' e sede vacante, 2r–v, 5v. See also Mario Vanti, Storia dell'ordine dei chierici regolari degli infermi, 3 vols. (Rome, 1943–45), 2:534–43. Paul Slack notes that one of the obstacles to effective plague measures in early modern London was the way they were financed, "Metropolitan Government in Crisis: The Response to Plague," in London 1500–1700: The Making of the Metropolis, ed. A. L. Beier and Roger Finlay (London, 1986), 67. For a contemporary drawing of the planned pesthouse outside Porta del Popolo see Guglielmo Matthiae, "Contributo a Carlo Rainaldi," Arti figurative 2 (1946): 48–49. I would like to thank Professor Joseph Connors for this reference.

Figure 11). As chief criminal magistrate his tribunal also prosecuted cases of contravention of the edicts of the Sanita'.[13]

While the Capitol and the governor of Rome protected the city's access points, other authorities—curial and lay—worried about sources of epidemic within Rome. Poisonous vapors might well arise inside the body social from garbage and rotting food, poor beggars and Jews, and wicked plague spreaders. The cardinal chamberlain and the two Roman gentlemen who served as street masters had to keep garbage out of the streets, using the conventional means at their disposal— edicts and fines. In the summer of 1630 they launched a hail of *bandi* against refuse, especially ashes, manure, pigs, and dead cats and dogs. They ordered Romans to dump putrefying matter into the river rather than the streets, being careful "that the stuff did not remain to give off a stench on the Tiber banks." The shops of butchers, fishmongers, and fruitsellers caused concern because decaying flesh or fruit might generate disease miasmas. "Much applause from the people" greeted the discovery of spoiled foodstuffs, which were promptly tossed into the river.[14] The street masters also tried to keep drains and sewers cleared.

While traditional measures were pursued, perhaps with more energy than usual, by other officials, the Sanita' congregation under Cardinal Francesco Barberini considered innovative ways of keeping the plague from erupting inside the walls. Poverty was a dangerous condition because it produced people with disagreeable odors. The commission therefore proposed that deputies be appointed to investigate each of the fourteen rioni "to make greater provision for the needs of the poor." Their job would be to question the "private" poor, those in want who were ashamed to seek alms in the street, about their sources of income, and to report what they lacked. At the same time the rione deputies were to divide the beggars—the "public" poor—they found into three groups. The first category, those who were blind, lame, or aged, should go to the hospital of San Sisto. Able-bodied youths should be instructed to find employment; if they refused, the *bargello* should confine them in the monastery of San Saba on the distant side of the Aventine hill; there they would be conveniently situated to be sent to labor in the fields. Younger boys were to be threatened with whipping. Finally, female beggars should be ordered to the hospital of San Giacomo degli Incurabili where they would be set to work.[15]

Something in the tone of these proposals suggests there was more than just fear

[13] ASR, Tribunale criminale del governatore, vol. 257, processi, 1630, includes several cases of contravention of health regulations. For the governor's edicts see ASV, arm. IV, vol. 61, edicts dated 15 July 1630 and 18 April 1630. For Carlo Rainaldi's drawing see BAV, Barb. lat. 4411, 16r. I am grateful to Professor Joseph Connors for making me aware of these drawings.

[14] BAV, Barb. lat. 4733, 372r; this is the fourth volume of a nine-volume manuscript life of Urban VIII by his official biographer Andrea Nicoletti. For the street masters' edict see ASV, arm. IV, vol. 61, edict dated 21 June 1630.

[15] BAV, Barb. lat. 5626, 9r–v, 103v–4v. San Saba was often called San Savo in seventeenth-century Roman dialect.

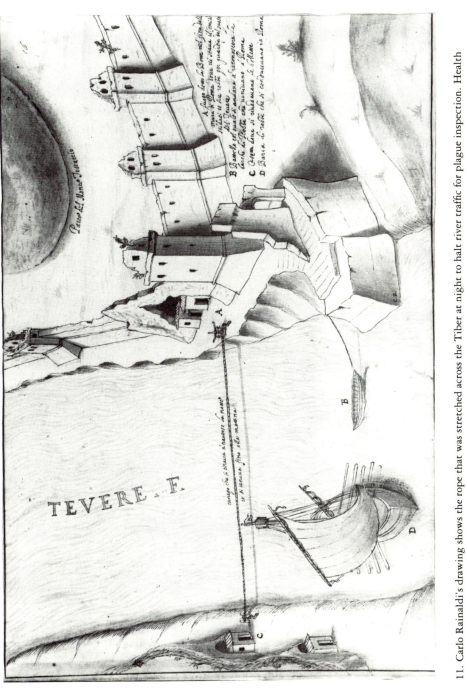

11. Carlo Rainaldi's drawing shows the rope that was stretched across the Tiber at night to halt river traffic for plague inspection. Health certificates were checked in the building at left indicated by the letter C.

of infection behind them; the Sanita' seemed to be hoping to rid the streets not just of smells but of behavior it did not like. The measures in themselves were not new. Putting up the disabled at public expense in San Sisto and forcing the young and healthy to labor were tried in the sixteenth century. What was novel in this plan was the notion of a full inquiry into the economic means of the population of each rione. This the commission eventually decided against. Only a short time before, in December 1629, a parish by parish fiscal survey had been ordered, and the Sanita' realized that so similar an investigation "could cause fright and terror to the inhabitants" as well as "jealousy and suspicion to outsiders."[16] Abandoning the rione visitation, the authorities nonetheless rounded up beggars by the usual haphazard methods and interred them in the three designated institutions. Carlo Rainaldi drew designs of the facilities for the beggars at San Giacomo and San Saba, where the Roman People provided bread for inmates.[17] (See Figures 12 and 13.) To deal with another category of poor, the Jews, since 1555 forced to live in the cramped conditions of the Ghetto, the Sanita' instituted a weekly inspection of the quarter.[18]

Another potential agent of the plague took the form not of a miasma, but of a poisonous unguent deliberately spread by evildoers. These wicked men, the *untori* or "smearers," some of whom were caught and executed in Milan in 1630, placed a deadly plague-causing ointment in fonts of holy water or on objects that people might touch unawares. The *untori* caused panic in Rome several times during the crisis years of 1629–1632, but since the city remained free of plague, no one was prosecuted for the crime. Popular violence almost finished off some suspects however. In one incident at the church of San Lorenzo in Damaso a sacristan noticed a poor man shake something around in the font of holy water. The sacristan whipped together a crowd to pursue him, but the man was lucky and before he could be lynched, he had a chance to explain that he was only trying to improve his sight with a special rock that he moistened in the font.[19]

A barrier of pesthouses and gentlemen gatekeepers protected Rome from exter-

---

[16] Ibid., 9v. For the parish survey see Gigli, *Diario*, 109. The idea of rounding up the poor was already in the air in 1627, well before the severe epidemic of the end of the decade. See the decree of the congregation of the apostolic visitation "to enclose the poor of Rome in some place," which is dated 26 August 1627 in Pagano, 429. See also Slack, 75, and Pastore, 141.

[17] BAV, Barb. lat. 4411, 14r–15r, 26r–27r; the governor of Rome prohibited begging on 9 June 1630, *Regesti* 4:110; ASC, cred. IV, vol. 112, mandati per sanita' e sede vacante, 10r. Spada's discussion emphasizes yet another source of concern about the poor: the fact that they were undernourished would make them an easier prey to disease. He also makes it clear that beggars of both sexes who could *not* work were housed at San Giacomo and San Saba; BAV, Barb. lat. 5626, 9r-v. I have not yet found specific evidence that San Giacomo and San Saba had ever been used to confine beggars prior to 1630. On measures to deal with beggars in Rome in the sixteenth century see Delumeau, *Vie* 1:403–16; Simoncelli, "Origini," and idem, "Note sul sistema assistenziale a Roma nel XVI secolo," in *Timore e carita': I poveri nell'Italia moderna*, ed. Giorgio Politi et al. (Cremona, 1982), 137–56.

[18] BAV, Barb. lat. 4733, 374r. Kenneth Stow, 31–36, shows that the papacy's fiscal demands were steadily impoverishing the Roman Jewish community in the sixteenth and seventeenth centuries.

[19] Gigli, *Diario*, 117; BAV, Barb. lat. 5626, 11v–12r. See also Preto's chapter on the *untori*.

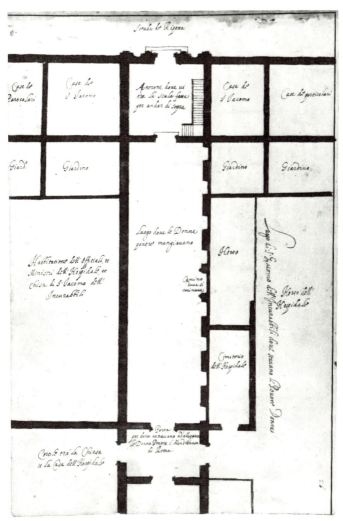

12. Carlo Rainaldi's plan of the quarters for poor women at San Giacomo degli Incurabili. The women ate in the large central room on
the ground floor where a hearth (*camino*) is indicated; they slept in a
dormitory above it.

nal contagion; measures of confinement, purgation, and watchfulness permitted
some feeling of security against internal infection. But no one in Rome thought
human efforts were sufficient defense against the plague. The pope organized an
appeal for divine help within four days of the first suspension of trade with plague-
stricken towns in northern Italy. On 18 November 1629 Urban VIII led the
cardinals, ambassadors, and Rome's regular and secular clergy in procession to

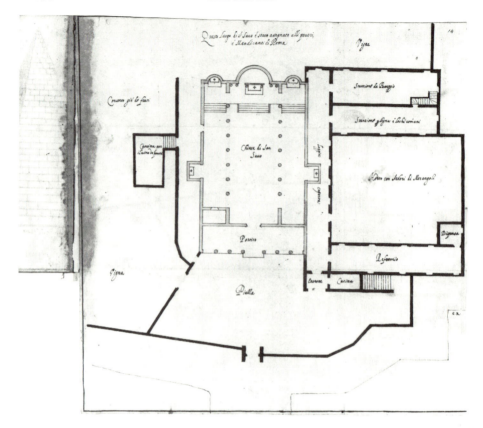

13. Carlo Rainaldi's plan of the ground floor of San Saba (San Savo) showing, to the left of the church, the *cantina* where wine for the poor was stored. The male beggars slept in dormitories on the second floor overlooking the garden (*horto*).

Santa Maria Maggiore, the home of the miraculous image that had saved the city from plague in 590. Throughout the duration of the threat, the pontiff crossed Rome almost every Sunday to say mass at the Madonna's basilica. This first papal procession had a pronounced courtly and ecclesiastical character; the ambassadors are the only laymen mentioned in Gigli's account of the event. With such a display Urban undoubtedly felt that he was mobilizing his most impressive suppli-cants. He promoted the spiritual contribution of the wider community not as a collectivity but as individuals. To anyone who visited the two churches on the processional route, fasted on three designated days, gave alms, took communion, and prayed to God for the cessation of the epidemic, the pope granted a jubilee indulgence.[20]

[20] Gigli, *Diario*, 108, 129. For an account of the procession of 590 CE see Jean-Noël Biraben, *Les hommes et la peste en France et dans les pays européens et méditerranéens*, 2 vols. (Paris, 1975–76), 1:29.

In the early months of 1630 Rome went about its business. While keeping a cautious eye on the plague's progress in the north, building quarantine quarters on the city perimeter, checking visitors, letters, and goods from the outside world, and rounding up beggars within the walls, Romans and their lay and papal authorities had energy left over to spar over new taxes. The plague aroused concern, but was still a safe distance away.

With the return of warm weather, however, the news grew more worrisome. On June 11th came the most serious announcement yet; plague had broken out within the Papal States in the city of Bologna. In the face of looming danger the prayers of the Romans had to be organized on a more systematic basis. On June 13th all parish churches were directed to recite the litanies of the saints each evening. Soon this order was extended to all Roman churches, with indulgences granted to those present, and this concession remained in effect for the next two years.[21]

In this anxious atmosphere religious associations took spiritual initiatives without waiting for orders from above. A notable example was the important confraternity of the Rosary, based at the Dominican church of Santa Maria sopra Minerva. The company, which enjoyed the patronage of the Barberini family, was particularly known for its processions. In keeping with its traditions, on 24 June 1630, the feast of St. John the Baptist, the confraternity of the Rosary organized a procession to pray for Rome's deliverance from the plague. This attracted a gathering that in its size and demeanor was without equal during Urban VIII's reign. Gigli estimated that 40,000 men and women, almost a third of the city, took part in the procession. There were so many people that the officials ordered the march to begin an hour and a half ahead of schedule because the narrow streets around the Minerva could not contain them all. Gigli was also struck by the comportment of the vast crowd and by their impact on bystanders. "It was remarkable with what modesty and devotion everyone walked . . . [The sight] was so moving that people who were just standing and watching the procession felt embarrassed and they too joined in and followed along."[22]

In the weeks that followed this outpouring of collective prayer the threat of plague grew more real. All through July and August grim tidings poured into Rome from the north. As Gigli recorded, "we heard of miserable events and the greatest destruction in the cities where the plague was, an infinite number of people, hundreds, thousands, dying every day."[23] On August 24th the Roman People voted to send a delegation of officials and gentlemen deputies with an

---

[21] Gigli, *Diario*, 113; ASV, arm. IV, vol. 61, edict of 11 June 1630. Parish priests had another job as well. They were asked to turn in weekly lists of parishioners who fell ill with a note on the nature of the illness; BAV, Barb. lat. 5626, 10r.

[22] Gigli, *Diario*, 88–91, 114. See also the contemporary pamphlet description by F[ra] Ambrosio Brandi, *Trionfo della gloriosa vergine del SSmo Rosario celebrato in Roma la prima domenica d'ottobre dell'anno Santo 1625 nella Processione solemne dell'Archiconfraternita del Rosario* (Rome, 1625).

[23] Gigli, *Diario*, 117.

offering to St. Sebastian at his chapel in San Pietro in Vincoli. The councils instructed their representatives to beseech the saint "to intercede with the Divine Majesty and to pray for the defense, preservation and liberation of the *Alma Urbe* [Rome] from the plague." The guilds took part in the spiritual effort as well; the butchers decided the next day to hire a priest to lead the litanies every evening at their church of Santa Maria della Quercia.[24]

Although in September the epidemic struck Florence, the cooler months brought a pause in the southward progress of the plague. Nevertheless Rome remained on the alert. The cardinal vicar ordered prayers at the end of December and the jubilee indulgence for supplications on the city's behalf was continually renewed. St. Sebastian drew special honors on his feast day in January 1631: the pope said the first mass at the church he had rebuilt on the Palatine hill and dedicated to the holy protector. Traditional Carnival races and masking were canceled. As Lent 1631 approached, it did not seem appropriate for Rome to amuse itself, in Gigli's words, "while many Italian cities wept." In place of the usual races and egg-throwing contests, many churches offered prayers and magnificent "Forty Hours" displays of the Holy Sacrament. As summer approached fears intensified; on 16 July 1631 the health authorities suspended commerce with Citerna in the Tiber valley on the Tuscan border, the closest the contagion had yet come.[25]

Remarkably, however, the plague advanced no further and in the fall and winter the sense of imminent danger abated. By December, after nearly two years of vigilance, Romans had begun to complain about the burdens of their volunteer gate duty. Many people found excuses not to take their turn so a new tax was levied and soldiers were hired to replace the Roman gentlemen and artisans who had hitherto stood guard. In February the Capitoline councils sent a delegation to Urban VIII to express their appreciation for his "paternal providence and exquisite diligence" in keeping the epidemic out of Rome and for the money he had contributed to the effort; the deputation also paid a visit of thanks to Cardinal Francesco Barberini.[26]

By late winter 1632 the Roman People felt they could celebrate the city's deliverance from the plague. The conservators decided to organize a huge demonstration of civic gratitude, which they scheduled for the time of the Madonna's great feast of the Annunciation. On March 24th, the vigil of the feast, they in-

[24] For the council decree see ASC, cred. I, vol. 33, decreti, 0097r (24 August 1630). For the butchers' action see ASR, 30 N.C., uff. 25 (Raymundus) 1630, pt. 4, 512r–v; they later rescinded their decision to pay for this, arguing that it was part of their chaplain's regular duties. For St. Sebastian's importance as a protector from plague see also Manlio Brusatin, *Il muro della peste: Spazio della pieta' e governo del lazzaretto* (Venice, 1981), 19.

[25] Gigli, *Diario*, 119; ASV, arm. IV, vol. 61, edict of 16 July 1631; *Regesti* 4:119.

[26] ASV, arm. IV, vol. 61, edict of 16 July 1631; ASC, cred. I, vol. 33, decreti, 0115r (9 February 1632).

vited the pope to celebrate mass at Santa Maria in Aracoeli.[27] It was Urban VIII's
first visit to the Capitoline hill since his *possesso* procession in 1623, and his last.
The church was richly decorated and in the morning the pope performed a low
mass. After he had departed a solemn mass was chanted in the Aracoeli in the
presence of the College of Cardinals, the representatives of the Roman People, and
a large crowd drawn in part by a plenary indulgence granted to everyone who took
communion. After mass the bells of the Capitol rang out and the drummers and
buglers of the Roman People made ceremonial noises as fireworks crackled.
Against this lively background, the civic magistrates dispensed bread, wine, and
money to the populace.

On the following afternoon, the feast of the Annunciation itself, the conservators planned an immense procession to honor Rome's patron saints, and particularly the Madonna. They began the celebration at St. Peter's by presenting a silver
lamp valued at 2,000 scudi to the altar of the apostles Peter and Paul. Both the
processional order and participants were minutely recorded by Giacinto Gigli.[28]
Standing at the window of the Vatican palace, the pope blessed the throng before
it snaked across the city to Santa Maria Maggiore, where the Virgin's powerful
image had once again saved the city from plague. Buglers led off, followed by the
lackeys of princes and cardinals with lighted candles. Five thousand artisans of
Rome marched along behind them, each grouped distinctly by guild, as they were
during the rounds of gate duty.

Immediately after the guilds came the gold brocade banner painted by Pietro
da Cortona, which was the Capitoline gift to the Madonna; it was carried by the
red-robed brothers of the confraternity of the Holy Sacrament at St. Peter's.[29]
Surrounding them were a few gentlemen with lighted tapers. After the standard
walked young boys clad in red, orphans, and then the religious orders of Rome.
The secular clergy and colleges proceeded next, and behind them, representing
episcopal authority, marched the vicegerent of the cardinal vicar. At the end of
the procession came the senator, the conservators' retainers in their red outfits
with painted batons, and finally the conservators themselves and the prior of the
caporioni dressed in long robes of gold brocade and surrounded by lighted candles. "All Rome" turned out to see and accompany this magnificent parade, which
did not arrive at its destination until after nightfall. They hung the golden banner, Gigli reported, in the middle of the basilica "as a perpetual memorial of the
grace received, that Rome had been spared plague, famine and war."

The thanksgiving procession was the grandest public ceremony sponsored by

---

[27] Gigli, *Diario*, 127.

[28] Ibid., 128–29.

[29] Accounts for the procession expenses include a payment of thirty scudi to Cortona for the painting ·
on the banner; ASC, cred. VI, vol. 30, registro di mandati, 309. For a contemporary pamphlet description see Antonio Gerardi, *Sommaria relatione della solenne processione dello stendardo benedetto dalla
S.ta' di N. S.re Urbano Papa VIII fatta dal Clero e Popolo Romano il giorno della Santissima Annuntiata*
(Rome, 1632).

the Roman People during Urban VIII's reign, and Gigli judged it worthy of "great praise." It stood out from other processions in Baroque Rome for several important reasons. The prominent participation of the guilds was most unusual in Roman public occasions of this epoch. While artisans took part in the senator's investiture procession, they did so not as guild members but as members of the civic militia. The unusual ceremonial appearance of the artisan guilds in 1632 reflected the recognition of their role in helping to protect the city from the plague. Their participation was not without a price, however, for each craftsman had to supply a candle at his own expense, a hardship of which a number complained. Gigli criticized the conservators for not providing candles from public funds.[30]

The Annunciation Day celebration was remarkable for what Gigli called its "plebeian" character. It was mainly a manifestation of popular rather than patrician gratitude. As the diarist noted disapprovingly, "apart from some gentlemen around the [Madonna's] banner there were none but servants and artisans" present.[31] Gigli again blamed the magistrates for "not inviting as many Roman gentlemen as possible."

While the conservators focused civic gratitude on the city's chief patron saints, St. Peter, St. Paul, and the Virgin, the pope also received thanks along the processional way. The notaries attached to the apostolic chamber and the guild of scribes both erected triumphal arches with inscriptions praising papal vigilance during the plague years.[32] As we have seen, the Roman People had not neglected to thank the Barberini either, and continued to credit Urban and his nephew for their good fortune in being spared. The conservators who entered office in January 1634 proposed to honor Urban VIII and Cardinal Francesco by putting up a memorial inscription to the pope in Santa Maria in Aracoeli and a statue to his nephew. In presenting their plans to the councils they particularly mentioned the cardinal's efforts as head of the Sanita'.[33]

Religious orders, confraternities, hospitals, civic magistrates, parish priests,

[30] Gigli, *Diario*, 129–30. A meeting of the vegetable sellers' (*ortolani*) guild on 23 March 1632 provides evidence both of the conservators' methods of organizing the procession and of the financial hardship it entailed for some artisans. The notary recording the meeting writes, "The order of the illustrious lord conservators sent to the guild consuls and chamberlain was read by me notary and in conformance with that [order] the lord consuls chose all the undersigned vegetable sellers to come next Thursday to the procession, warning them that whoever did not attend would be subject to the penalties contained in the conservators' order." Ninety-six men and the three guild officers were listed. An additional thirty-three men were excused from participation on the grounds of poverty. ASR, 30 N.C., uff. 2 (Bonanni) 1632, pt. 1, 496v–97v.

[31] Ibid.

[32] Andrea Brugiotti, chamberlain of the Roman People and the man who held the lease on the official printing press of the apostolic chamber—who thus printed all health certificates and plague edicts—erected a third triumphal arch praising Urban VIII along the route; Gigli, *Diario*, 128; for civic payments to Brugiotti see ASC, cred. IV, vol. 112, mandati per sanita' e sede vacante, 1r–2r.

[33] ASC, cred. I, vol. 33, decreti, 0137r (1 February 1634); Pastor, 29:370–71.

clerks of the chamber, papal nephews, and patron saints all had a role in protecting the city from pestilence. The key decisionmaking center for the whole state was the Sanita' commission, and important enforcement responsibilities outside Rome went to the curial employees associated with the apostolic chamber. Within Rome the Capitol had broad responsibilities for plague prevention. The Roman People mobilized unpaid lay labor and coordinated the disbursement of funds, working through the institutions traditionally under their jurisdiction—the civic staff, the guilds, and the rioni. Because the papal regime disliked any situation in which secular individuals gave orders to the clergy, however, the Capitoline authorities could not control everything. Thus the cardinalatial congregation of the Consulta directed the work of the religious orders that ran the quarantine areas, which were built and supplied at civic expense. In Rome clerics readily crossed the boundary between spiritual and temporal spheres; the parish priests, for example, led litanies and kept records of the sick. Laymen, except as members of confraternities, did so less easily.

When the plague actually hit Rome in 1656 and the congregation of health was reconstituted to deal with it, its first orders echoed the practices set up in 1630: "Delegate the gentlemen, restrict the poor."[34] Here I have highlighted the role of the "gentlemen," especially in their incarnation as the Roman People, to show how the complex structure of governmental authorities in Rome divided up the labor in an emergency and to underscore the dependence of the institutions of the central government on the work of the localities. I have emphasized those actors who are not always noticed in studies of plague measures that concentrate only on the highest levels of state. The Capitol organized and managed a great deal of activity in its role as executor of a papal congregation's instructions. The story of its share in fighting disease suggests again that our usual sense of what it means to "execute" orders may be too thin to do justice to the process in an early modern setting. This same story also illustrates very concretely, however, the way the real practice of government in Rome was embedded in social hierarchy, with gentlemen formally deputized to give orders to their artisan neighbors.

Although we cannot know how successful Rome would have been in limiting the epidemic if it had really broken out in 1630, a glance at cities where public officials were conspicuously less able to defend citizens from plague suggests that specific features of Roman administration worked to this city's advantage. There was a striking degree of coordination in the Roman effort of 1629–1632, a large number of "commandeered" and unremunerated services—not only by lay subjects but also by religious orders—and a flexible, responsive system of financing any extra expenditures required. We are justly warned not to be too "Whiggish" in our interpretation of government attempts to prevent disease.[35] Some of the

---

[34] Quoted by Pastore, 141.

[35] For London see Slack, 73; for Genoa and Rome in 1656 see Pastore; for Naples see Sonnino and Traina, 433.

variables favoring Rome were rooted in the historical fate that had placed the papacy there, with its advanced techniques of state finance, and made it the capital of Catholic Christendom, thus ensuring an ample supply of volunteers from the regular clergy. But in the context of an inquiry into the politics of jurisdiction, it is important to ask why the 1630 plague effort caused little jurisdictional conflict. Why was there such harmony about this division of labor among all the different magistracies, officers, and groups involved in facing the plague threat?

Naturally conflict, and not just over jurisdiction, was more likely to erupt in *real* incidents of epidemic, when people saw their property confiscated or their freedom curtailed. In the absence of anything but suspicions, tensions in Rome were brief and contained. On the institutional plane what also maintained peace between possible competitors were the separation of responsibilities inside and outside the city walls, the broad composition of the Sanita' congregation, its direction by the pope's second-in-command, Cardinal Francesco Barberini, and its ad hoc character. Walls, the focus of plague prevention, were a great clarifier of administrative competencies; in contrast to its market jurisdiction the Capitol had a virtually free hand inside a physically defined perimeter. Membership in the congregation of Sanita', which included civic and curial officials as well as Barberini friends, shared access to information and authority among potential rivals. The congregation could act quickly and decisively because the most powerful of Urban VIII's nephews gave it his full attention.

Most significantly, perhaps, the Sanita' was a body that came into being only episodically and left no permanent bureaucratic legacy to be nurtured or defended after it was gone. The comparison with the congregation of the Annona and Grascia, which we examined in Chapter 7, is again instructive. There the two clerks of the chamber, the prefect of the Annona and the president of the Grascia, did most of the ongoing work that fell under the aegis of the congregation. The congregation, even when headed by a Barberini cardinal after 1638, was low on his list of priorities and was not actively led. The clerks of the chamber had a great deal of independence as administrators and they inevitably developed a sharp sense of protectiveness about their privileged spheres. A jurisdictional boundary based on the same distinction between making policy and enforcing it that we saw operating between the Sanita' and the Capitol separated the clerks of the chamber from the conservators, but it was a more delicate boundary because two entrenched sets of officials were negotiating the same terrain, literally, day in and day out. When a plague crisis abated, by contrast, it left no new contenders for the right to print health certificates or stand guard at the city gates.

Issues of jurisdiction, the focus of these four chapters, highlight the political anxieties of actors who, temporarily at least, suspend their deference to the claims of hierarchy. Jurisdictional tensions, in contrast to other forms of conflict under absolutism, express competition along a horizontal axis. Although officials with unequal authority may in fact be disputing each other's privileges, the form of their dispute denies this inequality and pits them against each other as if they were on the same level. The "silent term" in jurisdictional conflict is thus the existence of an authority above this level who can determine the outcome. In the next section we focus on the "silent term" and examine hierarchically structured relations of authority. It is, of course, not the fact of unequal authority but the way that it is patterned that will absorb our attention in Part IV. The politics of patronage takes us from the horizontal to the vertical axis, as the Roman People negotiate the slippery rungs of the patron-client relationship.

The Politics of Patronage

ON 19 NOVEMBER 1623 Pope Urban VIII made his first great public procession through the city he had been chosen to rule three months before. It was the traditional *possesso* cavalcade, which took the pontiff from the Vatican across Rome to the seat of his bishopric at St. John Lateran. In his path was the Capitoline hill, which he would visit that day for the first time since his election. Prepared for their prominence in the festivities, the three conservators marched near the pope in togas of gold brocade (see Figure 8). Forty youthful pages, sons of the civic nobility, accompanied his litter while forty Roman gentlemen in fur-lined black velvet togas walked before it. The fourteen caporioni in white capes and red tunics preceded. Arriving at the foot of the Capitol, a chorus sang for the marchers. The pontiff then slowly ascended the ramp leading up to the Capitoline piazza between ten larger than life *faux-marbre* statues, each representing his special talents. They recognized his skill in Greek letters, poetry, legal training, knowledge of theology, and kindness (*humanita'* or *gentilezza*, says the probable author of the program), and they promised fortune, abundance, public happiness, fame, and glory from his reign.[1] In an allusion to an ancient triumph given by the Senate to an emperor, which was surely not lost on the classically educated Barberini, a triumphal arch next greeted the pontiff. On the side of the arch facing the city was a statue of the Church, "seated as a ruler," surrounded by four popes distinguished by their piety, learning, militance in propagating the faith, and zeal in preserving papal rights against secular monarchs. Statues symbolizing "political life" and "ecclesiastical life" made the point that both were subject to the supreme pontiffs. On the side of the arch facing the palaces of the senator and the conservators the niches were filled with figures drawn from Rome's classical past—Romulus, Cato the younger, Julius Caesar, and Trajan—above emblems of Magnificence and Faith. As the honored guest made his way down the back slope and through the Roman Forum, he saw inscriptions affixed to its antique monuments that praised him and wished him well.

The Capitoline authorities always put on a festive welcome for a new pope at his *possesso* procession and Urban VIII was no exception. Their celebratory display was a multilayered message that both flattered the pontiff and made the Roman People look good. Lest their efforts be forgotten when the wooden statues and canvas arch came down, civic officials paid the learned rhetorician Agostino Mascardi, who may have devised the iconography of the decor, to publish a description of how the Capitol appeared that day.[2] The adulatory tone of the spectacle

---

[1] Agostino Mascardi, *Le Pompe del Campidoglio* (Rome, [1624]), 10–39. Mascardi's text has been published in Diez, 123–56. See also Gigli, *Diario*, 80. On the ritual importance of the papal *possesso* see Burke, "Sacred Rulers," 174.

[2] ASC, cred. IV, vol. 96, istrumenti, 55r.

could not completely hide the self-promotion it also conveyed; praise was a demand for attention. The *possesso* ceremony reminds us that the conventional idiom in which the relations between the pope and the city were represented, and enacted, was the language of patronage. The patron and the client were unequal partners in a dialogue in which both hoped to benefit. Because of the asymmetry, however, the initiative for the relationship fell to the would-be client. The *possesso* was the first of many offerings the Roman People would make to their prince in order to attract and maintain his patronage.

To characterize the Roman People as operating within a matrix of patron-client relations presupposes a concept of patronage that includes, but goes beyond, the crude distribution of jobs or bribes. Patronage, it has been recently observed, was the lubrication that made it possible for early modern institutions to function.[3] I would go further and suggest that patronage was not only what enabled them to function, but was *how* they functioned. Patronage, as I conceive it here, is not just a matter of dispensing public resources to private persons, but a broader mode of social and political interaction. This mode of interaction aimed to accumulate or mobilize influence for varied purposes, immaterial as well as material. In a hierarchical social and political setting in which status, wealth, and power were, by definition, unequal, "influence" was instrumental; it was the way almost anything got done.

While creating and maintaining patron-client relationships was an essential part of doing business in the papal capital, it was not necessarily visible in such crude terms to participants. To them it was often indistinguishable from the activity of showing proper respect for superiors or magnanimity to inferiors. Status seemed to spontaneously evoke appropriate attitudes and conduct.[4] But appropriate conduct included advancing a client's petition or granting a favor, as well as using the right honorific titles of address and genuflecting the correct number of times.

Here we will look at what it meant for civic institutions to be located within a political culture structured as relations between patrons and clients. As we will see, what the Capitoline administration was called on to do—as a client, a patron,

---

[3] Anthony Molho, "Patronage and the State in Early Modern Italy," in *Klientelsysteme im Europa der frühen Neuzeit*, ed. Antoni Maczak (Munich, 1988), 241–42; see also Kettering, *Patrons*, 11. David Parker, 209, links the patronage system with the growth of royal absolutism in France, arguing that the king's role as "supreme arbiter" was fueled in part by the demands of his would-be clients. Other thoughtful reflections on the political dimensions of patronage include: Reinhard, *Freunde*; Werner L. Gundersheimer, "Patronage in the Renaissance: An Exploratory Approach," in *Patronage in the Renaissance*, ed. Guy F. Lytle and Stephen Orgel (Princeton, 1981), 3–23; F. W. Kent with Patricia Simons, "Renaissance Patronage: An Introductory Essay," in *Patronage, Art, and Society in Renaissance Italy*, ed. F. W. Kent and Patricia Simons (Oxford, 1987), 1–21; Weissman, "Taking Patronage Seriously;" Sharon Kettering, "Gift-Giving and Patronage in Early Modern France," *French History* 2 (1988): 131–51; and Victor Morgan, "Some Types of Patronage, Mainly in Sixteenth- and Seventeenth-Century England," in *Klientelsysteme im Europa der frühen Neuzeit*, ed. Antoni Maczak (Munich, 1988), 91–115.

[4] Bourdieu, 193.

and a broker—and the style, gestures, and language in which it did it, reflected the pervasive patronal system in which it was embedded. In Chapter 11 I examine the Roman People in their multiple roles as patron, client, and broker. In Chapter 12 I discuss financial negotiations between Urban VIII and the civic magistrates as a case study of relations between patron and client.

Chapter Eleven

THE NETWORK OF RELATIONSHIPS

THE PATRON-CLIENT system in which the Roman People operated dictated that they would exercise multiple roles.[1] Since they possessed certain patronage resources, they were sometimes patrons themselves. Doing favors for petitioners, however, gave them the occasional role as broker between their clients and their patrons. And finally, they had to be good clients in order to be of any use as patrons or brokers. Here we examine the Capitol in these three roles during Urban VIII's pontificate and then look in particular at its behavior as the pope's client.

PATRONS

What could civic officials or the civic councils offer as potential patrons? Closest to home, in the conservators' palace, they could respond to the requests of their servants and award living quarters, a rent subsidy, or a job promotion.[2] For wealthier clients, gentlemen from the very families that provided magistrates, they granted the favor of extending a life annuity (which took the form of a fictitious office or *vacabile*) belonging to one man to his brothers or sons. *Vacabili* paid a higher rate of interest than annuities that were technically inheritable (*non vacabili*), so the device of extending a *vacabile* to heirs netted the families in question a little extra income at the cost of the Capitoline treasury. *Vacabili* also carried the rights to the Christmas largesse or *regaglie* of sweetmeats, wax, pepper, and gloves, as we have seen, and grants of tax-free salt.[3]

The most important resource the civic administration dispensed, however, was not the immediately material cash or job. It was its seal of approval as a public body on a particular cause. Clients secured Capitoline patronage as part of a broader strategy to elevate the official status of something they were promoting. The Roman People were especially desirable as patrons when the goal was not a personal favor or private matter but rather a kind of public witness or testimony, often one in which the terrain being negotiated bridged the social and the sacred. What the Capitol could provide was rituals that conveyed formal recognition. Not surprisingly the clients able to tap into Capitoline patronage for such purposes were members of families who had a prominent tradition of civic office.

---

[1] Kettering, "Gift-Giving," 4.

[2] ASC, cred. I, vol. 32, decreti, 0270v; ASC, cred. I, vol. 33, decreti, 0126r, 0153v.

[3] ASC, cred. I, vol. 34, decreti, 0025v–26r, 0049v, 0053r, 0063r. For a slightly different perspective on seeking civic patronage see the proper forms of address to be used in writing to the conservators and other Capitoline officials in Marc'Antonio Rossi, *Il giardino de' scrittori* (Rome, 1598), 60.

The Albertoni sought the support of the Roman People for an ancestor whom they wanted to have accepted as a holy woman at a moment when the standards for holiness were being scrutinized and tightened. Actively pushing the cult of his distant relative Ludovica Albertoni, a Franciscan tertiary who had died in 1533, was Baldassare Paluzzi degli Albertoni (1568/69–1652), a wealthy former conservator and street master.[4] Ludovica was a patrician widow whose charity to the Roman poor had earned her a reputation for piety that endured beyond the grave. Her cult may have had a popular dimension but its fortunes were overwhelmingly a matter of family connections. The Albertoni were civic nobility of several centuries' standing in Rome and Ludovica's daughters and granddaughters had married into similar lineages, the Muti, Mattei, and Altieri. Such families were the backbone of the Capitoline government and could expect it to join them in honoring the memory of their kinswoman. Indeed since 1606 she had received an offering from the Roman People of a chalice and four large wax cierges each January 31st, the anniversary of her death.[5]

In 1622 Baldassare Paluzzi degli Albertoni opened a new front in the campaign to keep Ludovica's cult alive. He began extensive redecoration of the chapel in San Francesco a Ripa in which Ludovica was buried, hoping to draw attention to the cult, to show off Ludovica's good deeds and holy patrons, and to attract earthly ones. His painting and fresco commissions associated the matron with St. Anne and the recently canonized St. Charles Borromeo, and in March 1625 and January 1626 he organized ceremonies attended by ecclesiastical dignitaries and civic magistrates to climax the artistic campaign.[6]

Albertoni's activities were a traditional way to build a following for a holy person that might eventually culminate in canonization. But in these very years the cardinalatial congregation of the Holy Office or Inquisition, the highest body responsible for religious doctrine and practice below the pope himself, was taking a hard look at such traditions. Twice in 1625, and again in 1634, the Inquisition

---

[4] Shelley Perlove, "Gianlorenzo Bernini's *Blessed Lodovica Albertoni* and Baroque Devotion" (Ph.D. diss., University of Michigan, 1984), 18–34. The Franciscan Ludovico da Modena, author of an eighteenth-century chronicle of San Francesco a Ripa, seems to be the source for the mistaken identification of Baldassare as Ludovica's grandson (the passage is photo-reproduced in ibid., 207). Both were in fact descended from a common fourteenth-century ancestor, Pier Matteo I Albertoni (d. 1395); Visconti, 3:487–509. Baldassare was a member of the prestigious *regaglie* committee from before 1624 to 1644 and was also on several other Capitoline committees in these years, in addition to his civic offices.

[5] Perlove, "*Blessed Lodovica Albertoni*," 45 (no source given for this offering). The Franciscan chronicler Ludovico da Modena also asserted that at the time of Ludovica's death the Roman Senate commissioned the two extant frescoes of Ludovica Albertoni and Saint Clare in the chapel (passage photoreproduced in ibid., 209). In the absence of any other documentation for the commission, however, Perlove handles this claim cautiously (pp. 26, 45).

[6] Perlove, "*Blessed Lodovica Albertoni*," 29–34. The source for the civic representation at the exhumation of the corpse on 4 March 1625 and its translation on 31 January 1626 is given in Perlove, 34 nn. 58, 60, as Ugo Boncompagni Ludovisi, *Roma nel Rinascimento* (Albano, 1928), 4:482, but Boncompagni Ludovisi himself does not provide any documentation for his assertion.

published strict new regulations limiting devotions to persons who had not been authorized by the Church hierarchy. No new cults could be established without the pope's approval, unless they had existed for at least a century.

The language of the law was newly precise. Painting rays on the heads of un-official holy people, describing their miracles in print, or lighting lamps before their images was prohibited.[7] The actions of the Inquisition reflected a long-standing policy of the Counter-Reformation Church to keep control of all forms of religious expression in the hands of bishops and high ecclesiastical authorities, but the cardinals innovated in identifying exactly the practices that were no longer allowed. These changes had momentous implications for those promoting candidates for sanctity because they introduced difficult criteria that had not been in force universally before. How was a person's holiness now to be established if no signs of their special status could be placed before the public's eyes?

The first order of the Inquisition against cults of unauthorized individuals was promulgated a week after a ceremonial exhumation of Ludovica Albertoni's body in San Francesco a Ripa in March 1625. Exhumation itself, lamps kept burning before the refurbished altar, and two chapel inscriptions of 1625 calling the widow *beata* or "blessed" unabashedly pointed to the holiness of this particular Roman lady. Baldassare Paluzzi degli Albertoni was straddling the boundaries of the permissible in some of his devices for the Holy See had not approved any proceedings on behalf of Ludovica's beatification.

Against this background the Albertoni and their relatives sought additional Capitoline support for Ludovica's cult. Civic patronage was important at such an ambiguous moment for it suggested that the widow inspired devotion outside her family and that she was backed by people of social prominence whose rank attested to her virtue. Having patrons who were public officials served the further purpose of endowing Ludovica with a semipublic status herself. On 29 October 1625 the private council received a petition asking that the conservators suspend their audiences each January 31st, the day the Roman People made their offering of a chalice and candles to Ludovica. Baldassare Paluzzi degli Albertoni did not attend the meeting, but his son Antonio did and was no doubt satisfied with the favorable vote. To get the most mileage from the resolution Baldassare had it commemorated in a marble inscription on the wall of the burial chapel.[8] The family had effectively maneuvered the Roman People into declaring a holiday for an unauthorized "beata" in the very city and year in which the crackdown on unofficial cults began. Ludovica Albertoni's supporters either assumed the Inquisition orders were not meant for them or had high-level assurances that this particular gentlewoman was exempt.

---

[7] The Inquisition decision, dated 13 March 1625, permitted these practices for cults that had existed "since time immemorial." On 5 July 1634 a papal brief reiterated the 1625 ruling and added that "time immemorial" was to be understood as at least a century. For the relevant legislation see *Bullarium* 13:308–11 and 14:436–40, cited by Pastor, 29:10.

[8] ASC, cred. I, vol. 33, decreti, 0027v; Perlove, 45–46, 50.

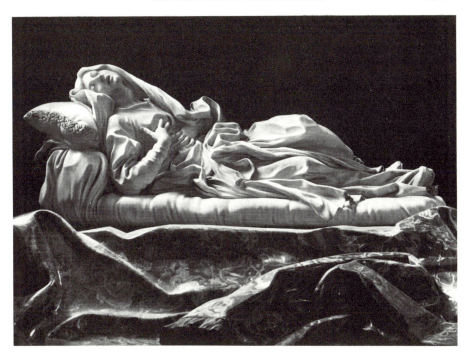

14. Gian Lorenzo Bernini's statue of Ludovica Albertoni (1671–1674) in the church of San Francesco a Ripa in Rome.

The Capitoline administration, always nudged by the Albertoni, remained loyal to Ludovica, commissioning her portrait for the conservators' chapel in 1645 and formally requesting the opening of hearings for her beatification in 1670.[9] This last date was anything but haphazard for an Albertoni had just become the adopted cardinal nephew of the new pope, Clement X, himself a member of the Roman Altieri family. A successful outcome for the proceedings was guaranteed and took place in late January 1671. The chapel inscription was cited along with other evidence to establish Ludovica's worthiness for the title of "blessed." Her family had skillfully employed civic patronage to widen her resonance and give her the all important testimony of public memory (see Figure 14).

A confraternity dedicated to the Madonna and the Immaculate Conception bid for civic sponsorship in the 1630s, and later, like Ludovica Albertoni's backers, returned to the Roman People when faced with new ecclesiastical restrictions. The company of the Immaculate Conception based in San Lorenzo in Damaso counted

---

[9] Perlove, *"Blessed Lodovica Albertoni,"* 46, 50–53. As Perlove notes, Antonio Albertoni was conservator in 1645. See also Pietrangeli, "Cappella," 11–17; the painting is attributed to Giovanni Francesco Romanelli. For more on the Albertoni's sacro-civic strategies see also Joseph Connors, "Alliance and Enmity in Roman Baroque Urbanism," *Römisches Jahrbuch für Kunstgeschichte* 25 (1989): 255–56.

a number of families of the civic nobility among its members; one of its officers, Bruto Gottifredo, was serving as conservator from July to September 1635.[10] On August 19th Gottifredo organized in the quarter an elaborate procession of the confraternity's prized possession, an image of the Madonna, to celebrate the re-decoration of the company's chapel. The Capitoline administration with Gotti-fredo at the helm was prominently represented, including the fourteen caporioni leading their artisan militia contingents, the "drummers of the Roman People" and, in a place of honor, the senator and conservators.[11]

The confraternity of the Conception was not the oldest or most prestigious Roman company, but it was hoping to be considered one of the most important by mounting events of this scale and splendor. It seems to have sought Capitoline support several times in the following years. A month after the great procession for the translation of the image in August 1635 the civic councils received a pe-tition asking that the conservators "adorn with their presence" the annual meeting of the confraternity to elect new officers.[12] Since this was the custom at the yearly elections of the venerable company of the Santissimo Salvatore ad Sancta Sancto-rum, the petitioners clearly hoped to be raised to the same status. They also wanted additional public demonstrations of civic patronage, requesting that the Capitoline buglers and the conservators' retainers, the *fedeli*, take part in their procession each year on the feast of the Immaculate Conception.[13]

Three years later in 1638 the company returned to the Capitol to seek an offer-ing of twelve large candles on August 19th, "the day of the translation of the image of the Immaculate Conception." They asked that the conservators, with papal approval, personally present the gift "in the name of the Roman People."[14] The offering of twelve candles associates their image of the Madonna of the Con-ception with the vision of a woman wearing a crown of twelve stars (*stelle*) that appeared to St. John in the Book of Revelation. A pious practice honoring the Virgin of the twelve stars (*stellario*) was popular in the seventeenth century and the last Sunday in August was her feast. In March 1640 the confraternity of the Conception and *Stellario* petitioned the councils to change the date of the civic gift to the final Sunday in August.[15]

---

[10] On the confraternity of the Concezione in San Lorenzo in Damaso see "Repertorio degli archivi delle confraternite romane," *RSRR* 6 (1985): 268–71. At a meeting of the confraternity on 4 January 1630, for example, members of the Velli, della Molara, Rossi, Tedellini, and Cinquini families were present; the Flemish lawyer Teodoro Ameyden was listed as one of the officers of the confraternity. ASR, 30 N.C., uff. 28 (Vespignani) 1630, pt. 1, 60r.

[11] Gigli, *Diario*, 157–60.

[12] ASC, cred. I, vol. 33, decreti, 0162v (22 September 1635).

[13] Ibid. New officers of the confraternity of the Salvatore were confirmed in the presence of the conservators, according to a legal document dated 1 April 1630, ASR, 30 N.C., uff. 18 (Bonincontro) 1630, pt. 2, 433r.

[14] ASC, cred. I, vol. 33, decreti, 0204v (27 April 1638).

[15] Antonio Cadlolo, "Compagnie, confraternite e pie unioni erette in S. Maria in Aracoeli di Roma," *Ara-coeli* 17 (1946): 43–44. ASC, cred. I, vol. 33, decreti, 0235v (21 March 1640). The

But the days of the Virgin of the twelve stars were numbered, as the petitioners surely knew. Two months earlier the Inquisition had moved to suppress this particular devotion by dissolving all confraternities with *stellario* in their titles. In what may have been a last desperate effort to keep it alive, the confraternity turned to the Roman People and won council approval for moving the date of the offering. Just as Baldassare Paluzzi degli Albertoni solicited civic support when the Church cracked down on unauthorized cults, the devotees of the *stellario* sought Capitoline backing at a moment when its status was, to say the least, ambiguous. To those who tried to obtain the patronage of the Roman People it was a form of public recognition that could enhance an effort to elevate the prestige of a cult or confraternity or that might help to keep it alive when threatened. [16]

BROKERS

The Roman People acted as patrons when they gave petitioners something they could give, like an extension to relatives of a Capitoline *vacabile*, the declaration of a public holiday for the conservators, or a civic delegation to a procession. They functioned as brokers when they facilitated the request of a client to patrons higher up. [17] As brokers the civic councils or magistrates were intermediaries, putting in a good word or adding their influence with patrons so that clients would receive favorable action. The Capitoline councils were the setting where petitions were brokered; they decided what further steps the Roman People would take with other authorities to support a client's cause. In the period 1623 to 1644 they rendered brokerage services to their own constituency of well-born lay families as well as to religious orders in the city.

In 1634 "some Roman families," who unfortunately remained nameless, sent a petition to the private council in defense of their rights in the main fish market. They collected a payment from their tenants, the fishmongers who rented stalls, which was called the fish market "piazzatico." Fearing that they would have to pay a tax on these fees, they pressed for Capitoline aid to stave it off. The councils responded warmly, directing that the conservators and the fiscal procurator

---

original petition addressed to the conservators is in ASC, cred. VI, vol. 60, giustificazioni, 353–54. It should be noted that, notwithstanding the council's approval of this petition, no funds were designated for the twelve candles in the 1641 *tabella*; ASC, cred. IV, vol. 106, 112v–38r. On the *Stellario* see Maroni Lumbroso and Martini, 218–19. While conceding an element of doubt, I do not follow these authors, or their eighteenth-century source, in identifying the petitioners of 1640 as a *different* confraternity of the Conception, one based at the church of Santa Maria in Aracoeli. Internal evidence links the two petitions of 1638 and 1640 and, as indicated above, the petition of 1638 refers explicitly to August 19th as "the day of the translation of the image of the Immaculate Conception." There is no evidence of the existence of a confraternity of the Conception at the Aracoeli in this period, while there is abundant documentation of one at San Lorenzo in Damaso, which sponsored a procession of its image on 19 August 1635.

[16] Cadlolo, 44.

[17] Kettering, *Patrons*, 4.

"should make every effort to continue the rights of these families, and if necessary, go in the name of the Roman People to Our Most Holy Lord [Urban VIII] and the Most Reverend Cardinal Francesco Barberini to preserve their continuation."[18] Although the petition recorded no names, we know from notarial documents that Roberto Capizucchi, member of an old family of the civic nobility, leased some stalls in the fish market to fishmongers in the 1630s and that the extinct patrician house of the Frangipani had owned others as late as 1614.[19] It is no surprise that the gentlemen who ran civic institutions occasionally used these institutions as added force in their efforts to protect their economic interests.

In the 1630s the Capitol was also twice called on by male religious orders to help raise the sacred status of one of their members. One man was a long-established saint from an ancient Roman senatorial family and the other was a recent immigrant who had chosen Rome as the recipient of innovative charitable efforts. While the two figures held vastly different rank in the Church's eyes—one was already canonized and the other the subject of an early beatification proceeding that failed—what they shared in the 1630s were supporters active in Rome who wanted to procure greater honors for them and for the monastic communities dedicated to them. The Hieronymite monks of the monastery of Saints Boniface and Alessio on the Aventine hill petitioned the Roman People in September 1635 to intercede with the pope to upgrade the feast of the "noble Roman," St. Alessio.[20] St. Alessio, the subject of an opera performed at the Barberini palace in 1632, was regarded in the seventeenth century as a special patron of the city of Rome and his painting was also commissioned for the chapel of the conservators' palace in 1645.[21] The monks played upon the contemporary obsession with aristocratic status in their appeal, counting on the Capitoline gentlemen to see this scion of an ancient patrician family as one of their own.

Promoters of the second holy man hoped that civic piety of a different sort would inspire the Roman People to support his cause. He was the Abbot Glicerio Landriani (1588–1618), a Milanese patrician associated with a very new religious order, the Piarists or Scolopi, from *scuole pie* or "pious schools," founded in 1617 by the Aragonese nobleman José de Calasanz (1556–1648). Calasanz had visited Rome in the late sixteenth century and been appalled by the religious ignorance he discovered among the Roman poor. In 1597 he opened a free primary school in the district of Trastevere and attracted followers who saw popular education as

---

[18] ASC, cred. I, vol. 33, decreti, 0141r (22 March 1634).

[19] ASR, 30 N.C., uff. 2 (Bonanni) 1636, pt. 2, 229r–30v; Cerasoli, "Diario," 278.

[20] ASC, cred. I, vol. 33, decreti, 0162v–63r (22 September 1635). They asked that his day be raised from a Simple to a Semi-Double feast. My thanks to Professor Patricia Fortini Brown for her assistance. For an interesting discussion of the hierarchy of public honors sought for seventeenth-century saints in southern Italy see Jean-Michel Sallman, "Il santo patrono cittadino nel '600," in *Per la storia sociale e religiosa del Mezzogiorno d'Italia*, ed. Giuseppe Galasso and Carla Russo, 2 vols. (Naples, 1980–82), 2:187–208.

[21] Magnuson, *Rome* 1:247–49; Pietrangeli, "Cappella," 15–17; the painting is attributed to Giovanni Francesco Romanelli.

an important work of charity. The Scolopi fathers urged the Capitoline councils in 1631 to petition the pope and the congregation of Rites for Landriani's beatification.[22] The Milanese religious had been one of Calasanz's closest disciples from the time of his arrival in Rome in 1612 and had provided the money that enabled the group to buy a house next to San Pantaleo to serve as its headquarters.[23] In addition to his efforts for the local poor, Landriani had family ties that recommended him to the civic magistrates for he was related to the aristocratic St. Charles Borromeo, reforming archbishop of Milan.

While Landriani's case seems to have had no more success before the congregation of Rites than St. Alessio's, both shed light on the role of civic brokering in a larger religio-political strategy. Clients turned to the Roman People as brokers when they thought the civic councils would see some reason to support their cause.

CLIENTS

The Roman People were most often patrons or brokers for causes dear to the hearts of particular families that played a role in civic institutions. As patrons they could offer public recognition, while as brokers they could help in private ways, using their influence informally by recommending a petition to Urban VIII or his nephews in a special delegation, by letter, or at one of the regular audiences that conservators had with the pope, or by interceding with a cardinalatial congregation like the congregation of Rites. But to act effectively as patrons and brokers the civic magistrates had to be sure that they were perceived by *their* patrons as good clients. Maintaining a favorable relationship with those who could offer help was as critical for the collective Roman People as for any individual family in Baroque Rome, and they did it in ways that were very like those of individuals. But the fact that they were a corporate or institutional client rather than an individual also set their client behavior apart in some respects, giving it particular features unlike the clientship of persons.

Capitoline officials spent a great deal of energy and resources oiling their bonds with key patrons. They made specific requests of their patrons relatively rarely; we will examine this kind of negotiation with one figure, the pope, in more detail in the next chapter. Most frequently we notice the Roman People cultivating a relationship with friends in high places rather than seeking a particular favor. Gifts and the language of piety and courtesy were the chief means they deployed to create a positive image of their affection for and loyalty to their patrons, earthly and celestial.

Routine gestures that elicited no special attention on the part of recipients

---

[22] ASC, cred. I, vol. 33, decreti, 0110v (6 September 1631).

[23] Carlo Bartolomeo Piazza, *Opere pie di Roma* (Rome, 1679), 84; Giovanni Giovannozzi, *Il Calasanzio e l'opera sua* (Florence, 1930), 8–9, 103; Leodegarius Picanyol, *Brevis conspectus historico-statisticus ordinis scholarum piarum* (Rome, 1932), 75, 296.

reveal how thoroughly institutional conduct was expected to conform to the standards of interpersonal relations. As we have seen, civic money funded presents or *regaglie* at Christmas to elected officers and the owners of Capitoline annuities (*vacabili*) as well as to many papal officials dispersed through the jurisdictional web of Roman government. Pepper, wax, sweetmeats, and salt went to the cardinal vicar, the rector of the university, all the clerks of the chamber, the auditor of the cardinal chamberlain, and the secretaries of all the important cardinalatial congregations.[24] These were not bribes; they were symbols of administrative politeness that also counted as part of the return on an investment or compensation for ill-paid public office. The Christmas gratuity was a sign of respect bearing the subtle assumption of continued, mutual, service. Granting the status of Roman citizen to foreign notables, especially those who came to staff the tribunal of the senator—the senator himself, his male kinsmen, and his collateral judges—was a form of recognition with the same purpose.[25]

Sometimes the Capitoline councils singled out a prestigious titled family or religious order for honor. To show their gratitude for "the immense love with which he had always attended the Roman People" they voted a memorial service for Cardinal Odoardo Farnese, a member of the ruling house of Parma, when he died in 1626. They decided to thank the Jesuits "for so much benefit and toil in educating all the sons of Romans and foreigners in knowledge and instruction" by presenting a chalice worth thirty scudi and four cierges to the church of the Annunziata, which served the Jesuits' Roman College before Sant' Ignazio was built, at the beginning of each academic year.[26] Although both gifts were public statements that were suitable for a public body to give, the language in which the civic gifts were expressed was the same elaborate, emotional rhetoric used between individuals. Anything less would have been perceived as lacking in respect.[27]

When there was a lack of respect between patron and client, it had to be carefully hidden. Capitoline offerings to the fiscal procurator, the "pope's man" on the Capitol, though expected, were slightly forced; often the fiscal procurator demanded them. Despite the element of coercion, or at least manipulation, in his requests, however, the Roman People responded in the proper affective terms. Voting to give Angelo Giardino and his son the extra Christmas *regaglie* he had asked for in 1643, they proclaimed their gratitude "for the benefits received through his efforts and for the singular affection he bears to the interests of the Capitol."[28] Their relationship with the fiscal procurator was delicate; the magis-

---

[24] ASC, cred. IV, vol. 106, tabella, 115r–26r.

[25] ASC, cred. I, vol. 32, decreti, 0275v; ASC, cred. I, vol. 33, decreti, 0188v, 0222r.

[26] ASC, cred. I, vol. 33, decreti, 0034r (10 March 1626); ASC, cred. I, vol. 32, decreti, 0280v (18 June 1624).

[27] Kettering, "Gift-Giving," 132–34; Orest Ranum, "Courtesy, Absolutism, and the Rise of the French State, 1630–1660," *Journal of Modern History* 52 (1980): 429–31.

[28] ASC, cred. I, vol. 34, decreti, 0043v (22 January 1643), 0049r (2 June 1643), 0055r (15 September 1643). For more on the complicated relationship with the fiscal procurator see Chapter 12.

trates cloaked their resentment at Giardino, waiting for a new pontiff and a chance to get rid of him.

As in the case of the fiscal procurator, the people whom the Capitoline administration had to please were only rarely freely chosen. The public status of the Roman People endowed them with obligatory patrons, a fact that was nowhere clearer than in their relationship to the Barberini, as we shall see. But they had obligatory celestial patrons as well, a function of their role as the corporate embodiment of the locality. The civic treasury provided a steadily increasing pantheon of holy persons with yearly offerings on the saints' feast days. Twelve churches had received annual donations of this kind in 1593, but the number had doubled by 1621 and had grown to a total of thirty-seven in the civic budget of 1641.[29] Averaging around 35 scudi, the value of the presents ranged from 2.5 scudi for two candles for the little church of San Biagio at the foot of the Capitoline hill to 70 scudi for a silver chalice and eight wax tapers for the great basilicas of St. Peter and St. John Lateran.

Sometimes the Roman People sought the special intervention of a saint for the welfare of the community. When plague raged in Italy in 1625 and 1630, the councils voted a chalice and cierges first to San Rocco and, in the latter year, to St. Sebastian, both famous for their salvific powers.[30] More often Capitoline gifts to saints were meant to maintain the city in the position of a faithful and grateful client, keeping the patron generally well-disposed to Romans. Civic officials made presentations to seven churches dedicated to the Madonna and to two institutions connected to Santa Francesca Romana, a local patrician matron who had died in 1440 and was canonized in 1608. Native saints like St. Cecilia, St. Agnes, St. Eustachio, and St. Alessio received the attention of the Capitoline government for similar reasons. Sometimes too civic officials emphasized a relationship with powers at once spiritual and sociopolitical. Chalices from the Roman People found their way not only to the Jesuit order but also to the Theatines, Dominicans, Barnabites, Franciscans, and Oratorians.[31]

When the civic councils made rules about how their contributions were to be treated, they sounded less like supplicants and more like donors. In 1629 they decreed that the chalices be engraved with the initials S.P.Q.R., the name of the reigning pontiff, and the year; they ordered church officials to keep the vessels in

[29] *Sommario dell'entrate e spese dell'Inclito Populo {sic} Romano* (Rome, 1593), which is found in ASV, arm. IV, vol. 32, 255v–58r. Most of the twelve churches were neighbors of the Capitol. For 1621 see Cametti, 115–16; for 1641 recipients see ASC, cred. IV, vol. 106, tabella, 114r, 133r–v, 137v–38r. It should be recalled that there were over 250 churches, oratories, monasteries, and convents in Rome in the 1640s; Pastor, 29:543. In 1565 eight churches had received chalices and wax from the Roman People; Francesco Cerasoli, "Commentario di Pietro Paolo Muziano relativo agli officiali del Comune di Roma nel secolo XVI," *Studi* 13 (1892): 121. In 1801 seventy-three churches received Capitoline gifts; ASC, cred. II, vol. 101, bilanci della camera capitolina, 246v.

[30] ASC, cred. I, vol. 33, decreti, 0024r (15 July 1625) and 0097v (24 August 1630). The offering to St. Sebastian was made at the chapel dedicated to him in San Pietro in Vincoli.

[31] ASC, cred. IV, vol. 106, tabella, 114r, 133r–v, 137v–38r.

perpetuity and to show them to the magistrates each year or the gifts would be withdrawn.[32] The Capitoline authorities wanted credit for their benefactions and saw no advantage in humility on that score; their donations were meant to honor both the saint and the Roman People. And indeed, what value would they have if neither community nor patron could see them? An institution operating in a patronal system needed to make its addresses in humble tones and to mask its criticisms just like an individual, but the signs of respect it could offer were different from those available to a person. They were necessarily public. When the conservators presented the chalice and wax on the saint's feast, dressed in their full regalia and accompanied by their liveried retainers, they were displaying civic piety, doing honor to the patron, and hoping for a sympathetic hearing when the city needed aid.

THE BARBERINI

Much the same constellation of motives underlay the client behavior of the Roman People in relation to the pope and his family. It was a mixture of reverence, self-promotion, and self-interest. Because they were civic representatives in a city with an elected monarch, the Capitoline authorities acquired a new set of patrons with each pontificate. From 6 August 1623 until his death on 29 July 1644 Urban VIII was the most important earthly patron the lay civic government could cultivate, followed by his nephew Cardinal Francesco Barberini and his other relatives.

The pope demanded a special fidelity from the Roman People; he expected to be the sole recipient of secular honors in his capital city. A Farnese cardinal could not have had a memorial service paid for by the civic treasury much later than 1626. Urban did not want the Capitol spreading its favors to other families or other monarchs, as his quashing of the proposed celebration for the Habsburg heir in 1637 demonstrated. He took civic clientage seriously.

Gifts of inscriptions, ceremonies, delegations, and statues flowed from the Capitol to the Barberini. "Applauding the glory and felicity of our lord Urban VIII and of his most excellent house," the civic councils would vote to give them a sign of their appreciation, fidelity, or devotion.[33] Gifts were material ways to honor the patron and they were also occasions for rhetorical display. As the ultimate "big man" in a patronal system, an absolute monarch expected elaborate marks of respect from subjects.[34] The language of civic address to the pope responds to such expectations. It is ornately reverential, typical of the prevailing

---

[32] ASC, cred. I, vol. 33, decreti, 0078r–79v (meetings of 18 and 22 September 1629).

[33] ASC, cred. I, vol. 33, decreti, 0107r (2 June 1631).

[34] Gundersheimer, 13; Ranum, 429–36; Peter Burke, "Languages and Anti-Languages in Early Modern Italy," in *Historical Anthropology*, 88, and idem, "Sacred Rulers," ibid., 181; Roland Mousnier, "Les concepts d'"ordres,' d'"états,' de 'fidélité' et de 'monarchie absolue' en France de la fin du XVᵉ siècle à la fin du XVIIIᵉ," *Revue historique* 247 (1972): 303–4.

idiom of clientage in its emotional tone and images. The honors offered by the Roman People to the early modern pontiffs, and especially to Urban VIII, have been misinterpreted and seen as a symbol of the decadence of civic institutions.[35] They are more usefully understood as an expressive and instrumental mode characteristic of contemporary patron-client discourse.

The Capitoline encomiums for the Barberini pope began, as we have seen, with his *possesso* procession past the statues, inscriptions, and triumphal arch that praised his virtue and talents and placed him within a Roman lineage of imperial and holy rulers. A few months later in June 1624 the civic councils made a more personal gesture; they recorded the death and merits of Virginio Cesarini, the pope's *maestro di camera* and a poet of some fame, by a memorial plaque in the palace of the conservators. During an international diplomatic crisis in early 1625 a special delegation to Urban VIII promised him the support of the Roman People. At the end of 1626 Capitoline representatives made their first present to Cardinal Francesco Barberini, profiting from their role as protectors of the city's antiquities to bestow a marble relief recently unearthed in the Forum.[36] They gave careful attention to the tastes of their patrons: Urban's love of poetry and his nephew's collecting instincts.

In 1630 the conservators convinced the Capitoline councils to make a demonstration of their sorrow at the death of the pope's brother Carlo Barberini that rivaled the *possesso* in its elaborateness. They organized a costly funeral at the church of Santa Maria in Aracoeli and commissioned an inscription and statue to honor him from Urban's favorite sculptor, Gian Lorenzo Bernini. Carlo Barberini had held the post of commander of the papal armies and the sculpture, a bust by Bernini affixed to an antique torso with limbs by Alessandro Algardi, emphasized his military role. The councils drew on a new Capitoline tradition, strongly influenced by ancient example; since 1593 three other papal generals had been recognized by a combination of inscriptions, ceremonies, and statues placed in the conservators' audience chamber. Giulio Cenci, the Capitoline legal counsel, gave the sermon at the memorial service on 3 August 1630, and as a sign of civic generosity bread was distributed by selected lay patricians to the poor in each of the fourteen neighborhood rioni.[37] In a subtle gesture of reciprocation the pope

---

[35] Hook, 214. For some sixteenth-century honors to the popes see Mitchell, 95–102, and Stinger, 257.

[36] ASC, cred. I, vol. 32, decreti, 0280r (18 June 1624); ASC, cred. I, vol. 33, decreti, 0021v (1 January 1625) and 0040v (3 December 1626). The council decrees do not mention the marble bust of Cesarini, which was eventually located in the audience chamber of the conservators; Pietrangeli, "Sala dei capitani," 645 n. 23. See also Pastor, 28:70–75.

[37] ASC, cred. I, vol. 33, decreti, 0092r–96v record details of their planning process between 5 March and the funeral itself on 3 August 1630. ASC, cred. VI, vol. 30, registro di mandati, 483–98 records payments by the papal treasurer Sacchetti. See also Gigli, *Diario*, 116. Pietrangeli, "Sala dei capitani," 645; Nicola Courtright, "Memorial to Carlo Barberini," in *Drawings by Gianlorenzo Bernini*, ed. Irving Lavin et al. (Princeton University Art Museum, 1981), 72–77; Irving Lavin, "Bernini's Memorial Plaque for Carlo Barberini," *Journal of the Society of Architectural Historians* 42 (1983): 6–8;

paid the Roman People back three weeks later by insisting, over their demurrals, that they send representatives to inspect for plague contagion the retinue of Cardinal Antonio Barberini when he returned from the infected north of Italy.[38]

The 12,000 scudi it took to produce Carlo Barberini's funeral came cheerfully, it seems, from the papal treasury, but the five months of preparations were volunteered by gentlemen of the civic nobility, led by the conservators. In this case Gigli allows us a privileged glimpse behind the scenes to see what probably drove much of the Capitol's client behavior.

> These obsequies were celebrated in the name of the Roman People, being authors the conservators of the chamber of Rome, who were obligated to the pope, particularly Valerio Santacroce and Vincenzo Muti, the former for having had a brother promoted to the cardinalate and the latter similarly for having had a brother made canon of St. Peter's.[39]

Families whose members were elected to the office of conservator exploited public resources to make their own special gestures of gratitude to the Barberini. Personal clients, they depended on papal patronage for jobs for themselves or their relatives.[40] Other gentlemen collaborated because they were also subsidized to look good in the patron's eyes and to play a patronal role themselves in relation to their needy neighbors.

Urban VIII perhaps found civic obeisance especially pleasing because his own family aspirations met resistance from the titled lords and princely houses of Italy. As we saw in Chapter 3, early in 1631 Urban had awarded the honorific title of prefect to his nephew Taddeo Barberini. The Roman People seized the opportunity to display their loyalty; they sent a delegation of congratulations and offered to make a "demonstration of rejoicing." Capitoline representatives thanked the pope and the Barberini cardinals for being invited to take part in the spectacular cavalcade that marked Taddeo's investiture in August and the conservators put up an inscription celebrating his new title in November.[41] By contrast, when Urban

Aikin, "Christian Soldiers," 222. For a comparative example of city-financed festivities of state see J. E. Varey, "Calderón, Cosme Lotti, Velázquez, and the Madrid Festivities of 1636–1637," *Renaissance Drama*, n.s., 1 (1968): 253–82.

[38] ASC, cred. I, vol. 33, decreti, 0097v–98r (24 August 1630).

[39] ASC, cred. VI, vol. 30, registro di mandati, 483–98; Gigli, *Diario*, 116.

[40] On behalf of a "Monsignor" Santacroce, Valerio Santacroce petitioned the Barberini for a post as governor in an undated letter, which may well have been written in the early to mid-1620s. (Since Santacroce's brother Antonio and son Marcello were both "monsignori" at one time or another, the date can only be speculative. However, only one of them, Antonio, ever held a post as papal governor and this was between 1623 and 1625; Cardella, 6:290–91.) The request is located in BAV, Barb. lat. 10634 prov. In another undated letter Giacinto del Bufalo, conservator in 1649, petitioned for a post in the household of Cardinal Francesco Barberini for his father; BAV, Barb. lat. 10633 prov. On Santacroce ties with the Barberini see also Stephen Pepper, *Guido Reni* (Oxford, 1984), 267.

[41] On the prefecture see Pastor, 28:46–47, and Gigli, *Diario*, 120–24. For the Capitoline response see ASC, cred. I, vol. 33, decreti, 0107r–8v; for civic expenses see ASC, cred. VI, vol. 30, registro di mandati, 291–93. A copy of the papal brief dated 19 November 1631, which gave the conservators

demanded that the new prefect take ceremonial precedence over all secular dignitaries, the highest-ranking aristocrats in the city were indignant and ambassadors of foreign powers broke off diplomatic relations with Rome. The prefecture crisis showed some of the concrete benefits the pope could draw from having the civic administration as a client. Special Capitoline deputations carried thanks to Urban VIII and Cardinal Francesco Barberini again in 1632, praising their efforts to safeguard Rome when plague threatened from the Tuscan border.[42]

The three conservators and prior of the caporioni who took office in January 1634 had a more daring idea of how "to gain favor," as Gigli put it, with the pope and his most powerful nephew: placing an inscription honoring Urban in the Aracoeli and putting up a statue of Cardinal Francesco with an inscription lauding his deeds.[43] Legislation of 1590 prevented the Capitoline authorities from indulging in a gesture of filial piety beloved of their sixteenth-century forebears: erecting a statue of the pope on the Capitol. Five pontiffs had received such homage, beginning with the first Medici pope, Leo X, in 1521. During the Vacant See that followed the death of Sixtus V in August 1590, however, the councils had forbidden further testimonials to "living princes" on the hill.[44]

The conservators obtained a papal brief rescinding the 1590 council decree on 15 January 1634, and two weeks later appeared before the private council to propose that it too vote to annul it. Between "the reefs of adulation and ingratitude," they explained, it was better to err on the side of the former, implying that, in any case, the bonds of natural law underlying their filial attachment to the pontiff should override any positive laws of their predecessors.[45] Their suggestion to offer a Capitoline statue of a cardinal nephew was unprecedented, and Cardinal Francesco evidently thought it unwise because he declined the gift, recommending that he merely be noted on the plaque planned for his uncle. The Roman People found a more satisfactory way to please him two years later when they voted to dismantle a tower above the arch of Septimus Severus in the Forum and give the

---

permission to put up an inscription congratulating Taddeo Barberini on the prefecture, is recorded in the council decrees, ASC, cred. I, vol. 33, 0113r. This inscription, which seems not to have been presented for approval to the councils, was also placed in the conservators' audience chamber. See also Scott, 55–56, fig. 146.

[42] ASC, cred. I, vol. 33, decreti, 0115r (9 February 1632).

[43] Gigli, *Diario*, 144. The three conservators and prior of the caporioni for the trimester beginning in January 1634 were Pietro Mazzarini, Angelo Incoronati, Serafino Cenci, and Valerio dei Massimi. ASC, cred. I, vol. 33, decreti, 0136v–37r (1 February 1634).

[44] For the prohibition against papal monuments see ASC, cred. I, vol. 29, decreti, 0253v (28 August 1590). Rodocanachi, *Capitole*, 167–69; Stinger, 527. Aikin suggests that the popes themselves ordered that these statues be erected, but does not supply evidence to support this contention, "Capitoline Hill," 163–64. See also Monika Butzek, *Die Communalen Repräsentationsstatuen der Päpste des 16. Jahrhunderts in Bologna, Perugia und Rom* (Bad Honnef: 1978).

[45] ASC, cred. I, vol. 33, decreti, 0136v (1 February 1634). They resolved to remove the marble inscription reminding them of the 1590 prohibition at the meeting of 23 June 1634; ASC, cred. I, vol. 33, decreti, 0145v–48r. A copy of the brief is included with their resolution.

material to the church of Saints Luke and Martina, which he was rebuilding nearby.[46]

But now that there was no bar to placing a monument to a "living prince" on the Capitol, why not a statue to the pontiff himself? A well-attended council meeting in September 1635 approved a resolution to commission a bronze sculpture of Urban VIII, the first new papal effigy on the Capitol since the 1580s. Although there is no record of it in the council decrees, planning must have been afoot for some time since a proposed inscription was submitted at the same session. Singling out the efforts of this "best prince" to avoid the dangers of war and plague, bring back the duchy of Urbino to the Papal States without bloodshed, maintain abundant food supplies, and construct new fortresses, the Senate and Roman People gave him public thanks.[47] The conservators turned the commission over to Gian Lorenzo Bernini, who used marble instead of bronze and completed the statue by the summer of 1640 (see Figure 15). Transported by torchlight, it was raised through the window of the main council chamber in the palace of the conservators. Late in September 1640 civic officials celebrated its installation with an oration, a mass at the Aracoeli, and a distribution of bread, medals, and coins.[48]

Earlier that year the conservators had had to concede one of their most singular forms of patronage to Taddeo Barberini. By long tradition the three magistrates had the exclusive right to the heads of any fish over forty inches long (5 *palmi*) caught in the Roman district; a marble plaque set up in the city fish market served as a public measure of the size of fish and a reminder of this regulation. The conservators gave the fish heads, considered a great delicacy, to people whom they wanted to impress or with whom they sought to cement ties.[49] Breaking with

[46] ASC, cred. I, vol. 33, decreti, 0140v (1 February 1634) and 0175r (9 September 1636). Gigli, *Diario*, 144.

[47] ASC, cred. I, vol. 33, decreti, 0162r–v (22 September 1635). Giovanni Andrea Borboni, *Delle statue* (Rome, 1661), 265, reports erroneously that approval came at a meeting of the private council on 13 October 1635, but the terms of the elected officers he lists as present at the meeting had in fact ended two weeks before.

[48] ASC, cred. I, vol. 33, decreti, 0238r–v (15 June 1640); Gigli, *Diario*, 192–94; Stanislao Fraschetti, *Il Bernini* (Milan, 1900), 151–53. In addition to the documents quoted by Fraschetti see payments in ASC, cred. VI, vol. 31, registro di mandati, 339–40. The three conservators printed the oration given on the occasion by Lelio Guidiccioni, *Adlocutio capitolina Laelii Guidiccioni statuam positam Urbano VIII Pont. Max.* (Rome, 1640).

[49] In a volume of *ricordi*, or memorable events of his time, the Roman patrician Orazio Altieri mentions that, while he was conservator in 1612, he and his two colleagues each received forty-two fish heads. According to the Altieri family biographer Pietro Visconti, Orazio kept a list of each person to whom he had given the fish heads, which were considered a culinary delicacy, and noted the motive for the gift: respect [*ossequio*], kinship, or friendship; Visconti, 3:569. Paolo Giovio's day-long pursuit of a choice fish is recounted by Lynn Lawner, *The Courtesan in the Venetian Republic* (New York, 1987), 29. I would like to thank Professor John Paoletti for this reference. After the conservators' privilege was abolished during the Napoleonic era, Pope Pius VII substituted the right to name a recipient of a

15. The statue of Urban VIII by Gian Lorenzo Bernini erected in the palace of the conservators in 1640.

custom in January 1640, however, the conservators permitted the pope's nephew
to keep the heads of large fish caught in his tuna fishing grounds at the little port
of Santa Marinella. In August 1641 the conservators were presented with a papal
order extending this right to fish taken from any of Taddeo's properties. The
message was clear: papal nephews could override long cherished civic privileges,
despite all the gestures of respect directed their way.[50]

As this concession warns us, Capitoline gifts to the pope were in part a defensive measure, meant to stave off damage as well as ensure a receptive audience
when the Roman People asked for a favor or expressed anxiety about something.
The expectation of getting something in return, we have been recently reminded,
was fundamental to the patron-client relationship.[51] But this opened it up to
potential disappointment and thus to feelings of resentment. The Roman People
never articulated such sentiments, but in small ways they sometimes revealed a
suppressed criticism. When Urban VIII recovered from a serious illness in 1637,
the Capitoline councils sent delegations to congratulate him and his nephews on
his return to health and ordered a mass of thanksgiving at the Aracoeli. But they
subtly commented on papal bread policy by distributing loaves of bread that
weighed twelve ounces in contrast to the eight-ounce loaf that had been the Annona's standard since 1621.[52]

Another incident in late 1641 disclosed their same preference for indirect expressions of irritation. Gigli tells of the discovery near the Corso of an antique
architectural fragment; Cardinal Francesco Barberini immediately notified the
conservators of the find, in recognition of Capitoline guardianship over the city's
antiquities. The diarist, who was serving as prior of the caporioni at the time,

dowry funded by the state lottery; Baldassare Capogrossi Guarna, *Il mercato del pesce in Roma. Cenni storici* (Rome, 1879), 13.

[50] *Statuta almae urbis*, bk. 3, chap. 67; ASC, protocollo no. 3495, registers the brief of 5 January 1640. Gigli refers to the order of 16 August 1641 in *Diario*, 199. To be fair, papal nephews could also help the Romans. Cardinal Francesco Barberini saved an ancient ruin from destruction at the hands of his uncle and civic officials in 1640. In order to rebuild the Trevi fountain, Urban VIII ordered the conservators on 15 May 1640 to contribute travertine taken from the tomb of Cecilia Metella on the Appian Way; Cesare D'Onofrio, *Acque e fontane di Roma* (Rome, 1977), 531. On 1 August the conservators met with the fountain's architect, Gian Lorenzo Bernini, to award the con-tract for dismantling the tomb. The contract went to the official Capitoline mason; ASC, cred. IV, vol. 96, istrumenti, 66v, 67r. On 25 August Ameyden reported that Bernini had indeed begun demolition, but, "the Roman People having become aware of it, he was stopped and the work ceased, so as not to cause an outcry." Oskar Pollak, *Die Kunsttätigkeit unter Urban VIII*, 2 vols. (Vienna, 1928–31), 1:14. However, an *avviso* of 1 September 1640 is more specific: "four gentlemen, lovers of an-tiquities, representing to Cardinal [Francesco] Barberini that this [demolition] would open the way to the destruction of the other antiquities, whose fame attracts almost the whole world to come to see them, and thus there would be fewer visitors, Cardinal Barberini, who has no other aim than the grandeur and good government of this city, has ordered that the demolition be suspended;" ibid., 1:14–15. See also John A. Pinto, *The Trevi Fountain* (New Haven, 1986), 41–42; Connors, "Alli-ance," 234.

[51] Kettering, "Gift-Giving," 151.

[52] Gigli, *Diario*, 54, 173; ASC, cred. I, vol. 33, decreti, 0188v (20 August 1637).

describes his remarkable candlelit visit to the excavation with the conservators, "I touched the marbles and the sculptures and took a piece of the yellow columns." But then the pope let it be known that he would like to receive the fragment. Rather than responding to their patron's hint, Capitoline officials interpreted this information as an indication that the papal treasurer would now bear the costs of digging up the piece. Nothing happened. With the arrival of the autumn rains the ruin was soon covered over again.[53]

The patronal system that patterned relations between persons in Baroque Rome also dictated the rules of comportment, the forms of address, and the kinds of expectations required of the Roman People. As a corporate or institutional actor, however, its resources differed somewhat from those of individuals tied by bonds of clientage. Although the Capitoline administration provided some brokerage services through informal channels, its main contribution to clients or patrons was publicity. Through delegations, inscriptions, ceremonies, and statues it could enhance their status by making public testimonials or giving public honors. Its institutional character also influenced its role in the patron-client network in other ways. Unlike individual clients the Capitol could not choose its patrons; the popes demanded civic loyalty and service. Nor, when they felt their gifts had not been adequately reciprocated, could the Roman People desert their prince in hopes of doing better elsewhere, although they could make oblique gestures of disapproval. Finally, the patronage of the Roman People as a collectivity was open to exploitation for private family goals by gentlemen who held high civic offices. In some Capitoline gifts to Urban VIII it was a little too easy to tell who the real client was.

In this chapter I have set Capitoline conduct towards the pope and the Barberini in a broader context of civic relationships with local religious orders, saints, and families. Prevailing assumptions of what was appropriate behavior between patrons and clients shaped all these relationships. In the next chapter we shall probe more deeply the interaction between Urban VIII and the Roman People, focusing on the issue of money and exploring the material basis for the clientage ties of pope and city.

[53] Gigli, *Diario*, 203.

Chapter Twelve

CIVIC REVENUES AND THE PAPACY

THIS CHAPTER examines the financial and political mechanisms available to the Roman People to raise money for "extraordinary expenses," the imposing category of public expenditures not covered by the ordinary revenues of the civic treasury, and the uses Urban VIII made of these mechanisms. Funding the extraordinary expenses of the city and the papacy takes us to the heart of the politics of fidelity. Neither the Capitoline chamber nor the apostolic chamber had much money left over to pay for the unexpected after fixed needs were met.[1] Plague prevention measures, an elaborate funeral, the outbreak of war, even routine maintenance of walls and flood control structures, all required fund-raising efforts by patron or client of varying degrees of difficulty. Some of these efforts were so routine as to seem like nothing more than accounting manipulations, although they were not that innocent in reality. Others involved negotiations between the Capitol and the pope that revealed the points of tension between, as well as the common interests of, patrician subjects and their prince.

SOURCES OF EXTRAORDINARY REVENUE

The Roman People had to provide for a regular list of ordinary expenditures, as we saw in Chapter 5, and they also had to finance extraordinary expenditures. Some of their so-called extraordinary obligations were long-established civic responsibilities, others were new initiatives, and still others were duties handed to them by the popes—showing the state's view of what the locality should fund. Like the officials of the apostolic chamber, Capitoline officers resorted to a range of devices of varying degrees of ingenuity to find money for items that did not figure in the ordinary budget. They delayed repayment to holders of civic bonds, drew on deposits in special accounts, raised new loans, and asked the pope for pecuniary contributions. Not all of these techniques were equally effective, but from the point of view of Roman gentlemen they all had one outstanding merit: they cost them nothing directly.

The most frequent method the Roman People employed to obtain extra sums of moderate size, anything from 75 to 12,000 scudi, was to postpone repayments of the public debt. This rather simple operation was encased in an elaborate terminology. As we saw in Chapter 5, most of the proceeds of the city's meat tax,

---

[1] For the civic budget see Chapter 5. On the papacy's extraordinary expenditures see Partner, "Financial Policy," 29; Lutz, 119; Reinhard, "Finanza," 371; Delumeau, *Vie* 2:757.

the Capitoline treasury's largest source of income, were earmarked for payments on bond issues called *monti*. In addition to the regular payment of interest, the system anticipated that every four months a certain number of bonds (*luoghi di monti*) would be extracted by lot and their owners repaid. With a papal chirograph giving permission, however, a scheduled extraction could be suspended and the amount that would have gone to reimburse bond holders made available for another specified purpose. Interest payments were not affected by this procedure, for extractions of *luoghi di monti* were repayments of the principal of the loan.[2]

From meat tax revenues freed up by suspending such extractions, the Roman People raised over 12,000 scudi to pay their part of the expenses of the pope's *possesso* procession in November 1623 and of his coronation earlier in the fall. This method also purchased new outfits for their officials during the Holy Year of 1625, fixed the clock on the palace of the senator, paid the Cavaliere d'Arpino for the paintings in the largest council chamber, and funded the inscription for the pope's friend, Virginio Cesarini.[3] In addition it provided money to fix the city walls.

Repairing the city walls illustrates a common type of financial transaction between the pope and the Capitol. In 1624, for instance, the street masters recommended that Urban VIII authorize funds for the civic authorities to use to fix sections of the wall outside three city gates. This resulted in a papal chirograph addressed to the conservators in which 1,000 scudi of the meat tax were diverted from repaying *monti* owners to patching up the walls. In a similar expenditure recorded in 1640 the magistrates paid the official civic mason for work "that we have had done by order of Our Lord [the pope]." The Capitol even provided small marble shields bearing the arms of three governing authorities, the pontiff, the cardinal chamberlain of the apostolic chamber, and the Roman People, to post on the recently revamped portion.[4] (See Figure 16.)

What these examples reveal is a normal mode of providing for extraordinary expenses. Although it was not registered as a regular budget item, the Roman People were responsible for maintaining the wall around the city and they did this with income from their meat tax. Suspending *monti* payments was a relatively painless way to produce sporadic sums for such a purpose, but the Capitoline magistrates did not have the authority to alter any terms related to the public debt. Thus a papal order was needed to release money that was technically civic money for a civic obligation undertaken by civic employees. It was also understood that both papal and civic officials would get acknowledgment for the work in the form of coats of arms at the site. Although they might seem complicated, the underlying relations between town and state finances expressed here would not surprise most historians of early modern government. Centralizing rulers ex-

---

[2] ASC, cred. IV, vol. 96, istrumenti, 49r–55v, record twelve chirographs diverting funds from the meat tax in this manner between 1623 and 1625.

[3] Ibid.

[4] Ibid., 51v (1624); ASC, cred. VI, vol. 31, registro di mandati, 347–48 (1640, 1642).

16. The coat of arms of the Senate and Roman People, the initials
S.P.Q.R. (*Senatus populusque romanus*), as it might appear on city
walls, fountains, and edicts.

ercised control over the credit mechanisms of their subject cities both to assure
their own tax base and to inspire confidence in would-be investors. That seventy
percent of the income of the Capitoline treasury already went towards debt service
and that this procedure lengthened the period of municipal indebtedness did not
concern any of the partners in the operation.[5]

[5] Partner, "Financial Policy," 28; Stumpo, *Capitale*, 264–67. On debt and relations between city
and state in the early modern Netherlands see James D. Tracy, *A Financial Revolution in the Habsburg
Netherlands* (Berkeley, 1985), 145, and in early modern France see Nora Temple, "The Control and
Exploitation of French Towns during the Ancien Régime," in *State and Society in Seventeenth-Century
France*, ed. Raymond Kierstead (New York, 1975), 69–71, and Gail Bossenga, "City and State: An

Did the pope ever order the Capitol to suspend *monti* extractions for items he wanted but that were not as clearly a civic duty as the walls? The answer would appear to be yes. In 1624 his chirographs released 2,000 scudi of meat tax revenue to the Roman People to contribute to housing pilgrims during the upcoming Holy Year of 1625 and another 1,000 scudi for draining the trenches surrounding the papal fortress near the Vatican. The Capitoline councils discussed neither expenditure; to Urban it must have seemed obvious that the civic government should help pay the costs of poor visitors during a jubilee year or of removing unhealthy pools of water around the Castel Sant'Angelo. In 1637 the pontiff ordered the conservators to take 1,000 scudi from the wine tax to repair the former Pantheon, which had been rededicated as the church of Santa Maria della Rotonda'. As custodians of city antiquities the Roman People could be construed to have a vague responsibility to protect the monument, but they certainly did not maintain every Roman church that had once been an ancient temple out of civic funds. None of these actions affected tax rates of course; when it was a question of increasing the meat tax, rather than of authorizing specific payments from it, the pope proceeded in a different manner, as we shall see.[6]

The Roman People had other expedients for financing extraordinary expenses that were less frequent than suspending debt repayments. One was taking funds on deposit in their name at the city's lending bank, the *monte di pieta'*. For example, when Pope Gregory XV gave the nuns of Sant'Ambrogio the right to pipe water from the Capitoline settling-tank in 1622, the civic treasurer made good the 200 scudi in income lost because of the pontiff's generosity from an account reserved for fountain repairs. The notaries who purchased the lucrative offices of the Thirty Capitoline Notaries paid sums into a fund at the bank designated for upkeep of the Capitoline palaces. It was from this account that the magistrates withdrew 2,000 scudi to pay Bernini for the marble statue of Urban VIII they erected in 1640.[7]

Still another method was raising new loans on the *monti* market, a procedure that required prior papal approval. In 1641 the Capitol was paying off eleven separate bond issues. Since this technique was rarely used during Urban's reign before the late 1630s, there must have been frequent recourse to it under his predecessors. Although our information is incomplete, we do know that between 1604 and 1641 the annual civic interest payments had risen from 62,000 to

---

Urban Perspective on the Origins of the French Revolution," in *The Political Culture of the Old Regime*, vol. 1 of *The French Revolution and the Creation of Modern Political Culture*, ed. Keith Michael Baker (Oxford, 1987), 119–23. *La fiscalité et ses implications sociales en Italie et en France au XVIIe et XVIIIe siècles*, a recent collection of essays devoted to fiscal relations between central and local government in France and Italy, is strangely silent on the subject of public debt.

[6] ASC, cred. IV, vol. 96, istrumenti, 53r–54v; ASC, cred. VI, vol. 52, registro di patenti, 0037v.

[7] ASC, cred. IV, vol. 96, istrumenti, 48v; ASC, cred. VI, vol. 48, ristretti di dare et avere, 95r; Fraschetti, 151–52. The receipt for the notaries' annual payment in 1635 is found in ASR, uff. 2 (Bonanni) 1635, pt. 3, 292r–v.

108,000 scudi. The first time that the councils approved new borrowing during the Barberini pontificate was in 1638, when they had to come up with 6,000 scudi to repair flood control structures on the Chiani, a river above Orvieto. To fund this project they sold sixty *luoghi di monti* valued at 100 scudi apiece on the Roman bond market. The interest payments on these loans, called "fruits" out of deference to the Church's anti-usury stance, were secured on income from the meat tax and from an earlier bond issue.[8] Floating a loan always had potential implications for taxation, since an assignment of specific funds to pay interest had to be made for each obligation.

These three methods, suspending debt repayment, drawing on special deposits, and issuing new loans, fall into the category of routine approaches to finding money because they required no particular effort outside the usual processes of financial administration. In a different category was soliciting funds directly from Urban VIII, a more delicate interaction, fraught with possible indiscretion or loss of face. It was at these sensitive moments that the fiscal procurator's role as intermediary between the pope and the Roman People took on a special importance. As we recall, this official, the pope's man on the Capitol, was also in these years a personal client of the Barberini. The pontiffs usually sent messages to the councils either via the conservators or the fiscal procurator, and the Capitol in turn used him to make requests of the monarch. When the councils needed 12,000 scudi for Carlo Barberini's obsequies in 1630, it was natural for them to dispatch the fiscal procurator, Pietro Colangelo, to Urban to ask for the sum.[9]

The pope granted the money for his brother's funeral, but he did not always respond positively when the Roman People appealed for funds. Their petitions to mount a celebration for the Habsburg heir in 1637 and to honor a local patron saint, Santa Francesca Romana, in 1638 were rebuffed.[10] Clearly Urban VIII's patronage favored Capitoline enterprises that glorified his own family. Significantly, however, when their hopes were disappointed it was not the patron but the go-between, the fiscal procurator, who bore the brunt of civic displeasure.

Giacinto Gigli, who as prior of the caporioni had participated in the negotiations to obtain money for a procession and altar for Santa Francesca Romana in April 1638, accused the fiscal procurator of wrecking the plan. Colangelo had in this instance "raised various impediments," according to Gigli, and was in fact guilty of years of attempts to undermine the Roman People.

> [He] was disliked by all, because, having been fiscal procurator of the Capitol for thirteen years, he had abused the People and, having acquired the ears of the Pope and Cardinal [Francesco] Barberino deceitfully, he had gained credit with them and

---

[8] Fraschetti, 151; ASC, cred. I, vol. 33, decreti, 0200v (20 April 1638). A year before this the pope had ordered the civic treasury to put 1,000 scudi from the wine tax "at the disposition" of Cardinal Francesco Barberini to spend on repairs to the flood *regolatore* and dikes along the Chiani, a dangerous tributary of the Tiber; ASC, cred. VI, vol. 52, registro di patenti, 0037v.

[9] ASC, cred. I, vol. 33, decreti, 0095r (26 March 1630).

[10] Ibid., 0197r–v, 0200v (15 and 20 April 1638); Gigli, *Diario*, 168, 178.

usurped so much of the authority of the magistrates that the conservators and other officials had to do what he wanted, or he crossed them, secretly and openly, in all their plans.[11]

Gigli's comments point up the tensions engendered by the ambiguous status of the fiscal procurator on the Capitol. If he really had the "ears" of the pope and his nephew, he was potentially valuable to the Roman People. Thus, despite bitterness like Gigli's, we find the councils voting citizenship and gifts for Colangelo and his successor, Angelo Giardino, entrusting them with civic business and tolerating their relatives in elected offices.[12] But that did not mean the gentlemen were fond of them. A non-Roman, dependent upon papal favor for advancement yet charged to know everything about their affairs and to be present daily at the Capitol, the fiscal procurator was a lightning rod for suppressed conflicts between the pontiff and the Roman People. Because of his behind-the-scenes influence and intimacy with the Barberini, he provoked special distrust and anger. But Colangelo was also a handy scapegoat in a city where rhetorical convention dictated that the patron could be addressed only with the greatest possible deference. The Capitoline authorities went to great lengths to be polite to Urban VIII and it would not have been appropriate to appear to criticize him. Negotiations over money might arouse passions, but patrician Romans preferred to shield the pope from confronting them directly; they attacked the agent rather than the author.

The gentlemen of Rome acting as the Roman People had a simple and unremarkable policy when it came to raising funds for extraordinary expenses: whenever possible they tried to moderate the flow of their possessions to the fisc, civic or papal. They did not object to those expenditures that could be financed by suspending repayment of loans, borrowing more money, or soliciting the pope, because these required no immediate outlay of cash. The *possesso* decorations, the statue of Urban VIII, the flood control measures, and the procession for Santa Francesca Romana were easy to approve because the money to pay for them did not come from their pockets, at least in the short term. They could, and did, ignore the long-term growth of muncipal debt and its larger implications for taxation.

FISCAL POLITICS

So far we have focused on the sources of extraordinary revenue available to the Capitoline treasury, but what happened when the apostolic chamber had to fi-

[11] Gigli, *Diario*, 185. However, the 1641 *tabella* suggests that some money was eventually found for a chapel; ASC, cred. IV, vol. 106, tabella, 131v. Colangelo's tenure as fiscal procurator was actually eleven years; he is documented in the post only from December 1627 to June 1638. ASC, cred. I, vol. 33, decreti, passim.

[12] Citizenship awarded to fiscal procurators and their male relatives: ASC, cred. I, vol. 33, decreti, 0058v (28 March 1628) and 0218r (21 February 1639). Gifts to the fiscal procurators: ASC, cred. I, vol. 33, decreti, 0083v, 0210v; ASC, cred. I, vol. 34, decreti, 0043v, 0049r–v, 0055r. For their elected offices see Chapter 2.

nance the unexpected? This was a vital question for Urban VIII since the costs of the Thirty Years War, especially the 1625 conflict in the Valtelline, an Alpine valley contested by France and Spain, the second war of the Mantuan succession from 1628 to 1630, and the war of Castro from 1641 to 1644 made "extraordinary" military needs an almost routine demand. To meet the extraordinary expenditures of the papacy in the years 1623 to 1644, Urban VIII turned to his subjects throughout the Papal States and to the bond market. He floated so many new loans that he doubled the papal debt in twenty years. Since loans were secured on specific revenues, however, state borrowing on this scale multiplied the number of taxes paid by all papal subjects. [13] In the late 1620s Romans began to feel the impact of these new burdens, which grew more intense in the early 1640s, as we shall see in Chapter 13.

The Roman People reacted to new fiscal demands in sharply contrasting ways. If they meant higher excises on consumption items, as they usually did, they accepted them without challenge. If they involved any departure from indirect taxes, however, they fought them. Patrician families wanted to preserve traditional Roman forms of taxation, even as they paid out more and more for Urban's military commitments. They opposed new kinds of imposts, not higher charges per se. In this they parted company with the common people of Rome, who complained vociferously about increases on the commodities they required for daily life. [14] The gentlemen of Rome saved their objections for fiscal innovations.

Urban VIII expected material support from the Roman People. The Capitol, with its special obligation of loyalty to the pontiff, had a distinctive role in his revenue raising plans. The popes did not, of course, simply help themselves to patrician pocketbooks or the civic treasury. In conformity with the conventions of clientage Capitoline aid was advanced as a freely proffered gift. [15] When war threatened papal troops stationed in the Valtelline in January 1625, for example, the conservators suggested that the Roman People give Urban "a sign of gratitude and fidelity . . . in these troubles." The civic councils obliged, decreeing that "Roman patricians are ready to offer themselves, their sons and their property to the service of His Holiness and the Apostolic See." [16]

The language of this declaration reflected in part the required formulae of courtesy, but it also implied that gentlemen had a say in the disposition of their property. At least when it came to their upper-class subjects, the popes accepted

[13] Lutz, 123–24; Rietbergen, 182, 187; Reinhard, "Finanza," 364; Partner, "Financial Policy," 27; Stumpo, *Capitale*, 124, 128–32; Gross, 134 n. 23.

[14] Gigli, *Diario*, 109; Angelo Contarini in Barozzi and Berchet, 1:258; Stumpo, *Capitale*, 97–98, 110–11; Gross, 126. Stumpo makes the point that where landowners dominated local government, consumption taxes were likely to be preferred to direct taxes. He also emphasizes the unique degree of dependence on indirect taxes in Rome, as contrasted with other parts of the Papal States.

[15] For the more coercive style of such "free gifts" to the king in early modern France see Kettering, "Gift-Giving," 135; Bossenga, 121; Temple, 83.

[16] ASC, cred. I, vol. 33, decreti, 0021v (10 January 1625); Pastor, 28:62, 70–75.

the principle that in fiscal matters "the law desires the consent of the whole people [*popolo*]," as the jurist Cardinal De Luca put it in 1673.[17] "The whole people" was naturally understood as the well-born and substantial property-holders. Since there was no parliament or meeting of estates in the papal domains, in individual towns "the people" (*popolo*)—narrowly defined—served as the vehicle for organizing consent. In Rome, from the point of view of the popes, this was one of the principal functions of the Roman People. And, again from the papal perspective, consent might take a range of forms, from a generic expression of willingness to contribute, as in the offer above, to gathering the civic councils for a vote of approval on a precise sum.

The process of choreographing Capitoline consent to papal financial requests, whether traditional or innovative, is nicely illuminated in a series of episodes between 1628 and 1630. When the second war of the Mantuan succession broke out in northern Italy early in 1628, the civic councils swiftly repeated the pledge they had given the pope during the Valtelline crisis of 1625. "As a sign of gratitude and fidelity," they declared themselves in April once again ready to expend their lives, sons, and fortunes in the defense of the Holy See.[18] On this occasion, unlike the previous one, Urban took them up on their proposition. On 2 July 1628 he signed a chirograph expanding the revenue generated by the meat tax by 25,000 scudi annually and assigning this sum to the apostolic chamber. The conservators publicized the new meat prices in an edict dated July 13th. On July 21st, in their first meeting since April, the Capitoline councils reassembled to hear a report on all this. According to the conservators who had held office from April to June, the pontiff had told them "that an offering from the Roman People would be very pleasing to him."[19] Urban had personally urged them to find a way to raise some funds for "unexpected necessities" as soon as possible. Hearing this, and "attentive to the intention and desire of Our Most Holy Lord," the councils conveniently agreed that increasing the meat tax was indeed "easiest and least injurious to the Roman People."

They were undoubtedly sincere; higher rates on foodstuffs made a much smaller

[17] De Luca, *Il Dottor Volgare*, bk. 15, pt. 3, chap. 34, p. 319. In this passage De Luca is referring specifically to the Capitoline councils. "Questo magistrato . . . in occasione di trattare delle alienazioni de beni delle Citta', e' di due specie: Una cioe' piu' generale, la quale rappresenta tutto il popolo, con l'amministrazione abituale, & anche con qualche sorte d'attuale in quelli atti gravi, nelli quali la legge desidera il consenso di tutto il popolo; come sono, le alienazioni de beni, l'imposizione delle gabelle, & altre gravezze, e cose simili; . . . [he neglects to say what the second 'specie' is]." For similar sentiments in early Bourbon Paris see Descimon, 117. For an interesting discussion of the role of consent among some theorists of absolutism see Robert Bireley, *The Counter-Reformation Prince: Anti-Machiavellianism or Catholic Statecraft in Early Modern Europe* (Chapel Hill, N.C., 1990), 222–23.

[18] ASC, cred. I, vol. 33, decreti, 0062v (11 April 1628). For the second war of the Mantuan succession see Pastor, 28:200–265.

[19] "S.mum D. N. in ultimo colloquio cum eorum antecessoribus habito, eis insinuavit sibi valde gratam fuisse oblationem per Romanum Populum factam erga S.tem Suam;" ASC, cred. I, vol. 33, decreti, 0065r (21 July 1628); the chirograph is reproduced on 0067v. See also *Regesti* 4:112.

dent in their pockets than in those of the majority of the population.[20] Yet why bother to approve a tax boost that had already been signed into law? The technical reason was that the meat tax was revenue belonging to the Capitoline treasury, not the papal fisc. But a political motive may have been more important. While the pope had sounded out the conservators before going ahead with his document of July 2d, he was not satisfied with the agreement of the magistrates alone. He wanted the councils to approve the increase, and its new destination, explicitly in a formal decree. The language of the chirograph makes this plain:

> the Senate and People of Rome having offered other times to give a subsidy to us and to this Holy See of all the money we should declare, which was approved by decrees of the said Senate, ordering for this that the meat tax be increased, as is contained in the said decrees, the tenor of which we wish to have clearly expressed, accepting with gratitude said offer, we have decided . . . to avail ourselves for now of an annual tax of 25,000 *scudi*.[21]

Perhaps Urban hoped to deflect, or confuse, critics by making this hike appear to be not merely an initiative of the Roman People but even an actual civic tax. In the stressful years of the war of Castro he often favored publishing new fiscal burdens under the aegis of the Capitol. In 1628, as he would do again in the 1640s, he built on the spontaneous expressions of support that news of a military threat elicited from the patricians. Having discussed the matter with top civic officials, Urban had them orchestrate a public statement of responsibility for an impost that henceforth showed up in papal coffers.

The popes had grown accustomed to turning to the Roman People for money long before Urban VIII came on the scene. In 1537 Paul III sought 96,000 ducats from the Capitol to fight the Turks; in 1567 Pius V asked for 115,000 scudi to aid French Catholics against the Huguenots; and in 1588 Sixtus V ordered civic officials to find 12,000 scudi a year to finance a papal navy. Between 1592 and 1599 Clement VIII requested 50,000 scudi for grain purchases, 45,000 for a new

---

[20] The butchers complained about the effects of the meat tax increase at a guild meeting on 13 October 1630; ASR, 30 N.C., uff. 25 (Raymundus) 1630, pt. 5, 449r.

[21] "Havendosi offerto altre volte il Senato e Popolo Romano di dare sovventione a Noi et a questa Santa Sede di tutta quella quantita' di danari che havessimo dichiarato, il che fu approvato per decreti de d.o Senato, ordinandosi per cio' che si accrescesse la gabella della carne come si contiene in d.i decreti, il tenore de quali vogliamo si habbi per espresso, accettando con grato animo d.a offerta, abbiamo deliberato in sovventione della nostra Camera et per supplire a molte spese straordinarie valerci per hora di una somma a prestatione annua di scudi venticinque milla;" ASC, cred. I, vol. 33, decreti, 0067v.

In the financial account of the apostolic chamber located in ASR, Archivio Santacroce, D 141, 182r, the following item is entered: "Augm.to della carne d'un q.no a llra [libbra] oltre quello ne cava il Po. Ro.—25,000 [scudi]." A new contract for the meat tax was drawn up on 14 July 1628 to include the recent increase. Since the tax–farmers were not scheduled to complete their present contract until the end of October 1629, the new lease was to begin 1 November 1629; it was awarded to Gasparo Rivaldi. ASC, cred. IV, vol. 96, istrumenti, 57r.

bridge, and 150,000 for the wars in Hungary from the Roman People.[22] As we have noted, the papal treasury was no more equipped to fund extraordinary expenditures from normal income than was the Capitoline. In 1628, as his predecessors had done many times before, Urban enlisted the civic government in raising revenue. Obviously the papacy thought it useful to have a vehicle through which its "unexpected necessities" could be translated into contributions from the Romans. For their part the Roman People did not mind higher consumption taxes and were content to accommodate the pontiff.

They showed a quite different spirit when a new method of paying for city street improvements was imposed that same spring. The usual way of covering such costs was a system of neighborhood taxes called *gettiti* that were administered by the two lay street masters and the curial president of the streets. When a building was torn down or a road widened, only proprietors close to the site were assessed for the work done. Early in 1628, however, the three street officials decided to levy a yearly paving tax on all city property owners. Patrician landlords were incensed at the unheard of notion of a charge that would be universal and perpetual. They gathered in council at the Capitol on March 23d and told the three street officials that they vehemently opposed the plan.[23] The assembly authorized a deputation to join the conservators in calling on the pope and the cardinalatial congregation of the streets to ask that "the old and usual custom" of neighborhood *gettiti* continue. The street officials dropped the paving tax in the face of this strident hostility.

A similar spirit of resistance surfaced two years later on an issue that involved the pope more directly. In January 1630, as the Mantuan war entered its third year, Urban returned to the Roman People for money to defend the Papal States. They had been quick to promise help early in the conflict and the meat tax hike had provided the pontiff with an extra 25,000 scudi a year. As imperial troops advanced into Italy in 1629, Urban readied 7,000 infantry and 800 cavalry. Soldiers were costly, however, and the pope who had been so careful about his first new impost was now constantly desperate for funds. By the end of 1629 he had boosted indirect taxes on oil, wine, salt, wood, cheese, notarized documents, and pawnbroking. Although the Capitol was silent, the populace of Rome was not. "Everyone complained greatly," Gigli reported, "especially in Rome, where the people, accustomed to the tranquil and abundant past, called to mind more than ever [the reign of] Paul V."[24]

[22] Delumeau, *Vie* 2:829–36; ASC, cred. I, vol. 30, decreti (table of contents: 1592, 1599); Rietbergen, 210. Stumpo presents the major items of papal extraordinary expenditure from 1570 to 1660, *Capitale*, 308, table 6.

[23] They took the unusual step of having a notary draw up a public record of their stance on the paving tax; ASC, cred. I, vol. 33, decreti, 0056v–57r. See also Rodocanachi, *Institutions*, 319; *Statuta almae urbis*, bk. 3, chap. 39; BAV, Urb. lat. 1098, pt. 1, 150v (*avviso* of 25 March 1628).

[24] Gigli, *Diario*, 109. Adding to the tension was the fact that these tax increases occurred at a time

Mobilizing traditional sources of revenue did not feed an army for long in the seventeenth century, however, and even as the common people "murmured," Urban was exploring new ways of raising money. Just before Christmas Roman parish priests went the rounds of the householders in their parishes in order to estimate their wealth; it looked like papal officials were considering imposing some kind of direct tax.[25] Instead, early in January 1630, the pontiff sent word to the Capitol that he would welcome a voluntary contribution from those able to pay.

On January 8th Vincenzo Muti, first conservator, presented the pope's new fund-raising plan to a council session attended by about sixty people. Urban did not want to levy another tax, Muti reported, and so he was asking for individual donations. The council dragged its feet. They voted to send the conservators and four gentlemen, chosen by the conservators from a list of twenty-six suggested names, back to the pope with the message that, although the Roman People were ready to offer him their lives, property, and sons, they would refer his request to another meeting.[26]

The official decrees do not record the real agenda of this delegation, but it emerges clearly from the report they made on their return, at the council meeting of February 1st. Speaking again to a group of sixty people, Muti described the deputation's discussion with Urban VIII. They had communicated their good will to the pope and their readiness to sacrifice, but they beseeched him not to impose this particular contribution.[27] They asked instead to be allowed to find a way of raising the money in the least harmful manner possible. Urban told them that he was determined that the contribution be voluntary and that the Roman People choose the means they thought most appropriate.

On hearing this account the council reacted more decisively. Not following the usual method of leaving the choice to the conservators, they immediately named six gentlemen to return with the magistrates to the pope. This time the minutes clearly expressed the purpose of the delegation. The deputies "should represent [to the pope] the great need in which all the [Roman] People found themselves and should humbly ask that he deem it worthwhile to relieve and free the People from the aforesaid contribution."[28] The council also ordered its spokesmen to ask Cardinal Francesco "strenuously" to intercede with his uncle to obtain this favor.

There is no precedent during Urban VIII's reign for such polite but determined resistance by the Capitol to the pope's express wishes. The councillors understood that a "contribution" based on ability to pay would hit a different constituency from the one that bore the main burden of new taxes on food and drink. It was

when the price-controlled bread loaf eaten by the poor had declined in weight due to the rising price of grain. See also Pastor, 28:237.

[25] Gigli, *Diario*, 109.
[26] ASC, cred. I, vol. 33, 0082v–85v (8 and 11 January 1630).
[27] Ibid., 0089r (1 February 1630).
[28] Ibid., 0089v.

one thing to approve increased charges for consumption items, quite another to ask men of their own rank to reach voluntarily into their purses.

The recording scribe at the two council meetings following the February 1st resolution gave up after noting several dozen names, and wrote "and many others." Patrician Romans were taking unusual interest in these negotiations. On February 8th they heard that their second deputation had failed in its attempt to get the pope's request withdrawn. Urban repeated that he was unwilling to compel them and that he wished their "dutiful generosity" to be voluntary.[29]

The ensuing reaction was too indecorous for the scribe to document, but Gigli is less circumspect. He describes a rare tumultuous moment at the Capitol.

> In this month of February the Roman People were called to council on the Capitol many times, at which it was put forward that the Pope wanted a universal contribution from all the people, who voluntarily ought to give whatever they could according to their ability, to help maintain troops and the defences of Rome, but . . . the people did not wish to go along with this contribution, indeed the conservators, who endeavored to bend the people in every way possible to give their consent, were several times forced to leave their tribunal and withdraw from the people, who had already begun to riot, and the fiscal procurator, who at one point began to browbeat the people to force them to obey, heard the response, which was given to him publicly, that if he didn't watch himself he would get to test the height of the windows of the palace.[30]

From Gigli's account it is clear that "the people" who figure in these events were not the populace, who could have gotten no closer to the council chamber than the piazza outside. These "people" were all from that class of respectable citizens who had the right to a place in the Capitoline councils. The councils had turned on the go-betweens who bore the pope's wishes before them: they ignored the entreaties of the conservators and they threatened the fiscal procurator with defenestration. Antagonism broke through the customary decorum of Roman gentlemen in the Baroque age.

In the face of such heated opposition, the conservators abandoned the attempt to get the council's approval for the contribution. At the end of February they simply proclaimed by public edict that anyone with an income above 120 scudi a year should offer to pay whatever he could within ten days. They still spoke of a "spontaneous contribution," but they warned that the names of those who did not come forward would be reported to the pope. Gigli was clear on the implications,

---

[29] Ibid., 0090v–91v (4 and 8 February 1630). "Et quod ad hoc sua sanctitas eis respondit ipsum summopere expetere, et optare istud munus et largitionem voluntarie ab eodem Populo faciendam et quod in hoc aliquem invitum cogere non intendit;" ibid., 0091v. For the first time the term *munus*, with its connotations of obligation, is used by the scribe to describe the pope's request.

[30] Gigli, *Diario*, 110.

"[for] whomever does not obey . . . there will be an investigation into his wealth and he will be rigorously forced to pay by compulsion."[31]

The conservators, intermediaries between Urban and their fellow patricians, had an unenviable task. They seem to have solicited funds, from the guilds as well as individuals, and they levied a large sum on themselves and on the other Capitoline officials. Many Romans did meet their obligations, Gigli reported, but resistance continued, and Urban VIII drew sharp criticism.

> There were also those who did not on any account want to offer anything, saying that they would sooner pay a hundred *scudi* by force than ten unwillingly. They added that it was not true that the Pope had need [of the money], since he continually gave huge sums to his brother and nephew, who had the command of the papal army, and also purchased principalities and manors for his nephews.[32]

Popular complaints about Barberini nepotism may well have predated the Mantuan war. Nevertheless, it is significant that Gigli comments on Urban's gifts to his family for the first time in connection with the unpopular levy the pope demanded from propertied Romans in 1630. This tax particularly burdened people of Gigli's own social rank, the families who were most directly represented by the Roman People. Their recalcitrance was reflected in the edicts that the papal treasurer published continually throughout the summer and fall, demanding payment of the next two installments of the "voluntary" contribution. The last of these orders followed by some weeks the news that the second war of the Mantuan succession was over.[33]

The Capitol's financial negotiations with the papacy in the 1620s show clearly that the Roman People had something to offer their patron besides ceremonies

---

[31] Ibid., 111; ASV, arm. IV, vol. 38, edict of 21 February 1630. A meeting of the butchers' guild refers also to a "second" edict of the conservators dated 11 March 1630: ASR, 30 N.C., uff. 25 (Raymundus) 1630, pt. 2, 162r–63v. To give an idea of the kind of person upon whom the voluntary contribution paid by those earning 120 scudi a year might fall, here are some examples of annual incomes: a parish priest in a poor parish might have a stipend of 45 scudi; an apprentice doughnut maker who did not live with his master might earn 50 scudi; and a spy could be hired for 120 scudi. Fiorani, "Visite," 121; ASC, cred. XI, vol. 14, lettere, 93r; BAV, Barb. lat. 4901, 47r. Gigli himself had a yearly income of around 1,000 scudi; a clerk of the chamber expected 3,000 scudi annually from the office he had purchased. Ademollo, *Gigli*, 61; Visconti, 3:518. See also Gross, 112–13.

[32] Gigli, *Diario*, 111. Taddeo Barberini purchased fifteen fiefs; Stumpo, *Capitale*, 273–74. The magistrates' pressure on the guilds emerges from notarial sources. At the butchers' meeting on 14 March 1630 it was reported that the fiscal procurator had told guild officers that "all those who can should contribute spontaneously and make this contribution;" ASR, 30 N.C., uff. 25 (Raymundus) 1630, pt. 2, 162r–63v. At a meeting on 13 March 1630 the fishmongers' officers similarly announced that they had been asked by the fiscal procurator "by order of the *Signori* conservators, whether the fishmongers' guild wanted to make an offering to the pope like the other guilds." The matter was discussed and the fishmongers agreed, many signing pledges on the spot. ASR, uff. 2 (Bonanni) 1630, pt. 1, 652v, 685r.

[33] Gigli, *Diario*, 118; Pastor, 28:265–66; ASV, arm. IV, vol. 38, treasurer's edicts dated 21 February, 22 April, 19 August, and 20 November 1630.

and statues. On many occasions Urban VIII needed and sought their material support. Civic institutions were useful to the pontiffs in part because they offered a way of legitimating, of gaining "consent" for, new fiscal demands. However, if they did not produce polite agreement the pope backed away. Urban distanced himself from his requests, leaving them to subordinate officials to execute and tacitly permitting the recalcitrant to disobey, or dropping them altogether. Although heavily pressed financially, the Barberini pope did not resort to confrontation with the Capitol in the way some of his predecessors or successors did. Both Sixtus V (1585–1590) and Innocent X (1644–1655), for example, took a hard look at the salaries the apostolic chamber paid out to civic officials and suppressed them, though in Sixtus's case only temporarily and in Innocent's only partially. Sixtus V also tussled with the Roman People over who had the right to sell certain Capitoline offices.[34] In the end, however, savings from salaries and gains from new *vacabili* produced relatively little for the papal treasury. Urban VIII was more clever, at least in the short run; he opted for amassing huge sums by going into debt and deploying civic resources as promissory notes. He avoided attacking income the Capitoline government thought of as privileged and he was careful to appear to consult the Roman People when he moved in on their terrain. The politics of fidelity was based on reciprocal benefits for patron and client; it is no wonder that the Capitol led no protests against this pope or his fiscal policy. That he was mortgaging their future and burdening those least able to pay did not concern the gentlemen of Rome, at least in their corporate incarnation.

[34] Rodocanachi, *Institutions*, 316–18; Gigli, *Diario*, 264.

PART V

The Politics of Accommodation and Protest

THE ROMAN PEOPLE and Pope Urban VIII faced intense challenges in the final years of the Barberini pontificate. War and interregnum dominated political life in Rome from 1640 to 1644, dramatically reshaping the context in which ruler and subjects, both patrician and plebeian, operated. The focus of these two chapters is the key crises of this period for the city of Rome, the war of Castro and the Vacant See. Drawing back from the close analysis of fictitiously "stable" civic institutions, the perspective opens to embrace the actions and reactions of a broader sweep of papal subjects caught up in swiftly changing circumstances. The Roman People are one group among many called on for new sacrifices and offered novel opportunities in this dynamic political environment. Their moments of passivity and silence, as well as of civic self-assertion, are especially eloquent in this larger narrative of events.

Urban VIII had been elected pope in 1623 at the unconventionally youthful age of fifty-five. The cardinals preferred candidates who were advanced in years; they wanted to make sure that no one family could monopolize the power and wealth of the papal office for too long. As Urban's reign stretched out past its fifteenth and towards its twentieth year there was a subtle change of mood in Rome. Those with close ties to the Barberini knew they had only a brief period to profit from their patrons' position; those who had found their advancement blocked bided their time in frustration and expectation. The pope's nephews experienced the passage of years with particular urgency, for their influence and resources disappeared the instant their uncle died.

Against this background of anticipation and anxiety the pope led his subjects into the greatest danger and imposed on them the heaviest burdens of his pontificate. The reason was the war of Castro, which from 1641 to 1644 pitted Urban VIII against a papal descendant, Odoardo Farnese, duke of Parma and Piacenza, who was the pope's vassal through his possession of the rich grain-growing fief in northern Lazio known as the duchy of Castro. The war of Castro was different from the other wars in which the papacy had participated in the sixteenth and seventeenth centuries. It was local; it had no religious dimension; and it started in Rome, not in the court of some distant European monarch. The dispute was really a family quarrel, with the rising papal nobility, the Barberini, pitted against the haughty great-great-great-grandson of Pope Paul III; but it rippled out to engage the other Italian powers, France, and the Holy Roman Emperor, and penetrated down to the silk weavers and leather workers of Rome.

The war of Castro did not turn out well for Urban VIII and in the process it fatally disfigured the image of authority and magnificence he had so carefully cultivated. In the collapse of his state's defenses and the emptying of its coffers many of his subjects read bad government. When Urban died a few months after signing the peace treaty in 1644, his death released not merely the normal impatience provoked by a long pontificate but an added charge of popular anger built up during the three years of war. The interregnum or Vacant See that followed every papal reign was the traditional period in which the old pope was mourned and a new pope was elected. In Rome in 1644, however, the Vacant See was the chance many had been longing for to give vent to their criticisms of the rule of the Barberini.

Chapter Thirteen

THE WAR OF CASTRO

LIKE NO OTHER contemporary event, the war of Castro from 1641 to 1644 throws the political life of Baroque Rome into high relief. Stretching his resources, both material and immaterial, to the utmost, Urban VIII tested the affection and loyalty of his subjects and had to contend for the first time with outspoken enemies. His most serious political disadvantage was that the papal dignity alone was not enough to maintain support for the campaign, especially after it began to entail sacrifices. When the pope had to reach out to his public, "selling" his cause or defending it against opponents, it was a sign that he had used up his most valuable asset: the reverence of their unconscious respect.

The war began as a family matter, but it became a threat and a burden to the city of Rome as well as to other communities in the Papal States. The Roman People played a substantial role in the local effort, responding both to the concerns of patrician families and to the demands of Urban VIII. Unlike others in Rome, civic spokesmen did not express opposition to papal policies; they remained faithful, if silent, allies of the pope and his cause. They were not much help to the pontiff, however, in the difficult political task he faced. The gentlemen of Rome either could not, or would not, bridge the gap that opened up between the Barberini and their critics.

THE ROAD TO WAR

The war of Castro originated between 1639 and 1641 in an escalating exchange of discourtesies that reflected the social tension between new papal dynasties and older ones.[1] In 1639 the duchy of Castro was the largest and richest feudal terri-

---

[1] For treatments generally sympathetic towards Urban VIII see the following: Gigli, *Diario*; Nicoletti, BAV, Barb. lat. 4738 (volume nine of his nine-volume manuscript biography of Urban VIII, this is entirely devoted to the war of Castro); Pastor, 29:382–401; Pietro Romano, 119; and Delumeau, "Progrès," 406. For more critical judgments of the pope see the following: Ameyden, "Diario," Biblioteca Casanatense, cod. 1831–32, passim; Giacinto De Maria, "La guerra di Castro e la spedizione dei presidi (1639–1649)," in *Miscellanea di storia italiana* (Turin, 1898), 191–256; and Caravale and Caracciolo, 438–39. The most detailed published accounts of the war of Castro are those of Pastor and De Maria. Pastor relied heavily on Nicoletti, who was commissioned by Cardinal Francesco Barberini to write the life of Urban VIII; on Nicoletti's work see Pastor, 29:584–90. De Maria, on the other hand, drew on the Venetian ambassadors' dispatches; these are not the more public "relazioni" that were read aloud to the Senate after an envoy had returned from his post, but the more informative, private "dispacci" that kept the Venetian government apprised of what was happening on a regular basis.

tory still remaining within the borders of the Papal States. Granted by Paul III (1535–1549) to his son Pierluigi Farnese in 1537, the duchy encompassed both the ancestral holdings of the Farnese family in upper Lazio and a fertile agricultural region around Lake Vico (see Map 4). In addition to being papal vassals, however, the Farnese were also dukes in their own right, thanks again to Paul III. He had removed a portion of the Papal States from the Church's patrimony and created the independent duchy of Parma and Piacenza in the Po valley for his son.

At Urban VIII's election in 1623 the reigning duke of Parma was the eleven-year old Odoardo Farnese, who had acceded to his father's state the year before. As a youthful ruler growing up during the Thirty Years War, Odoardo Farnese found himself tempted by opportunities for military glory and political gain from many directions, a necessarily expensive avocation. The duke did not hesitate to go into debt for his ambitions, raising loans in Rome, for example, to pay for his participation in the campaign of 1635 against the Spaniards. His recourse to the Roman *monti* market was the same device used by the Roman People, the apostolic chamber, and local aristocrats in need of funds. As security for the borrowed sums and to cover the interest payments, Duke Odoardo pledged the revenues of the duchy of Castro.[2]

Like most Italian rulers the duke of Parma leased the privilege of collecting taxes in Castro to private bankers or tax-farmers. Their advances furnished Farnese with the money to pay his creditors, the owners of *monti Farnesi* in Rome and elsewhere. In 1638 a group of bankers close to Urban VIII, Giovanni Battista and Alessandro Siri and Giovanni Francesco Sacchetti, held the lease of Castro's revenues. It was thought that Taddeo Barberini was also a partner, though because of his rank his participation was kept secret. The following year falling grain prices diminished Castro's income below the level the bankers had expected. This fact, according to a later account, "caused the Siri, whose name cloaked that of the Barberini, jointly to press for compensation and a reduction of the contract."[3] Meanwhile, Farnese, lacking the tax-farmers' advances, could not pay the interest on the *monti*. In the face of this dilemma the duke left his state in north Italy in September 1639 and made a visit to his villa at Caprarola twenty-eight miles north of Rome. He hoped to find the Siri more tractable in person.

As early as 1635 the Barberini family had sought to purchase the duchy of Castro from Farnese, but the duke, despite his financial need, had rebuffed their offer. In the fall of 1639 they again hoped to draw some family advantage, perhaps a marriage alliance, from Farnese's difficulties. Taking advantage of his proximity in Caprarola, they urged the duke to come to Rome. Farnese resisted the invita-

---

[2] Pietro Romano, 70; Stumpo, *Capitale*, 269. See also Maurice Aymard and Jacques Revel, "La famille farnèse," in *Le palais farnèse*, 3 vols. (Rome, 1981), vol. 1, pt. 2, 695–715.

[3] "Relatione delle vere cagioni de' presenti disgusti fra il Signor Duca di Parma e signori Barberini," quoted in De Maria, 198 n. 1, 197. Whatever their "occult" connections with Taddeo Barberini, the Siri bankers clearly had close ties to the papacy; by December 1640 they were "general depositaries" of the apostolic chamber. See *Regesti* 5:25. See also Nicoletti, BAV, Barb. lat. 4738, 66r.

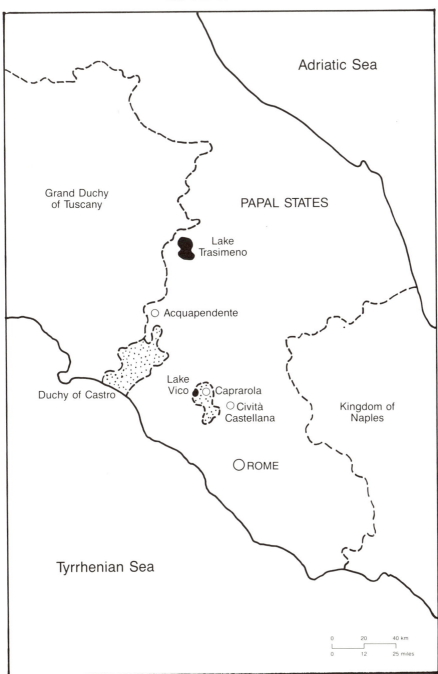

Map 4. Northern Lazio with the Duchy of Castro

tion at first, but finally agreed on two conditions, that he not be forced to give ceremonial precedence to Taddeo Barberini as prefect of Rome and that Urban VIII grant him a reduction in the interest payments he owed to the owners of the *monti Farnesi*.[4]

Odoardo Farnese's two-month stay in Rome from November 1639 to January 1640 was a fiasco. The situation was fraught with tension from the outset. The duke of Parma, who reportedly made fun of his own mother because she was descended from the Aldobrandini pope Clement VIII (1592–1605), regarded the Barberini as social upstarts. Yet he respected the pope's dignity and needed his approval to ease his financial burdens. On the other hand, the Barberini nephews, rich and powerful thanks to Urban VIII's long reign, hoped by an alliance with a princely house or the acquisition of a fief like Castro, to assure their family's position after the pope's death. While they did not have their hearts set exclusively on Castro, they were indeed looking to benefit from the hardships afflicting the duke of Parma, a fact that presumably was not lost on the haughty Farnese. Moreover, the Barberini had successfully allied themselves by marriage to the highest Roman nobility, the Colonna, and saw no reason to think Odoardo Farnese's son too good for them.

Against this charged background the duke of Parma and the pope greeted each other with mutual flattery; Farnese even went to the trouble of reading Urban's poetry and of making a special visit to the new fortifications at the harbor of Civitavecchia, of which the pontiff was very proud. But the duke refused to treat Cardinal Francesco with the same deference and ridiculed the cardinal's suggestion of a marriage alliance. He then found to his annoyance that the agreement allowing him to reduce the interest payments on his loans was unaccountably held up. Over the next several weeks Farnese and the Barberini cardinals inflicted on each other a series of breaches of court etiquette: failing to accompany the guest to his carriage or refusing to make the proper visits.[5]

When Farnese left Rome in late January 1640, after bursting into the pope's inner chambers with a band of armed retainers to express his outrage at Cardinal Francesco, he asked the pope not to pay attention to what his nephews would say about him. Urban agreed, but the duke himself kept the furnaces stoked by ordering his envoy not to attend Cardinal Francesco's regular audiences. As one scholar succinctly put it, "the quarrel and discourtesies had reached such a point that there was no longer an authority powerful enough to calm the hatreds aroused."[6] The seeds of the war of Castro were sown in Rome early in 1640.

Over the next fifteen months Urban VIII, despite his promise, turned against Farnese. On 20 March 1641 the pope permitted the apostolic chamber, headed since 1638 by his nephew Cardinal Antonio Barberini, to revoke the right of the

---

[4] De Maria, 197–98.

[5] Ibid., 199; Pastor, 29:384.

[6] De Maria, 200; Ferdinand de Navenne, *Rome et le Palais Farnèse*, 2 vols. (Paris, 1923), 1:173–74.

duchy of Castro to export grain. The papal authorities immediately confiscated a ship laden with cereals as it departed from the harbor of Montalto.[7] This was a serious blow, for without the ability to sell Castro's grain abroad the duke of Parma had no money with which to pay the interest on the *monti* he had raised in Rome. The Roman financial market panicked and protested in the most strident terms.

Although at Farnese's request the pope had authorized a reduction in interest payments less than two years before—an event that Gigli had reported with dismay—Urban now warmed up to the cause of the *monti* owners who were the duke of Parma's creditors. Many Roman religious institutions as well as individuals owned shares in the duke's debt. Gigli spoke for them all when he complained that Farnese's inability to pay the *montisti* caused "heavy loss [to] an infinite number of persons and holy places."[8]

Events came to a head in August 1641. The Siri brothers reported to the pope that the duke of Parma was arming Castro and Ronciglione. Urban VIII dispatched two notaries to take sworn testimony in the two towns where Farnese had ordered the fortifications. On August 21st the pope directed the auditor of the apostolic chamber to command the duke to dismantle Castro's defenses and discharge the troops he had gathered; this monitory was sent to Farnese in Piacenza and posted in Rome's four major basilicas. Now determined to use force, Urban tried to justify his decision to the College of Cardinals. He reminded them of Farnese's repeated refusals to obey him and claimed that the duke had left creditors to the tune of 1.5 million scudi in Rome without any security.[9]

"THE CAUSE OF ST. PETER"

Urban VIII probably hoped that a short march north to Castro and quickly seizing it would turn the duke of Parma back into a decorous vassal with whom he could then negotiate on more polite terms. And in late August and September 1641 that hope looked very plausible. In the context of such expectations the Roman People moved swiftly to offer support to the pope, as they always had done when he faced a military threat. On September 9th and 10th the private and public councils agreed that, in recognition of "the bond of gratitude" they owed Urban, they would finance a contingent of 3,000 infantry at a cost of 150,000 scudi. As Gigli put it, "it was argued that this could be done by finding a way to increase the income of the [Roman] People, without imposing excise taxes or burdening anyone, and giving this increase to the Pope as long as the war lasted, after which it would return to the People."[10]

---

[7] For the pope's sentiments towards Odoardo Farnese at this time, see De Maria, 201 n. 1. Edict of 20 March 1641 summarized in *Regesti* 5:27; Nicoletti, BAV, Barb. lat. 4738, 58v.

[8] Gigli, *Diario*, 195–96, 199; Navenne, 1:175.

[9] Nicoletti, BAV, Barb. lat. 4738, 66r–67v.

[10] Gigli, *Diario*, 199; ASC, cred. I, vol. 34, decreti, 0025r–v.

Two days later a delegation composed of the conservators and prior of the caporioni, six other gentlemen, and Monsignors Giulio Cenci and Domenico Cecchini, the two prelates who gave the Capitol legal counsel as "advocates of the
Roman People," presented this offer to the pontiff. Gigli was the prior of the
caporioni during this trimester and his diary provides a unique eyewitness account
of a meeting between Urban VIII and a deputation from the Roman People.

> [Giulio] Buratto, first conservator, spoke for everyone and said that the Roman People
> had commanded that we offer to pay for a regiment of infantrymen during the war.
> The Pope was moved and tears came to his eyes, and he thanked the People very
> much, and several times made a gesture with his hand to the [kneeling] magistrates
> that they rise to their feet.[11]

Urban spoke at length to the civic representatives, telling them how deeply he
regretted having to go to war after what he described as "eighteen years of peace,"
and recounting the many acts of ingratitude and the injuries done him by the
duke of Parma. In a city where even artisan guilds might own *luoghi di monti*, he
made much of the hardship caused by Farnese's failure to pay the interest on the
bonds he had sold. The pope chose not to mention the fact that he himself had
authorized a reduction of 300,000 scudi in these interest payments just two years
before. Urban claimed that he had been too patient with Duke Odoardo, extending the time limit for disarming Castro even when Farnese ignored it. The pope
played up his role as an ecclesiastical rather than a secular ruler. He told the
delegation that

> he had done what he could to preserve peace, granting delays and extensions as the
> style and custom of the Church demanded, although he knew that it was little to his
> personal honor, [and] that a secular prince, without so much ceremony, would already
> have taken an army and attacked the enemy, not wasting time in words, but he being
> pontiff could not do that.[12]

In conclusion, the pontiff said that he hoped for God's help "because it was His
cause and that of St. Peter."

Despite Urban VIII's justifications, however, and the prompt support of the
Roman People, some observers in Rome were already voicing misgivings about
the whole enterprise. On August 31st Teodoro Ameyden, the hispanophile Flemish attorney who tended to regard Urban with suspicion because of his pro-French
sympathies, described the nighttime removal from the city of thirty ammunition
wagons, fifteen bronze artillery pieces, and ten pairs of oxen. He commented that
"the people of Rome, seeing such preparations for war, are talking a lot, saying
that the State of Castro does not require such efforts, but that there are bigger

---

[11] Gigli, *Diario*, 200.
[12] Ibid.

thoughts."[13] A few of the cardinals had cautioned against a large display of military force precisely because they worried that if the pope appeared to have "bigger thoughts" the other Italian princes might intervene in the conflict. Urban VIII rejected this counsel in favor of an impressive show of strength.

On 25 September 1641 the papal troops led by the Roman nobleman Marchese Luigi Mattei, 12,000 infantrymen and 3,000 cavalry, set out for Castro. They met very little resistance and on 12 October Castro surrendered. The very next day the first cold winds blew, marking the close of the 1641 campaign season. The army was split three ways, two parts marching north to Bologna and Ferrara, and the third returning to winter in Rome. At the end of October Taddeo Barberini, commander-in-chief of the papal armies, headed for Bologna to review the strength of the border fortresses of the Papal States.[14]

The structure of command for the war effort in the Papal States was already in evidence, with the Barberini nephews in the key positions. In his role as superintendent of the Papal States Cardinal Francesco Barberini oversaw everything, but concerned himself especially with troop recruiting and discipline; Taddeo, as general, was early in the field, concentrating on the area around Bologna because it was close to Farnese's state of Parma and Piacenza; the younger Cardinal Antonio remained in Rome heading the apostolic chamber, but in a pinch also led military forces. The members of the papal bureaucracy who were most prominent in the war were the treasurer general, who organized provincial villages to lodge soldiers and gave orders about some new taxes, and the clerk of the chamber who had charge of arms supplies and outfitting fortresses in the Papal States. The governor of Rome tried to keep soldiers from disrupting life in the city too much. As for the Roman People, their customary supervision of hay and straw supplies, as well as many food prices, made a contribution on the home front, and in the second year of the war they formed a civic militia. Some patricians also joined the papal army. But from the council meeting of early September 1641 until the spring of 1644, their chief task was raising money.

As the Roman gentlemen had divined before they made their offering of 150,000 scudi to the pope, even the briefest and most successful military enterprise had financial repercussions. Within two weeks of Urban VIII's order to Farnese to disarm Castro in August 1641, two new indirect taxes were imposed in the Papal States. Already in September the common people reportedly "complained loudly that they were incapable of greater hardships." Though Castro had been captured by mid-October, troops still had to be fed and paid, at a cost to the papal treasury that the same source, Ameyden, estimated was 50,000 scudi a

---

[13] "Il Popolo di Roma vedendo tanto apparecchio e provisioni di guerra fa' massi discorsi dicendo che tant'apparecchio non corrisponde al Stato di Castro, ma' che ci siano pensieri molto maggiori"; Ameyden, "Diario," Biblioteca Casanatense, cod. 1831, 99r.

[14] Ludovico Frati, "Poesie satiriche per la guerra di Castro," *Archivio storico italiano*, 5th ser., 37 (1906): 393; Gigli, *Diario*, 201.

month.[15] In Rome revenues controlled by the apostolic chamber rose first: the customs duties paid on products entering the city and taxes on salt and firewood. Despite the wish not to "burden anyone," however, the Capitol soon found itself as involved as the papal treasury in the hailstorm of new imposts. To make good on their promise to aid the pope, the Roman People instituted fresh levies under their own name and then turned the proceeds over to the apostolic chamber for the war effort.

They began in January 1642 with a tax on bullets (*palle di piombo*), whose collection they leased to a Florentine for 2,000 scudi a year. Then on April 11th civic officials raised the charge on grain measured outside the Campo dei Fiori, the city's central grain market, by five baiocchi (one *grosso*) per *rubbio*. Their edict announced the increase in terms that would be repeated frequently over the next two years. They claimed to act "in execution of the resolution made in public council 10 September 1641 and of the powers obtained from Our Lord to subsidize the costs that the Roman People need to pay in the present war." The proclamation went on to say that the conservators had ceded the power to collect the tax to the apostolic chamber and the Annona, the papal grain provisioning authority, and the cardinal chamberlain or the prefect of the Annona would prescribe its exact form. An edict of April 26th did just this. The revenue from both bullets and grain measuring was deployed for interest payments on the 200,000 scudi the pope borrowed from a group of Genoese bankers.[16]

Three new excises followed in May 1642 and another in July. Not surprisingly, the two main Capitoline taxes, on wine and meat, were not spared and now had their chance to contribute to papal coffers. Without the politicking of his first encroachment on the civic meat levy in 1628, in July Urban simply raised the rate by one *quattrino* per *libbra* and added the proceeds to the apostolic chamber. More controversial was the change in the wine impost, for it hit the locally grown *vino romanesco*, the drink of the populace, for the first time. Announced in May, the wine charge went into effect in July, but by September the pope had been convinced to lift it. Military and political circumstances alike dictated that this unpopular tax must go.[17]

[15] "Il popolo senza follo [?] stripita molto come incapace di maggior gravezza"; Ameyden, "Diario," Biblioteca Casanatense, cod. 1831, 100r, 148r; Alessandro Ademollo, "Il macinato a Roma," *Rivista europea*, n.s., 8 (1877): 427.

[16] ASR, Bandi, vol. 436, Campidoglio, edicts of 13 January 1642 and 11 April 1642; ASV, arm. V, vol. 233, edict of 26 April 1642; Ademollo, "Macinato," 427.

[17] For the meat tax hike, dated 16 July 1642, see *Regesti* 5:46. The towns of the Papal States were given the responsibility for collecting it. In Rome the increase seems to have been added to the tax-farming contract of Francesco Ravenna, a former conservator and son of a Genoese banker. When the tax was raised by another *quattrino* on 22 July 1644, it was leased to him again, both times for 22,000 scudi a year. ASC, cred. VI, vol. 30, registro di mandati; BAV, Chigi, H III 68, 84r. For other taxes see Ademollo, "Macinato," 427; Gigli, *Diario*, 208. The tax on *vino romanesco* was leased on 15 May 1642 for 30,889 scudi to the man who held the new contract for the civic wine tax (*gabella dello Studio*),

The War Widens

The great strategic issue that hissed beneath the surface of mounting taxes in the first half of 1642 was whether to take the war north and attack the duke of Parma on his home ground. Neither the pope nor Farnese appeared inclined to come to terms. In January the apostolic chamber announced that the duke of Parma's property in Rome would be auctioned off to the highest bidder. Farnese responded by exiling all foreign members of religious orders from the duchy of Parma and Piacenza and pawning his wife's jewels to raise a new army.[18] Merely capturing Castro, a territory within the Papal States, had settled nothing. A successful campaign against the duchy of Parma and Piacenza itself might prove more decisive, but it was also risky.

Since 1598 the other Italian states, among them Venice, Modena, and Tuscany, had watched the Papal States peacefully absorb the lands of two great princely houses, the Este's Ferrara and the Della Rovere's Urbino. The annexations had increased both the extent and the cohesion of the papal territories, an expansion that was not lost on its neighbors. As we recall, when Urban VIII first readied his forces to march on Castro in August 1641, there had already been speculation that the pope had "bigger thoughts." In the months that followed the defeat of Castro it was these thoughts that the other Italian powers intently tried to read.

What the pope and his family weighed in 1642 was the danger that an attack on Farnese in his north Italian duchy might be interpreted elsewhere as a move to enlarge the Papal States. Such a reading could provide the duke of Parma with a number of powerful new allies. On the other hand, as the papal commanders Taddeo Barberini and Marchese Mattei surveyed the disorder reigning in the duke of Parma's army, they judged him an easy target.[19]

At the end of July 1642 Taddeo made his move, placing a garrison in the independent fortress of Mirandola, fifty miles from Parma (see Map 5). Meanwhile, Cardinal Francesco Barberini ordered fortifications between the duchy of Castro and the Tuscan border. The Venetians and the duke of Modena were uneasy about the papal garrison; the Medici grand duke of Tuscany worried about the pope's intentions along his southern frontier. None were surprised when Urban VIII announced on August 11th that he would force the duke of Parma to surrender. Three weeks later Venice, Modena, and Tuscany concluded a mutual defense pact.[20]

As Gigli's diary entry suggests, from Rome the alliance appeared formidable indeed. "The emperor, the king of France, the king of Spain, the Venetians, the

---

Arrigo Arigoni; it would have almost doubled the revenues he collected. ASC, cred. VI, vol. 58, giustificazioni diverse, 47r.

[18] De Maria, 211; *Regesti* 5:39, 42. The properties did not find eager purchasers.

[19] De Maria, 211.

[20] Ibid., 211–12. See also Fulvio Testi, *Lettere*, ed. M. L. Doglio, 3 vols. (Bari, 1967), 3:293. Testi was in the service of the duke of Modena. See also Pastor, 29:390–91.

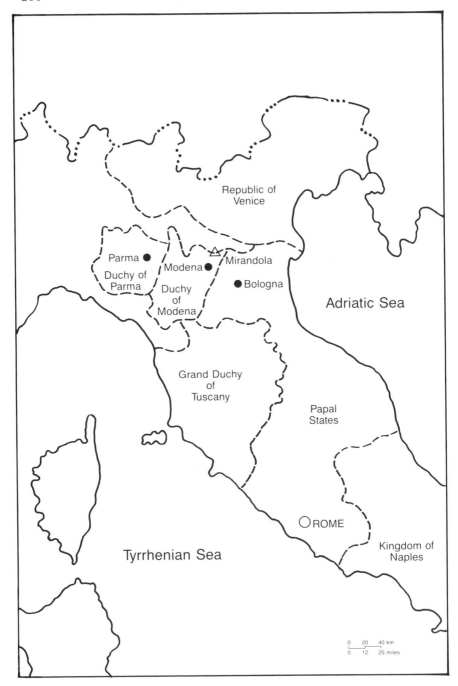

Map 5. The Duchy of Parma and the Papal States

grand duke of Tuscany and the duke of Modena have joined together and made known to the pope that they do not want him to make war in Italy, that the pope should make peace with the duke of Parma." Before any such peace negotiations could get underway, however, the duke of Parma, buoyed by this opposition to the papal campaign and fueled by cash support from France, Venice, and Tuscany, took matters into his own hands. On 10 September 1642 he invaded the Papal States near Bologna.[21]

In Rome the news provoked the first real panic of the war. Although a military guard had stood watch at the city gates since July, the duke's offensive took Romans by surprise. On September 17th Cardinal Antonio Barberini left Rome at the head of a military contingent directed toward the fortress of Civita Castellana thirty miles north of the city on the strategically important Via Flaminia. Accompanying him with troops they had outfitted at their own expense were a number of prominent Roman patricians, among them Marchese Prospero Santacroce, Marchese Alfonso Teodolo, Tiberio Astalli, Antonio Altieri, and the street master Virgilio Cenci.[22]

The day after Cardinal Antonio's departure ninety-five gentlemen gathered on the Capitol in the largest council meeting recorded during Urban VIII's reign. They met to organize a militia to defend Rome. Although the Roman People clearly took the initiative in this decision, they tried not to offend the pope and his nephew by voting to send the usual delegation to make the suggestion to them. The spokesmen were

> to ask that His Blessedness and the eminent Lord Cardinal Barberino should wish to give execution to this thought of the People. . . . And also, if it appears appropriate to His Holiness and His Eminence, this delegation should choose captains and other officers from the *rioni* to carry out the orders given to the soldiers; and at the same time should request to have an overall head to manage and instruct them.

To themselves the Roman People represented their action as intended "not only [for] the service of His Holiness, but also for the greater security of this city."[23]

---

[21] Gigli, *Diario*, 212; Pastor, 29:390.

[22] Gigli, *Diario*, 212.

[23] The conservators' proposal was, unusually, rendered by the scribe in the vernacular rather than in Latin: "negli ultimi consegli tenuti da questo Inclito Popolo fu risoluto che si offerisse alla S.ta di N. S. tutto quello che esso Popolo havesse possuto dare con la vita istessa come fu eseguito, et dalla S.ta sua et Em.mi Padroni fu sommamente gradito l'offitio; riconoscendo in questa attione la solita obedienza et devoto affetto del Popolo: Ma perche' non solo per servitio della Santita sua medesima, ma anco per maggior sicurezza di questa citta e conveniente che vi sia una militia destinata per d.o effetto, come in ogni altra citta ben governata si osserva, si propone di fare deputati.ne particolare ad effetto di supplicare sua Beat.ne et l'Em.mo Sig.r Card.l Barberino, che voglia dare esequtione a questo pensiero del Popolo et far quel piu che giudicaranno espediente et opportuno, et anco se pareva a sua S.ta et sua eminenza possa questa deputatione elegger Capitani et altri offitiali nelli soliti rioni per governare conforme gli ordini che gli saran dati la sua soldatesca; et insieme far istanza di haver un Capo Generale che la governi et istruischi"; ASC, cred. I, vol. 34, decreti, 0036v–37r (18 September 1642). Cf. Gigli, *Diario*, 212, 220.

At this same meeting Domenico Cecchini, legal advocate of the Roman People, announced that he had convinced Cardinal Francesco to remove the hated tax on *vino romanesco* imposed in May. According to his own account, no one believed him until the tax-farmer himself came forward and confirmed it, but Cecchini was then cheered wildly by those attending the meeting. The pope made another gesture of goodwill to the Capitol by formally canceling the Roman People's offer of 150,000 scudi from the year before.[24] Urban obviously did not feel he could afford widespread disaffection in Rome at the very moment in which Farnese was marching through Romagna, meeting virtually no resistance. Although the duke had a combined infantry and cavalry force of only 6,000 men, and no artillery, the 18,000 papal troops at the fortress the pope had built between Bologna and the Modenese border reputedly "scattered like chaff" before him.[25] Bologna, Imola, and Faenza then surrendered without a fight. The road to Rome lay open.

Meanwhile, on September 19th and 20th the Roman People carried out a house-to-house registration of all artisans and gentlemen in the city capable of bearing arms. Four days later the first contingent of workingmen collected their weapons at the Capitol. According to Gigli, the conservators and the four gentlemen they had picked to aid them chose militia officers and assigned to each a group of the new recruits. Monsignor Cecchini, who claimed that he was put in charge of the arrangements, used papal stocks and funds to provide the material supplies the militia needed, from drums to firearms. Five colonels and forty captains were appointed from the ranks of the patricians to lead 6,000 soldiers. Gigli did not think much of these "soldiers": they were "common people" (*plebe*) who could not even handle a sword, much less a musket or pike; many of them had been inscribed on the muster rolls by other people and had no wish to join.[26]

Creating a cavalry force was, if anything, more difficult, because it meant persuading the upper echelons of urban society to contribute their horses. Cecchini complained, "I had more trouble with this than with the footsoldiers; and I had some very unfriendly responses and heard some extravagant slanders; in short I returned home humiliated more than once." Nevertheless he collected five hundred animals and found five captains and a colonel to command the mounted troops. But Gigli criticized the way the horses were chosen. "They took whatever they could find from people who kept carriages, without determining whether they were good or bad." Finding men to put on them was another problem. The same artisans who could not manage a gun were equally inexpert when it came to a bridle; "they did not know how to make the horse go . . . and many fell off and broke their legs, and had to ride off like that dejected and in pain." Many people

---

[24] Ranke, 3:410–11; Fumi, 306. Although neither Ranke nor Fumi gives a date for this gathering, the council meeting of 18 September 1642 was the only one between May and December at which Cecchini was listed as present; ASC, cred. I, vol. 34, decreti, 0035v.

[25] Pastor, 29:392.

[26] Gigli, *Diario*, 212–13, 220; Fumi, 305–6.

asked themselves, he added, "if these are the soldiers of the pope, how will the lands of the Church and Rome itself be defended?"[27]

It was no secret that Farnese's advance was causing consternation at the papal palace. Urban seems to have been unprepared for the collapse of his defenses on the border with Modena. Outraged, he accused Taddeo of betraying him, having had money for 30,000 soldiers and yet only raising 10,000, and he denounced Cardinal Francesco for covering up for his brother. He vowed henceforth to excommunicate anyone in his entourage who lied to him. Meanwhile he called on heavenly aid. On September 22d the pope ordered litanies in all Roman churches to pray for help in "the cause of St. Peter." He also directed that a special prayer "against rebels of the Church" be intoned at every mass. Romans attending divine service heard Urban's point of view on the duke of Parma: "We beg, Lord, by the strength of thy right hand, knock down the arrogance and stubbornness of our enemies." Neither spiritual nor military defenses made as forceful an impression on his subjects, however, as the pontiff's transfer from the Quirinal palace to the better-fortified Vatican on September 25th. As he crossed Rome, a large crowd surrounded his carriage shouting "Viva Pope Urban! Peace Holy Father!" The pope wept, as Gigli heard the story, and blessed those who had gathered at St. Peter's to await his arrival. But his move touched off a general flight from town and a run on the banks.[28]

By the end of September Farnese had traversed the Apennines and encamped at Lake Trasimeno, less than a hundred miles from Rome. He marched south in the early days of October, plundering the cities in his path. Rome, which had not been attacked since 1527, waited in trepidation, while Cardinal Antonio Barberini, at the head of the second papal army, made his way north to meet him from Civita Castellana. Upon hearing this news, however, Farnese's troops, weighed down by booty, decided to go home. On October 9th, forty-five miles from Castro, the duke of Parma had to turn back.[29]

Gigli, who, like many Romans, had an exaggerated image of the duke of Parma's strength, was extremely relieved that Farnese had not heeded the advisers who urged him to march on Rome. Totally discounting the papal army, the diarist commented that the duke "could have taken [the city] easily because there was no one who could have stopped him."[30] Though absolutely loyal to Urban VIII's cause, Gigli felt they had all had a narrow escape. The pathetic performance of the papal troops in the north under Taddeo Barberini and the incompetent city defense measures did not redound to the government's credit.

Ignoring Cardinal Antonio Barberini's role in arresting Farnese's advance, Gigli

---

[27] Fumi, 306; Gigli, *Diario*, 220.

[28] Gigli, *Diario*, 212–15, 219–20.

[29] Pastor, 29:390–94; Gigli, *Diario*, 212–13, 220–21.

[30] Gigli, *Diario*, 221; Pastor and Gigli differ in their interpretations of the duke of Parma's sudden departure from Acquapendente. Pastor, 29:393–94, says that Cardinal Antonio Barberini and his new French general Achille d'Estampes-Valençay "constrained Farnese . . . to break up his camp."

blamed the pope's family for the misconduct of the war and quoted Urban VIII himself on his nephews' failings. The Flemish observer, Teodoro Ameyden, voiced similar suspicions. He noted that, as commander-in-chief, Taddeo handled 30,000 scudi a month; with malicious innocence he claimed that he personally did not believe Taddeo was pocketing the money, "because this *signore* was already rich enough."[31] His comment highlights a commonplace of political talk in Rome: the opinion that papal relatives profited from papal wars. After all, the pope's brothers and nephews held important state offices, both lay and ecclesiastical, from which they derived handsome revenues; it was a fine line indeed that separated their peacetime from their wartime earnings. During the war of Castro, as unprecedented amounts of money were consumed by the papal treasury, the conviction of Barberini corruption hardened in the minds of many subjects. It was against this background that Urban set up a commission of theologians to study the implications of papal gifts to relatives in November 1642.[32] Interestingly, there was little public criticism of the profits being made by the Genoese bankers to whom the papacy leased its tax revenues in exchange for advances.

THE HOME FRONT: PRESSURES AND PROTEST

If war hysteria peaked in Rome in the frantic weeks of September 1642, the final eighteen months of the conflict wreaked a different sort of havoc. New consumption taxes, forced silver collections, higher grain prices, scarce specie, and a general head-tax brought the costs of the conflict ever more painfully into local households. Although the gentlemen did not desert him, for the first time in his reign Urban VIII found himself facing outright opposition among the Roman populace.

After Farnese's retreat the married soldiers in the papal army were released to plant their crops and the unmarried men were sent north to Bologna. In Rome the commander of the civic militia, Marchese Marc'Antonio Lante, suggested to Cardinal Francesco Barberini that there be a general review of the entire company. After getting approval from the pope, Lante posted the announcement on October 30th, only to find that he had offended Cardinal Francesco, who thought the edicts should not have gone up without his order and commanded that they be removed. Gigli reported that there was talk that Lante would resign and the militia be disbanded, "which annoyed a lot of people because both captains and soldiers had gone to a lot of expense to appear honorably and it seemed that they had been deluded." No general review took place, but several smaller ones occurred in early November at Monte Testaccio and at Termini, in which Roman

[31] Ameyden, "Diario," Biblioteca Casanatense, cod. 1831, 148r; Gigli, *Diario*, 90, 215, 231; Bastiaanse, 306.

[32] Much of their report is included in Josef Grisar, "Päpstliche Finanzen Nepotismus und Kirchenrecht unter Urban VIII," *Miscellanea historiae pontificiae* 7 (1943): 205–365; the first session met 11 November 1642 (p. 300).

patricians and artisans presumably got to display their outfits.[33] In January Cardinal Francesco published a list of rules and privileges for the militia that suggested what their duties were. Men of the laboring classes had the unusual right to carry weapons, and they were immune from debt seizures or civil suits while engaged in active service as sentinels, in camp, or as guards of the gates, walls, and bridges of the city.[34]

With the military campaign once again suspended for the winter and Romans no longer in immediate fear of their lives, the pope in November imposed new taxes on salt, meat, and oil. In January 1643, notwithstanding Urban's cancellation of their financial offering the previous September, the Roman People were called on to order a new series of levies on basic foodstuffs: grain, barley, broad beans, and oats. The pontiff, the edict stated, had granted this power to the conservators "so that with this imposition the Roman People can bring into effect the offer made to His Holiness in the present war." It was up to the conservators to specify the "orders and provisions" of the exaction to the apostolic chamber, but the cardinal chamberlain and prefect of the Annona would be responsible for assuring its collection. The absence in this document of any specific reference to the council meeting of September 1641 that had voted the original offering suggests that the magistrates were no longer maintaining the fiction that the civic contribution would be limited to 150,000 scudi. They had accommodated themselves to an open-ended commitment.[35]

The military-strategic development that dominated the final year and a half of the war was the entry of Venetian, Modenese, and Tuscan troops, not just money, into the lists on the side of the duke of Parma. When the fighting season resumed in the spring of 1643, the pope's soldiers for the first time faced hostile armies on several fronts: Farnese's in southern Tuscany, the Venetians in the Po delta, an allied force at Ferrara, and the Tuscans near Lake Trasimeno. Urban VIII threatened to excommunicate anyone who lent support to the duke of Parma. The Italian powers countered by defending their joint action not as an attack on the papacy but as an effort to restore peace after its rupture by the pope's family. They claimed "that they made war not against the Holy Church but against the Barberini," wrote Gigli disapprovingly.[36]

The Roman diarist did not think much of this argument, but his rebuttal shows little regard for the papal nephews. The devil had deceived the allies, Gigli argued, for "they do not attack the cities or towns of the House of Barberini, but

---

[33] Gigli, *Diario*, 221–22; ASV, arm. IV, vol. 80, edict of 8 October 1642; *Regesti* 5:49.

[34] The five Roman tribunals were each to receive a copy of the militia roll so that if someone charged with carrying a weapon was inscribed as a soldier, he could be released and his arms returned to him. ASR, Bandi, vol. 18, edict of 17 January 1643. Men on the muster roll were not permitted to hold guild office.

[35] Gigli, *Diario*, 222; ASR, Bandi, Campidoglio, vol. 436, edict of 16 January 1643 (cf. edict of 11 April 1642, ibid.).

[36] De Maria, 227–28; Gigli, *Diario*, 226, 228, 230–31; Pastor, 29:395–96.

the cities of the Holy Church." Moreover, "they do the Barberini, their enemies, a service rather than harm because, while the war lasts, the Barberini collect huge sums as captains of the ecclesiastical army and instead of suffering they double their gain."[37]

Salt charges had increased in the spring of 1643, but the outbreak of war in June finally pushed the pope beyond the usual indirect taxes that had hitherto prevailed in Rome. Up to this point both the apostolic chamber and the Capitol had stuck to traditional modes of taxation. Although forced silver collections had taken place at the time of the Valtelline crisis in 1625, none had yet occurred during the war of Castro. On 12 June 1643, however, Romans with silver worth more than a hundred scudi received orders to bring it to Castel Sant'Angelo to be beaten into coins. As in 1625 the treasurer of the apostolic chamber promised to pay them with *monti* shares. On August 28th a second edict reached deeper: all silver valued at fifty scudi or more should be brought to the mint. Orders issued over the next two weeks threatened a house-to-house search if residents did not come forth with their silver. Propertied Romans "muttered" their opposition, and a few, notably the hard-hit silversmiths, "complained aloud." Some obeyed the orders "unwillingly," while others hid their silver. "And all waited to see how things would turn out, saying that if [agents] were sent searching the houses to remove silver by force, you could say Rome had already begun to be sacked." In the end the government backed down and did not make good its threat. As Gigli reported it, "whoever wished to turn in his silver did so, whoever did not was not bothered."[38]

Perhaps papal authorities felt they could ease the pressure on well-to-do Romans because they had discovered a better way to raise funds from the populace. Although a number of early modern Italian rulers had found a tax on flour-milling, called the *macinato*, highly profitable, the popes had suppressed it in 1583 after several decades. Pressed by defense costs during the second war of the Mantuan succession, however, Urban VIII had resuscitated the milling levy for the Papal States in 1630; as had been the case in Rome in the sixteenth century, the *macinato* was given to town governments to collect. On 12 August 1643 Romans learned that the milling tax would rise sevenfold from three to twenty baiocchi (two *giuli*) per *rubbio* of grain ground. The new charge arrived with some warning: it followed four days after the pope's declaration of a plenary indulgence for city residents who visited the four patriarchal basilicas. By now, "when the people heard that a jubilee was to be announced, they immediately knew they were about to face higher taxes."[39]

---

[37] Gigli, *Diario*, 231.

[38] Ibid., 229–30; "Per tali Editti il Popolo mormorava . . . et io sentii alcuni, che per le strade si lamentavano ad alta voce"; ibid., 235; cf. ibid., 86–87. *Regesti* 5:59, 62.

[39] Gigli, *Diario*, 253, 234. On the *macinato* in the sixteenth century see Delumeau, *Vie* 2:794–96, 828; Reinhard, *Papstfinanz* 2:175; Stumpo, *Capitale*, 115–16. Ademollo categorically denies that the *macinato* was collected in Rome before 1643, "Macinato," 435–36. But see ASV, arm. IV, vol. 63,

Against this background of increasing fiscal pressures, the involvement of the Florentines in the war on the side of the duke of Parma created the first opening for outspoken criticism of the war in Rome. The papal capital was the home of men and women of many "nations," some of whom blatantly took the side of Urban VIII's enemies. The grand duke of Tuscany's declaration of war against the "House of Barberini" made a big impression, for the wealthy and influential Florentine community in Rome rallied behind the Medici. The Florentines, who had once displayed such pride in having a fellow countryman elected pope, now openly lambasted Urban VIII and made fun of his excommunication. Imitating the use the duke of Parma had made of printed propaganda pamphlets, Grand Duke Ferdinand II also exploited the medium to publicize Tuscan victories over the "Barberini troops."[40]

The appearance of a vocal opposition to the war within Rome had repercussions in a town that usually discussed government policy *sotto voce*, in murmurs or complaints. An incident that Gigli reported in the fall of 1643 affords a rare glimpse of public debate in Rome and of the means the papacy used to court popular opinion. To counter propaganda about Florentine victories, the apostolic chamber put out a circular in September bearing the title: "New Report of the Deeds Done by the Ecclesiastical Army against the Florentines, Enemies of the Holy Church."

> This having been brought into the public squares by some people who pronounced the title aloud, you saw that many people openly laughed at it and did not want to hear the Florentines called "enemies of the Holy Church;" in many places you saw people disputing, some defending the pope and others the Florentines, but what was very clear was that the pope had many against him in Rome.[41]

The news from the battlefields between June and September was mixed and it was difficult for Romans, already inclined to think little of papal troops, to know how the war was going. In the absence of objective reports they relied on rumors. Interestingly, although the army in the north under Cardinal Antonio Barberini acquitted itself well during the summer against the Venetians and Modenese, Gigli did not dwell on these victories. Instead he, and probably many Romans, worried more about the Tuscan army that was fighting papal troops nearby at

---

edicts of 12 September 1639 and 18 January 1642, which seem to indicate that a lower tax of three baiocchi (compared to the standard elsewhere of one *giulio*, or ten baiocchi) was imposed in Rome.

[40] Gigli, *Diario*, 235–36, 216. For some of the anti-Barberini writings produced in Italy at this time see Spini, 188, 191. See also Giovanni Battista Petrucci, *Stratagemme militari da diversi autori brevemente raccolte . . . per servitio & uso degl'eserciti pontificij della Santita' di N. S. Papa Urbano VIII*, with a false title page indicating it was printed in Viterbo in 1643.

[41] Gigli, *Diario*, 236. For the French kings' use of letters announcing military victories in this period, see Michèle Fogel, "1620–1660. Constitution et fonctionnement d'un discours monarchique sur la guerre: L'information comme cérémonie," in *L'État baroque: Regards sur la pensée politique de la France du premier XVIIᵉ siècle*, ed. Henry Méchoulan (Paris, 1985), 335–52, and, more generally, Hélène Duccini, "L'État sur la place: Pamphlets et libelles dans la première moitié du XVIIᵉ siècle," ibid., 289–300.

Lake Trasimeno and in the area around Perugia. He reported in detail the losses inflicted on the ecclesiastical army by the Florentines after one battle in September, and later bemoaned the "treachery" of the papal captains there.[42]

In fact, when the campaign season ended in November the military balance-sheet of the war was roughly equal; neither the allies nor the papacy were clearly ahead. After two extraordinarily expensive years the dispute between Urban VIII and Odoardo Farnese was no closer to a military solution. Negotiations for a peace treaty, which had continued sporadically throughout the conflict, now took a more serious turn.

Perhaps Urban VIII hoped to "win" the peace by making another show of strength in late November 1643. Perhaps the prospect of maintaining an army over the winter called for more funds than the treasury had raised by previous measures.[43] For whatever reason, it was at this point, with the military contest at a draw and doubts increasing about the possibility of a military resolution to the conflict, that the Romans were called on to make their greatest financial sacrifices of the war.

The bad news came via the Capitol. On November 25th the civic councils met for the first time since Farnese's invasion fourteen months before. They learned that the pope had requested that the Roman People raise 600,000 scudi a year for him for the duration of the war. At the meeting the first conservator Marco Casale urged, "we ought in these necessities to be ready to give [His Holiness] not only this sum but all we have and our very persons." But he added pragmatically, "we should all the more agreeably respond to the desires of His Holiness as we are certain that we will the more easily achieve peace with the good preparation of war."[44]

In their usual manner the Roman People entrusted the onerous task of finding a way to raise the money to the conservators and six specially deputed gentlemen. Their job was all the more challenging in that the war had caused a dramatic shortage of coins. Teodoro Ameyden reported that when the pope had initially made his fiscal needs known to civic officials, they had asked, since grain was abundant and money scarce, that the new tax not be imposed on bread. Shrewdly, however, "His Holiness had referred the whole matter back to the Roman magistrates [saying] that they might put it where they wished, provided that 600,000 scudi a year were forthcoming." The six deputies and officials, Ameyden continued, "are attempting to obtain this money with the least discomfort to the people possible [but] I think they will meet many and insuperable difficulties." Meanwhile, "Rome shrieked to the skies, not only the poor but also well-to-do citizens

[42] Gigli, *Diario*, 234, 236–37.

[43] Pastor, 29:397.

[44] Gigli, *Diario*, 237. "Doviamo in questi bisogni esser pronti a dar non solo detta somma ma ogni nostro havere con le proprie persone. E tanto piu gratamente doviamo correspondere alli desiderij di sua santita quanto che siamo certi che facilmente si acquista la Pace, con il ben prepararsi alla Guerra"; ASC, cred. I, vol. 34, 0057r (25 November 1643).

and even the nobility, that famine came not from heaven but from the disposition of men [for there is] such a scarcity of money that not even a *quattrino* can be found."[45]

On November 29th the Capitoline delegation met with Cardinal Francesco Barberini to discuss what to do. Conditions in 1643 were not those of 1630, however, and the pope had no time for extended negotiations with the Roman People. With less compassion for the magistrates' predicament than Ameyden, Gigli commented acidly, "but it had already been fixed at the [Vatican] Palace what they wanted them to do and calling the People to council was only for ceremony and to show that the People went along." Indeed, the day before Urban had signed the chirograph in which the milling tax was raised by 120 baiocchi (12 *giuli*). Thus, on December 2d, it was from a Capitoline edict that Romans learned that the *macinato* on each *rubbio* of grain ground into flour had increased sixfold overnight.[46] The tax-farmer for the new sum, estimated at 150,000 scudi, was none other than the former conservator Francesco Ravenna, who had picked up several other wartime taxes in addition to his contract with the Capitol to collect the civic meat impost.[47]

The next day, to add to popular tensions, the weight of the state-supported loaf of bread, whose price was fixed at one baiocco, dropped for the first time in Urban VIII's reign. Not surprisingly, Gigli reported that the populace "complained greatly" at this action of the apostolic chamber. In a pattern that Romans had come to recognize, however, the pope followed up these harsh measures two weeks later with a plenary indulgence for all city inhabitants.[48]

Notwithstanding such spiritual largesse, stories began to circulate in Rome that suggested how deeply some residents wished Urban would hear their griev-

[45] Ameyden quoted by Ademollo, "Macinato," 437–38. The copper *quattrino* was the smallest coin used in Rome; there were five *quattrini* in a baiocco and 500 in a scudo. On the long-term causes of the shortage of specie in Rome see Gross, 143.

[46] Gigli, *Diario*, 238. For the chirograph of 28 November 1643 see Biblioteca Corsini, ms. 1654, 167–68; see also ASV, arm. IV, vol. 63, 228, edict of 1 December 1643. Gigli's statement that the pope called the council only "per cerimonia" can be compared to similar dismissals in other Italian political settings quoted by Peter Burke in "The Repudiation of Ritual in Early Modern Europe," in *Historical Anthropology*, 235–36.

[47] Gigli, *Diario*, 238. BAV, Chigi, H III 68, 79v–84v. The *macinato* proceeds were to go to the apostolic chamber, but the Roman People were to protect the rights of the tax-farmer and enforce its collection. For the contract with Ravenna, dated 11 December 1643, see ASC, cred. IV, vol. 97, istrumenti, 259r–64v. The bond issue supported by the new tax, the *Monte del Macinato del Popolo Romano*, paid eight percent interest and ultimately had a capital sum of 200,000 scudi; ASV, arm. IV, vol. 41, 241–44.

[48] At this time a loaf of state-regulated *pane a baiocco* weighed eight *oncie*. According to Ademollo, there is some uncertainty about whether the decrease in the weight of the *pane a baiocco* that occurred in December 1643 was 1, 1.5, or 2 *oncie*. There is also some evidence that bread simultaneously rose in price. Ademollo, "Macinato," 438. Perhaps the poor person's bread—*pane a baiocco*—grew lighter, while the more costly, better-quality *pane a decina*, whose price was not fixed by the apostolic chamber, became more expensive. Gigli, *Diario*, 238.

ances. Gigli recounted one of these anecdotes, giving it full credence. On December 21st the pope's personal preacher, a Jesuit named Luigi Albrizzi, inspired by the feast of the doubting apostle, allegedly suggested to him that "the prince at times ought to condescend to the questions of his subjects, even if they were impertinent, as Christ did when he allowed St. Thomas to touch his rib."[49]

But the pope pressed on with his extraordinary fund-raising measures, which now, for the first time, included a direct tax, a so-called *gabella personale*, to be paid by each of his subjects. For this highly charged measure Urban VIII chose not to rely on laymen but on the clergy, who were hopefully more obedient. As had occurred once before, in 1629, Rome's eighty-odd parish priests were ordered on December 26th to make a house-to-house census of what each of their parishioners could pay. The return for the parish of Santa Dorotea in Trastevere survives and shows that one-quarter of the heads of households were assessed by the priest for a total of just over 800 scudi. The highest amount, 60 scudi, was owed by a tavernkeeper at Porta Settimiana, while a policeman (*sbirro*) and some members of the lower clergy (*sacerdoti*) were deemed too poor to contribute anything at all. By early January the parish priests had turned in their reports, against a background of popular alarm about these "strange innovations." Unlike 1629, however, when the plan for a direct tax was not carried through, this time Urban decided to go ahead with it.[50]

For the delicate task of collecting the sums from each household papal authorities preferred to call on officials of the Curia rather than parish priests. Each of Rome's fourteen rioni was assigned to a prelate, mostly those who held the office of clerk of the chamber.

> These men went from house to house telling each head of the household how much he had to pay. Those who had means were urged to buy public bonds for 100 *scudi* each. Those who could not reach this amount were rated a goodly sum of *scudi*. Some were induced to go along unwillingly, others did not want to pay and used the excuse that they could not. The prelate, to do his job well, had to act almost like a policeman, intimidating and threatening and taxing almost by force; in so doing many talked back to him and shouted and every day the difficulties increased. They let no

---

[49] Gigli, *Diario*, 239. Father Albrizzi was born in Piacenza and thus was originally a subject of the dukes of Parma. Modern authorities dispute Gigli's assertion that Albrizzi was removed from his post after this sermon. See *Dizionario Biografico degli Italiani*, s.v. "Albrizzi, Luigi," by Pietro Pirri.

[50] Gigli, *Diario*, 239; for 1629 see ibid., 109. "Si va facendo la descrition per la gabella personale con rigor grande . . . e il Popolo tutto parla molto liberam.te che potrebbe essere principio di strane novita' "; Ameyden, "Diario," Biblioteca Casanatense, cod. 1832, 3–4 (2 January 1644). For Santa Dorotea's assessment see ASVR, S. Dorotea e Silvestro, status animarum, no. 7, 8r–15r (1644), cited in Sbrana, Traina, and Sonnino, 443 nn. 6–7 (and reproduced in part, fig. 8). Of a total of 441 heads of household, 104 were assessed. In the lower range of assessments were a painter (3 scudi), vegetable seller (4.5 scudi), silk weaver (6 scudi), and a female tavernkeeper (4.5 scudi). The total was 821.1 scudi. Sbrana, Traina, and Sonnino, 442 n. 6.

one off, but rated even poor persons, and needy artisans, and there were great complaints and much murmuring.[51]

The disadvantages of having a militia of workingmen became evident when feisty leather-workers in the dense artisan rione of Regola poured out to chase the prelate away by force of arms. When the authorities countered by printing an edict ordering everyone with firearms to turn them in at the Castel Sant'Angelo, the Romans openly complained and, surprisingly, the edict was suppressed before it could be put up. The tax collections continued, however, though the clerks of the chamber now refused to go door-to-door. Instead of assessing inhabitants on the basis of their wealth, the tax became a fixed rate per head. As Gigli wrote disapprovingly, "the father of a family is rated according to how many children he has, regardless of whether he is poor or rich."[52]

The apostolic chamber then hit upon the novel device of sending the tax bills to parish priests to deliver to their parishioners. These printed slips ordered heads of households to bring one-third of the amount owed to the papal depositary within three days or the constables would be sent to the house. When some of the local clergy objected, "saying that their duty consisted in bringing the Eucharist, extreme unction, and recommending the souls of the dying, not acting as policemen," the papal authorities warned they would be imprisoned if they disobeyed.[53]

In January 1644, however, within a few days of these threats, the apostolic chamber abandoned the attempt to collect the direct tax. Romans speculated about the reasons. Some, according to Ameyden, thought that the head-tax had been suppressed because the pope was gravely ill. "Others said that was not the cause but rather that it had met too much resistance."[54] For whatever reason, the papal government drew back, unwilling to push its Roman subjects further.

Peace negotiations intensified in February. In March, after a final military engagement at the mouth of the Po in which Cardinal Antonio Barberini narrowly escaped a Venetian ambush, a treaty was signed. A month later the peace settlement was printed and distributed in Rome. The papal celebration was distinctly understated. A *Te Deum* mass was sung at St. Peter's and a few cannons were fired as Romans learned that Castro had been returned to the duke of Parma and was restored to its status before the war.[55]

But the new taxes continued. In May the milling levy went up again and on August 1st came increases on salt and meat. By now the reign of Urban VIII was drawing to a close and, in expectation of a violent interregnum, the conservators were finally permitted to lower the *macinato* by six *giuli* a few days before the

[51] Gigli, *Diario*, 240.

[52] Ibid.

[53] Ibid.

[54] Ameyden, "Diario," Biblioteca Casanatense, cod. 1832, 4.

[55] Gigli, *Diario*, 241–42, 245. The final battle occurred at Ponte Lagoscuro on the Po River near Ferrara; Pastor, 29:398.

pope's death on July 29th. One source estimated the total intake from wartime fiscal levies in Rome at over 400,000 scudi, all used to secure fresh loans. To finance the war of Castro the pope had also withdrawn about one-third of the gold stocks left in the treasury that Sixtus V had set up as a safety net for the papacy. The war had cost over five million scudi, and, thanks to the government's sophisticated credit mechanisms, its burden would weigh on subjects for decades to come.[56]

The inhabitants of Rome had felt sharply the burdens of the military venture. Although they had not experienced at firsthand the devastation of an enemy army, their contribution to the apostolic chamber, just under a tenth of the cost of the war, was sizable, though proportional to what provincials paid. What especially provoked their sense of grievance, however, was not the total outlay or any single increase, but the combination of fiscal innovation and papal nepotism. As we have seen, they reacted most vigorously to the violation of customary modes of tax collection, such as forced silver levies in the summer of 1643 and the personal tax of December 1644. Their behavior thus encouraged the papacy to resort to loans based on indirect taxes rather than risky confrontations with its subjects.

Nepotism gave angry taxpayers a target that was safer, psychologically if not politically, than the pope himself. Perceiving the Barberini nephews as incompetent and corrupt, their management of the war as a disaster, and their control of state resources a scandal made the citizens' own sacrifices seem less than worthwhile. Indeed, the more certain Romans became that the war was a family matter, the more illegitimate their burdens appeared.

How widespread was this disapproval? The Roman People as a collectivity did not express it. They accommodated themselves to power, leading no opposition and playing the role thrust upon them by the pope obediently. But their support for the war was relatively passive after the initial moment, when a short campaign looked likely, and they did not go out of their way to praise the Barberini during these years of strain. Moreover, as substantial property holders, they benefited from the regressive way new taxes were imposed in Rome. Despite expressions of concern for the common people, they always opted for, or at least went along with, excises on foodstuffs rather than some other form of exaction. When we can hear an individual voice, such as Gigli's, the Roman gentleman sounds loyal to the pontiff but critical of his kinsmen. Indeed it is only in grumbling about the effects of nepotism that Gigli can articulate a critique of papal government. As for the populace, their perceptions mostly come to us through the lenses of Gigli and Ameyden, who were not above using them as mouthpieces for their own views. We see and hear the common people directly only in a few actions: sur-

[56] ASR, Bandi, vol. 18, edict of 24 July 1644; Stumpo, *capitale* 280, 123–24. In 1663 Cardinal Giulio Sacchetti gave a much higher estimate; Rietbergen, 42, 210. Between 1590 and 1644, 1.4 million of a total of 3 million scudi left the Sistine gold stockpile; half of this amount was withdrawn between 1639 and 1644; Rietbergen, 172–73. For war of Castro tax increases and new loans see BAV, Chigi, H III 68, 74r–86v.

rounding Urban's carriage and calling for peace or chasing curial officials from their streets at the point of arms.

The war of Castro was not only a litany of discontent, of course; it was also a patriotic civic mobilization, if not for the very poor, at least for the patricians and laboring classes. While the gentlemen, however reluctantly, provided horses and captains to the militia, or went off to take up commands in the papal army, the artisans and their journeymen and apprentices mustered for gate duty and drilled at Monte Testaccio. Urban VIII had tried to promote the war against the duke of Parma as an act to protect owners of shares in the Farnese debt, the middling as well as the upper layers of urban society. But it was never very clear that seizing Castro had made a difference to the small Roman creditor. And what *was* clear was that widow, monastery, landlord, and guild member were paying more for meat, salt, grain, oil, and flour. Some Romans may have once seen the pope's cause as their own and most wanted to defend themselves from another sack, but neither motive could prevent a growing restiveness in the face of taxation and military stalemate. The depth of their impatience emerged in the summer of 1644, when the news of the pope's death tolled forth from the belltower on the Capitol.

Chapter Fourteen

THE VACANT SEE

THE VACANT SEE or interregnum between the death of one pope and the election of the next changed the normal rules governing politics in the papal capital. A hierarchical structure of authority with the pontiff and his key nephews at the top had suddenly lost its head. This was never a light matter in an absolute monarchy, but it had especially powerful effects on one whose ruler was elected and not the long-designated heir of a dynasty. The fact that Rome had an elective monarchy was what produced the peculiar phenomenon of the Vacant See, which, as we shall see, was quite literally a different kind of regime from the one that existed while the pope lived. Naturally this altered regime affected the character of political comportment during its brief life. The expectations of deference and courtesy flowing upward from inferiors to superiors who dispensed favors and protection in exchange were suspended. The demand that subjects obey the will of the prince no longer had meaning; there was no one figure to be courted, placated, or accommodated. Political styles did an about-face; insults and self-assertion replaced compliments and submission. Roman traditions of political protest, rituals of inversion tenaciously observed over the centuries, open—even violent—jurisdictional conflict, and satire and mockery swept to the fore. In this stormy force-field with many new actors the Capitol acquired novel symbolic dimensions, not entirely controlled by the Roman People, and civic jurisdictions took on an expanded signficance in public life.

THE RITES OF THE VACANT SEE

When the pontiff died, the "plenitude of apostolic power" ceased until the Holy Spirit designated his successor. This ritually and juridically distinct interval was known as the *sede vacante*, the vacant seat or see. Its duration, usually a month or two in the seventeenth century, depended on how long it took the College of Cardinals to elect the next pope. During the Vacant See government mints turned out coins bearing a special emblem and cardinals and civic officers changed the color of their dress (see Figure 17). No new laws could be promulgated, all papal tribunals halted, and most curial officials lost their powers.[1]

[1] The papal bull establishing the rules for the Vacant See during the early modern period was Pius IV's *In eligendis* (1562); *Bullarium* 7:230–36. For a useful summary see Del Re, *Curia*, 459–69. Lorenzo Spinelli deals with the Vacant See before the time of Pius IV in *La vacanza della sede apostolica dalle origini al Concilio Tridentino* (Milan, 1956). The Vacant See following the death of Pope Alexander

17. The emblem on coins and on edicts emanating from
the cardinals during the Vacant See was a canopy, called
the *pavilion* or *ombrellino*, over the crossed papal keys.
The canopy stood for the secular power of the papacy.

Here was absolutism with a built-in, if temporary, hiatus. What replaced it in
the interregnum certainly had ties to the preexisting structures of government
and society, but could not help but articulate itself differently. The Vacant See
was no formless anarchy. It had its own enduring customs, rites, and institutions,
and it had at least two practical tasks: to bury the dead pope and to preserve
enough order for the cardinals to meet and choose a new one. But the first item
on the agenda was revenge.

Romans in the early modern period saved all kinds of grievances for the interregnum. A man of letters threatened the prefect of the Annona by telling him he
would get even with him when the Vacant See came. A courtesan defended herself
from a violent acquaintance with the warning, "Watch out, Paolo, it's no longer
the Vacant See!" Murders, beatings, and break-ins were common fare as people

VIII in 1691 lasted an exceptional five months; Pastor, 32:561. Edoardo Martinori, *Annali della zecca
di Roma: Gregorio XV e Urbano VIII*, 2.14 (1919): 17–19, 2.15 (1919): 1. De Luca, *Il Dottor Volgare*,
bk. 15, pt. 3, chap. 3, pp. 34–35. *The Ceremonies of the Vacant See. Or a True Relation of What Passes at
Rome upon the Pope's Death*, trans. J. Davies (London, 1671), 6 [9]. Cerasoli, "Commentario," 126–
30. I am grateful to Professor John Beldon Scott for information on the iconography of the coat of
arms of the Vacant See.

hurried to settle old scores while papal justice was in abeyance.[2] An anonymous English pamphlet of 1671 evoked the legendary freedom of Rome during the Vacant See.

> If the Murtherers or other mischievous persons be not surpriz'd in the very Facts, and can make a shift to abscond themselves and keep out of the way till the creation of a new Pope, they return to their habitations as if they had committed those crimes in some other Countrey.[3]

At specific historical moments some of those scores were political as well as personal. In the early 1530s, for example, although two years of grain shortages had caused discontent in the city, it was only at Pope Clement VII's death in September 1534 that residents rioted and assaulted grain warehouses belonging to his personal banker Filippo Strozzi. In 1559, Romans who were outraged at the crimes of the nephews of Paul IV (1555–1559) again waited for the Vacant See, and then decapitated the pope's statue on the Capitol and dragged it through the streets. In 1590 crowds threatened the sculpture of Sixtus V there and chanted for the deaths of his banker and architect. Now, after the difficult years of the war of Castro and the unusually long twenty-one year reign of Urban VIII, many wanted to get even with the Barberini pope.[4]

July 1644 was drawing to a close when Romans saw the Barberini carriages leave the Vatican and make their way to the residence of Cardinal Francesco in the Cancelleria. On July 25th rumors told that Urban VIII had received the sacrament of extreme unction. Two nights later, a procession of prisoners in chains was led from prisons on the east bank of the Tiber to the fortress of the Castel Sant'Angelo. People who could recall the early 1620s knew these signs: the long Barberini era was coming to an end. The city that they had dominated stirred in anticipation of the pope's death.[5]

Even before Urban passed away the bonds of deference began to dissolve. At court an aristocrat, peeved at not getting permission to publish a manuscript, insulted Cardinal Francesco to his face. Near his palace on the Via del Pellegrino commoners, annoyed at him for the eleventh-hour tax levies on salt and meat and for a miniscule increase in the size of bread, jeered the "Cardinal of the Half-Ounce" as he passed. Giacinto Gigli noted that "Cardinal Barberino gave people

---

[2] Gigli, *Diario*, 329, 77. ASR, Tribunale del governatore, processi, bu. 134 (1559). I am indebted to Professor Thomas V. Cohen for the courtesan's comment; he and Elizabeth S. Cohen are publishing the full trial testimony in which it occurred. For concern about provoking crowd violence in the Vacant See of 1676 see *Specchio di Roma barocca: Una guida inedita del XVII secolo*, ed. Joseph Connors and Louise Rice (Rome, 1990), 118–20.

[3] *The Ceremonies of the Vacant See*, 21–22.

[4] Melissa Bullard, "Grain Supply and Urban Unrest in Renaissance Rome: The Crisis of 1533–34," in *Rome in the Renaissance*, ed. P. A. Ramsey (Binghamton, N.Y., 1982), 282; Delumeau, *Vie* 2:889; Pecchiai, *Roma*, 158; Butzek, 276–78, 467–74.

[5] Ameyden, "Diario," Biblioteca Casanatense, cod. 1832, 99. Gigli gives the date July 25th, *Diario*, 252. The *avvisi* give July 28th; ASV, Segreteria di Stato, Avvisi, vol. 96, 203r.

much to talk about because one saw clearly that it was he who imposed the taxes and not the pope, who was about to die."[6] This was only a prelude, however, for once Urban expired on Friday morning, July 29th, "the knots by which the Barberini had tied everyone's tongues for so many years came loose."[7] What erupted first was popular fury, and later public laughter, at the government of Urban and his nephews. On its heels, however, came the eager tread of those ready to put a new, if temporary, government in its place: the Roman People and the College of Cardinals.

Ritual, formal and informal, sacred and secular, was the vehicle that created the new context for populace, patricians, and churchmen. Until Urban's last breath it was clear who was in charge, the same people who had been managing Church and state for twenty years: the pope, his nephews, and their clients. With his passing all was abruptly different. The central message of the official rites—both sacred and secular—that ushered in the Vacant See was this break with the past. They declared discontinuity and the arrival of a new regime. On the next question, who governs, they were more discordant.

The ecclesiastical ritual focused first on the pontiff's legal attributes and only later on his status as someone to pray for and mourn.[8] Within minutes of Urban's death on the morning of July 29th, an elaborate and time-honored ceremony got underway that dramatized the transition to the Vacant See. The clerks of the apostolic chamber gathered around the pope's bed, while the cardinal chamberlain, one of only three curial officials who retained his powers in the *sede vacante*, removed the "ring of the fisherman" from the dead pontiff's hand. He then broke the ring, which the pope used to seal his briefs, and shattered the matrix in which the lead stamps for papal bulls were molded. This symbolized that no new legislation could appear until a new pope had been chosen. The fundamental principle that underlay the Vacant See was that while the living pope was omnipotent, no institution, family, or individual inherited this power at his death.[9] No pontifical

---

[6] Ameyden, "Diario," Biblioteca Casanatense, cod. 1832, 104. For the reactions to these new taxes elsewhere in the Papal States see the fascinating letters sent by papal officials to the College of Cardinals during the Vacant See, "Conclave per la Morte di Urbano VIII anno 1644," ASV, Conclavi, 1644, 79r–133r. Gigli, *Diario*, 252. A letter of Cassiano dal Pozzo supplies more details on Count Castel Villano's ill feelings towards Cardinal Francesco Barberini; Lumbroso, 187.

[7] Pietro Romano, 99.

[8] On mourning and burial rites see Laurie Nussdorfer, "The Vacant See: Ritual and Protest in Early Modern Rome," *Sixteenth Century Journal* 18 (1987): 175–76. These rites ended nine days after the pope's death. On the tenth day the cardinals entered the conclave. See also BAV, Vat. lat. 12323 and 12327. For informal rites see Carlo Ginzburg, ed., "Saccheggi rituali: Premesse a una ricerca in corso," *Quaderni storici* 65 (1987): 615–36.

[9] *Bullarium* 7:230–36; Girolamo Lunadoro, *Relatione della corte di Roma* (Venice, 1661), 188–99; *The Ceremonies of the Vacant See*; De Luca, *Il Dottor Volgare*, bk. 15, pt. 3, chap. 3. Prodi, *Pontefice*, 188. The Venetian aristocracy expressed a similar concern in their interregnum rites; see Edward Muir, "The Doge as *Primus Inter Pares*: Ducal Interregnum Rites in Early Sixteenth-Century Venice," in *Essays Presented to Myron P. Gilmore*, ed. Sergio Bertelli and Gloria Ramakus, 2 vols. (Florence, 1978), 1:147. For rituals that stressed the continuity of royal justice rather than its rupture see Ernst Kan-

judges functioned and few curial officials could exercise jurisdiction because their powers were granted by the pontiff himself; they did not inhere in an office. These rituals underscored the personal character of papal authority and the fact that the law and judgment of the late pope were over. They left a vacuum, which others would attempt to fill.

Across the Tiber from the Vatican the temporal realm asserted the break with the past in rites of its own, with the Capitol as their focus. The knell of the great bell on the senator's palace told the waiting city that Urban VIII was dead and signaled to the laity that their turn had come. In keeping with the central message that papal justice was no more, a secular ritual was enacted, opening the city jails and freeing their prisoners (see Figure 18). Only the papal fortress, the Castel Sant'Angelo, remained aloof. In 1644 it was Gigli's job, as caporione of the district of Campitelli in which the Capitol was located, to free the inmates of the Capitoline prisons. The tolling bell alerted the tailor Giovanni Battista de Rocchi, *capotoro* or captain of the Campitelli rione guard, that it was time to muster his contingent of fellow artisans and set out for Gigli's house in the Via delle Botteghe Oscure.

Gathering themselves together, Gigli and his men marched with drums beating to the senator's palace, where a large crowd was waiting. Once there the cells were opened and the prisoners called before him. "It was the custom," Gigli wrote in recounting the episode, "for the last of the prisoners, following the *caporione* to his house, to carry away the rope [*corda*]" used in the strappado punishment. The prison warden then had to pay fifteen *giulii* to the men of the guard to get it back. This time however the keeper paid the rione troop in advance so they would not remove the hated symbol of lower class oppression.[10] The other two city prisons, Tor di Nona and Corte Savelli, were emptied of inmates by their respective caporioni in a similar fashion. Then the three caporioni returned to the Capitol, where the Roman People were assembling in council.

The Capitol had already that morning been the scene of a traditional political ritual of more informal character, which conveyed not just the end of the old regime but a specific critique of its dominant figure. Popular murmuring and complaints about taxes during the war of Castro had left little doubt about the sentiments of the populace towards Urban VIII. Now freed from fear of judicial reprisals, they could openly express their anger at his government. Local custom dictated their target in 1644 as it had in 1559, 1590, and would again in 1798: the pope's statue on the Capitol.[11]

torowicz, *The King's Two Bodies* (Princeton, 1957), 418, and Ralph Giesey, *The Royal Funeral Ceremony in Renaissance France* (Geneva, 1960), 56.

[10] Gigli, *Diario*, 253–54; idem, BNC-VE, Sess. 334, 214r. The *corda* or strappado was the typical form of punishment for plebeian offenders in Rome who could not afford stiff fines. It entailed tying the arms behind the back, hoisting the person in the air by a rope attached to the wrists, and "dropping" them (part way) a specified number of times. Often the arms were dislocated. I am grateful to Professor John Beldon Scott for his assistance in obtaining photographs of the conclave plans.

[11] Pecchiai, *Roma*, 158; Butzek, 276–78, 467–74; for the fate of another papal statue during the

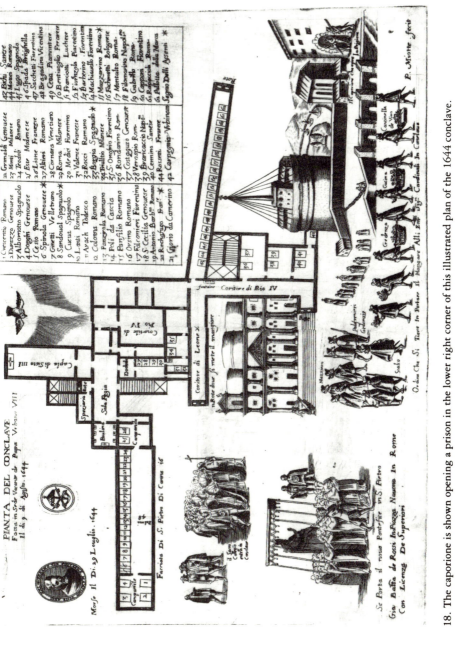

18. The caporione is shown opening a prison in the lower right corner of this illustrated plan of the 1644 conclave.

Bernini's marble statue of Urban VIII, erected by the Roman People in 1640, stood in the great chamber of the conservators' palace where the public council met. It was on the *piano nobile* or second floor, but the room had large windows that opened out onto the plaza. No sooner had the news of the pope's passing rung out than a crowd stormed the hill. The conservators, however, knew to expect such an attack and had taken steps to protect the statue by boarding up the windows and doors of the palace. Providing the teeth was an armed force of villagers from the fiefs of the great baron Filippo "Contestabile" Colonna, whose daughter was married to Taddeo Barberini. The angry mob halted briefly before the pikes and muskets of the Colonnesi. But harangued by an aristocratic Roman prelate who, playing on the similarity between *barbari* and *Barberini*, urged them "to take revenge on the barbarian tyrants," they immediately found a substitute target. Descending on the nearby Jesuit college where a stucco image of Urban had been set up in a courtyard, they turned it to dust. Or as Ameyden dryly put it, "the pope died at quarter past eleven and by noon the statue was no more."[12]

In their actions the crowd amply demonstrated that the "license" of the Vacant See was no fiction, but also that it was connected to, in this case as a critique, precise relationships within the normal political structure. The freedom of the interregnum offered those to whom vertical ties were the dominant context for social identity the opportunity for revenge and mockery. Such behavior was an inversion of what was normally expected by social or political superiors of their servants, clients, or subjects. Indecorous acts of vengeance and satire were political "truth telling" of a sort traditional in Rome, especially seductive to those embedded in hierarchical relations of dependence. The Capitol reveals a new layer of meaning when we see its potent symbolism for these interregnum critics.

Other political players mobilized in novel ways during the Vacant See according to a logic that was similarly anchored in the existing institutional structure. The license of the Vacant See had a somewhat different resonance for someone who, while possibly also dependent on a patron, was at the same time a possessor, as an official or member of a privileged body, of some fragment of authority in public life. For those exercising an office or representing a corporate body, interregnum freedom was a jurisdictional cockfight. It meant trampling not a statue, but the rights of other bodies, or risk being trampled on. Jurisdictional disputes

French occupation of Rome in 1799 see Aikin, "Capitoline Hill," 167. The custom of attacking papal statues was not confined to Rome. In 1511 the Bolognese destroyed Michelangelo's bronze statue of Pope Julius II; Stinger, 239. Nor were papal statues the only targets; Gigli reports that the statue of a commander who was thought to have betrayed the city of Perugia during the war of Castro was burned there in 1643, *Diario*, 237.

[12] Ameyden, "Diario," Biblioteca Casanatense, cod. 1832, 111–12; this passage is published in Fraschetti, 154. See also Gigli, *Diario*, 254, 241. The prelate in question is identified only as Monsignor Cesarini, but he may perhaps be Filippo Cesarini, whom Ameyden describes elsewhere as "abate, giovane di molto spirito"; *La storia delle famiglie romane di Teodoro Amayden*, ed. Carlo Augusto Bertini, 2 vols. (1910; Bologna, 1979), 1:302. The Cesarini came from the highest ranks of the Roman aristocracy.

were not an inversion of norms but rather a more blatant expression of tensions that usually existed, but were held in check by the presence of the monarch. Such normal tensions did change, however, when they were expressed more openly; during the Vacant See competition for prestige became contests over power. This was the understandable outcome of the shift in political reference from ruler to ruled. Without its head the polity had no authoritative arbiter of prestige; when the actors became autonomous they reached for the next best thing. This was not power in an absolute and unlimited sense, of course, but in the sense that people accustomed to a network of overlapping institutions understood: more room in their own domain. The Vacant See gave the guardians of civic jurisdictions, the Roman People, a different kind of license than the truth tellers. A much larger domain, both in juridical and geographical terms, became theirs, and they rose swiftly to the challenge to protect it from other militant predators.

THE NEW POLITICS OF JURISDICTION

With the populace diverted to the streets below, patrician Romans, nearly ninety strong, gathered at the conservators' palace for a meeting of the public council. They had control, not revenge, on their minds. This council session, filled with faces that ordinarily did not appear and in numbers three or four times greater than normal, marked the beginning of the expanded role the Roman People played in the Vacant See.[13] No article of their statutes described their powers during the interregnum, but by long tradition it was they alone who could exercise justice in the city of Rome. While papal tribunals ceased, the senator could continue to hold court as long as the public council granted him this right.[14] The Roman People could not take their privileges in the Vacant See for granted, however; they had to defend them vigilantly, in 1644 as in other years. Their swift mobilization on July 29th was both to do a job and to communicate that they had the authority to do it. On the other side of the Tiber the College of Cardinals would soon dispute that.

The council met only once. Its task was to approve a list of forty gentlemen who would assist civic officials in keeping order during the Vacant See. Preserving "order" was the purpose that legitimated their assembly in the first place, as the

---

[13] ASC, cred. I, vol. 34, decreti, 0069v–71r (29 July 1644). In addition to the three conservators and fourteen caporioni, there were eight other officials, sixty-four citizens, "and many others," whom the scribe did not have time to list by name. Gigli indicates that civic offices were eagerly sought when a Vacant See was anticipated, *Diario*, 446. See also Amydenus [Ameyden], *Pietate*, in Bzovio, ed., 20:561.

[14] ASC, cred. I, vol. 6, decreti in *sede vacante*, 0286r (12 July 1623). In theory the governor of Rome's tribunal did not function during the Vacant See; Del Re, *Curia Romana*, 467. However, in practice the College of Cardinals sometimes ordered the governor to execute punishment upon certain offenders; during the *sede vacante* of 1644, for example, they ordered the hanging of some counterfeiters. In this instance, of course, the Sacred College, not the governor, was acting as judge. ASV, Conclavi, 1644, 297r (1 September 1644).

first conservator Ottaviano Acciaioli appreciated when he told the council that, "to provide against the tumults that could arise," they must "take measures to keep the city quiet."[15] The practice of designating forty "deputies of the Vacant See" was consistent with the gentlemen's firm commitment to order, for henceforth, as long as the interregnum lasted, none but these forty would be allowed to meet with the conservators and caporioni to conduct civic business.

Restricting access to Capitoline deliberations during the Vacant See was not new in 1644, but it is a useful reminder that patrician Romans were no more comfortable with the idea of lively group assemblies than their sovereign. Their predecessors had made this explicit after the death of Gregory XIV in 1591, when, following the custom of that time, they limited the number of deputies to twenty "to avoid tumults that could arise in calling frequent councils." By tightly controlling attendance at their sessions during the Vacant See the Roman People ensured that they did not become embarrassing free-for-alls. Were anxieties about conflict within the conservators' palace exaggerated by the middle decades of the seventeenth century? Neither in 1623 nor 1644 did more than half of the deputies show up at meetings, even with the expansion from twenty to forty. In August 1644 a quorum had to be defined as fifteen, so that business could be handled despite nonattendance.[16] On the other hand, as we saw in 1630, "tumults" still did take place on the Capitol, and absenteeism might be seen as a sign of success; choosing genuinely uninterested deputies guaranteed that sessions would go smoothly.

The use of specified deputies had another, less obvious but perhaps more vital, political purpose. It sent a message that civic officials could not act entirely on their own in the interregnum. This was the same point made by the custom of issuing Capitoline edicts jointly by the conservators and the forty deputies, not just by the magistrates alone as they were normally. During the Vacant See the families that looked on the Capitol as their means of playing a public role in Rome made sure that their elected officers were embedded in a larger, if no less exclusive, collectivity. This predisposition may have also reflected the shrewd judgment that the greater the number of important men associated with the Roman People the stronger their claims would be. Both in 1623 and 1644 the gentlemen chosen as "deputies of the Vacant See" came overwhelmingly from the most prestigious Capitoline families, especially those who provided conservators. Half of these men did not even show up at the public council in which they were appointed; they were gentlemen to whom one assigned civic authority, whether or not they were present, by virtue of who they were.[17]

---

[15] ASC, cred. I, vol. 34, decreti, 0071r.

[16] ASC, cred. I, vol. 6, decreti in *sede vacante*, 0292v; ASC, cred. I, vol. 29, decreti, 0304v (16 October 1591).

[17] See, for example, the edict of 4 August 1644, ASV, arm. IV, vol. 80. For names of deputies and attendance at the public council see ASC, cred. I, vol. 32, decreti, 0268r–v (9 July 1623), and cred. I, vol. 33, decreti, 0071r–v (29 July 1644).

As soon as the public council had approved the list of forty deputies to the Vacant See, it disbanded. That very day, however, the officials of the Roman People immediately took their first action to manifest their governance and preserve urban peace. They issued a series of edicts to ensure order on their side of the Tiber: banning the carrying of firearms; ordering householders to keep a light burning at one window during the night; prohibiting games of chance, which might lead to brawls, and dressing in disguise, which made it harder to identify malefactors; demanding that barbers and surgeons report the names of anyone whose wounds they treated to the notary of the conservators; and requiring innkeepers to turn in a list of their overnight lodgers each day to the same notary.[18]

Although officials rightly feared an outbreak of crime in the notorious license of Rome's Vacant See, their quick publication of these regulations had a political as well as policing aim. By issuing public edicts about law and order the Roman People proclaimed their role as keepers of the city and tried to preempt their ecclesiastical rivals, the College of Cardinals. As we shall see, they had reason to be prompt.

On August 1st, the Monday following Urban VIII's death, Capitoline officials and thirty-three of the deputies of the Vacant See reconvened in the first of their regular meetings. Their main business was to elect a patrician as captain of the Roman People, who would be in charge of guarding the urban perimeter and entry gates during the interregnum. Ludovico Casale, the son of a conservator from a family established in Rome for several centuries, defeated Giovanni Francesco Alberici, a more recent arrival and nephew of a clerk of the chamber, in the balloting. Though Casale was named by the Roman People, he took orders also from the College of Cardinals, who were equally concerned about protecting the city from attack.[19]

The Roman People then moved to execute their newly expanded jurisdiction over policing and justice. At the top of the civic hierarchy the three conservators each had specific and enlarged responsibilities. One remained always at the Capitol supervising the judicial activity of the caporioni and serving as judge of appeals from their decisions. As soon as the cardinals entered conclave, ten days after the pope died, another conservator was posted at the Vatican palace for the duration of the election process. The third conservator captained a force of two hundred armed men who patrolled within the walls, arresting and punishing suspected criminals. He was supported at night by the fourteen artisan *capotori* who each led a number of *contestabili* from his rione on the rounds of their district. While the governor of Rome retained his police force during the Vacant See, their activities

---

[18] ASV, arm. IV, vol. 80, edicts of 29 July 1644; ASR, Bandi, vol. 12, edicts of 9 July 1623; ibid., vol. 18, edicts of 29 July 1644.

[19] ASC, cred. I, vol. 6, decreti in *sede vacante*, 0291v (1 August 1644). ASV, Conclavi, 1644, 275r. The meetings of officials and deputies were called *congregazioni* rather than *concilii*. Their resolutions are recorded in a volume of decrees of the Vacant Sees from 1555 to 1670: ASC, cred. I, vol. 6.

were curtailed by the limitations on the governor's authority during these periods.[20]

The caporioni themselves presided over fourteen small-scale courts of law; their jurisdiction over their districts now extended to cases involving Jews, who were normally required to appear before the cardinal vicar's tribunal. In the caporione's house a legal expert and a notary whom he had chosen assisted him in hearing cases and dispensing punishments. The fines collected were distributed to the poor or to charitable institutions. Although they did not necessarily go on the nightly rione patrols with the craftsmen, the caporioni gave commands to the *capotori* and were responsible for their actions.[21]

On the other side of the Tiber an aristocrat of Roman feudal stock, who was not part of the Roman People, had inherited the title of "Marshal of the Holy Church" and guardian of the conclave. Prince Bernardino Savelli's specific task was to protect the conclave that would soon begin at the Vatican palace and he had a temporary barracks constructed for his men in front of St. Peter's. But in the seventeenth century the protection that Savelli offered was directed not so much to the cardinals' safety as to their independence, controlling communication between them and the world outside. He held the three keys that locked the main door to the conclave at the top of the Scala Regia in the Vatican and also kept a watchful eye on the four or five wheels (*ruote*) by which food was passed into the churchmen by teams of prelates.[22]

While the Roman People took charge of justice and police on their side of the river, the cardinals, summoned by special couriers as soon as the pope's death was announced, were gathering in Rome for the conclave to begin August 7th. The Sacred College as a body now administered the Roman Catholic Church, though precisely what that meant was subject to dispute. By papal decision the college was explicitly denied judicial and legislative powers during the Vacant See so that

[20] ASC, cred. I, vol. 33, decreti, 0052r (26 August 1627); ASV, Segreteria di Stato, Avvisi, vol. 96, 222v (20 August 1644); Del Re, *Maresciallo*, 99. For the capotori's permits to carry lights and arms at night see ASV, arm. IV, vol. 32. According to Gigli, de Rocchi had ten soldiers at first and then reduced the number to seven and finally to six, BNC-VE, Sess. 334, 214r–v.

[21] ASV, arm. IV, vol. 80, edicts of 10 July 1623 and 4 August 1644; ASC, cred. I, vol. 6, decreti in *sede vacante*, 0286v (29 July 1623); ASV, arm. IV, vol. 80, edict of 4 August 1644. In 1644 Gigli appointed Francesco Stefanonio, doctor of laws, as his legal consultant (*assessore*) and Francesco Egidio as his notary; Gigli, BNC-VE, Sess. 334, 214v.

[22] Del Re, *Maresciallo*, 99; the barracks for the marshal's force are shown in a print of the conclave of 1721; ibid., facing 48. For the marshal's dispute with the ecclesiastical governor of the Borgo in 1644 over the exclusive retention of these keys see ASV, Conclavi, 1644, 378r–87r. The keys to the conclave were a potent symbol; in 1676 the Roman People proudly commemorated their possession of two keys to the *ruote*, and the privilege of opening and closing them, in an extant inscription on the wall of the main staircase in the conservators' palace. Forcella, 1:65, no. 170. The *ruote* are indicated on two conclave plans from 1644 (see Figures 18 and 19). The *avvisi* report that Savelli marched to his post in front of St. Peter's at the head of a troop of 500 men, but most of these "soldiers" were sent home that evening and only a small core of paid troops remained; ASV, Segreteria di Stato, Avvisi, vol. 96, 215v (13 August 1644). See also Gigli, *Diario*, 407.

it could not draw any advantages from delaying the election of a new pope. Yet contemporary jurists argued that the College of Cardinals could act in the capacity of three of the pope's four formal titles: patriarch of the West, bishop of Rome, and secular prince of the lands of the Church. This last attribute clearly implied at least some authority over the temporal domain, and in practice the cardinals did indeed keep in close touch with papal governors in the many towns of the Papal States during the Vacant See. An open question in 1644, however, was what their responsibility for the temporal domain meant in Rome.[23]

Subordinate to the pope while he lived, the Sacred College transformed itself into a self-governing corporate body with rotating leadership after his death. At its head was a four-man executive committee made up of the cardinal chamberlain and the chief of each of the three "orders" of cardinals: bishops, priests, and deacons. The "chief" (capo) of each order was the oldest churchman in each rank, though after the conclave began the post of chief changed daily. The four cardinal capi di ordine, as the members of this committee were called, met frequently both prior to and during the conclave. After the conclave began, it was they who received petitioners and officials and issued orders in the name of the Sacred College. General business meetings of the entire College of Cardinals also took place, beginning, in 1644, the day after Urban VIII's death.

The first assembly of the cardinals on July 30th had an analogous purpose to that of the Roman People the day before, to announce a new structure of power. They asserted their control over the Papal States, including Rome, during the Vacant See. They immediately let the Barberini cardinals know who was in charge by debating vigorously whether or not to remove Taddeo from his military command as general of the Church. As was their right, they confirmed the Genoese Monsignor Giovanni Girolamo Lomellino as governor of Rome and appointed a prelate from Lucca, Monsignor Girolamo Bonvisi, to the office of governor of the Borgo and conclave.[24]

In a move consistent with the message sent to the Barberini, they then annulled the edicts the Roman People had issued the day before. The cardinals explicitly

[23] ASV, Conclavi, 1644, 79r–133r; Prodi, Pontefice, 188. See also n. 14 above. De Luca also states that the congregation of the Consulta, an appeals court for cases arising outside Rome and its district, continued to receive criminal cases on appeal from those parts of the Papal States subject to its jurisdiction, Il Dottor Volgare, bk. 15, pt. 3, chap. 22, p. 180.

[24] Ameyden, "Diario," Biblioteca Casanatense, cod. 1832, 106. During the first half of the seventeenth century the office of governor of the Borgo was normally held by a layman while the pontiff was alive, but by an ecclesiastic during the Vacant See; Del Re, Governatore, 46 n. 109. This change reflected a shift in functions that took place after the pope's death. The governor of the Borgo's usual duties were to serve as judge in civil and criminal cases arising in the Borgo or Vatican precinct. During the sede vacante, however, this court did not operate and the governor of the Borgo's main task was overseeing the sending in of provisions to the cardinals while they were in the conclave; these were prepared at home by the servants of each cardinal and carried to the Vatican (see Figure 18). ASV, Conclavi, 1644, 387r. By the sixteenth century it was customary to prefer clerics to laymen in service posts involving close physical contact with high Church dignitaries; Hurtubise, 340.

denied that the Vacant See altered the normal configurations of authority in Rome. In an edict of their own they commanded "that there be observed precisely what it is customary to observe when the see is occupied [*in sede plena*], while the pontiff is alive, and that no innovations be made."[25] Not only did the Sacred College attack the Capitol's power to enforce order, it also pursued its jurisdiction in matters of justice. The cardinals forbade the officials of the Roman People to pass judgment in civil or criminal cases involving corporal punishment or fines over twenty-five scudi.

This battle of the edicts showed that both the Roman People and the Sacred College had long memories for it had been joined for the first time more than twenty years before in the Vacant See of 1623, which ended with Urban VIII's election. At that time it was the then governor of Rome, Monsignor Giovanni Benini, who had first objected to the activities of the Capitoline officials. Three weeks into the interregnum, in a letter to the secretary of the Sacred College dated 1 August 1623, Monsignor Benini complained,

> This morning I saw a new edict published in the name of the conservators and now I am advised that they are arranging to publish another. Issuing edicts presupposes having jurisdiction in the matter which they treat, and I have said several times at meetings that the conservators do not have [this jurisdiction] and that the tradition which they adduce [in its defense] is mere corruption, not to be permitted to continue.[26]

The Roman People's exercise of judicial powers in criminal matters, especially those entailing corporal punishment, was what particularly bothered the governor of Rome. Benini made the argument that the Sacred College repeated in 1644: if the conservators did not enjoy a given privilege *in sede plena*, they had no right to claim it during the Vacant See. The edict that had aroused the governor had appeared the week before on July 24th. In it the civic magistrates had ordered youths not to throw stones or get into fights and demanded that doctors who treated the wounded report their patients not only to the governor but also the notary of the conservators. Benini read this as an unmistakable sign that the magistrates planned to begin proceedings against offenders, which, should they be convicted, would lead to the usual application of physical penalties. Inspired by the latest Roman law reasoning, the governor protested strenuously. "It is certain that to acquire jurisdiction, especially in corporal matters, a privilege of the prince is needed and ancient usage is not sufficient, even when not explicitly prohibited by the prince." In any case, according to Benini, the actions of the Roman People were unprecedented. "Today I have been alerted by experts that there is no memory of such practices and that edicts of the conservators regarding

---

[25] ASR, Bandi, vol. 18, edict of 30 July 1644.

[26] "Lettere spedite per la morte di Clemente VIII, Leone XI, Paolo V e Gregorio XV," ASV, Conclavi, 1623, 298r (1 August 1623). The Vacant See had begun three weeks earlier. ASV, arm. V, vol. 233, edict of 24 July 1623. ASR, Bandi, vol. 12, edicts of 9 July and 24 July 1623.

crimes and government have never been seen in any vacant see." Following Benini's complaints the conservators were summoned before the Sacred College on
August 3d and forbidden to issue any edicts without the cardinals' express permission.[27] But before their compliance could be put to the test, Maffeo Barberini
was elected pope on August 6th.

Twenty years later, when the test came, the Roman People demonstrated by
their haste to publish their edicts that they had no intention of complying. Their
reaction to the ban the cardinals imposed on 30 July 1644 was to ignore it. On
August 4th they issued several more edicts: forbidding anyone to molest the Jews,
wear a disguise, or organize occasions for gambling.[28] The Sacred College countered with a sharply worded announcement on August 8th.

> Having ourselves sufficiently provided, with a detailed edict on July 30th, and the
> monsignor governor of Rome also, with other edicts especially published at our order,
> for the quiet existence of the city of Rome in the present Vacant See; notwithstanding,
> having received notice of other edicts published by order of the *signori* conservators of
> Rome concerning in part the same things for which we had provided by our own order
> as above; so that, on account of the multiplication of said edicts the people remain in
> doubt about which to obey, which causes not only confusion, but much prejudice to
> justice and the public quiet. With the present public edict we revoke and annul the
> aforesaid edicts ordered by the conservators, and others which in any way they might
> publish in the future concerning the government of the city of Rome.[29]

Unlike the first, this second edict hit home. Reporting its contents in his journal, Gigli noted bitterly, "Everyone muttered that, all the authority having been
taken away from the People by the popes, now the college of cardinals wished to
remove that dominion that remained to them in the period of the Vacant See."
Two days later Capitoline officials and deputies convened to decide how to respond to the challenge. As usual Gigli's eyewitness account of the meeting adds
details omitted by the civic scribe's terse record. The group,

> [discussing how] to remedy this injury, complained of Angelo Giardino, fiscal proc-
> urator of the Capitol, [because] in order to gain the favor of the cardinals and the
> governor of Rome he participated in these things against the Roman People, and

[27] ASV, arm. V, vol. 233, edict of 24 July 1623; ASV, Conclavi, 1623, 298r, 302r. It is difficult
to test Benini's claim that this was a striking innovation. While I have not found any such edicts
emanating from the conservators before 1623, not all edicts survive and those that do are dispersed in
many Roman archives and libraries; earlier ones may exist. Jean Bodin makes an interesting distinction
between issuing edicts, which falls within the powers of a magistrate, and issuing laws, which belongs
to the powers of a sovereign, in bk. 1, chap. 10, of his *Les six livres de la république* (Paris, 1576); see
Jean Bodin, *Six Books of the Commonwealth*, trans. M. J. Tooley (New York, 1967), 43.

[28] ASV, arm. IV, vol. 80.

[29] Ibid., edict of 8 August 1644. For the cardinals' resolution (in their meeting of 7 August) to
annul the conservators' edicts, see ASV, Conclavi, 1644, 197r.

those were not lacking who said that when he came to the Capitol he should be thrown out the windows.[30]

Unable to lay their hands on Giardino, the Roman People instead did what they did normally when the pope was alive, dispatched a delegation of their officials and four gentlemen to the cardinals to discuss the situation. They requested that the "usual jurisdictions" of the Capitol be retained in the Vacant See and promised "to employ them only for the good government of the city and in service to the Sacred College."[31]

The deputation made an appearance outside the conclave the next day, but was not received. They returned again the following day, August 12th. At that time, according to Gigli, who was a caporione and sensitive to any possible slight to his office,

> they were graciously listened to by the cardinals, who responded that no wrong or prejudice would be done to the Roman People, but it seems that in fact they felt otherwise, for they proposed that the governor of Rome send his sheriff and constables through the city after the *caporioni* had made their rounds, which the conservators opposed saying that the *caporioni* were sufficiently diligent.[32]

Again, as with the edicts regarding public order, policing was seen as a crucial attribute of jurisdiction, which the cardinals did not want to surrender to lay authorities. At this point in the conversation at the conclave window, the Roman nobleman and imperial ambassador Duke Federico Savelli, who was standing nearby, suddenly spoke up to defend "with great efficacy" civic privileges. The Roman People were so impressed with this gratuitous and timely assistance that the next day they voted to send two gentlemen to thank him.[33]

The next public edicts issued by the Roman People, repeating the earlier ones regulating soldiers at the city gates and forbidding—once again—molesting the Jews, reflected a compromise between the Capitol and the Sacred College. Duke Savelli had performed a valuable service in publicly lending his aristocratic prestige to the Roman People's cause, but Monsignor Lomellino, governor of Rome, played the crucial mediating role behind the scenes. Lomellino, the bulk of whose normal duties as the head of Rome's chief criminal court were suspended, acted as the eyes and ears of the cardinals while they were locked in the conclave. In audiences at the wheels where food was passed inside and through regular correspondence, he kept them informed of the city's worst disturbances. Lomellino had a copy of the edicts that the Roman People planned to publish brought to him. He then passed them on to the cardinals suggesting, in a letter of August 16th, the addition of the phrase "with the consent and participation of the Sacred Col-

---

[30] Gigli, *Diario*, 255; ASC, cred. I, vol. 6, decreti in *sede vacante*, 0293r–v (10 August 1644).

[31] ASC, cred. I, vol. 6, decreti in *sede vacante*, 0293r (10 August 1644).

[32] Gigli, *Diario*, 255.

[33] Ibid., 255–56; ASC, cred. I, vol. 6, decreti in *sede vacante*, 0294r–v.

lege." By this compromise the Capitol retained its right to issue orders relevant to the city's government provided it acknowledge the cardinals' approval, and the Sacred College accepted this activity in exchange for a gesture of public obeisance. Evidently Lomellino's plan was tolerable to both parties for the civic edicts of August 16th did bear the suggested addition.[34]

Relations between the Capitol and the Vatican seem to have been more cooperative during the remaining weeks of the Vacant See. Acting on another bone of contention, the conservators ordered the caporioni to turn in written reports of the cases they handled; these were then dispatched to the cardinals for their perusal. At the same time the Sacred College showed their acknowledgment of the judicial authority of the Roman People by ordering the Capitoline tribunal to begin legal proceedings against some unruly Neapolitans.[35]

The compromise between cardinals and lay patricians in 1644 was only one round in a conflict that flared in one Vacant See after another in the seventeenth and eighteenth centuries.[36] While in the Middle Ages the Roman barons had fought over the city during the interregnums between popes, new contenders for power emerged with the strengthened state administration, staffed by clerics, in the sixteenth century. Rather than the bloody clashes of Orsini and Colonna, cardinals and curialists now fought a verbal war over jurisdiction with Roman gentlemen.

Public words in the society of Baroque Rome were not to be taken lightly, however, and though the style of combat was less destructive, what was at stake was no less keenly felt. Beneath the dispute between the Capitol and the Sacred College in 1623 and 1644 lay frustrations rooted in the triumph of papal absolutism. The College of Cardinals was itself a casualty of the papacy's successful consolidation of power in the fifteenth and sixteenth centuries. Once the representative organ of Christendom, by 1600 the cardinals as a body had lost all their deliberative and consultative functions. While they still served the pope, they did so, in Paolo Prodi's analogy, as bureaucrats rather than as senators.[37] Thus the seventeenth-century Vacant See was for the cardinals, as it was for the Roman People, a rare opportunity to exercise "dominion."

Although laymen were willing to fight more openly for their privileges during the interregnum than when the pope was alive, it would be wrong to see their actions as purely defensive. The governor of Rome in 1623 may have been right;

---

[34] ASR, Bandi, vol. 18; ASV, Conclavi, 1644, 280r–81r.

[35] ASC, cred. I, vol. 6, decreti in *sede vacante*, 0295v (16 August 1644); ASV, Conclavi, 1644, 305r (10 September 1644).

[36] For the cardinals' continued attempts to control the judicial activity of the conservators and caporioni, see ASV, arm. IV, vol. 26, 241r–46r (1655–1700). See also ASC, cred. I, vol. 35, decreti, 0193r–94r (1691), and Francesco Valesio, *Diario di Roma*, ed. Gaetana Scano, 6 vols. (Milan, 1977–79), 6:299 (1740). In the ASC are two large eighteenth-century manuscript "treatises" devoted to the jurisdiction of the conservators during the Vacant See: cred. XIV, vol. 148 (1758), and cred. XVI, vol. 27 (n.d. but after 1765).

[37] Prodi, *Pontefice*, 169–80, 189; Alvise Contarini in Barozzi and Berchet, 1:355–57.

the Roman People may not have issued police edicts before the Vacant See of that year. Both patricians and prelates were ready to encroach in imaginative new ways on the terrain of others if they saw an opportunity, though laymen were perhaps quicker to claim "tradition" as their source of legitimacy.

In 1644 Monsignor Girolamo Bonvisi, governor of the Borgo, challenged Prince Bernardino Savelli, marshal of the Holy Roman Church and guardian of the conclave, over possession of the keys to the door of the conclave. Savelli, brother of the duke who had spoken up for the Roman People in their struggle with the cardinals, reiterated his family's ancient and exclusive right to lock and unlock the main entrance into the cardinals' enclosure against the claim of the governor of the Vatican area.[38] He argued successfully that the ecclesiastical official could hold keys to the wheels or *ruote* where food was passed to the churchmen, but not to the great door at the top of the Scala Regia, which was the privilege of his family alone.

Although it was ostensibly over keys, the contest between the lay Roman aristocrat with his deep local roots and the prelate from Lucca holding a relatively new curial office bore some similarity to that between Capitoline officials and cardinals. In both cases, stirred by the Vacant See, lay members of the city's upper classes defended their "ancient rights" against churchmen. A clash was inevitable, for the clerics, whether advancing in careers in a developing state bureaucracy or waiting it out in the Sacred College, increasingly expected laymen to obey *in sede vacante* just as *in sede plena*.

At a lower level in the social and institutional hierarchy the caporioni spearheaded jurisdictional conflicts with each other during the Vacant See. We have already seen how miffed Gigli, caporione of Campitelli, was at the suggestion by the cardinals that the governor of Rome should send his police around after the nightly patrols by the rione guard. He perceived it as a muscling in on a privilege that belonged to him and his fellow district officers. However, Gigli was equally sensitive to threats to his jurisdiction from lay officials. He refused to allow an injunction issued by civic judges in a homicide that had occurred in rione Campitelli to be delivered because it had been signed by the caporione of the adjacent district of Pigna. Although his *capotoro*, de Rocchi the tailor, was thrown in jail for preventing execution of the order, he was eventually supported by the conservators, who released de Rocchi and dropped charges against him.[39]

In some rioni civic officials expressed their enhanced sense of jurisdiction by making life difficult for people on their borders. A series of incidents occurred where the rione of Regola partially overlapped the Jewish ghetto. At the beginning of the Vacant See the Jewish community had tried to protect itself—an act of defense with a hint of defiance—by bolting the ghetto gates at night. But Francesco Cardello, the *capotoro* who headed the guard for Regola, objected and

[38] Ameyden, "Diario," Biblioteca Casanatense, cod. 1832, 117. The dispute is documented in ASV, Conclavi, 1644, 378r–87r.

[39] ASC, cred. XI, vol. 14, lettere, 132v.

seized the bars. He claimed that he had to enter the ghetto, as all the other streets in his district, to make sure that residents were keeping a light at each window. That same evening he locked up the Jew Salamone di Romano for "wandering at night without a light." A few nights later his troop rounded up "a quantity of Jews gathered together in a conventicle," while a ghetto inhabitant yelled out the window to them, "Cunning thieves! This is how you lead poor men to the slaughter!" From these episodes, recounted before the caporione of Regola, Benedetto Finocchietti, who was sitting as judge in the cases, one gets an intimate sense of the unsavory ways by which the caporioni acquired their increased judicial business during the Vacant See.[40] They throw some light too on the cardinals' desire to supervise this activity.

Finocchietti and the Regola guard clashed with the caporione of Parione and his men in a more serious incident on the night of August 14th. The two bands met head-on in the plaza in front of the city loan bank and a dozen shots were fired. One member of Parione's guard was killed, as was a notary who had the misfortune to look out his window at the wrong moment. Finocchietti demanded that Cardello be suspended as *capotoro* after this melee, but his men got into a similar shooting spree some weeks later when they crossed paths with the rione guard of Sant'Angelo district. This time the conservators clapped Finocchietti in prison, releasing him only after he posted a bond of 4,000 scudi.[41]

Long-standing district jealousies do not account for the violence of rione conflict during the Vacant See. Although there had been festive and athletic competition between urban districts in earlier centuries, there were few occasions for rivalry in the seventeenth century and little evidence of a sense of rione loyalty sharp enough to end in blows.[42] Fights over boundaries between city neighborhoods, as between laymen and clerics, and Christians and Jews, arose because the Vacant See gave privileged subjects, who already participated in a culture with a keen sensitivity to jurisdiction, a need to defend and a chance to expand their turf.

JUDGING THE OLD POPE

Observers of the Roman scene during the Vacant See of 1644 were amazed by the outpouring of hostility against Urban VIII, despite signs of discontent during the

---

[40] ASR, Tribunale del senatore, processi, vol. 147 (1644). This volume contains a series of bundles (*buste*) consisting of cases heard by various caporioni, not the senator, during the Vacant See of 1644. These events took place on 30 July and 9 August and are found in bu. 134, 1r–2v, and bu. 143, 1r–v. Rione Sant'Angelo also bordered on the ghetto.

[41] ASV, Conclavi, 1644, 279r–v, 298r; Gigli, *Diario*, 258; ASC, cred. I, vol. 6, decreti in *sede vacante* (16 August 1644).

[42] Nussdorfer, "City Politics," 323–34. For the agonistic festivities of the earlier Roman Carnival, which involved rione competition, see Martine Boiteux, "Chasse aux taureaux et jeux romains de la Renaissance," in *Les jeux à la Renaissance*, ed. Philippe Ariès and Jean-Claude Margolin (Paris, 1982), 38, and, more generally, Filippo Clementi, *Il carnevale romano nelle cronache contemporanee* (Rome, 1899), and Alessandro Ademollo, *Il carnevale di Roma nei secoli XVII e XVIII* (Rome, 1889).

war of Castro. Urban, the new Nero, should have been buried alive in Nero's tomb. He had denied Christ in his pursuit of wealth. A heretic, the pope had befriended the protestant forces during the Thirty Years War. He should be cursed to the stars for the torments he had inflicted on Rome for more than twenty years. He was an impious, unjust tyrant who was a rebel to God and destined for the eternal flames, where he would await his equally damned nephews. "The multitude of pasquinades and great infamies spoken and written against all the popes that ever were are not equal to the number said of Urban alone," gloated the hispanophile Ameyden.[43]

Several days after the pontiff died, Cardinal Francesco Barberini still feared for his uncle's statue on the Capitol. But the prelate Domenico Cecchini, lawyer for the Roman People, when asked by the cardinal to speak with his "friends," was able to reassure him. "What happened at first could not . . . happen in cold blood."[44] Cecchini read the atmosphere correctly; in the following weeks the mode of protest shifted from crowd action to talk, verse, and song. The refined touch of more elite critics was evident in this new key, for much of the output was highly literate, if not literary. According to Gigli,

> During this time the people vented themselves against dead Pope Urban VIII and the Barberini, with injurious words, and with the pen, writing of him every evil; wherewith were published an infinite number of compositions in Latin and in the vulgar tongue, in prose and in verse, so that I do not believe there has ever been anything like it. Some were bizarre and facetious, others satirical and stinging, and others too sharp and unworthy of a Christian. In sum, whoever had a fine wit and was an eloquent writer or good poet showed it in speaking ill of Urban and his nephews.[45]

As Gigli somewhat sarcastically suggested, a sense of injury was not all that was operating in this flood of compositions; a delight in satirical invention also found the freedom of the Vacant See very much to its taste. Both factors undoubtedly help to account for the presence of ecclesiastics among the rabble-rousers and authors of witty verses. As we recall, one of them, Monsignor Cesarini, had urged the mob that stormed the Capitol on the day of the pope's death to avenge themselves on the "barbarian tyrants." Cesarini's cousin, the duke of Ceri, had been imprisoned several years earlier for killing one of the governor of Rome's constables, and the prelate apparently still held a grudge against Urban VIII for this treatment of his kinsman. The author of witty verses directed at the Barberini, Cesarini was also credited with a mischievous request to the pontiff's favorite sculptor. In one anecdote circulating during the Vacant See, he allegedly accosted the sculptor Bernini and told him to make "a large Christ" to put in the apse of

---

[43] Pietro Romano, 103–6. Ameyden, "Diario," Biblioteca Casanatense, cod. 1832, 135.

[44] Ameyden and Cecchini's comments are published in Pietro Romano, 112, 115.

[45] Gigli, *Diario*, 256.

St. Peter's between the tombs of those two "thieves," Urban VIII and Paul III Farnese.[46]

Another cleric, Monsignor Stefano Vaio, author of a nuptial eulogy to Taddeo Barberini and an erstwhile Barberini client, was famous for writing the words to a song mocking the pope that was printed and chanted through the streets. Gigli, who thought him ungrateful and a bit mad, could not find any motive of revenge to explain Vaio's creativity. "He professed to be a free spirit [*huomo libero*] and enjoyed composing verses and songs."[47]

The populace could enjoy and participate in some of this learned play, of course. Song, in particular, was a vehicle of public criticism shared by the upper and lower classes. Boys in the street, laboring women, and gentlemen in carriages all sang about the misdeeds of Urban VIII, according to Ameyden. The most famous song of the Vacant See of 1644 was "Papa Gabella" (Pope Tax), which had an easy structure that lent itself to the invention of new verses. "Serenades with music and instruments take place all night from a great number of carriages, singing the ballad 'Papa Gabella,' which daily grows in stanzas." Although some copyists were arrested with handwritten copies of the song and swore that Monsignor Cesarini was the author, the prelate himself denied the attribution, while laughingly composing another verse that blamed Monsignor Vaio.[48]

"Papa Gabella" may not have been printed, although other songs were, but its celebrity was widely attested in Rome. An existing manuscript copy shows it to have been a full catalogue of the issues that aroused Roman disapproval of Urban VIII's government. Taxes, bread, and the wealth of the Barberini nephews all figure among its rhymes.[49] The gist of the judgment against the Barberini was summed up in the famous mock epitaph that played on the family's heraldic emblem, the bee.

[46] Ibid., 254. Diary of Marc'Antonio Valena, quoted in Fraschetti, 154. The allusion is to the tombs of Paul III and Urban VIII that faced each other on either side of the apse of St. Peter's. After his actions on 29 July, Cesarini was put under house arrest by the College of Cardinals to avoid further "scandal;" ASV, Conclavi, 1644, 277r. See also Ameyden's comment on the involvement of *curiali* in the satire of the Vacant See in Pietro Romano, 100.

[47] Gigli also reproduces a stanza of the song in *Diario*, 257. For Vaio's writings see Leone Allacci, *Apes Urbanae* (Rome, 1633), 237.

[48] Ameyden, "Diario," Biblioteca Casanatense, cod. 1832, 131, 145; Pietro Romano, 107–8, 112–13. One of the other songs went: "Papa Urbano della barba bella, doppo il giubileo mette la gabella," recorded by Ameyden and published in Bastiaanse, 357. Christiane Klapisch-Zuber discusses traditions of "nocturnal vagabondage to musical accompaniment" in her essay on the charivari of north-central Italy, and it may be that there is a connection between this set of customs and the "serenate" of the Vacant See, "The 'Mattinata' in Medieval Italy," in *Women, Family, and Ritual in Renaissance Italy*, trans. Lydia Cochrane (Chicago, 1985), 268.

[49] Some sample verses include: "In the time of Urban the big breadloaf (*pagnotta*), lightweight and badly baked, became an oil cake (*panella*)," and "They did more damage, Urban and his nephews, than the Vandals and Goths to my beautiful Rome;" Pietro Romano, 108–11. See also Gigli, *Diario*, 257.

On the tomb of Urban VIII a few words appeared,
He fattened the bees and flayed the flock.[50]

The upside-down pleasures of the Vacant See, the release of anger following the decapitation of the normal political hierarchy, and the revelry that succeeded it expressed a startling fact. As Taddeo Barberini put it, somewhat plaintively, Romans were acting as if "Urban, *mero politico* [a purely political ruler], never had religion nor anything divine or humane about him." Gigli also remarked on this, saying it was as if "an impious and wicked tyrant" had died rather than a holy father.[51] For many subjects Urban's efforts to maintain his state may have had too much in common with those of his rival princes.

Making the New Pope

"Never has Pasquino chattered as much as at the death of this pope," said Ameyden, referring to the loquacious statue on which Romans were accustomed to post anonymous lampoons. As the outpouring continued, it was clear that Urban VIII was not the only absorbing topic of conversation. Beginning ten days after the pope's death, the tongues of the city and the world turned to the conclave and the choice of the next ruler. Papal elections took place according to strict procedures designed to ensure that the seventy members of the College of Cardinals had the greatest independence possible in making their choice. The very notion of a conclave enclosing the cardinals in an area with limited access to and from the outside world, which dates from the early thirteenth century, expressed this desire in physical terms. When the popes first returned to Rome in the fifteenth century, conclaves had taken place in city churches, but by the sixteenth century they had moved to the more detached Vatican.[52] The election was supposed to be isolated and secret, but Rome and the world participated in it to a surprising extent through clandestine messages, gossip, chants, processions, and prayers.

In any case physical separation was certainly no guarantee of genuine freedom from outside influences. European rulers had an intense interest in who controlled the Church and their ambassadors lobbied vigorously to promote sympathetic

---

[50] Ameyden records both a Latin and Italian version of these lines, published in Bastiaanse, 360:

Pauca haec Urbani scribantur verba sepulchro:
Tam male pavit oves, quam bene pavit apes; [and]

Questo d'Urban' si scriva al monumento:
Ingrasso' l'api e scortico' l'armento.

[51] Ameyden, "Diario," Biblioteca Casanatense, cod. 1832, 130; Gigli, *Diario*, 256–57. See also Nicolai Rubinstein, "The History of the Word *Politicus* in Early-Modern Europe," in *The Languages of Political Theory in Early-Modern Europe*, ed. Anthony Pagden (Cambridge, 1987), 54–55.

[52] Ameyden published in Bastiaanse, 360. The generally accepted date of the first conclave is the papal election of 1216 in Perugia; Del Re, *Curia Romana*, 465 n. 1. For fifteenth-century conclave locations see Gigli, BNC-VE, Sess. 375, 288r–89v; Stinger, 83.

candidates among the "papabili," the cardinals who were likely subjects for election. The task of the foreign agents did not cease after the official closing of the conclave, ten days after the pope's death, though it did become more challenging.[53]

Several means of penetrating the sealed conclave presented themselves to determined diplomats and cardinals. Bribing a construction worker beforehand to make a hole in the wall of one's cell for passing messages was one possibility. Such a hole was discovered connecting Cardinal Francesco Barberini's conclave room to the palace's exterior; the cardinals who opposed him made a fuss, the hole was quickly sealed up, and a worker went to jail (see Figure 19). Sending concealed notes with the food that was sent into the cardinals was another method by which the outside world could keep in touch with the cardinals. The two staff members or *conclavisti* who accompanied each cardinal into the conclave had the job of finding ways to send notes back out.[54]

There was also licit communication: the audiences that the four cardinal *capi di ordine*, who ran the Sacred College during the Vacant See, held at the wheels where food was sent in to the conclave. Here they met with ambassadors, the governor of Rome, and other officials, and received deputations like that of the Roman People on August 12th. The space around the wheels and in the palace courtyard functioned just like the antechamber to a normal audience hall. People hung around talking, and were the first to know what had transpired inside at each of the twice daily votes that took place. This is where Ameyden spent much of his time in the summer of 1644, collecting news for his Spanish patrons. The Sacred College could have limited access to the Vatican much more severely by simply closing the Tiber bridge that connected the Borgo with the rest of the city. At several threatening points during these weeks in fact they did so. This was the exception, however, and a generous exchange of information between the cardinals and the outside world was the rule.[55]

Romans indulged themselves in the kind of open discussion that they did not allow themselves during a papal reign. In place of whispers and murmurs, they commented on the qualities of their many possible future rulers. As Gigli reported,

> Many [verses] . . . and jokes and gossip and judgments were heard about all the cardinals, divulging the habits, vices, inclinations, and defects of each one, especially those who aspired to the papacy, with defamatory discussion [*discorso giudiciario*] of the consequences, should so-and-so become pope.[56]

[53] Prodi, *Pontefice*, 187.

[54] Gigli, *Diario*, 255. According to a memorandum of the marshal of the conclave in 1644, "se le Rote restat.o ap[er]te, si potrebbe trasmettere, e polize [notes] et altro;" ASV, Conclavi, 1644, 380r. On the ease of passing notes through the *ruote* in the conclave of 1623 see the "avviso segreto," BAV, Urb. lat. 1093, 576r [n.d. but sometime after 24 July 1623].

[55] Ameyden, "Diario," Biblioteca Casanatense, cod. 1832, 121, 130, 134–35.

[56] Gigli, *Diario*, 257.

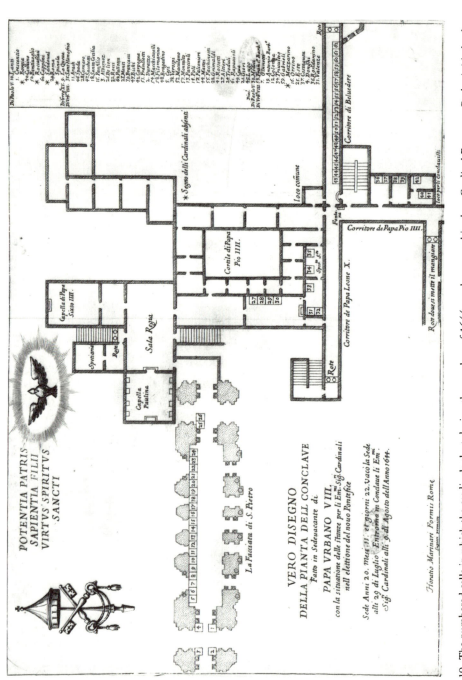

19. The numbered cells in which the cardinals slept during the conclave of 1644 are shown on this plan. Cardinal Francesco Barberini lodged in room 53 in the Belvedere corridor of the Vatican palace.

Those talented with the written word added their contribution, often employing professional copyists rather than risking the more easily discovered printing press to disseminate their works. After several weeks of such freedom of tongue and pen the governor of Rome could not stand it any longer. Lomellino wrote to the four cardinal *capi di ordine* that the writings touching the eminent persons of their colleagues were so frequent that he thought it was time to take matters in hand. It was not enough to control the places where it was customary to post pasquinades, he complained, because the scribbled compositions were passed from hand to hand. He asked permission to imprison some of the copyists so as to cut off the flow of criticism, if not at the source, at least before it swelled any higher.[57]

Many Romans worried that Cardinal Giulio Sacchetti, a member of the Florentine banking and tax-farming family who was the favorite candidate of Cardinal Francesco Barberini, might be elected. In the seventeenth century the outcome of papal elections was frequently determined by arrangement between the cardinal nephews of the preceding popes, each of whom acted as head of a faction of "creatures," cardinals promoted by their uncles. Urban VIII's remarkably long reign had produced a sizable Barberini faction, but not quite enough to dictate the election of Sacchetti. As the days passed Sacchetti's name dominated the talk outside the wheels, however, and on August 31st it looked as if he would win. "The courtyard published Pope Sacchetti with great certainty," Ameyden reported. But an angry crowd gathered outside the conclave. "If you make Sacchetti Pope," they shouted to the windows above, "Rome will be sacked!"[58] The Sacred College remained undecided.

Jokes, gossip, and threats were not the only ways for Romans to try to influence the election. One method the cardinals actually encouraged was collective prayer to secure the help of the Holy Spirit in making their choice. For the pious, and any others he could divert from crime or conversation, the cardinal vicar of Rome arranged a busy program of prayer, processions, and alms-giving in which clergy and laity could participate together. Four days after the beginning of the conclave the vicar's office ordered a week of special services, in which the Holy Sacrament was exposed for twenty-four hours at seven different city churches. On the designated day two confraternities were scheduled at widely spaced intervals to visit the church where the Sacrament was on display. They were urged "to pray to God insistently for the quick, unanimous and useful election of the Supreme Pontiff." City residents as a whole were also urged to add their prayers, fasts, and works of piety to the holy enterprise. The Sacred College even authorized the payment of 1,200 scudi from the apostolic treasury to the poor and to a number of city convents so that these groups might contribute their highly valued prayers to the creation of the future pontiff.[59]

[57] ASV, Conclavi, 1644, 290r (24 August 1644).

[58] Ameyden, "Diario," Biblioteca Casanatense, cod. 1832, 137; Gigli, *Diario*, 257. Cf. Muir, 147, 157 n. 12.

[59] ASV, arm. IV, vol. 80, edict of 13 August 1644; ASV, Conclavi, 1644, 230r–31r (15 August

The seven churches seem to have been chosen to touch every part of the city. They included Santa Maria del Popolo at Rome's northern gate, Santa Prassede in the newly settled Monti district, and Santa Maria della Scala in Trastevere. At the same time the fourteen confraternities honored with the privilege of making processions to the Sacrament ranged socially from the patrician company of the Gonfalone to the artisan brotherhoods of the tailors and weavers. Their assignment to a given church seems to have been dictated by the desire to make their procession visible in neighborhoods throughout Rome rather than by convenience or proximity. The company of the Madonna del Carmine in rione Monti was not directed to nearby San Marco, but marched down the processional artery, the Via Papale, which led through the heart of town. Its final destination was the church of the Oratorian fathers, Santa Maria in Vallicella. In addition to the confraternity processions, which mixed laymen and clerics, the religious orders and parish priests of Rome made a separate march each day from San Lorenzo in Damaso in the city center to St. Peter's.[60]

Whether due to prayers or threats, the members of the Sacred College held out successfully against Cardinal Francesco's hand-picked candidate until mid-September. The victor on 15 September 1644 was a compromise figure, a Roman, Giovanni Battista Pamphili, whose brother and nephew had been conservators and who took the hopeful name of Innocent X. The Romans had reservations about Pamphili—"he was considered a severe man and not very generous"—and greeted the announcement of their new pope without much enthusiasm. Gigli, however, reported with relief that Innocent X had only one nephew, though he predicted that Pamphili's sister-in-law would be the "la Dominatrice" of the regime.[61]

Rejoicing in one of the new pontiff's first acts, removing the unpopular Angelo Giardino from his job as fiscal procurator, the Roman People exerted themselves to honor Innocent. First they celebrated a solemn mass and distributed bread to the poor; a few days later the conservators attended the pope's coronation in St. Peter's. Civic magistrates put their greatest energy, however, into lavish display for the *possesso* procession on 23 November 1644, when the pontiff made his first official visit to his see at St. John Lateran. Outfitting dozens of gentlemen, pages, and officials in dazzling cloth of silver, they erected a festive arch on the Capitol and provided a banquet for the strong-minded sister-in-law, Donna Olimpia Maidalchini. It was back to the business of cultivating the patronage of the city's new leading family.[62]

Whether as popular violence, jurisdictional squabbles, mocking verses, or ir-

---

1644). The *avvisi* reported that the continuing expositions of the Sacrament were "frequented by a great number of people;" ASV, Segreteria di Stato, Avvisi, vol. 96, 234v (3 September 1644).

[60] ASV, arm. IV, vol. 80, edict of 13 August 1644; ASV, Segreteria di Stato, Avvisi, vol. 96, 234v (3 September 1644).

[61] Gigli, *Diario*, 259.

[62] Ibid., 259–60, 262–63.

reverent serenades, the Vacant See took the normal political relationships and structures of a princely age and either inverted them or freed them from constraints.[63] In so doing it opened up a space for criticism and expanded participation in public life not only for the Roman People but for groups they excluded from civic institutions. Unseemly and indecorous as it often was, the notorious license of the Vacant See sometimes pressed uncomfortable meanings out of courtly and patrician symbols. Much as the well-born citizens who met in the palace of the conservators might disapprove, the statues of popes on the Capitoline hill were repeatedly singled out for physical assault in preference to any other papal likenesses. In 1644—not for the first or last time—the Capitol was, for at least some subjects, a symbol of opposition to papal misgovernment. In choosing targets that had been civic gifts to reigning pontiffs, however, the Roman populace may have been conveying more than one message. Perhaps they were expressing their resentment not only at the pope but also at the gentlemen who had usurped the name of the Roman People.

[63] For classic explorations of the meanings of ritual challenge to hierarchy in other early modern settings see Natalie Zemon Davis, "The Reasons of Misrule," in *Society and Culture in Early Modern France* (Stanford, 1975), 107, and Keith Thomas, *Rule and Misrule in the Schools of Early Modern England* (Reading, England, 1976), 33–34. I am grateful to Professor Peter Brown for bringing the latter reference to my attention.

CONCLUSION

"POLICY," as the seventeenth century termed it, was a ruler's prerogative. The pope, his close male relatives, and his court were the epicenter of decisionmaking. If Urban VIII chose to go to war with a vassal, subjects funded it, and often did the fighting, whether or not they thought it was a good idea. He did not have to consult them, he did not, and they did not ask to be consulted. The monarch's rights to make law and exercise the final say even in minute matters of administration were unchallenged. He did not have to demand obedience for it was given without question.

It would be wrong to equate policy with politics, however, and to assume that the only serious topic for political analysis in an absolutist regime was the "mind" of the prince and his advisers, or that one could get access to that mind by studying the ruler's deeds and decrees alone. Political history, as opposed to the history of "policy," must attend to setting—social, institutional, economic, cultural—for it makes rulers and subjects do what they do in a particular way. This book has looked closely at one of the crucial milieux in which papal absolutism operated, its capital city, and at the political institutions of the local landed classes with which it cooperated.

In the age of the absolute monarch there were many treatises on the powers of the prince and many handbooks on how to be a good courtier or a worthy royal officer.[1] There was virtually no discussion in seventeenth-century Italy of the purpose of municipal office or the aims of membership on a town council. If there had been a contest between the state and the city for the attention of early modern political thinkers, it would have been won by the dazzling sovereign, not the humble citizen. In the absence of contemporary reflection on the goals and significance of municipal administration, what the men who composed the Roman People might have thought about what they were doing remains obscure. But documentary traces of their activities allow us to know something about who they were and what they did, and to understand better the practice, if not the theory, of civic politics in an absolutist state.

The Senate and Roman People was a notion to which Romans in the early modern period attached duties and meanings of many sorts. Water, walls, statues, chalices, and edicts were some of the physical manifestations of this entity. More elusive and more deeply embedded were attitudes, processes, and symbols.

---

[1] For relevant bibliography see among others Bireley; Elliott; Vittor Ivo Comparato, *Uffici e societa' a Napoli (1600–1647): Aspetti dell'ideologia del magistrato nell'eta' moderna* (Florence, 1974); Cesare Mozzarelli, "Principe, corte e governo tra '500 e '700," in *Culture et idéologie dans la genèse de l'état moderne* (Rome, 1985), 367–79.

Chicken sellers who yearned to sell eggs along with chickens had one kind of experience of the municipal magistrates and their market police; patricians who wanted to raise the spiritual status of a kinswoman looked upon the Roman People differently; taxpayers who attacked a statue of the pope on the Capitoline hill responded to other resonances. In the reality of daily life the men and buildings and rules and traditions associated with the Capitol were palpable and taken for granted. This social and institutional tissue of chicken sellers, police, gentlemen, influence, taxes, and memory, what we call "local government," was a vital if reticent presence in the Baroque city.

As a vehicle of public activity for patrician laymen, the Senate and Roman People also had more specific work to do on behalf of the urban upper classes. It buttressed claims to noble status, helped to integrate immigrants into a heterogenous "elite," and promoted the interests of landed estate-owners whose family strategies might also include advancing in the local bureaucracy of the Church or Curia. It performed these tasks at the same time that it had to accommodate a resident prince who was also the pope. No other civic administration in seventeenth-century Europe took orders from an elected, celibate ruler who headed an international ecclesiastical organization. The peculiarities of this political regime left their mark on Roman civic politics.

The fact that the popes were elected monarchs influenced political dynamics in Rome in several ways. It structured a period of interregnum into city life, which gave regular play to jurisdictional claims by lay and ecclesiastical bodies and provided opportunities for overt criticism by unhappy subjects. The Vacant See exercised voices and muscles that were muted and flaccid during papal reigns. Electoral monarchy also meant that the prince and his family were a temporary dynasty; whether generous or grasping, efficient or bungling, they came and went. One consequence was that the pope's relatives were easy scapegoats for all the frustrations experienced under a given pontificate. Commanding no particular loyalty from papal subjects, they drew off criticism that might have been aimed at the ruler, much as "evil councillors" did in dynastic regimes. Finally, the fact that any member of the College of Cardinals could conceivably become the next pope complicated strategies for political advancement, even among laymen with no prospects at the papal court. It dispersed the attention of would-be clients among many cardinals in ways that flowed into the civic world. Instead of being able to put one's money on a clearly designated royal heir one had to place bets on a number of potential candidates, some of whom were brothers, uncles, or nephews of officials of the Roman People. Even at the Capitol therefore one could make or break the future of one's family by a well-aimed favor or a misspoken phrase. Thus the manner in which popes were chosen contributed to a broadly politicized atmosphere outside the court as well as within it.

Other features of papal government also had an impact on the civic sphere. The papacy was a lure that directly affected the composition of city society and indirectly the profile of municipal office. Its manpower needs were filled by well-born, wealthy, or well-educated young men drawn from all over Italy, giving Rome's upper strata a regular infusion of new families and fostering a relatively open urban elite. Other royal bureaucracies may have exercised a similar attraction on their provincials, but there were differences. The papacy recruited over a relatively wide geographic area and preferred unmarried officeholders, who were of course accompanied by kinsmen. One effect of papal employment patterns therefore was to turn the energies of a constant stream of ambitious foreign families loose on the city of Rome, where they explored many forms of social capital accumulation including civic office.

In seventeenth-century Rome there were significant distinctions between municipal and papal officials. Both in precept and practice civic office was restricted to laymen. In contrast, the curial bureaucracy that managed the affairs of the Catholic Church and the Papal States was by this time composed mainly of clerics. The existence of this division in the personnel of city and state administration set Rome apart from a capital like Paris, for example, where judges in the king's tribunals gradually took over the municipal government. Civic officials in Rome were not the same men who staffed the papal administration, although, as we have seen, they might be their relatives. Civic offices remained immune from the patrimonial pressures affecting offices in the papal bureaucracy; they were not venal and they resisted becoming a form of family property. They continued to be filled by election and to circulate among a rather loosely defined cast of "gentlemen."

This separation of the officers of state and city did not, of course, translate itself into an autonomous civic politics. Drawn from the same families as papal officials or ones very similar in socioeconomic character, and channeled ideologically to think of political action in terms of jurisdiction and patronage, the lay patricians of the Roman People did not reflect critically on absolutist government. They may have opposed specific policies of Urban VIII, but they did not mount a theoretical challenge to papal rule. It has been one of the aims of this book to show why it was in their material and immaterial interest to work with the papacy rather than against it.

The Roman People dealt in the currency of a society transfixed by the hierarchy of birth and the spectacle of a seventeenth-century court. Like Urban VIII himself, like the foreign ambassadors to the Holy See, like the individual families of which they were composed, and like the city's laboring women and men, they worked hard to construct an honorable image and they worried about actions that might tarnish that image. Capitoline officials participated in a public culture of deference that favored demonstrations of gratitude and loyalty to those in superior positions of authority, especially the pontiff and the cardinal nephew. Showing sufficient gratitude and loyalty was difficult when resources were limited and the throng of would-be clients immense. It took effort and imagination to think up a constant flow of honors the civic treasury could afford. Maintaining an image of nobility and magnificence made the gifts of the Roman People more valuable and helped stretch their investment further.

Administration was primarily a political activity. Officials of one tribunal did not share common goals with officials of another tribunal; they viewed representatives of other public bodies as their competitors and they were more concerned to preserve or improve their position relative to those other officers than they were to promote order or justice. What Capitoline edicts, permits, trials, and processions did was make tangible and visible the "jurisdiction" of the Roman People. Jurisdiction was a quality that institutions had in infinitely varied degrees, and which could be usurped, even lost, by microscopic shifts in procedure or obligations. Since there was no deeper rationale for their existence, their identity—what they might have thought of as their honor—was at stake in every interaction they had. This made administrative functions not only conveyors of messages about status, dignity, and respect but also instruments for their construction.

The pope, as the ultimate arbiter of rank, played a crucial role in such a system and it was this, not just his coercive powers or autocratic personality, that made him so compelling a "charismatic center."[2] The Roman People depended on an absolute monarch to uphold their prerogatives, as their struggles during the Vacant See attest. No other figure had his capacity to do a favor. This dependence grounded their fidelity firmly in interest and further inhibited any inclination they might have had to challenge or criticize.

If "self-interest" is perhaps overstressed as a motive here, it is in part to correct the prevailing view that the Roman People in the Baroque age were simply "decadent," a residual vessel somehow emptied of historical vigor. In fact, civic institutions were always engaged in a process of mutual interaction both with the institutions of papal government and with broader cultural movements. The local lay elite put civic resources to work in old and new ways as structures and values changed. The activism of the clerks of the chamber was met by lay officials with a vigorous invocation of their civic jurisdictional privileges. The seventeenth century's obsession with aristocratic rank prompted the Roman People to pass fresh exclusions on civic officeholding and to force recognition of status via new forms of public memory. When we look at the varied ways civic institutions could have meaning and the multiple uses to which they were put, they appear supple perhaps, and polyvalent, but hardly decadent.

If this assessment of the Capitol in the Baroque age is valid, we have to credit the sturdiness of a particular kind of urban political tradition that was widespread in Italy in the Middle Ages and that left an important legacy to the early modern period. It included the right to be regulated by locally initiated statutes, the recourse to election to fill magistracies, and the elaboration of a notion that hold-

---

[2] Clifford Geertz, "Centers, Kings and Charisma: Reflections on the Symbolics of Power," in *Culture and Its Creators: Essays in Honor of Edward Shils*, ed. J. Ben-David and T. Clark (Chicago, 1977), 151. See also Beik, 323.

ing civic office was honorable. While no one would deny that most of Italy's free cities had been profoundly transformed by the acquisition of princely rulers in the sixteenth century, they had kept from their past much of this legacy and the habit of active participation by local landed families in urban affairs.[3]

It may be startling to claim this inheritance for Rome, a city that had never been an independent commune and that had always been subordinate to one degree or another to the pope. Yet, as we have seen, Rome's civic institutions shared in these traditions of recognized public statutes, electoral recruitment to office, and conferral of noble status, and may, if anything, have allowed greater participation by newcomers than other early modern Italian towns. To highlight the significance of this legacy we might cast a glance at Bourbon Paris, the capital of the French monarchy, which was a fief of the king without published statutes, where civic offices were bought and sold, and where royal judges and river merchants, not landed estate owners, vied for control.[4] Seen from this perspective Baroque Rome was indeed a city in the Italian manner.

The popes had approved this type of local administration in their capital early in the fifteenth century and they showed little inclination to change it over the succeeding centuries. For their part Roman gentlemen continued to profit from the social, political, and symbolic role it provided. Despite occasional conflicts, pontiffs and patricians both found ways to bend and stretch civic institutions to further their own ends. Perhaps this elasticity was the ultimate strength of the Roman People, permitting them to outlast papal monarchs just as they had ancient emperors.

[3] See also *Fiscalite'*, ix.
[4] Descimon, 113–50.

BIBLIOGRAPHY

ARCHIVAL AND MANUSCRIPT SOURCES

(All archives and libraries are in Rome)

Archivio Storico Capitolino (ASC)

FONDO CAMERA CAPITOLINA

cred. I, vol. 1	cittadini romani
cred. I, vol. 4	cittadini romani
cred. I, vol. 5	cittadini romani
cred. I, vol. 6	decreti in sede vacante
cred. I, vol. 13	matricole dei consigli
cred. I, vol. 15	decreti dei consigli
cred. I, vol. 28	decreti dei consigli
cred. I, vol. 29	decreti dei consigli
cred. I, vol. 32	decreti dei consigli
cred. I, vol. 33	decreti dei consigli
cred. I, vol. 34	decreti dei consigli
cred. I, vol. 35	decreti dei consigli
cred. I, vol. 38	decreti dei consigli
cred. I, vol. 40	decreti delle congregazioni
cred. II, vol. 101	bilanci della camera capitolina
cred. III, vol. 22	testamenti e donazioni
cred. IV, vol. 2	decreti delle congregazioni
cred. IV, vol. 16	cartoni delle regaglie del sale
cred. IV, vol. 90	statuto della citta' di Magliano
cred. IV, vol. 91	statuto della citta' di Cori
cred. IV, vol. 92	catasto della terra di Barbarano
cred. IV, vol. 96	istrumenti, brevi e lettere patenti
cred. IV, vol. 97	istrumenti diversi della camera capitolina
cred. IV, vol. 106	tabelle di entrata et uscita del Pop. Romano
cred. IV, vol. 112	mandati per sanita' e sede vacante
cred. IV, vol. 113	mandati per sanita' e sede vacante
cred. IV, vol. 128	cedole di sussidii dotali
cred. VI, vol. 30	registro di mandati
cred. VI, vol. 31	registro di mandati
cred. VI, vol. 48	ristretti di dare et avere
cred. VI, vol. 52	registro di patenti, brevi e chirografi
cred. VI, vol. 58	giustificazioni diverse
cred. VI, vol. 60	giustificazioni diverse
cred. VI, vol. 63	interessi diversi della camera capitolina
cred. VI, vol. 88	invenzioni dagli straordinari (1695–1735)

cred. VI, vol. 108   relazione del tumulto accaduto in Roma, 1736
cred. VI, vol. 114   uffici capitolini
cred. IX, vol. 21   pene (1683–1684)
cred. XI, vol. 13   registro di lettere (1595–1603)
cred. XI, vol. 14   registro di lettere (1632–1647)
cred. XI, vol. 15   registro di lettere (1648–1704)
cred. XI, vol. 19   lettere patenti (1615–1630)
cred. XI, vol. 20   lettere patenti (1632–1645)
cred. XI, vol. 40   statuto della terra di Barbarano
cred. XI, vol. 49   statuto della citta' di Magliano
cred. XI, vol. 64   statuto della terra di Vitorchiano
cred. XI, vol. 73   statuti, universita' dei saponari (soapmakers)
cred. XI, vol. 103   statuto della terra di Barbarano
cred. XIII, 1st. ser.,
    vol. 30   edicts
cred. XIV, vol. 148   giurisdizione in sede vacante
cred. XVI, vol. 27   giurisdizione in sede vacante

Archivio di Stato di Roma (ASR)

BIBLIOTECA
Bandi, vol. 12
Bandi, vol. 18
Bandi, Campidoglio, vol. 436
Statuti, 449/7, universita' dei pescivendoli (fishmongers)
Statuti, 571, universita' dei materassari (mattress makers)
Statuti, 795/1, *Statuta civitatis corae* (Rome: 1732)

ARCHIVIO
Archivio Santacroce, D 141 "Entrate che la sede app.ca cava ogn'anno della citta' di Roma"
Camerale I, Mandati camerali, vol. 1008
Camerale II, Arti e mestieri, vol. 15
Camerale II, Conti di entrata e uscita, bu. 1
Presidenza delle strade, vol. 8
Presidenza delle strade, vol. 446
30 Notai Capitolini
    uff. 2 (1626–27, 1630–36)
    uff. 15 (1630)
    uff. 18 (1630, 1645)
    uff. 20 (1630)
    uff. 25 (1630, 1645)
    uff. 26 (1630)
    uff. 28 (1630)
Tribunale dei conservatori, vol. 49
Tribunale dei conservatori, vol. 57
Tribunale dei conservatori, vol. 59
Tribunale criminale del governatore, vol. 257
Tribunale criminale del senatore, vol. 147

.

Archivio Segreto Vaticano (ASV)

arm. II, cod. 150 [Teodoro Ameyden], "Relatione seu Raguaglio compitissimo di tutte le Nobilità delle Famiglie antiche"

Archivum Arcis

    arm. IV, vol. 26

    arm. IV, vol. 32

    arm. IV, vol. 38

    arm. IV, vol. 52

    arm. IV, vol. 61

    arm. IV, vol. 63

    arm. IV, vol. 80

    arm. V, vol. 233

Conclavi, "Lettere spedite per la morte di Clemente VIII, Leone XI, Paolo V e Gregorio XV"

Conclavi, "Conclave per la morte di Urbano VIII"

Segreteria di Stato, avvisi di Roma, vol. 96

Archivio Storico del Vicariato (ASVR)

S. Dorotea e Silvestro, stati di anima, no. 7

Biblioteca Apostolica Vaticana (BAV)

STAMPATI

R. G. Storia. IV 9253 (8): Statuti (ms.), universita' dei muratori (masons)

MANOSCRITTI

Barb. lat. 2211–23 bussula officialium Populi Romani

Barb. lat. 4411 Carlo Rainaldi drawings of hospitals

Barb. lat. 4649 conclave plan of 1644

Barb. lat. 4730–38 Andrea Nicoletti, "Vita di Papa Urbano Ottavo"

Barb. lat. 4751 conclave plan of 1644

Barb. lat. 4835 count of number of horses, artisans, shops

Barb. lat. 4901 memorie di Monsignore Herrara

Barb. lat. 5626–29 Giovanni Battista Spada, lettere ed istruzioni della congregazione della sanita', 1629–1634

Barb. lat. 9910 Giacinto Gigli's illustrated poem

Barb. lat. 10633–36 (provisional) Barberini carteggio

Chigiani, H II 55 (1–6) list of gentlemen by rioni

Chigiani, H III 56 (1–7) bussula officialium Populi Romani

Chigiani, H III 68 apostolic chamber account

Chigiani, N III 84 "Modo per tor via che i prezzi delle cose magnative non stiano alti in Roma"

Urb. lat. 1093–98 avvisi di Roma

Vat. lat. 12323 diaria caeremoniarum Pauli Alaleonis

Vat. lat. 12327 diaria caeremoniarum Fulvii Servanti

Biblioteca Casanatense

cod. 1831–32 Teodoro Ameyden, "Diario di Roma," 1640–1647

Biblioteca Corsini

ms. 1654 "Relatione da darse nella Congregazione dell'Abbondanza"

Biblioteca Nazionale Centrale-Vittorio Emanuele II (BNC-VE)

MANOSCRITTI

Sess. 334 Giacinto Gigli, "Cronologia dei consoli, priori e magistrati di Roma"
Sess. 375 Giacinto Gigli, "Cronologia romana di Giacinto Gigli"

PRINTED SOURCES

Ackerman, James. *The Architecture of Michelangelo.* 2 vols. London, 1961.
————. "Marcus Aurelius on the Capitoline Hill." *Renaissance News* 10 (1957): 69–74.
Ademollo, Alessandro. *Il Carnevale di Roma nei secoli XVII e XVIII.* Rome, 1883.
————. *Giacinto Gigli ed i suoi diarii del secolo XVII.* Florence, 1877.
————. "Il macinato a Roma." *Rivista europea,* n.s., 8 (1877): 421–45.
Gli affreschi del Cavalier D'Arpino in Campidoglio: Analisi di un'opera attraverso il restauro. Rome, 1980.
Ago, Renata. *Carriere e clientele nella Roma barocca.* Bari, 1990.
————. "Conflitti e politica nel feudo: Le campagne romane del Settecento." *Quaderni storici* 63 (1986): 847–74.
Aikin, Roger. "The Capitoline Hill during the Reign of Sixtus V." Ph.D. diss., University of California, Berkeley, 1977.
————. "Christian Soldiers in the Sala dei Capitani." *Sixteenth Century Journal* 16 (1985): 206–27.
Albèri, Eugenio, ed. *Le relazioni degli ambasciatori veneti al senato durante il secolo decimosesto.* 15 vols. Florence, 1839–63.
Alberini, Marcello. *I ricordi di Marcello Alberini.* Vol. 1 of *Il sacco di Roma del M.d.xxvii.* Edited by Domenico Orano. Rome, 1901.
Allacci, Leone. *Apes Urbanae.* Rome, 1633.
Altieri, Marc'Antonio. *Li nuptiali.* Edited by E. Narducci. Rome, 1873.
Amelang, James S. *Honored Citizens of Barcelona: Patrician Culture and Class Relations, 1490–1714.* Princeton, 1986.
Ameyden, Teodoro. *La storia delle famiglie romane di Teodoro Amayden.* Edited by Carlo Augusto Bertini. 2 vols. Rome, 1910.
Amydenus [Ameyden], Theodorus. *De pietate romana.* Rome, 1625. Reprinted in vol. 20 of *Annales ecclesiastici,* 526–62. Edited by Abramo Bzovio. Cologne, 1641.
Anderson, Perry. *Lineages of the Absolutist State.* London, 1974.
Argan, Giulio Carlo. *The Europe of the Capitals 1600–1700.* Translated by Anthony Rhodes. Geneva, 1964.
Ashby, Thomas. *La Campagna romana al tempo di Paolo III.* Rome, 1914.
Aymard, Maurice, and Revel, Jacques. "La famille farnèse." In *Le palais farnèse,* vol. 1, pt. 2: 695–715. 3 vols. Rome, 1981.
Balani, Donatella. *Il vicario tra citta' e stato: L'Ordine pubblico e l'annona nella Torino del Settecento.* Turin, 1987.
Barcia, Franco. *Bibliografia delle opere di Gregorio Leti.* Milan, 1981.
Barozzi, Niccolo', and Berchet, Guglielmo, eds. *Relazioni degli stati europei lette al Senato*

dagli ambasciatori veneti del secolo decimosettimo. Series 3, *Italia, Relazioni di Roma.* 2 vols. Venice, 1877–78.

Bastiaanse, A. *Teodoro Ameyden (1586–1656): Un neerlandese alla corte di Roma.* The Hague, 1967.

Becchetti, Piero. "L'Acqua Mariana." In *Il Tevere.* Edited by Bruno Brizzi. Rome, 1989.

Beik, William. *Absolutism and Society in Seventeenth-Century Languedoc.* Cambridge, 1985.

Beneš, Mirka. "Villa Pamphilj (1630–1670): Family, Gardens and Land in Papal Rome." Ph.D. diss., Yale University, 1989.

Berce', Yves-Marie. "Troubles frumentaires et pouvoir centralisateur: L'émeute de Fermo dans les Marches (1648)." Parts 1, 2. *École française de Rome. Mélanges d'archéologie et d'histoire* 73 (1961): 471–505; 74 (1962): 759–803.

Berengo, Marino. "La citta' di antico regime." *Quaderni storici* 27 (1974): 661–92.

Berengo, Marino, and Diaz, Furio. "Noblesse et administration dans l'Italie de la Renaissance. La formation de la bureaucratie moderne." *XIII International Congress of Historical Sciences,* vol. 1: 151–63. Moscow, 1970.

Bevilacqua, Mario. *Il Monte dei Cenci: Una famiglia romana e il suo insediamento urbano tra medioevo ed eta' barocca.* Rome, 1988.

Biraben, Jean-Noël. *Les hommes et la peste en France et dans les pays européens et méditerranéens.* 2 vols. Paris, 1975–76.

Bireley, Robert. *The Counter-Reformation Prince: Anti-Machiavellianism or Catholic Statecraft in Early Modern Europe.* Chapel Hill, N.C., 1990.

Black, C. F. "Perugia and Papal Absolutism in the Sixteenth Century." *English Historical Review* 96 (1981): 509–39.

Boas, George. *Vox Populi: Essays in the History of an Idea.* Baltimore, 1969.

Bodin, Jean. *Six Books of the Commonwealth.* Translated by M. J. Tooley. New York, 1967.

Boiteux, Martine. "Carnaval annexé. Essai de lecture d'une fête romaine." *Annales* 32 (1977): 356–80.

———. "Chasse aux taureaux et jeux romains de la Renaissance." In *Les jeux à la Renaissance,* edited by Philippe Ariès and Jean-Claude Margolin, 33–53. Paris, 1982.

———. "Les Juifs dans le Carnaval de la Rome moderne." *Mélanges de l'École Française de Rome—Moyen âge/temps modernes* 88 (1976), pt. 2: 745–87.

Boncompagni Ludovisi, Ugo. *Roma nel Rinascimento.* 4 vols. Albano, 1928.

Bonney, Richard. "Absolutism: What's in a Name?" *French History* 1 (1987): 93–117.

Borboni, Giovanni Andrea. *Delle statue.* Rome, 1661.

Borromeo, Cardinal Federico. *La peste di Milano.* Milan, 1987.

Bosher, J. F. *French Finances 1770–1795.* Cambridge, 1970.

Bossenga, Gail. "City and State: An Urban Perspective on the Origins of the French Revolution." In *The Political Culture of the Old Regime,* vol. 1 of *The French Revolution and the Creation of Modern Political Culture,* edited by Keith Michael Baker, 115–40. Oxford, 1987.

Botero, Giovanni. *The Greatness of Cities.* Translated by Robert Peterson and edited by P. J. Waley and D. P. Waley. New Haven, 1956.

Boüard, Alain de. *Le régime politique et les institutions de Rome au moyen-âge, 1252–1327.* Paris, 1920.

Bourdieu, Pierre. *Outline of a Theory of Practice.* Translated by Richard Nice. Cambridge, 1977.

Brandi, Ambrosio. *Trionfo della gloriosa vergine del SSmo Rosario celebrato in Roma la prima domenica d'ottobre dell'anno Santo 1625 nella Processione solenne dell'Archiconfraternita del Rosario.* Rome, 1625.

Braudel, Fernand. "Pre-modern Towns." In *The Early Modern Town*, edited by Peter Clark, 53–90. London, 1976.

Brentano, Robert. *Rome before Avignon: A Social History of Thirteenth-Century Rome.* New York, 1974.

Brown, Judith C. "Prosperity or Hard Times in Renaissance Italy?" *Renaissance Quarterly* 42 (1989): 761–80.

Brusatin, Manlio. *Il muro della peste: Spazio della pieta' e governo del lazzaretto.* Venice, 1981.

Bullard, Melissa. "Grain Supply and Urban Unrest in Renaissance Rome: The Crisis of 1533–34." In *Rome in the Renaissance*, edited by P. A. Ramsey, 279–92. Binghamton, N.Y., 1982.

Bullarium diplomatum et privilegiorum sanctorum Romanorum pontificum. 25 vols. Turin, 1857–72.

Burke, Peter. "Insult and Blasphemy in Early Modern Italy." In *The Historical Anthropology of Early Modern Italy*, 95–109. Cambridge, 1987.

———. "Languages and Anti-Languages in Early Modern Italy." In *The Historical Anthropology of Early Modern Italy*, 79–94. Cambridge, 1987.

———. "The Repudiation of Ritual in Early Modern Europe." In *The Historical Anthropology of Early Modern Italy*, 223–38. Cambridge, 1987.

———. "Sacred Rulers, Royal Priests: Rituals of the Early Modern Popes." In *The Historical Anthropology of Early Modern Italy*, 168–82. Cambridge, 1987.

Burroughs, Charles. *From Signs to Design: Environmental Process and Reform in Early Renaissance Rome.* Cambridge, Mass., 1990.

Butzek, Monika. *Die Communalen Repräsentationsstatuen der Päpste des 16. Jahrhunderts in Bologna, Perugia und Rom.* Bad Honnef, 1978.

Cadlolo, Antonio. "Compagnie, confraternite e pie unioni erette in S. Maria in Aracoeli di Roma." Parts 1, 2. *Ara-coeli* 17 (1946): 20–23, 43–44; 18 (1947): 9–11, 27–30.

Calvi, Giulia. *Histories of a Plague Year: The Social and the Imaginary in Baroque Florence.* Berkeley, 1989.

Cametti, Alberto. "I musici di Campidoglio." *Archivio della Societa' Romana di Storia Patria* 48 (1925): 95–135.

Capogrossi Guarna, Baldassare. *Il mercato del pesce in Roma. Cenni storici.* Rome, 1879.

Caracciolo, Alberto. "Sovrano pontefice e sovrani assoluti." *Quaderni storici* 52 (1983): 279–86.

Caravale, Mario. *La finanza pontificia nel Cinquecento: Le province del Lazio.* N. p., 1974.

Caravale, Mario, and Caracciolo, Alberto. *Lo stato pontificio da Martino V a Pio IX.* Turin, 1978.

Cardella, Lorenzo. *Memorie storiche intorno ai cardinali di santa romana chiesa.* 10 vols. Rome, 1792–97.

Carsalade du Pont, Henri de. *La municipalite' parisienne à l'époque d'Henri IV.* Paris, 1971.

Caselli, Virgilio. *Il Vicariato di Roma.* Rome, 1957.

Cerasoli, Francesco. "Censimento della popolazione di Roma dall'anno 1600 al 1739." *Studi e documenti di storia e diritto* 12 (1891): 169–99.

————. "Commentario di Pietro Paolo Muziano relativo agli officiali del Comune di Roma nel secolo XVI." *Studi e documenti di storia e diritto* 13 (1892): 101–31.

————. "Diario di cose romane degli anni 1614, 1615, 1616." *Studi e documenti di storia e diritto* 15 (1894): 263–301.

————. "Lista di uffici di Campidoglio (a. 1629)." *Archivio della Societa' Romana di Storia Patria* 12 (1889): 373–76.

The Ceremonies of the Vacant See. Or a True Relation of What Passes at Rome upon the Pope's Death. Translated by J. Davies. London, 1671.

Chambers, D. S. "Studium Urbis and *gabella studii*: The University of Rome in the Fifteenth Century." In *Cultural Aspects of the Italian Renaissance: Essays in Honour of Paul Oskar Kristeller*, edited by Cecil H. Clough, 68–110. New York, 1976.

Chartier, Roger, and Neveux, Hugues. "La ville dominante et soumise." In *La ville classique de la Renaissance aux Révolutions*, edited by Emmanuel LeRoy Ladurie, 16–285. Vol. 3 of *Histoire de la France urbaine*, edited by Georges Duby. Paris, 1981.

Chittolini, Giorgio. "Stati padani, 'Stato del Rinascimento': Problemi di ricerca." In *Persistenze feudali e autonomie comunitative in stati padani fra Cinque e Settecento*, edited by Giovanni Tocci, 9–29. Bologna, 1988.

Cipolla, Carlo M. "The Decline of Italy." *Economic History Review*, 2d ser., 5 (1952): 178–87.

————. *Fighting the Plague in Seventeenth-Century Italy.* Madison, 1981.

Clementi, Filippo. *Il carnevale romano nelle cronache contemporanee.* Rome, 1899.

Coffin, David. *The Villa in the Life of Renaissance Rome.* Princeton, 1979.

Colliva, Paolo. "Bologna dal XIV al XVIII secolo: 'Governo misto' o signoria senatoria?" In *Storia della Emilia Romagna*, edited by Aldo Berselli, 2:13–34. Bologna, 1977.

Comparato, Vittor Ivo. *Uffici e societa' a Napoli (1600–1647): Aspetti dell'ideologia del magistrato nell'eta' moderna.* Florence, 1974.

Connors, Joseph. "Alliance and Enmity in Roman Baroque Urbanism." *Römisches Jahrbuch für Kunstgeschichte* 25 (1989): 209–94.

————. *Borromini and the Roman Oratory: Style and Society.* Cambridge, Mass., 1980.

Coste, Jean. "I casali della Campagna di Roma all'inizio del Seicento." *Archivio della societa' romana di storia patria* 92 (1969): 41–115.

Courtright, Nicola. "Memorial to Carlo Barberini." In *Drawings by Gianlorenzo Bernini*, by Irving Lavin, Pamela Gordon, Linda Klinger, Steven Ostrow, Sharon Cather, Nicola Courtright, and Ilana Dreyer, 72–77. Princeton, 1981.

Crostarosa, Fortunato. *Le milizie urbane della citta' di Roma.* Rome, 1897.

D'Agostino, Guido. "Citta' e monarchie nazionali nell'Europa moderna." In *Modelli di citta': Strutture e funzioni politiche*, edited by Pietro Rossi, 395–418. Turin, 1987.

D'Amelia, Marina. "La conquista di una dote: Regole del gioco e scambi femminili alla Confraternita dell'Annunziata (secc. XVII–XVIII)." In *Ragnatele di rapporti: Patronage e reti di relazione nella storia delle donne*, edited by Lucia Ferrante, Maura Palazzi, and Gianna Pomata, 305–43. Turin, 1988.

————. "La crisi dell'egemonia urbana: Approvigionamenti e consumo della carne a Roma nel XVIII secolo." *Mélanges de l'École Française de Rome—Moyen âge/temps modernes* 87 (1975), pt. 2: 495–534.

D'Amico, John F. *Renaissance Humanism in Papal Rome: Humanists and Churchmen on the Eve of the Reformation.* Baltimore, 1983.

Darricau, Raymond. "Princes et peuples dans leur reciproque fidélité chez les docteurs catholiques de Bellarmin à Muratori." In *Hommage à Roland Mousnier: Clientèles et fidélités en Europe à l'époque moderne*, edited by Yves Durand, 42–55. Paris, 1981.

Davis, Natalie Zemon. *Society and Culture in Early Modern France*. Stanford, 1975.

De Gregori, Luigi. "Cariche da burla del comune di Roma." *Strenna dei romanisti* 3 (1942): 268–74.

Del Re, Niccolo'. "L'Abbate Ottavio Sacco ed una singolare magistratura romana." *Studi romani* 3 (1955): 12–26.

―――. *La curia capitolina*. Rome, 1954.

―――. *La curia romana: Lineamenti storico-giuridici*. 3d ed. Rome, 1970.

―――. "La curia Savella." *Studi romani* 5 (1957): 390–400.

―――. *Il maresciallo di santa romana chiesa, custode del conclave*. Rome, 1962.

―――. *Monsignor Governatore di Roma*. Rome, 1972.

―――. *Il Vicegerente del Vicariato di Roma*. Rome, 1976.

De Luca, Giovanni Battista. *Il Dottor Volgare overo il compendio di tutta la legge civile, canonica, feudale, e municipale, nelle cose piu' ricevute in pratica*. Rome, 1673.

Delumeau, Jean. "Rome: Le progrès de la centralisation dans l'État pontifical au XVI siècle." *Revue historique* 226 (1961): 399–410.

―――. *Vie économique et sociale de Rome dans la seconde moitié du XVIe siècle*. 2 vols. Paris, 1957–59.

De Maria, Giacinto. "La guerra di Castro e la spedizione dei presidi (1639–1649)." In *Miscellanea di storia italiana*, 191–256. Turin, 1898.

Descimon, Robert. "L'échevinage parisien sous Henri IV (1594–1609): Autonomie urbaine, conflits politiques et exclusives sociales." In *La ville, la bourgeoisie et la genèse de l'état moderne (XIIe-XVIIIe siècles)*, 113–50. Paris, 1988.

Dessert, Daniel. *Argent, pouvoir et société au Grand Siècle*. Paris, 1984.

Dethan, Georges. *Mazarin et ses amis: Étude sur la jeunesse du Cardinal*. Paris, 1968.

De Vries, Jan. *The Economy of Europe in an Age of Crisis*. New Haven, 1976.

―――. *European Urbanization 1500–1800*. Cambridge, Mass., 1984.

Diez, Renato. *Il trionfo della parola: Studio sulle relazioni di feste nella Roma barocca 1623–1667*. Rome, 1986.

Dizionario biografico degli italiani, s.v. "Albrizzi, Luigi," by Pietro Pirri. Rome, 1960–.

Donati, Claudio. *L'Idea del nobilta' in Italia, secoli XIV–XVIII*. Bari, 1988.

D'Onofrio, Cesare. *Acque e fontane di Roma*. Rome, 1977.

―――. *I vassalli del Campidoglio*. Rome, 1965.

Duccini, Hélène. "L'État sur la place: Pamphlets et libelles dans la première moitié du XVIIe siècle." In *L'État baroque: Regards sur la pensée politique de la France du premier XVIIe siècle*, edited by Henry Méchoulan, 289–300. Paris, 1985.

Dupre' Theseider, Eugenio. *Roma dal comune di popolo alla signoria pontificia (1252–1377)*. Vol. 11 of *Storia di Roma*. Bologna, 1952.

Durand, Yves, ed. *Hommage à Roland Mousnier: Clientèles et fidélités en Europe à l'époque moderne*. Paris, 1981.

Elliott, J. H. *Richelieu and Olivares*. Cambridge, 1984.

Erythraeus, Ianus Nicius [Giovanni Vittorio Rossi]. *Eudemiae libri VIII*. N. p., 1637.

Esch, Arnold. *Bonifaz IX und der Kirchenstaat*. Tübingen, 1969.

―――. "La fine del libero comune di Roma nel giudizio dei mercanti fiorentini. Lettere romane degli anni 1395–1398 nell'Archivio Datini." *Bullettino dell'Istituto Storico Italiano per il Medioevo* 86 (1976–1977): 235–77.

Esposito, Anna. "Famiglia, mercanzia e libri nel testamento di Andrea Santacroce (1471)." In *Aspetti della vita economica e culturale a Roma nel Quattrocento*, 197–220. Rome, 1981.

Fanfani, Amintore. *Storia del lavoro in Italia*. 2d ed., enl. and illust. Milan, 1959.

Fanti, Mario. "Il governo e classi sociali di Bologna." *Strenna storica bolognese* 11 (1961): 133–79.

Fanucci, Camillo. *Trattato di tutte l'opere pie dell'alma citta' di Roma*. Rome, 1601.

Farr, James R. *Hands of Honor: Artisans and Their World in Dijon, 1550–1650*. Ithaca, N.Y., 1988.

Fasano Guarini, Elena, ed. *Potere e societa' negli stati regionali italiani fra '500 e '600*. Bologna, 1978.

Fenzonio, Giovanni Battista. *Annotationes in statuta, sive ius municipale romanae urbis*. Rome, 1636.

Finley, Moses. *Politics in the Ancient World*. New York, 1983.

Fiorani, Luigi. "Religione e poverta': Il dibattito sul pauperismo a Roma tra Cinque e Seicento." *Ricerche per la storia religiosa di Roma* 3 (1979): 43–131.

―――. "Le visite apostoliche del Cinque-Seicento e la societa' religiosa romana." *Ricerche per la storia religiosa di Roma* 4 (1980): 53–148.

La fiscalité et ses implications sociales en Italie et en France au XVIIe et XVIIIe siècles. Rome, 1980.

Fogel, Michèle. "1620–1660. Constitution et fonctionnement d'un discours monarchique sur la guerre: L'information comme cérémonie." In *L'État baroque: Regards sur la pensée politique de la France du premier XVIIe siècle*, edited by Henry Méchoulan, 335–52. Paris, 1985.

Forcella, Vincenzo. *Iscrizioni delle chiese e d'altri edifici di Roma dal secolo XI fino ai giorni nostri*. 14 vols. Rome, 1869–84.

Fosi, Irene Polverini. *La societa' violenta: Il banditismo dello Stato Pontificio nella seconda meta' del Cinquecento*. Rome, 1985.

Franceschini, Michele. "La magistratura capitolina e la tutela delle antichita' di Roma nel XVI secolo." *Archivio della Societa' Romana di Storia Patria* 109 (1986): 141–50.

Franza, Gerardo. *Il catechismo a Roma e l'arciconfraternita della dottrina cristiana*. Alba, 1958.

Fraschetti, Stanislao. *Il Bernini*. Milan, 1900.

Frati, Ludovico. "Poesie satiriche per la guerra di Castro." *Archivio storico italiano*, 5th ser., 37 (1906): 388–403.

Frommel, Christoph L. "Papal Policy: The Planning of Rome during the Renaissance." In *Art and History: Images and Their Meaning*, edited by Robert I. Rotberg and Theodore K. Rabb, 39–65. Cambridge, 1988.

Frugoni, A. "Sulla 'renovatio senatus' del 1143 e l''ordo equestris.' " *Bullettino dell'Istituto Storico Italiano per il Medioevo* 62 (1950): 159–74.

Fumi, Luigi. "Il Cardinale Cecchini romano secondo la sua autobiografia." *Archivio della Societa' Romana di Storia Patria* 10 (1887): 287–322.

Geertz, Clifford. "Centers, Kings and Charisma: Reflections on the Symbolics of Power." In *Culture and Its Creators: Essays in Honor of Edward Shils*, edited by J. Ben-David and T. Clark, 150–71. Chicago, 1977.

―――. *Negara: The Theatre State in Nineteenth-Century Bali*. Princeton, 1980.

Geertz, Clifford. "Religion as a Cultural System." In *The Interpretation of Cultures*, 87–125. New York, 1973.

Gennaro, Clara. "La 'Pax Romana' del 1511." *Archivio della Societa' Romana di Storia Patria* 90 (1967): 17–60.

Gerardi, Antonio. *Sommaria relatione della solenne processione dello stendardo benedetto dell S.ta' di N. S.re Urbano Papa VIII fatta dal Clero e Popolo Romano il giorno della Santissima Annuntiata.* Rome, 1632.

Giacomelli, Alfeo. "La dinamica della nobilta' Bolognese nel XVIII secolo." In *Famiglie senatorie e istituzioni cittadine a Bologna nel Settecento*, 55–112. Bologna, 1980.

Giesey, Ralph. *The Royal Funeral Ceremony in Renaissance France.* Geneva, 1960.

Gigli, Giacinto. *Diario romano (1608–1670).* Edited by Giuseppe Ricciotti. Rome, 1958.

Ginzburg, Carlo, ed. "Saccheggi rituali. Premesse a una ricerca in corso." *Quaderni storici* 65 (1987): 615–36.

Giovannozzi, Giovanni. *Il Calasanzio e l'opera sua.* Florence, 1930.

Girouard, Mark. *Cities and People: A Social and Architectural History.* New Haven, 1985.

Gramsci, Antonio. *Selections from the Prison Notebooks.* Edited and translated by Quintin Hoare and Geoffrey Nowell Smith. New York, 1971.

Gregorovius, Ferdinand. "Alcuni cenni storici sulla cittadinanza romana." *Atti della R. Accademia dei Lincei*, 3d ser., 1 (1876–1877): 314–46.

————. *History of the City of Rome in the Middle Ages.* Translated by Annie Hamilton. 4th ed. 8 vols. London, 1894–1902.

Grendler, Paul. *Schooling in Renaissance Italy: Literacy and Learning, 1300–1600.* Baltimore, 1989.

Grisar, Josef. "Päpstliche Finanzen Nepotismus und Kirchenrecht unter Urban VIII." *Miscellanea historiae pontificiae* 7 (1943): 205–365.

Gross, Hanns. *Rome in the Age of Enlightenment: The Post-Tridentine Syndrome and the Ancien Regime.* Cambridge, 1990.

Guasco, Luigi. *L'archivio storico capitolino.* Rome, 1946.

Guidiccioni, Lelio. *Adlocutio capitolina Laelii Guidiccioni statuam positam Urbano VIII Pont. Max.* Rome, 1640.

Gundersheimer, Werner L. "Patronage in the Renaissance: An Exploratory Approach." In *Patronage in the Renaissance*, edited by Guy F. Lytle and Stephen Orgel, 3–23. Princeton, 1981.

Gurreri, Fabrizia. "La liquidazione dell'Asse Ecclesiastico nella Campagna romana: Vecchi e nuovi proprietari, cambiamenti e permanenze." *Storia urbana* 12 (1988): 85–144.

Güthlein, Klaus. "Der 'Palazzo Nuovo' des Kapitols." *Römisches Jahrbuch für Kunstgeschichte* 22 (1985): 83–190.

Hallman, Barbara McClung. *Italian Cardinals, Reform and the Church as Property, 1492–1563.* Berkeley, 1985.

Harris, Ann Sutherland. *Andrea Sacchi.* New York, 1977.

Haskell, Francis. *Patrons and Painters: A Study in the Relations between Italian Art and Society in the Age of the Baroque.* Rev. and enl. ed. New Haven, 1980.

Haskell, Francis, and Penny, Nicholas. *Taste and the Antique: The Lure of Classical Sculpture, 1500–1900.* New Haven, 1981.

Hess, Jacob. *Kunstgeschichtliche Studien zu Renaissance und Barock.* 2 vols. Rome, 1967.

Hill, Christopher. "The Poor and the People in Seventeenth-Century England." In *History from Below*, edited by Frederick Krantz, 29–52. Oxford, 1988.

Hobsbawm, Eric. "From Social History to the History of Society." In *Historical Studies Today*, edited by Felix Gilbert and Stephen R. Graubard, 1–26. New York, 1972.

Hook, Judith. "Urban VIII: The Paradox of a Spiritual Monarchy." In *The Courts of Europe: Politics, Patronage, and Royalty 1400–1800*, edited by A. G. Dickens, 213–31. New York, 1977.

Hughes, Steven C. "Fear and Loathing in Bologna and Rome: The Papal Police in Perspective." *Journal of Social History* 21 (1987): 97–116.

Hurtubise, Pierre. "Familiarité et fidélité à Rome au XVIᵉ siècle: Les 'familles' des cardinaux Giovanni, Bernardo et Antonio Maria Salviati." In *Hommage à Roland Mousnier: Clientèles et fidélités en Europe à l'époque moderne*, edited by Yves Durand, 335–50. Paris, 1981.

Kantorowicz, Ernst. *The King's Two Bodies*. Princeton, 1957.

Kaplan, Steven L. *Provisioning Paris: Merchants and Millers in the Grain and Flour Trade during the Eighteenth Century*. Ithaca, N.Y., 1984.

Kaplow, Jeffry. *The Names of Kings: The Parisian Laboring Poor in the Eighteenth Century*. New York, 1972.

Kent, F. W., with Patricia Simons. "Renaissance Patronage: An Introductory Essay." In *Patronage, Art, and Society in Renaissance Italy*, edited by F. W. Kent and Patricia Simons, 1–21. Oxford, 1987.

Kettering, Sharon. "Gift-Giving and Patronage in Early Modern France." *French History* 2 (1988): 131–51.

———. *Patrons, Brokers and Clients in Seventeenth-Century France*. Oxford, 1986.

Klapisch-Zuber, Christiane. "An Ethnology of Marriage in the Age of Humanism." In *Women, Family, and Ritual in Renaissance Italy*, translated by Lydia Cochrane, 247–60. Chicago, 1985.

———. "The 'Mattinata' in Medieval Italy." In *Women, Family, and Ritual in Renaissance Italy*, translated by Lydia Cochrane, 261–82. Chicago, 1985.

Knapton, Michael. "City Wealth and State Wealth in Northeast Italy, 14th-17th Centuries." In *La ville, la bourgeoisie et la genèse de l'état moderne*. Paris, 1988.

Kociemski, Leonard. "Un fattaccio di cronaca del Seicento." *Strenna dei romanisti* 23 (1962): 184–87.

Kolsky, Stephen. "Culture and Politics in Renaissance Rome: Marco Antonio Altieri's Roman Weddings." *Renaissance Quarterly* 40 (1987): 49–90.

Kraus, Andreas. "Amt und Stellung des Kardinal Nepoten zur Zeit Urbans VIII (1623)." *Römische Quartalschrift für Christliche Altertumskunde und Kirchengeschichte* 53 (1958): 239–43.

———. "Der Kardinal-Nepote Francesco Barberini und das Staatssekretariat Urbans VIII." *Römische Quartalschrift für Christliche Altertumskunde und Kirchengeschichte* 64 (1969): 191–208.

Krautheimer, Richard. *Rome Profile of a City, 312–1308*. Princeton, 1980.

Labrot, Gérard. *Un instrument polémique: L'image de Rome au temps du schisme (1534–1667)*. Paris, 1978.

Ladner, Gerhart B. "The Concepts of 'Ecclesia' and 'Christianitas' and Their Relation to the Idea of Papal 'Plenitudo Potestatis' from Gregory VII to Boniface VIII." In *Sacerdozio e regno da Gregorio VII a Bonifacio VIII*. Rome, 1954.

Lane, Frederic C. *Venice: A Maritime Republic*. Baltimore, 1973.

Laurain-Portemer, Madeleine. "Absolutisme et népotisme: La surintendance de l'état ec- clésiastique." *Bibliothèque de l'école des chartes* 131 (1973): 487–568.

Lavin, Irving. "Bernini's Memorial Plaque for Carlo Barberini." *Journal of the Society of Architectural Historians* 42 (1983): 6–10.

Lavin, Marilyn Aronberg. *Seventeenth-Century Barberini Documents and Inventories of Art.* New York, 1975.

Lee, Egmont. "Foreigners in Quattrocento Rome." *Renaissance and Reformation*, n.s., 7 (1983): 135–46.

LeRoy Ladurie, Emmanuel. "L'Histoire immobile." *Annales* 29 (1974): 673–92.

Leti, Gregorio. *Il nipotismo di Roma: O vero, Relatione delle raggioni che muovono i pontifici all'aggrandimento de' nipoti.* Amsterdam, 1667.

Litchfield, R. Burr. *Emergence of a Bureaucracy: The Florentine Patricians 1530–1790.* Princeton, 1986.

Lloyd-Jones, K. "Du Bellay's Journey from *Roma Vetus* to *La Rome Neufve.*" In *Rome in the Renaissance*, edited by P. A. Ramsey, 301–19. Binghamton, N.Y., 1982.

Lodolini, Armando. "Il tribunale dell'Agricoltura." *Agricoltura* 2 (1953): 79–80.

Lombardo, Maria Luisa. *La camera urbis: Premesse per uno studio sulla organizzazione amminis- trativa della citta' di Roma durante il pontificato di Martino V.* Rome, 1970.

Lumbroso, Giacomo. "Notizie sulla vita di Cassiano dal Pozzo." *Miscellanea di storia ital- iana*, 1st ser., 15 (1876): 129–388.

Lunadoro, Girolamo. *Relatione della corte di Roma.* Venice, 1661.

Lutz, Georg. "Rom und Europa während der Pontifikats Urbans VIII." *Rom in der Neuzeit*, edited by R. Elze, H. Schmidinger, and H. S. Nordholt, 72–167. Vienna, 1976.

Mackenney, Richard. *Tradesmen and Traders: The World of the Guilds in Venice and Europe c. 1250–1650.* London, 1987.

Magnuson, Torgil. *Rome in the Age of Bernini.* 2 vols. Stockholm, 1982–86.

Maire-Vigueur, Jean-Claude. "Classe dominante et classes dirigeantes à Rome à la fin du Moyen Âge." *Storia della citta'* 1 (1976): 4–26.

Malatesta, Sigismondo. *Statuti delle gabelle di Roma.* Rome, 1885.

Marangoni, Giovanni. *Istoria dell'antichissimo oratorio o cappella di S. Lorenzo nel Patriarchio lateranense.* Rome, 1747.

Maroni Lumbroso, Matizia, and Martini, Antonio. *Le confraternite romane nelle loro chiese.* Rome, 1963.

Marrara, Danilo. "Nobilta' civica e patriziato. Una distinzione terminologica nel pensiero di alcuni autori italiani dell'eta' moderna." *Annali della Scuola Normale Superiore di Pisa*, 3d ser., 10 (1980): 219–32.

Martin, Gregory. *Roma sancta (1581).* Edited by George Bruner Parks. Rome, 1969.

Martini, Antonio. *Arti, mestieri e fede nella Roma dei Papi.* Bologna, 1965.

Martinori, Edoardo. *Annali della zecca di Roma: Gregorio XV e Urbano VIII.* Rome, 1919.

Marucci, Valerio; Marzo, Antonio; and Romano, Angelo, eds. *Pasquinate romane del Cin- quecento.* 2 vols. Rome, 1983.

Mascardi, Agostino. *Le pompe del Campidoglio.* Rome, [1624].

Matthiae, Guglielmo. "Contributo a Carlo Rainaldi." *Arti figurative* 2 (1946): 49–59.

McGinness, Frederick J. "Preaching Ideals and Practice in Counter-Reformation Rome." *Sixteenth Century Journal* 11 (1980): 108–27.

Mettam, Roger. "Two-Dimensional History: Mousnier and the Ancien Régime." *History* 66 (1981): 221–32.

Miglio, Massimo. "Il leone e la lupa: Dal simbolo al pasticcio alla francese." *Studi romani* 30 (1982): 177–86.

———. "L'immagine dell'onore antico: Individualita' e tradizione della Roma municipale." *Studi romani* 31 (1983): 252–64.

Mistruzzi, Carlo. "La nobilta' dello Stato Pontificio." *Rassegna degli Archivi di Stato* 23 (1963): 206–44.

Mitchell, Bonner. "The S.P.Q.R. in Two Roman Festivals of the Early and Mid-Cinquecento." *Sixteenth Century Journal* 9 (1978): 95–102.

Molho, Anthony. "Patronage and the State in Early Modern Italy." In *Klientelsysteme im Europa der frühen Neuzeit*, edited by Antoni Maczak, 233–42. Munich, 1988.

Morelli, Gonippo. *Le corporazioni romane di arti e mestieri dal XIV al XIX secolo*. Rome, 1937.

Morgan, Victor. "Some Types of Patronage, Mainly in Sixteenth- and Seventeenth-Century England." In *Klientelsysteme im Europa der frühen Neuzeit*, edited by Antoni Maczak, 91–115. Munich, 1988.

Moroni, Gaetano. *Dizionario di erudizione storico-ecclesiastica*. 103 vols. Venice, 1840–61.

Moscati, Laura. *Alle origini del comune romano. Economia, societa', istituzioni*. [Rome], 1980.

Mousnier, Roland. "Les concepts d''ordres,' d''états,' de 'fidélité' et de 'monarchie absolue' en France de la fin du XVᵉ siècle à la fin du XVIIIᵉ." *Revue historique* 247 (1972): 289–312.

———. *The Institutions of France under the Absolute Monarchy, 1598–1789*. 2 vols. Chicago, 1979.

Mozzarelli, Cesare. "Principe, corte e governo tra '500 e '700." In *Culture et idéologie dans la genèse de l'état moderne*, 367–79. Rome, 1985.

———. "Strutture sociali e formazioni statuali a Milano e Napoli tra '500 e '700." *Societa' e storia* 3 (1978): 431–63.

Muir, Edward. "The Doge as *Primus Inter Pares*: Ducal Interregnum Rites in Early Sixteenth-Century Venice." In *Essays presented to Myron P. Gilmore*, edited by Sergio Bertelli and Gloria Ramakus, 1:145–60. 2 vols. Florence, 1978.

Mumford, Lewis. *The City in History*. New York, 1961.

Muto, Giovanni. "Gestione del potere e classi sociali nel Mezzogiorno spagnolo." In *I ceti dirigenti in Italia in eta' moderna e contemporanea*, 287–301. Udine, 1984.

Natale, A. "La felice societa' dei Balestrieri e dei Pavesati e il governo dei Banderesi dal 1358 al 1408." *Archivio della Societa' Romana di Storia Patria* 62 (1939): 1–176.

Navenne, Ferdinand de. *Rome et le Palais Farnèse*. 2 vols. Paris, 1923.

Nicora, Maria. "La nobilta' genovese dal 1528 al 1700." *Miscellanea di storia ligure* 2 (1962): 217–310.

Nussdorfer, Laurie. "City Politics in Baroque Rome, 1623–1644." Ph.D. diss., Princeton University, 1985.

———. "The Vacant See: Ritual and Protest in Early Modern Rome." *Sixteenth Century Journal* 18 (1987): 173–89.

———. "Writing and the Power of Speech: Notaries and Artisans in Baroque Rome." In *Culture and Identity in Early Modern Europe, 1500–1800*, edited by Barbara Diefendorf and Carla Hesse. Forthcoming.

Otto of Freising. *Ottonis episcopi Frisingensis Chronica sive Historia de duabus civitatibus.* Edited by Adolf Hofmeister. Hannover, 1984.

Pagano, Sergio. "Le visite apostoliche a Roma nei secoli XVI–XIX: Repertorio delle fonti." *Ricerche per la storia religiosa di Roma* 4 (1980): 317–464.

Paglia, Vincenzo. *La Pieta' dei carcerati: Confraternite e societa' a Roma nei secoli XVI-XVIII.* Rome, 1980.

Parker, David. "Class, Clientage and Personal Rule in Absolutist France." *Seventeenth-Century French Studies* 9 (1987): 192–213.

Partner, Peter. "Appunti sulla riforma della Curia romana." In *Libri, idee e sentimenti religiosi nel Cinquecento italiano,* edited by Rolando Bussi, 77–80. Modena, 1987.

———. *The Lands of St. Peter: The Papal State in the Middle Ages and the Early Renaissance.* London, 1972.

———. "Papal Financial Policy in the Renaissance and Counter Reformation." *Past and Present* 88 (1980): 17–62.

———. *The Papal State under Martin V.* London, 1958.

———. *The Pope's Men: The Papal Civil Service in the Renaissance.* Oxford, 1990.

Pasquali, Susanna. "Il patriziato romano secondo il 'libro d'oro' di Benedetto XIV." In *L'Angelo e la citta',* 2:41–43. 2 vols. Rome, 1987.

Pastor, Ludwig von. *The History of the Popes.* Translated by Ernest Graf et al. 40 vols. London, 1891–1953.

Pastore, Alessandro. "Tra giustizia e politica: Il governo della peste a Genova e Roma nel 1656/7." *Rivista storica italiana* 100 (1988): 126–54.

Pecchiai, Pio. *I Barberini.* Rome, 1959.

———. *Il Campidoglio nel Cinquecento.* Rome, 1950.

———. *Roma nel Cinquecento.* Vol. 13 of *Storia di Roma.* Bologna, 1948.

Pelliccia, Guerrino. *La scuola primaria a Roma dal secolo XVI al XIX.* Rome, 1985.

———. "Scuole di catechismo e scuole rionali per fanciulle nella Roma del Seicento." *Ricerche per la storia religiosa di Roma* 4 (1980): 237–68.

Pepper, Stephen. *Guido Reni.* Oxford, 1984.

Perlove, Shelley. "Bernini's Androclus and the Lion: A Papal Emblem of Alexandrine Rome." *Zeitschrift für Kunstgeschichte* 45 (1982): 287–96.

———. "Gianlorenzo Bernini's *Blessed Lodovica Albertoni* and Baroque Devotion." Ph.D. diss., University of Michigan, 1984.

Petrocchi, Massimo. *Roma nel Seicento.* Vol. 14 of *Storia di Roma.* Bologna, 1970.

Petrucci, Giovanni Battista. *Stratagemme militari da diversi autori brevemente raccolte . . . per servitio & uso degl'eserciti pontificij della Santita' di N. S. Papa Urbano VIII.* Viterbo, 1643.

Piazza, Carlo Bartolomeo. *Opere pie di Roma.* Rome, 1679.

Picanyol, Leodegarius. *Brevis conspectus historico-statisticus ordinis scholarum piarum.* Rome, 1932.

Pietramellara, Giacomo. *Il libro d'oro del Campidoglio.* 2 vols. Rome, 1893–97.

Pietrangeli, Carlo. " 'Cappella vecchia' e 'cappella nuova' nel Palazzo dei Conservatori." *Capitolium* 35, no. 2 (1960): 11–17.

———. "Iscrizioni inedite o poco note dei Palazzi Capitolini." *Archivio della Societa' Romana di Storia Patria* 71 (1948): 123–37.

———. "La 'Madonna delle Scale' nel Palazzo dei Conservatori." *Strenna dei romanisti* 17 (1956): 243–47.

————, ed. *Rione X—Campitelli.* 2d ed. Guide rionali di Roma. Rome, 1979.

————. "La sala dei capitani." *Capitolium* 37 (1962): 640–48.

Pietrangeli, Carlo, and De Angelis D'Ossat, Guglielmo. *Il Campidoglio di Michelangelo.* Milan, 1965.

Pinto, John. *The Trevi Fountain.* New Haven, 1986.

Piola Caselli, Fausto. "Aspetti del debito pubblico nello Stato Pontificio: Gli uffici vacabili." *Annali della facolta' di scienze politiche dell'Universita' degli studi di Perugia,* n.s., 1 (1973): 99–170.

Pisano, G. "L'ultimo prefetto dell'Urbe: Don Taddeo Barberini, e le relazioni tra la corte di Roma e la repubblica veneta sotto il pontificato di Urbano VIII." *Roma* 9 (1931): 103–20, 155–64.

Pollak, Oskar. *Die Kunsttätigkeit unter Urban VIII.* 2 vols. Vienna, 1928–31.

Pompili Olivieri, Luigi. *Il senato romano nelle sette epoche di svariato governo.* 3 vols. Rome, 1886; repr., Bologna, 1972–73.

Ponnelle, Louis, and Bordet, Louis. *St Philip Neri and the Roman Society of His Times.* Translated by Ralph Francis Kerr. London, 1932; repr., 1979.

Preto, Paolo. *Epidemia, paura e politica nell'Italia moderna.* Bari, 1987.

Prodi, Paolo. *Il sovrano pontefice: Un corpo e due anime: La monarchia papale nella prima eta' moderna.* Bologna, 1982.

Pullan, Brian. "The Roles of the State and the Town in the General Crisis of the 1590s." In *The European Crisis of the 1590s,* edited by Peter Clark, 285–300. London, 1985.

Ranke, Ludwig von. *History of the Popes.* Translated by E. Fowler. Rev. ed. 3 vols. New York, 1901.

Ranum, Orest. "Courtesy, Absolutism, and the Rise of the French State, 1630–1660." *Journal of Modern History* 52 (1980): 426–51.

Rapp, Richard T. *Industry and Economic Decline in Seventeenth-Century Venice.* Cambridge, Mass., 1976.

Re, Emilio. "Maestri di strada." *Archivio della Societa' Romana di Storia Patria* 43 (1920): 5–102.

Regesti di bandi, editti, notificazioni, e provvedimenti diversi relativi alla citta' di Roma e dello Stato Pontificio. 7 vols. Rome, 1920–58.

Reinhard, Wolfgang. "Finanza pontificia e Stato della Chiesa nel XVI e XVII secolo." In *Finanze e ragion di stato in Italia e in Germania nella prima eta' moderna,* edited by Aldo De Maddalena and Hermann Kellenbenz, 353–87. Bologna, 1984.

————. *Freunde und Kreaturen: 'Verflechtung' als Konzept zur Erforschung historischer Führungsgruppen Römische Oligarchie um 1600.* Munich, 1979.

————. *Papstfinanz und Nepotismus unter Paul V (1605–1621).* 2 vols. Stuttgart, 1974.

Reinhardt, Volker. *Kardinal Scipione Borghese, 1605–1633: Vermögen, Finanzen und sozialer Aufstieg eines Papstnepoten.* Tübingen, 1984.

Renazzi, Filippo. *Storia dell'universita' di Roma.* 4 vols. Rome, 1803–6.

"Repertorio degli archivi delle confraternite romane." *Ricerche per la storia religiosa di Roma* 6 (1985): 175–413.

Revel, Jacques. "A Capital City's Privileges: Food Supplies in Early-Modern Rome." In *Food and Drink in History,* translated by Patricia M. Ranum and edited by Robert Forster and Orest Ranum, 37–49. Baltimore, 1979.

Reynolds, Anne. "Cardinal Oliviero Carafa and the Early Cinquecento Tradition of the Feast of Pasquino." *Humanistica Lovaniensia* 34A (1985): 178–208.

Rice, Louise. "The Altars and Altarpieces of New St. Peter's (1621–1653)." Ph.D. diss., Columbia University, 1992.

Rietbergen, Peter J. A. N. *Pausen, Prelaten, Bureaucraten: Aspecten van de geschiedenis van het Pausschap en de Pauselijke Staat in de 17e Eeuw.* Nijmegen, 1983.

Robertson, Ian. "Neighborhood Government in Malatesta Cesena." In *Patronage, Art, and Society in Renaissance Italy,* edited by F. W. Kent and Patricia Simons, 99–110. New York, 1987.

Rodocananchi, Emmanuel. *Le Capitole romain antique et moderne.* Paris, 1904.

———. *Les corporations ouvrières à Rome depuis la chute de l'empire romain.* 2 vols. Paris, 1894.

———. *Les institutions communales de Rome sous la papaute'.* Paris, 1901.

Romani, Mario. *Pellegrini e viaggiatori nell'economia di Roma dal XIV al XVI secolo.* Milan, 1948.

Romano, Pietro [Pietro Fornari]. *Quod non fecerunt barbari . . . (Il pontificato di Urbano VIII).* Rome, 1937.

Romano, Ruggiero. "L'Italia nella crisi del secolo XVI." *Studi storici* 9 (1968): 723–41.

———. "Tra XVI e XVII secolo: Una crisi economica, 1619–1622." *Rivista storica italiana* 74 (1962): 480–531.

Rossi, Marc'Antonio. *Il giardino de' scrittori.* Rome, 1598.

Rubinstein, Nicolai. *The Government of Florence under the Medici (1434–1494).* Oxford, 1966.

———. "The History of the Word *Politicus* in Early-Modern Europe." In *The Languages of Political Theory in Early-Modern Europe,* edited by Anthony Pagden, 41–56. Cambridge, 1987.

Ruggiero, Maria Grazia Pastura. *La Reverenda Camera Apostolica e i suoi archivi (secoli XV–XVIII).* Rome, 1984.

Salimei, Alfonso. *Senatori e statuti di Roma nel medioevo.* Rome, 1935.

Sallman, Jean-Michel. "Il santo patrono cittadino nel '600." In *Per la storia sociale e religiosa del Mezzogiorno d'Italia,* edited by Giuseppe Galasso and Carla Russo, 2:187–208. 2 vols. Naples, 1980–82.

Savio, Pietro. "Ricerche sulla peste di Roma degli anni 1656–1657." *Archivio della Societa' Romana di Storia Patria* 95 (1972): 113–42.

Saxl, Fritz. "The Capitol during the Renaissance—A Symbol of the Imperial Idea." In *Lectures.* 2 vols. London, 1957.

Sbrana, Carla; Traina, Rosa; and Sonnino, Eugenio. *Gli 'stati delle anime' a Roma dalle origini al secolo XVII: Fonti per lo studio della popolazione di Roma.* Rome, 1977.

Scaduto, Mario. *L'Epoca di Giacomo Lainez.* Vols. 3 and 4 of *Storia della compagnia di Gesu' in Italia,* edited by P. Tacchi-Venturi. Rome, 1964–74.

Scavizzi, Paola. "Considerazioni sull'attivita' edilizia a Roma nella prima meta' del Seicento." *Studi storici* 9 (1968): 171–92.

———. "La rete idrica urbana in eta' moderna." *Storia della citta'* 29 (1984): 77–96.

Schudt, Ludwig. *Le guide di Roma.* Vienna, 1930.

Scott, John Beldon. *Images of Nepotism: The Painted Ceilings of Palazzo Barberini.* Princeton, 1991.

Sereni, Emilio. *Storia del paesaggio agrario italiano.* 3d ed. Bari, 1976.

Siebenhüner, Herbert. *Das Kapitol in Rom.* Munich, 1954.

Silvestrelli, Giulio. *Citta', castelli e terre della regione romana.* 2d ed. 2 vols. Rome, 1940; repr., 1970.

Simoncelli, Paolo. "Note sul sistema assistenziale a Roma nel XVI secolo." In *Timore e carita': I poveri nell'Italia moderna,* edited by Giorgio Politi, Mario Rosa, and Franco Della Peruta, 137–56. Cremona, 1982.

———. "Origini e primi anni di vita dell'ospedale romano dei poveri mendicanti." *Annuario dell'Istituto Storico Italiano per L'Eta' Moderna e Contemporanea* 25–26 (1973–1974): 121–72.

Slack, Paul. "Metropolitan Government in Crisis: The Response to Plague." In *London 1500–1700: The Making of the Metropolis,* edited by A. L. Beier and Roger Finlay, 60–81. London, 1986.

Soliday, Gerald L. *Community in Conflict: Frankfurt Society in the Seventeenth and Early Eighteenth Centuries.* Hanover, N.H., 1974.

Solmi, Arrigo. *Il senato romano nell'alto medio evo.* Rome, 1944.

Sonnino, Eugenio, and Traina, Rosa. "La peste del 1656–57 a Roma: Organizzazione sanitaria e mortalita'." In *La demografia storica delle citta' italiane,* 433–52. Bologna, 1982.

Sparti, Donatella L. "Carlo Antonio dal Pozzo (1606–1689). An Unknown Collector." *Journal of the History of Collections* 2 (1990): 7–19.

Spaziani, Antonio. *Cenni sul potere del senato di Roma considerato in rapporto allo statuto del S. P. Gregorio XIII e alle vigenti leggi comunali.* Rome, 1864.

Specchio di Roma barocca: Una guida inedita del XVII secolo. Edited by Joseph Connors and Louise Rice. Rome, 1990.

Spinelli, Lorenzo. *La vacanza della sede apostolica dalle origini al Concilio Tridentino.* Milan, 1956.

Spini, Giorgio. *Ricerca dei Libertini: La teoria dell'impostura delle religioni nel Seicento italiano.* Rev. and enl. ed. Florence, 1983.

Statuta almae urbis Romae. Rome, 1580.

Statuta civitatis corae. Rome, 1732.

Statuta nobilis artis agriculturae urbis. Rome, 1627.

Gli Statuti dell'Agricoltura. Rome, 1718.

Statuti della citta' di Roma. Edited by Camillo Re. Rome, 1880.

Stinger, Charles. *The Renaissance in Rome.* Bloomington, Ind., 1985.

Stow, Kenneth R. *Taxation, Community and State: The Jews and the Fiscal Foundations of the Early Modern Papal State.* Stuttgart, 1982.

Stumpo, Enrico. *Il capitale finanziario a Roma fra Cinque e Seicento.* Milan, 1985.

———. "I ceti dirigenti in Italia nell'eta' moderna. Due modelli diversi: Nobilta' piemontese e patriziato toscano." In *I ceti dirigenti in Italia in eta' moderna e contemporanea,* 151–98. Udine, 1984.

Talbert, Richard J. A. *The Senate of Imperial Rome.* Princeton, 1984.

Temple, Nora. "The Control and Exploitation of French Towns during the Ancien Régime." In *State and Society in Seventeenth-Century France,* edited by Raymond Kierstead, 67–93. New York, 1975.

Testi, Fulvio. *Lettere.* Edited by M. L. Doglio. 3 vols. Bari, 1967.

Theiner, Augustin, ed. *Codex diplomaticus domini temporalis S. Sedis.* 3 vols. Rome, 1861–62.

Thomas, Keith. *Rule and Misrule in the Schools of Early Modern England*. Reading, England, 1976.

Tittoni, Maria Elisa. "Gli affreschi di Tommaso Laureti in Campidoglio." In *Roma e l'antico nell'arte e nella cultura del Cinquecento*, edited by Marcello Fagiolo, 211–34. Rome, 1985.

Totti, Pompilio. *Ritratto di Roma moderna*. Rome, 1638.

Toubert, Pierre. *Les structures du Latium médiéval*. 2 vols. Rome, 1973.

Tracy, James D. *A Financial Revolution in the Habsburg Netherlands*. Berkeley, 1985.

Trevor-Roper, H. R. "The General Crisis of the Seventeenth Century." *Past and Present* 16 (1959): 31–64.

Trexler, Richard. *Public Life in Renaissance Florence*. New York, 1980.

Valentini, Roberto, and Zucchetti, Giuseppe, eds. *Codice topografico della citta' di Roma*. 4 vols. Rome, 1940–53.

Valesio, Francesco. *Diario di Roma*. Edited by Gaetana Scano. 9 vols. Milan, 1977–79.

Vann, James Allen. *The Making of a State: Württemberg, 1593–1793*. Ithaca, N.Y., 1984.

Vanti, Mario. *Storia dell'ordine dei chierici regolari degli infermi*. 3 vols. Rome, 1943–45.

Varey, J. E. "Calderón, Cosme Lotti, Velázquez, and the Madrid Festivities of 1636–1637." *Renaissance Drama*, n.s., 1 (1968): 253–82.

Vicens Vives, Jaime. "The Administrative Structure of the State in the Sixteenth and Seventeenth Centuries." In *Government in Reformation Europe 1520–1650*, edited by Henry J. Cohn, 58–87. London, 1971.

Visconti, Pietro. *Citta' e famiglie nobili e celebri dello stato pontificio*. 3 vols. Rome, 1847.

Vismara, Giulio. "Le istituzioni del patriziato." In *Il declino spagnolo (1630–1706)*, vol. 11 of *Storia di Milano*, edited by Giovanni Treccani degli Alfieri, 226–86. Milan, 1958.

Voelkel, Markus. "Haushalt und Gesellschaft. Römische Kardinalsfamilien des 17. Jhs. Unter besonderer Berücksichtigung der Borghese, Barberini und Chigi." Habilitation thesis, University of Augsburg, 1991.

Volpi, Roberto. *Le regioni introvabili: Centralizzazione e regionalizzazione dello Stato Pontificio*. Bologna, 1983.

Walker, D. P. *Spiritual and Demonic Magic: From Ficino to Campanella*. London, 1958; repr., Notre Dame, Ind., 1975.

Waquet, Jean Claude. *De la corruption: Morale et pouvoir à Florence au XVIIe et XVIIIe siècles*. Paris, 1984.

Weber, Max. *The City*. Translated and edited by Don Martindale and Gertrud Neuwirth. Glencoe, Ill., 1958.

Weil-Garris, Kathleen, and D'Amico, John F. "The Renaissance Cardinal's Ideal Palace: A Chapter from Cortesi's *De Cardinalatu*." In *Studies in Italian Art and Architecture, 15th through 18th Centuries*, edited by Henry A. Millon, 45–123. Rome, 1980.

Weissman, Ronald. "Taking Patronage Seriously: Mediterranean Values and Renaissance Society." In *Patronage, Art and Society in Renaissance Italy*, edited by F. W. Kent and Patricia Simons, 25–45. New York, 1987.

Westfall, Carroll. *In This Most Perfect Paradise: Alberti, Nicholas V, and the Invention of Conscious Urban Planning in Rome, 1447–1455*. University Park, Pa., 1974.

Wittkower, Rudolf. *Art and Architecture in Italy 1600–1750*. Harmondworth, England, 1958.

Zenobi, Bandino Giacomo. *Tardo feudalita' e reclutamento delle élites nello Stato Pontificio (secoli XV–XVIII)*. Urbino, 1983.